Salvador Dalí

MASTER of MODERN ART

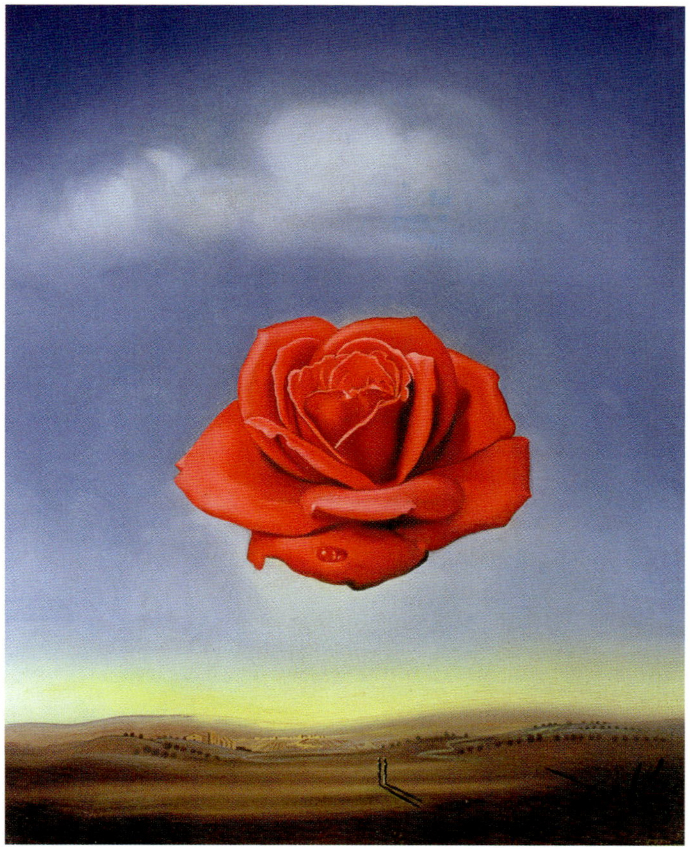

Publisher and Creative Director: Nick Wells
Commissioning Editor: Polly Prior
Senior Project Editor and Picture Research: Laura Bulbeck
Art Director and Layout Design: Mike Spender
Copy Editor: Ramona Lamport
Proofreader: Amanda Crook
Indexer: Amanda Leigh
Special thanks to: Gillian Whitaker, Jenna Cordisco and Frances Bodiam.

Publisher's Note: The quotes included on the pages featuring photographs of Dalí have not necessarily been sourced from the same books which the photographs were first printed in. These pages have been designed as artistic features, creating their own narrative.

FLAME TREE PUBLISHING
6 Melbray Mews
Fulham, SW6 3NS
United Kingdom

www.flametreepublishing.com

First published 2016

18 20 19
3 5 7 9 10 8 6 4 2

A CIP record for this book is available from the British Library upon request.

ISBN: 978-1-78361-993-1

Printed in China | Created, Developed & Produced in the United Kingdom

Salvador Dalí

MASTER of MODERN ART

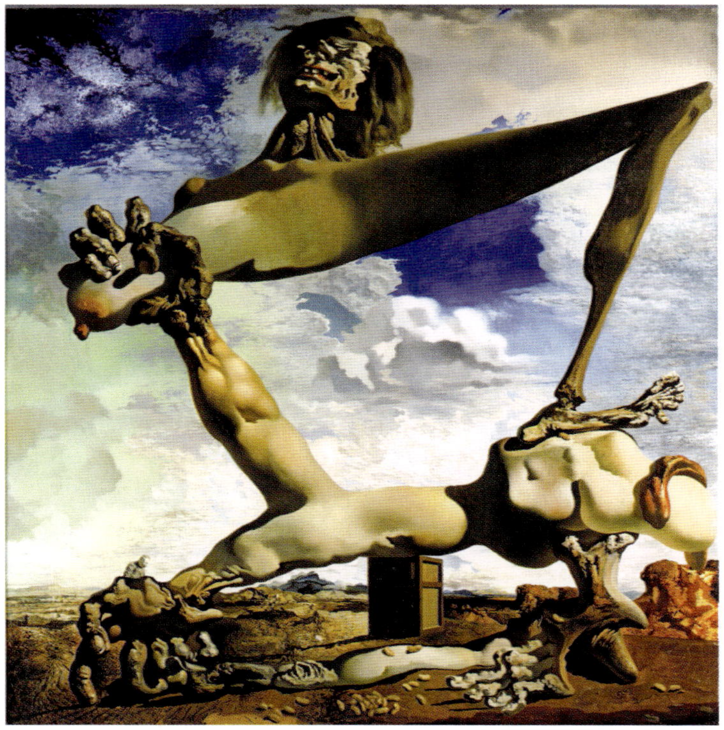

Julian Beecroft

FLAME TREE
PUBLISHING

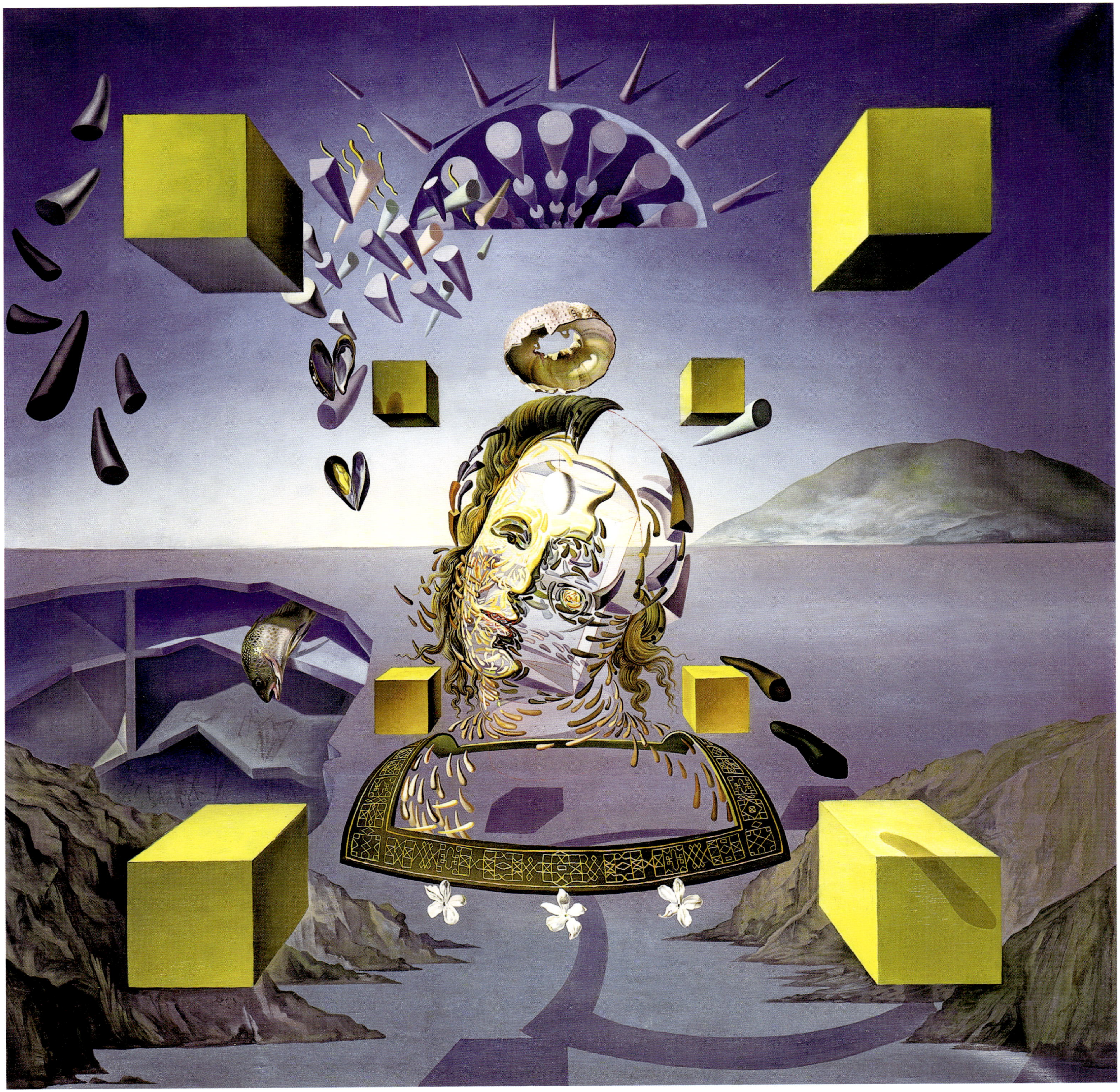

Contents

Introduction to Dalí: a Master of Visual Theatre

Perhaps no one in the annals of modern art has been more in the public eye in his own lifetime, or written with such candour about his own life, than the Surrealist artist Salvador Dalí (1904–89). And yet we can never be quite sure that what Dalí is telling us is either not made up or an unwitting delusion. This leads to the conclusion that Dalí himself may not have been sure who he meant by the artist he referred to as Dalí; that Surrealism for Dalí may not have been simply an aesthetic proposition but a psychological fact of life. As he puts it in his autobiography, *The Secret Life of Salvador Dalí*, published in 1942 when the artist was just 38 and at the height of his fame: 'I'm in a constant interrogation: where does the deep and philosophically valid Dalí begin, and where does the looney and preposterous Dalí end?'

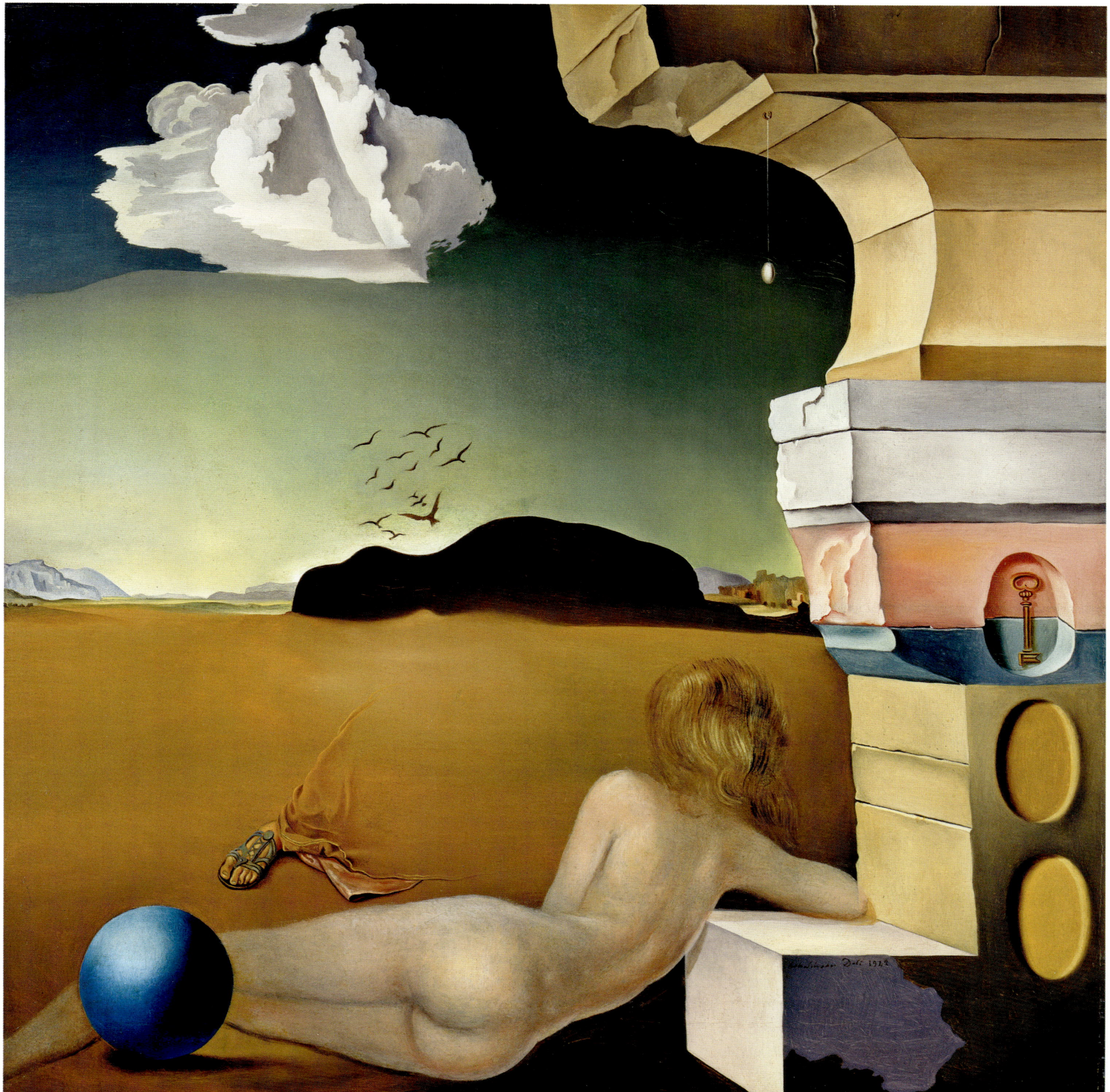

Nude on the Plain of Roses, **1942** | Medium: Oil on canvas | Dimensions: 50 x 50 cm (19¾ x 19¾ in) | Location: Private Collection

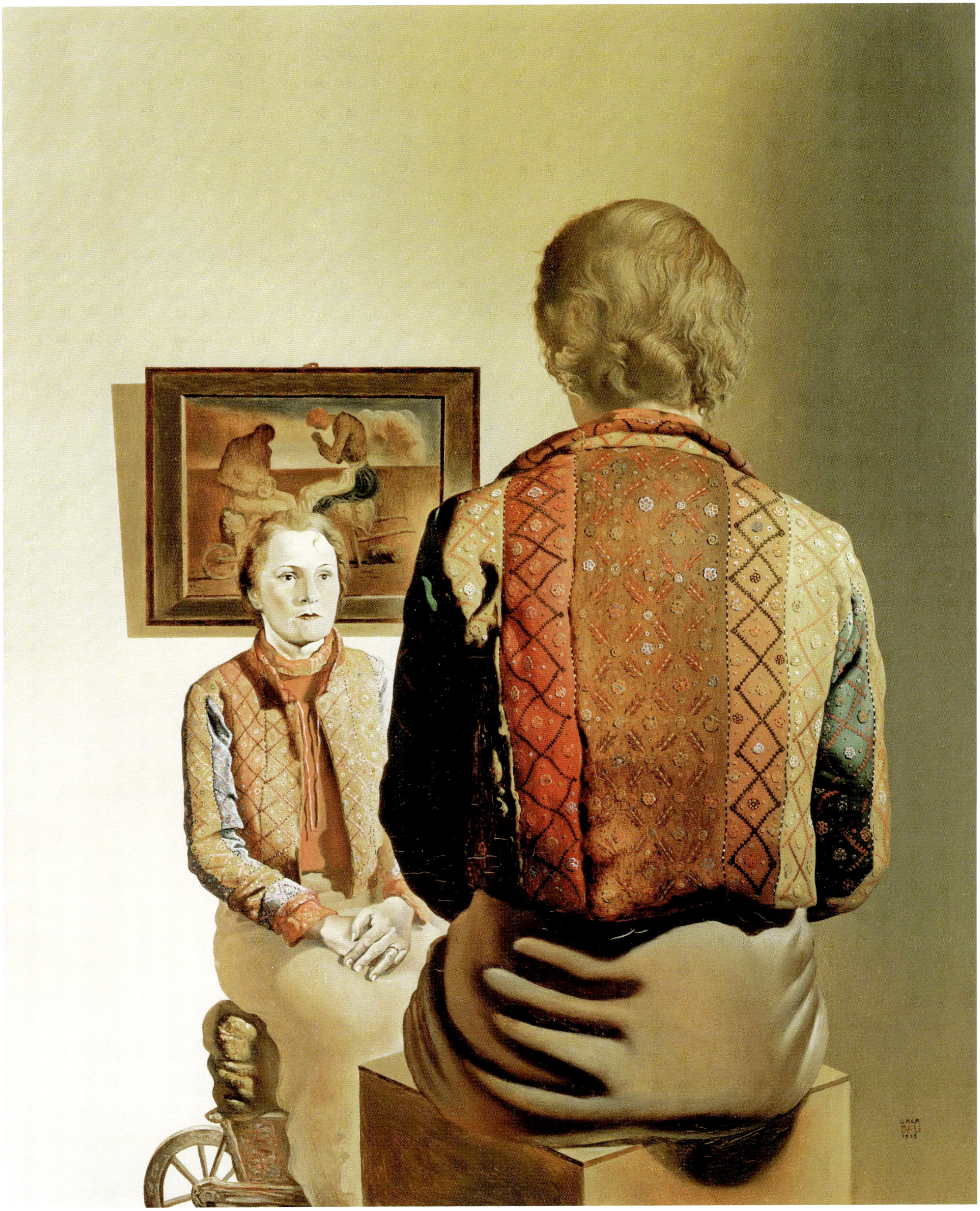
GALA
DALI

Surrealist Objects

It is a question that anyone would be minded to ask, having visited the Dalí Theatre-Museum in Figueres in northern Catalunya in the north-east corner of Spain. A compendium of Dalí's interests and achievements in so many forms of visual art, the Theatre-Museum is also a creation in itself, a Surrealist object that Dalí even came to describe as his greatest work. As with everything he made or painted or wrote, the Theatre-Museum is full of contradictions that take us closer to the soul of this master of illusion at the same time as they dispel the very idea of there being a soul to discover. The more he tells us, it seems, the less we can ever hope to know who Dalí was. It is quite probable that he never knew himself.

As we walk the corridor that encircles the central courtyard, we come across famous works, not only paintings and prints but other pieces – strange composite objects that reveal Dalí's knack, time and again, of dreaming up images whose implausibility is not simply bizarre but utterly compelling. Works like *Retrospective Bust of a Woman* (1933, *see below*) defy a conventional analysis, being rooted in the unconscious, the bottomless pit of irrationality that Dalí and his fellow Surrealists had made it their mission to explore. Nevertheless, we know from what Dalí wrote about his work and his life, and by comparing the *Retrospective Bust* with his paintings, that this object, to take just one example, bears many of the hallmarks and psychological obsessions that we find in his paintings from the same period.

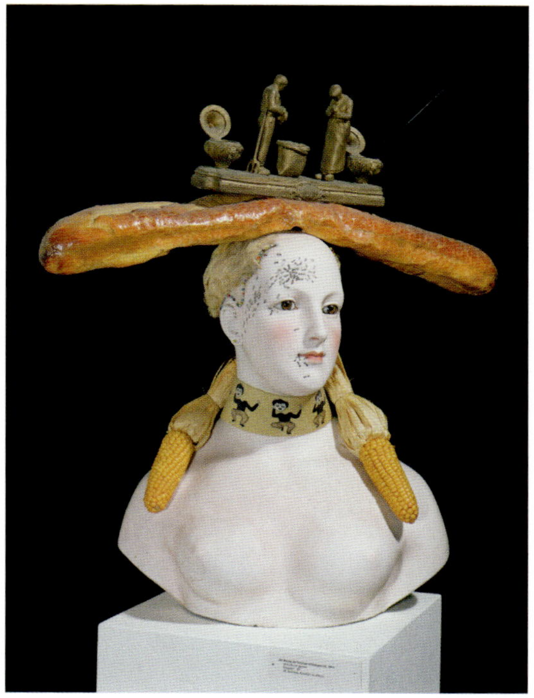

A *Retrospective Bust*

Despite his assertion of having invented the Surrealist object, Dalí was in fact extending a tradition of absurdist *objets trouvés* (found objects) that went back at least to the *Fountain* (1917) of Marcel Duchamp (1887–1968), the readymade urinal he signed with a fictitious signature to mock the exalted pretensions of fine art. But the power of *Retrospective Bust of a Woman*, so typical of Dalí, is rooted not in an impersonal critique of social and aesthetic convention but in his own personal neuroses, which lie at the heart of nearly all his most powerful work.

(Left)

Portrait of Gala, 1935
Medium: Oil on wood
Dimensions: 32.4 x 26.7 cm (12¾ x 10½ in)
Location: Museum of Modern Art, New York

(Above)

Retrospective Bust of a Woman, 1933
Medium: Painted porcelain, bread, corn, feathers, paint on paper, beads, ink stand, sand, and two pens
Dimensions: 73.9 x 69.2 x 32 cm (29 x 27¼ x 12⅗ in)
Location: Museum of Modern Art, New York

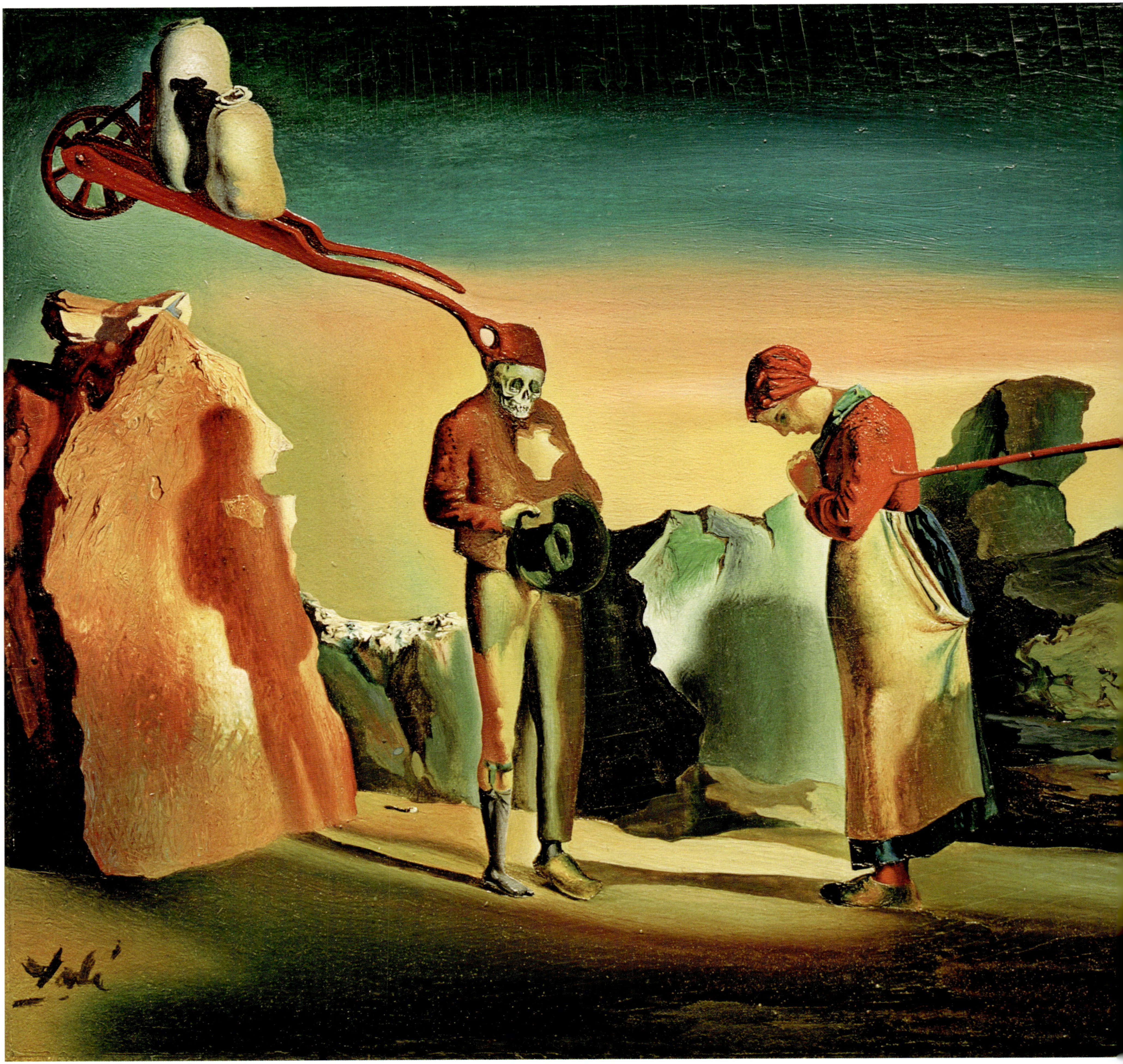
Dalí

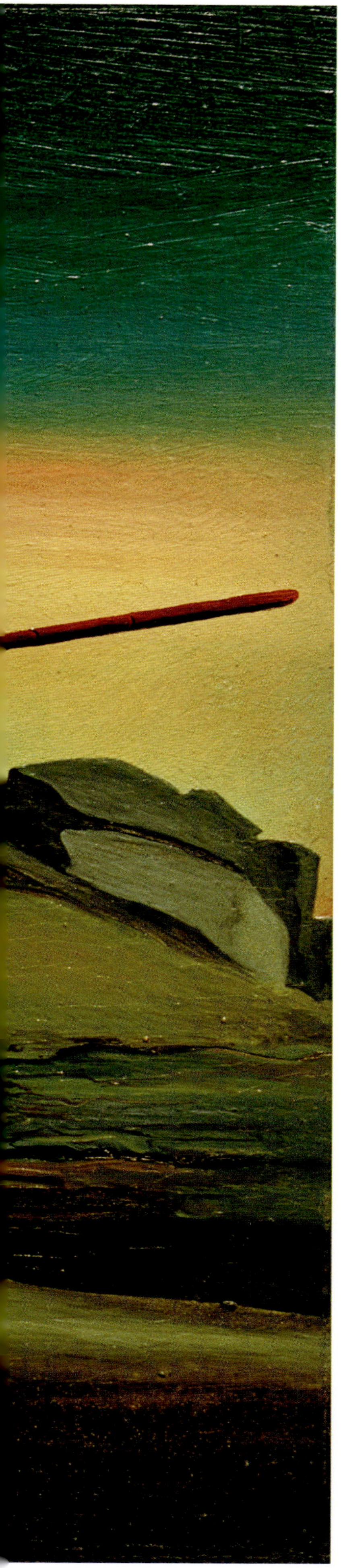

'My painting is the least important thing about me.'

Above all, this classic Surrealist piece is topped by the two figures from the *Angelus* (1859) of Jean-François Millet (1814–75), a painting that had held Dalí in thrall as a child. In 1932 it had resurfaced as a powerful memory, giving rise to one of his most important essays, 'The Tragic Myth of Millet's *Angelus*' (1933), in which he gave the first explanation of the paranoiac-critical method, his most significant artistic perception and the technique – as much psychological as technical – which in one form or another he would make use of throughout his career. The same discovery also led to some of the most troubling images Dalí would ever paint, such as *Meditation on the Harp* (1932–34, *see* page 14) and *Atavism at Twilight* (1933–34, *see* left), as well as the *Retrospective Bust of a Woman*.

A Prayer and a Loaf of Bread

Having come across an inkwell decorated with an image of the praying couple from Millet's painting (whom in the essay as well as in numerous paintings on this theme he depicted as eroticised figures), in the *Retrospective Bust of a Woman* Dalí embeds a symmetrical pair of inkwells and pens in a baguette, together with figurines of the scene from the *Angelus*. The bread, in turn, straddles with surprising fitness the head of a mannequin, as if it were a bicorn hat. The baguette is real, as – according to Dalí's account in *The Secret Life* – at the work's

(Left)

Atavism at Twilight, 1933–34

Medium: Oil on wood
Dimensions: 13.8 x 17.9 cm (5⁵⁄₁₆ x 7 in)
Location: Kunst Museum, Bern

first exhibition a dog belonging to Pablo Picasso (1881–1973) proceeded to eat it. (The version in the Theatre-Museum is not the original one.)

But why a mannequin? Dalí was acutely alive both to tradition and modernity, and here he teases us by posing an apparently antique bust that looks somehow mass-produced, as if she has been taken from the shop window of some chichi department store. Across her forehead and face, a colony of ants can be seen crawling, a deliberate insult to beauty. This is yet another familiar Dalínian motif, rooted in a childhood memory of seeing a dead lizard rotting and swarmed over by ants. It is as if the purity of the beautiful woman has been corrupted by the putrefaction of death; as if the woman herself were as edible, and as perishable, as the bread.

But who is she? Do those corn cobs dangling from her shoulders indicate a goddess of fertility, or are the cartoon figures on the zoetrope strip around her neck, to which the cobs are attached, a send-up of the very idea of gods, goddesses and a world that might differ from the one in which we earn our daily bread?

A Fondness for Fetish

In an object such as this we see not only how the Surrealist movement – of which by 1933 Dalí was a leading member – had sought to ridicule and unsettle conventional ways of making and understanding art, but also how Dalí had a particular ability to make disturbingly familiar images by reassembling reality according to his own neurotic whims. Indeed, it was natural that someone who, as we shall see, routinely fetishized objects in his paintings would soon end up making them; exploring or perhaps exploiting his own feelings of erotic alienation through the strangeness of the objects he created, as is the case with *Retrospective Bust of a Woman*. As Dalí himself put it in *The Secret Life*: 'The Surrealist object is one that is absolutely useless from the practical and rational point of view, created wholly for the purpose of materializing in a fetishistic way, with the maximum of tangible reality, ideas and fantasies having a delirious character.'

Lobsters and Sofas

Throughout the 1930s, Dalí made three-dimensional pieces that still possess this delirious and startling character, even today.

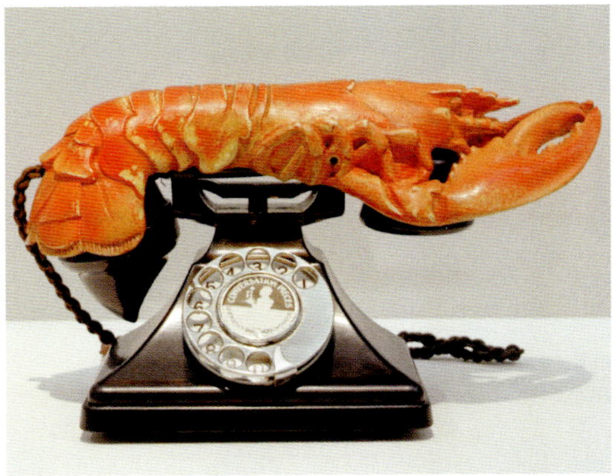

(Above)

Lobster Telephone, 1936

Medium: Telephone with lobster (made of painted plaster) on the handset
Dimensions: 18 x 12.5 x 30.5 cm (7 x 5 x 12 in)
Location: Museum für Kommunikation, Frankfurt

The *Lobster Telephone* (1936, *see* left) makes a purely morphological connection between the shapes of a crustacean and a telephone – at the time still a fairly new technology – as if this apparently beneficial device had a sinister side that we had not seen until Dalí had pointed it out to us. Such a sense of threat indeed seems to be the case with the telephones that appear in his paintings in the late 1930s. And having painted *Mae West's Face Which May Be Used as a Surrealist Apartment* (1934–35), Dalí then created another enduring object that very quickly entered the popular imagination, the *Mae West Lips Sofa* (1936–37, *see* page 16). This in turn led to his three-dimensional re-creation of the original picture as a room in the Theatre-Museum in Figueres, complete with the two illusionistic paintings in the original picture, double images which are both cityscapes as well as the Hollywood siren's eyes (*see* page 17). This flamboyant theatricality, the sheer populist chutzpah of some of his 3D

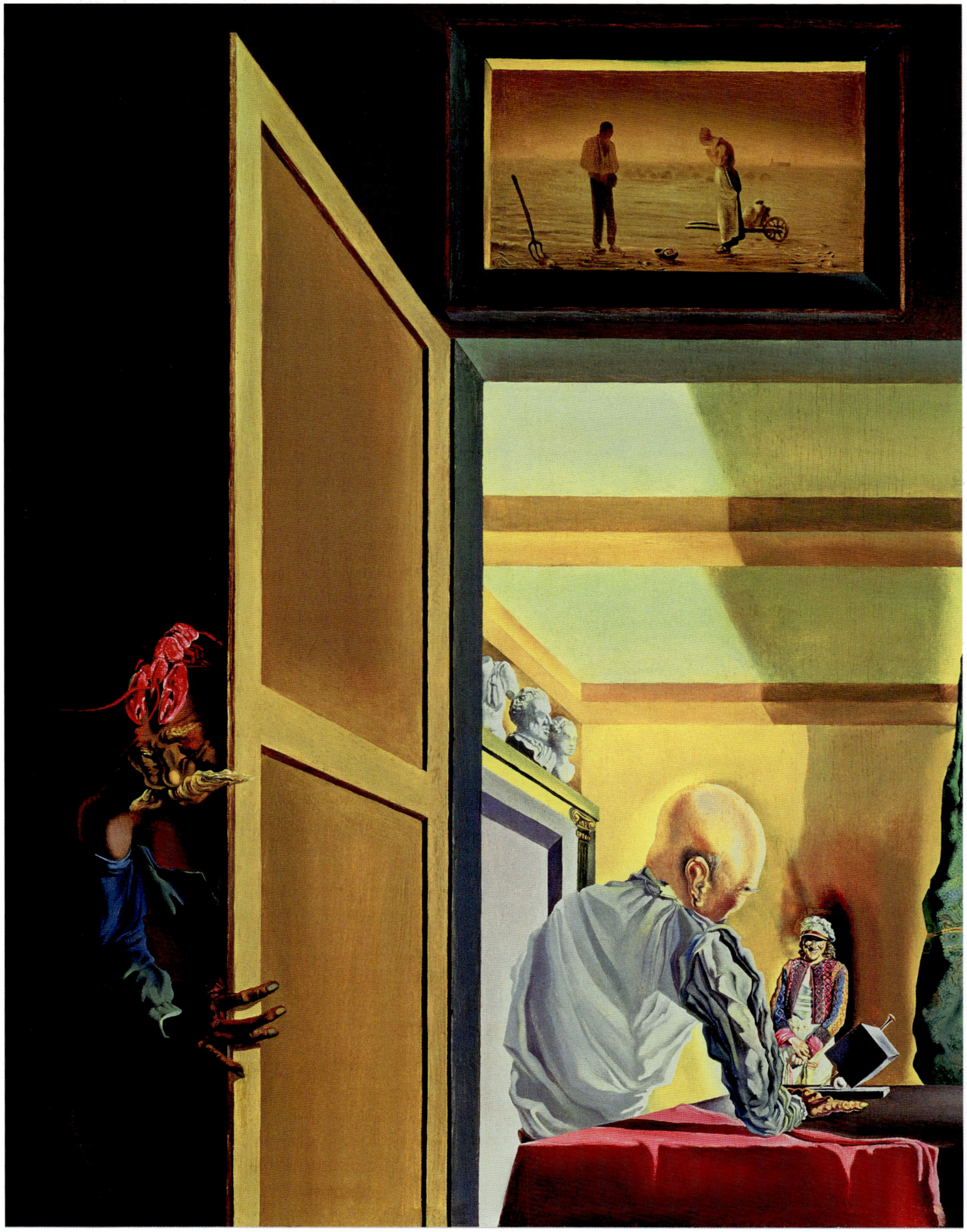

(Right)

Gala and the Angelus of Millet Before the Imminent Arrival of the Conical Anamorphoses, 1933

Medium: Oil on panel
Dimensions: 24 x 18.8 cm (9½ x 7½ in)
Location: National Gallery of Canada, Ottawa, Ontario

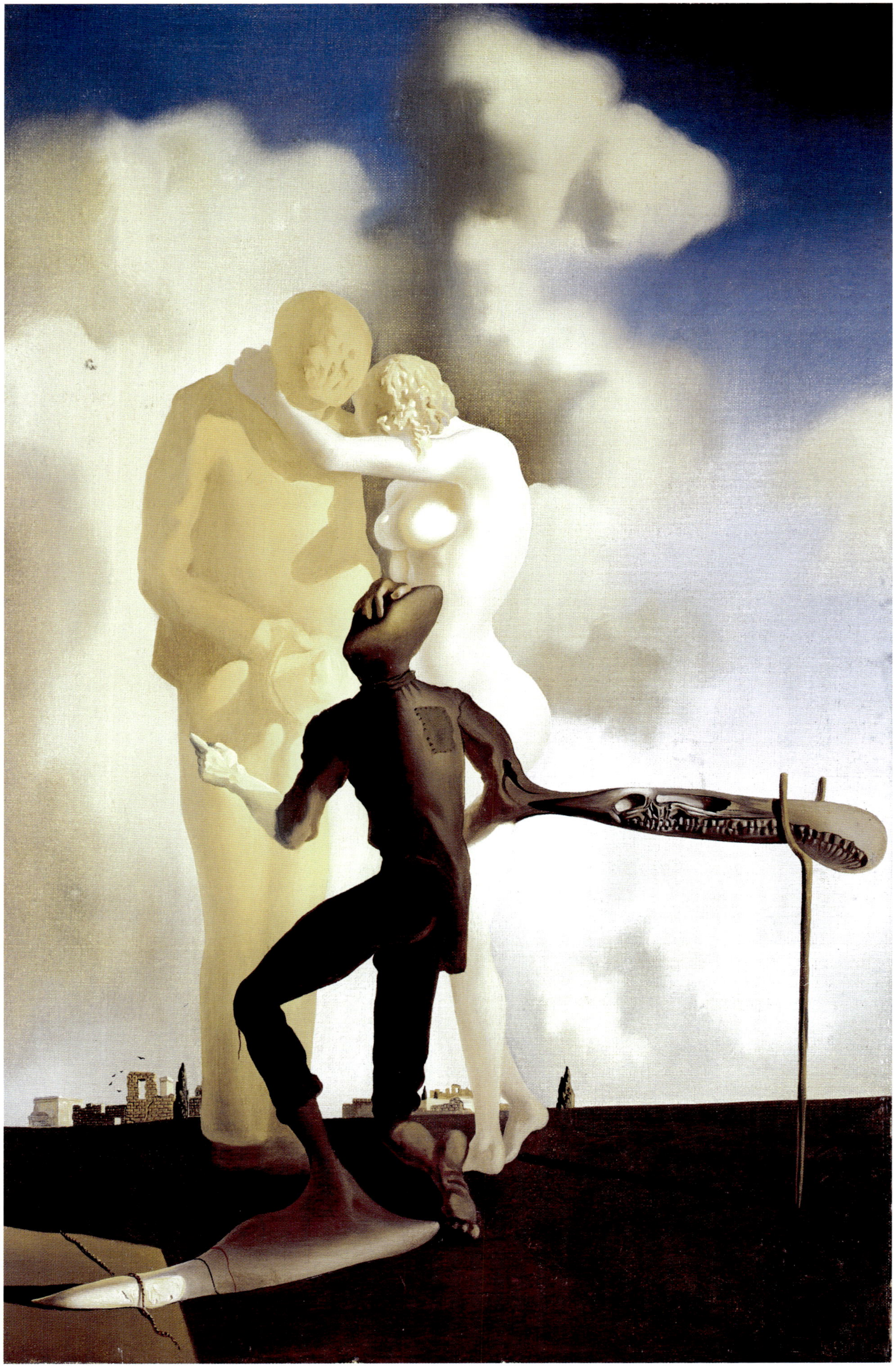

work, is something unique to Dalí among artists of the time and set an obvious precedent for the fetishized kitsch of some of the leading artists of our own day, such as Jeff Koons (b. 1955) and Damien Hirst (b. 1965). Koons, for one, credits Dalí, whom he met as a young artist living in New York, as having a big impact on his own work, singling out in particular the *Retrospective Bust of a Woman* (see page 9).

The *Rainy Taxi*

Looking into the courtyard of the Theatre-Museum, we see a black Cadillac – a present from Dalí to his wife, Gala (1894–1982) – which he had had shipped over from the United States so that in the late 1940s, by then a picture of worldly success, he could turn up in swanky elegance at his father's house in Figueres. But if we push a coin into the slot by the door, it begins to rain inside the cab – a typical twist. This is the famous *Rainy Taxi* (1938), another show-stopping exhibit which features a mannequin driver and similar backseat passenger, an elegant female done up to the nines but with snails oozing their slimy flesh all over the woman's body and her sopping-wet hairdo. In the original version exhibited at the Salon des Surindépendants in Paris that year, the cab driver had a shark's head in place of a human one, and the same idea was one that Dalí made use of in a different form the following year in *The Dream of Venus* (1939), a spectacular pavilion he designed for the New York World's Fair, which opened just as Europe was gearing itself up for another disastrous war.

The Dream of Venus

In the event, the spectacle Dalí came up with included live bare-breasted mermaids complete with fishes' heads instead of the more conventional tails. Set in a large pool amid a backdrop of giant reproductions of classic Renaissance images, including a cut-out of the goddess from *The Birth of Venus* (1482–85) by Sandro Botticelli (*c.* 1445–1510), it was not so much the titillating nudity the sponsors objected to – far from it – but the seemingly perverse reconfiguration of the mermaids' fish anatomy relative to their human parts, with the result that behind his back the sponsors reversed Dalí's reimagining to the normal mermaid format, which they felt the public would more readily accept. Dalí issued a famously robust manifesto, his 'Declaration of the Independence of the Imagination and the Rights of Man to His Own Madness', but beyond this wholly justifiable defence of his artistic integrity he would also have seen a priceless opportunity for the kind of self-promotion in which he never ceased to indulge. In this, as also in conceiving an artwork as installation – even performance – he was clearly a godfather to the sensibility of our own age.

> 'In the first place my work was violent and audacious.'

Schiaparelli and the Shoe Hat

Having courted controversy and fame in America throughout the later 1930s, Dalí became one of many European artists and intellectuals driven there by war at the end of the decade. He not only lived in the US throughout most of the 1940s but thereafter was in the habit of returning for several months every winter, where he and Gala would install themselves in a suite at the St Regis Hotel in New York

(Left)

Meditation on the Harp, 1932–34
Medium: Oil on canvas
Dimensions: 67 x 47 cm (26⅜ x 18½ in)
Location: Salvador Dalí Museum, St Petersburg, Florida

City. And following the World's Fair and other spectacular incidents that invariably made the newspapers, Dalí was never short of work in a variety of fields, from covers for *Vogue* to advertisements for any manufacturer who would pay him a big enough fee, to set and costume designs for the theatre and for his own ballets.

By then, Dalí had already made his mark on fashion, having designed the celebrated shoe hat which in 1937 Elsa Schiaparelli (1890–1973) turned into a fashion classic. It was one of a number of Dalí's ideas from which the great Italian designer made daring couture, though Schiaparelli was not the only couturier whose friendship the Dalís enjoyed. They were also on intimate terms with Coco Chanel (1883–1971), the doyenne of twentieth-century fashion having invited them to stay at her villa in the South of France for several months in early 1939. Chanel also made some of the costumes for Dalí's first ballet, *Bacchanale* (1939), which was staged in New York to great acclaim later that year. It was one of many theatre projects, both his own and those of others, in which Dalí would immerse himself over the following decade.

Un Chien Andalou

However, the art form which throughout his life teased him more than any other with its possibilities was film, which at one point Dalí felt held the greatest potential for the creation of Surrealist images, given its capacity for the metamorphosis of images and objects over time. In truth, though he was never short of projects he wanted to tackle, his involvement in the medium would be a frustrating experience following a single, astonishing early success. The film was called *Un Chien Andalou* (1929), a 20-minute silent movie that still has the power to shock. Moreover, despite its brevity and the minimal resources used in its production, this quintessential Surrealist masterpiece has exerted a profound influence on the history of the cinema, not to mention the medium of the art film. The scenario was conceived jointly with his friend Luis Buñuel (1900–83) in a process that Buñuel himself later described as both harmonious and creatively liberating: 'Our only rule was very simple: no idea or image that would lend itself to a rational explanation of any kind would be accepted. We had to open all the doors to the irrational and keep only those images which surprised us, without trying to explain why.'

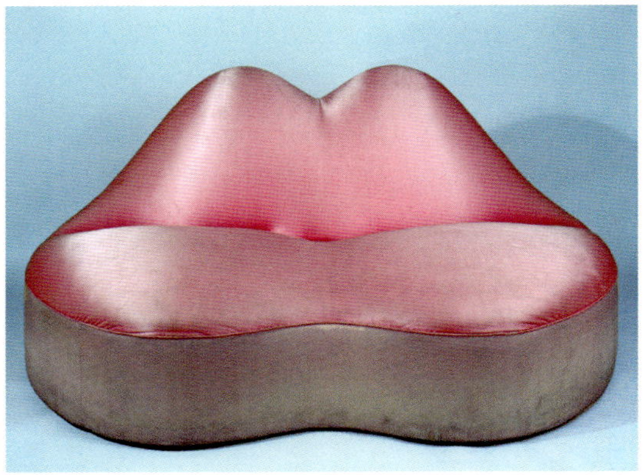

(Above)

Mae West Lips Sofa, 1938

Medium: Wood carcass upholstered in pink satin
Dimensions: 86.5 x 183 x 81.5 cm (34 x 72 x 32⅛ in)
Location: The Trustees of The Edward James Foundation, Chichester

(Right)

Reconstruction of the image known as 'Mae West's Face Which May be Used as a Surrealist Apartment', 1934–35

Medium: Mixed media
Location: Teatre-Museu Dalí, Figueres

Rotting Donkeys

Beyond the initial fleshing out of scenes, Dali also appears in the film as one of two priests being dragged along the floor by a rope tied around his middle. But his most telling involvement was the preparation of the heads of two putrefying corpses of donkeys that lie beneath the lid of a grand piano in one of the film's most dramatic and disturbing scenes – the same one in which he appears. Dali describes it with typical attention to revolting detail in *The Secret Life*. 'The shooting of the scene of the rotten donkeys and the pianos was a rather fine sight, I must say. I "made up" the putrefaction of the donkeys with great pots of sticky glue which I poured over

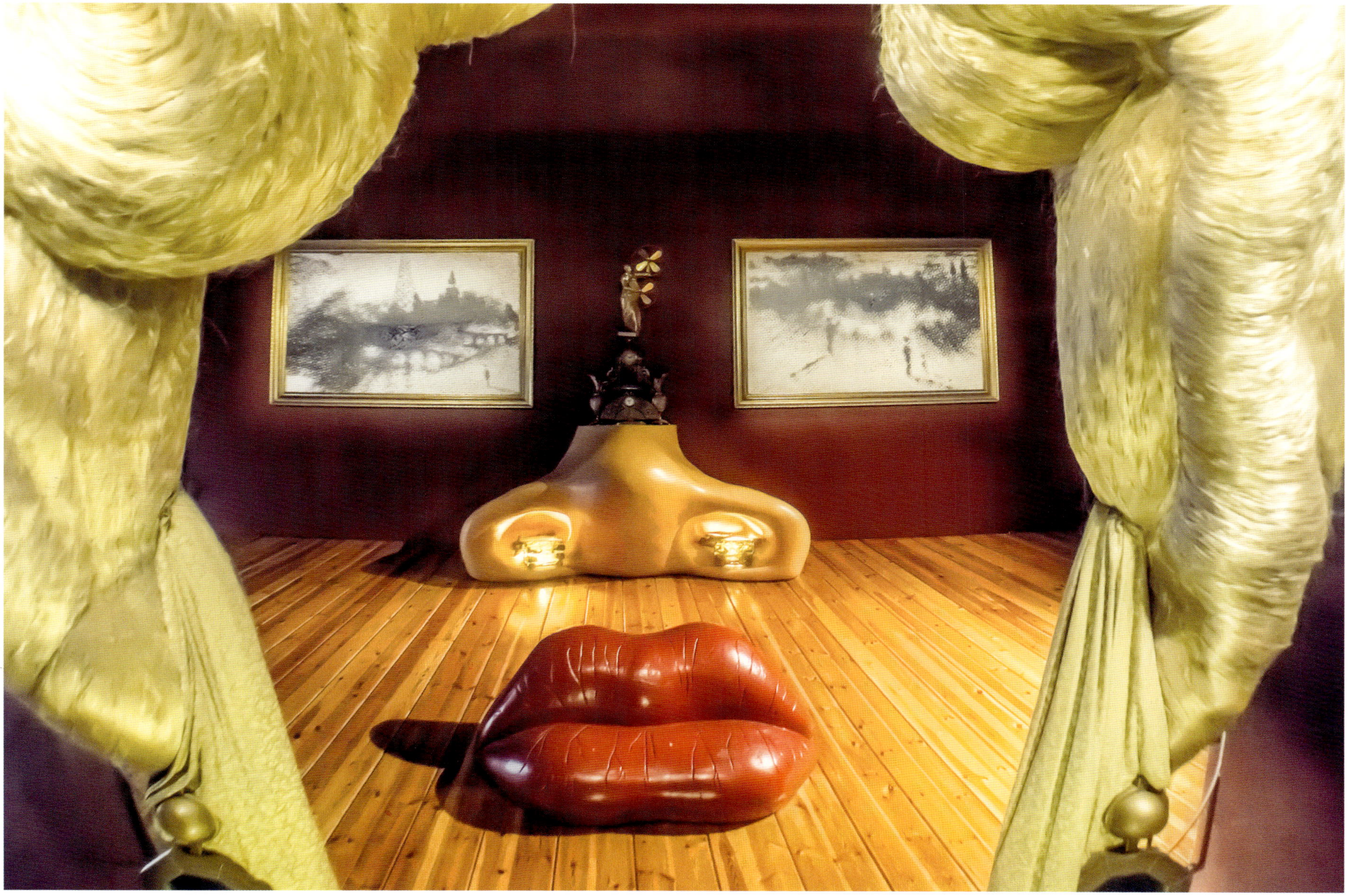

them. Also I emptied their eye-sockets and made them larger by hacking them out with scissors. In the same way I furiously cut their mouths open to make the white rows of their teeth show to better advantage, and I added several jaws to each mouth so that it would appear that although the donkeys were already rotting they were still vomiting up a little more of their own death, above those other rows of teeth formed by the keys of the black pianos. The whole effect was as lugubrious as fifty coffins piled into a single room.'

'The one thing the world will never have enough of is the outrageous.'

Spellbound

The resulting film shocked the Parisian avant-garde, a success that was topped, at least in scandal, the following year by *L'Age d'Or* (1930), another collaboration with Buñuel. Dalí would later more or less disown his involvement in this project, describing the film in *The Secret Life* as 'crudely anti-clerical', an estimation which by then fitted with his ever more conservative, even reactionary view of politics and human affairs. In fact, it would not be until Hollywood came calling in the mid-1940s that Dalí would get another opportunity to work in the medium, specifically when asked by Alfred Hitchcock (1899–1980) to design the dream sequence of his film, *Spellbound* (1945). Hitchcock chose the painter because Dalí's images were always sharply defined, belying conventional wisdom

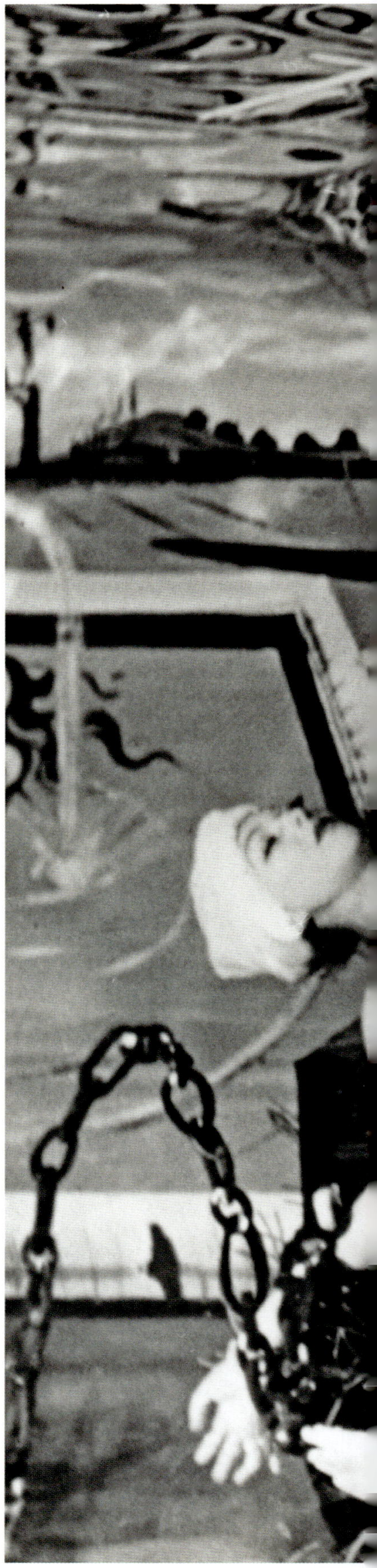

(Right)

The Dream of Venus, Pavilion Built for the New York World's Fair, 1939
Photograph by Eric Schaal (1905–94)

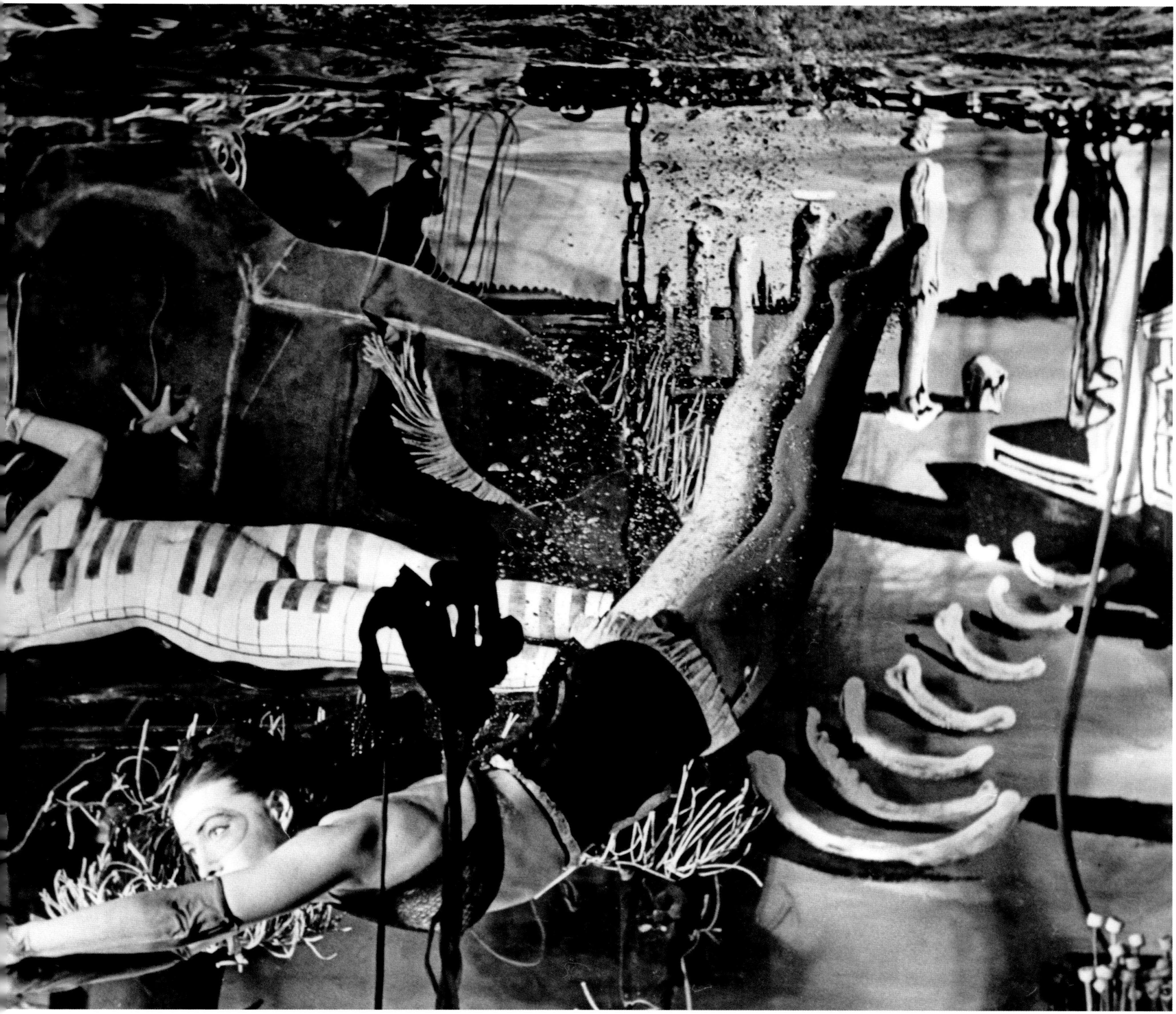

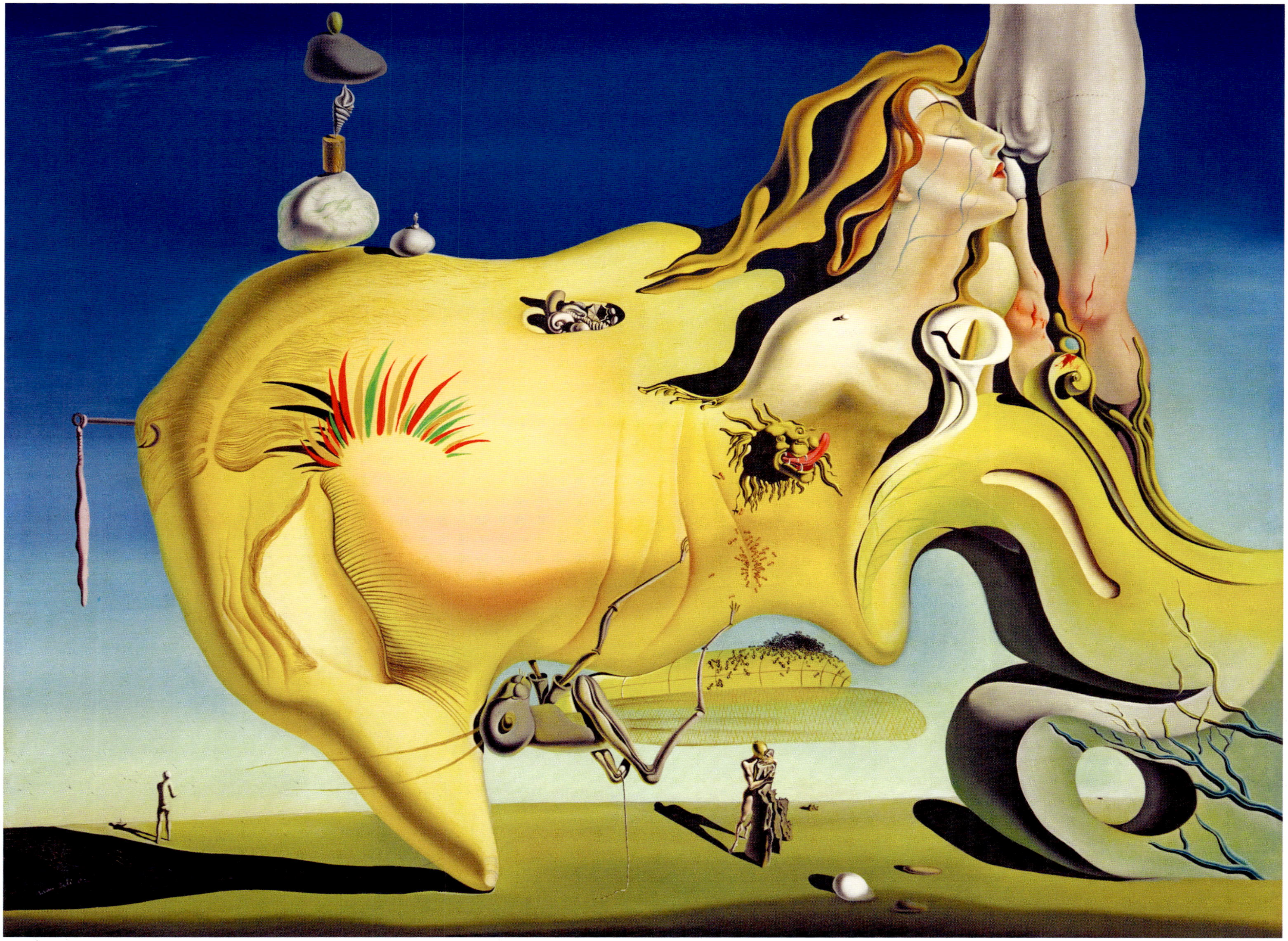

concerning the visual content of the images that appear in dreams. The one sequence, separated into three short scenarios, which made the final cut would have been many people's first glimpse of the Dalinian imagination. But those who knew Dalí's paintings would have noted familiar themes: melting wheels echoing the clocks of his most famous painting, *The Persistence of Memory* (1931, *see* page 84); a grossly distorted head inclined towards the ground, as if dreaming, evoking the one in *The Great Masturbator* (1929, *see* left) and other works of his early Surrealist period; and an eye cut with a pair of scissors, recalling the most shocking scene from *Un Chien Andalou*. In fact, what remains in the film is far less than either Hitchcock or Dalí had wanted, and when another collaboration – an animated film for Walt Disney – came to nothing despite the months the artist had spent working on it, he became fairly disillusioned with the collaborative nature of film-making.

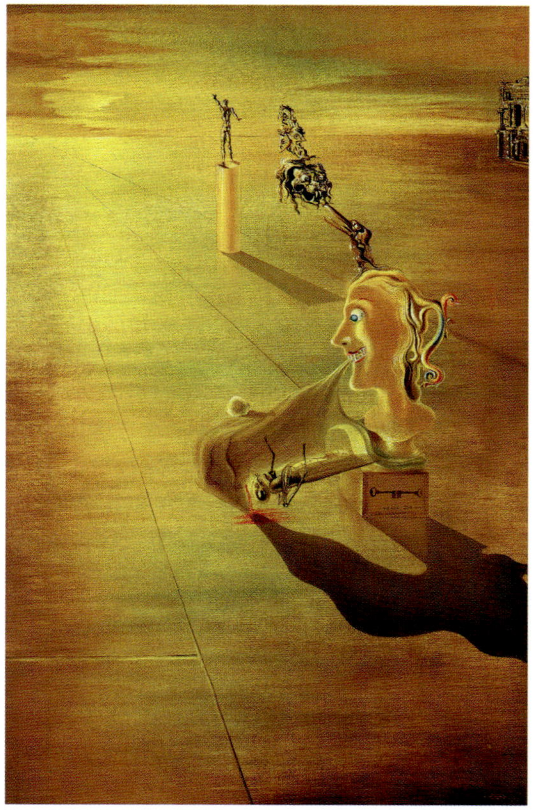

'For me, then, the erotic must always be ugly.'

Dalí's Jewels

By this point Dalí had also started making jewellery, some examples of which can be seen today in a separate part of the Theatre-Museum in Figueres. Among these remarkable artefacts, which in many cases are quite obviously too large and impractical to be worn as jewellery, are *The Space Elephant* (1956), a golden elephant with long spider's legs and an emerald obelisk on its back, echoing the motif of the *Elephant and Obelisk* sculpture by Gian Lorenzo Bernini (1598–1680), erected in 1667, which had appeared in several paintings over the previous decade; and *The Royal Heart* (1953), a piece Dalí made apparently in memory of his mother, no doubt partly in penance for the way he had insulted that memory in an image made some 20 years earlier, which had also featured a Sacred Heart.

It is clear then that Dalí's work in other media derived its content principally from

(Left)

The Great Masturbator, 1929

Medium: Oil on canvas
Dimensions: 110 x 150.5 cm (43 1/3 x 59 in)
Location: Museo Nacional Centro de Arte Reina Sofía, Madrid

(Above)

Phantasmagoria, 1929

Medium: Oil on panel
Dimensions: 69 x 44 cm (27 1/4 x 17 1/3 in)
Location: Private Collection

the obsessions he explored as a painter. It was in painting that all these themes were first worked out, and it was to painting that he returned time and again whenever he tired of his addiction to publicity – what he referred to in *The Secret Life* as 'the tragical sequence of exhibitionism' which by then defined the public man. It was a compulsion – a performer's curse, if you like – that Dalí would only escape when as a rather broken old showman he was no longer able to perform – a need that would lead him to declare more than once that 'My painting is the least important thing about me.'

Dalí's Moustache

This seems an inexplicable statement to anyone who knows his art, but then, as with so much that Dalí wrote and said, it is hard to know whether he really meant it. But it is also clear that the creation he felt most compelled to thrust before the public eye, the most persistent Surrealist object of them all, was the persona of Dalí himself. Indeed, he routinely referred to himself in the third person, a living caricature complete with wide, rolling eyes and an ever-growing moustache whose two ends, turned absurdly skywards, he referred to as his 'antennae'. This facial appendage was immortalized in a book of brilliant but ridiculous images called simply *Dalí's Mustache* (1954), created by Dalí and his long-time collaborator, the photographer Philippe Halsman (1906–79). The same man also took *Dalí Atomicus* (1948, *see* right), the infamous photo of a jumping Dalí and the flying cats about to be drenched with water, a typically dramatic Surrealist image, complete with the casual cruelty towards animals for which Dalí and Gala were notorious.

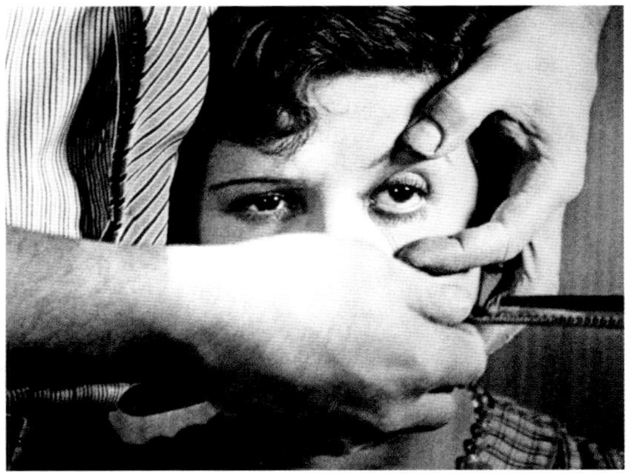

(Above)

Film still from *Un Chien Andalou*, 1929

But the exhibitionist Dalí, a carefully crafted portrait of immorality which increasingly came to dominate the public's view of him in his final decades, was an idea he had nurtured through so many activities beyond painting. It was also perhaps as much a smokescreen as an exercise in seeking attention. And therein lies the paradox of Dalí: no other artist of his time courted the public imagination like he did, and in controlling it so completely succeeded in hiding in plain sight. It is only perhaps through his paintings that we might hope to understand the man behind the mask of genius, who desperately needed to be understood yet perhaps also lived in dread that one day this was exactly what would happen.

(Right)

Dali Atomicus, 1948

Photograph by Philippe Halsman (1906–79)

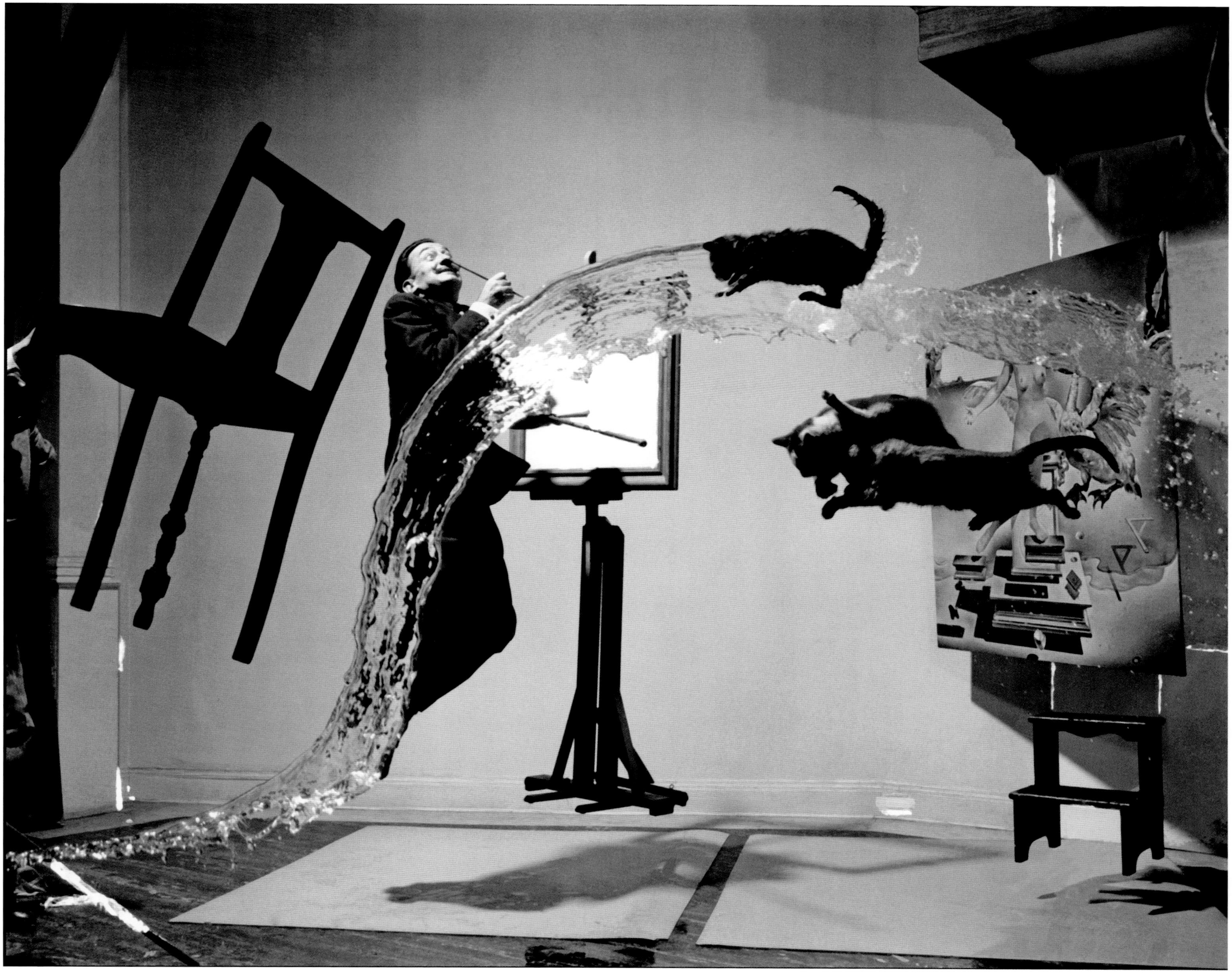

The Boy Who Would Be King

Salvador Dalí was born on 11 May 1904 in the provincial town of Figueres in Catalunya in northern Spain. His sister, Anna Maria, remembers their childhood as having been largely harmonious. His father, after whom he was named, was the notary of the town, an important and well-respected position that brought with it a good income which afforded the family a comfortable life. As a result, in addition to the spacious apartment they occupied in the heart of Figueres, the family also owned a house in the coastal village of Cadaqués, where young Salvador spent the long hot summers of his childhood.

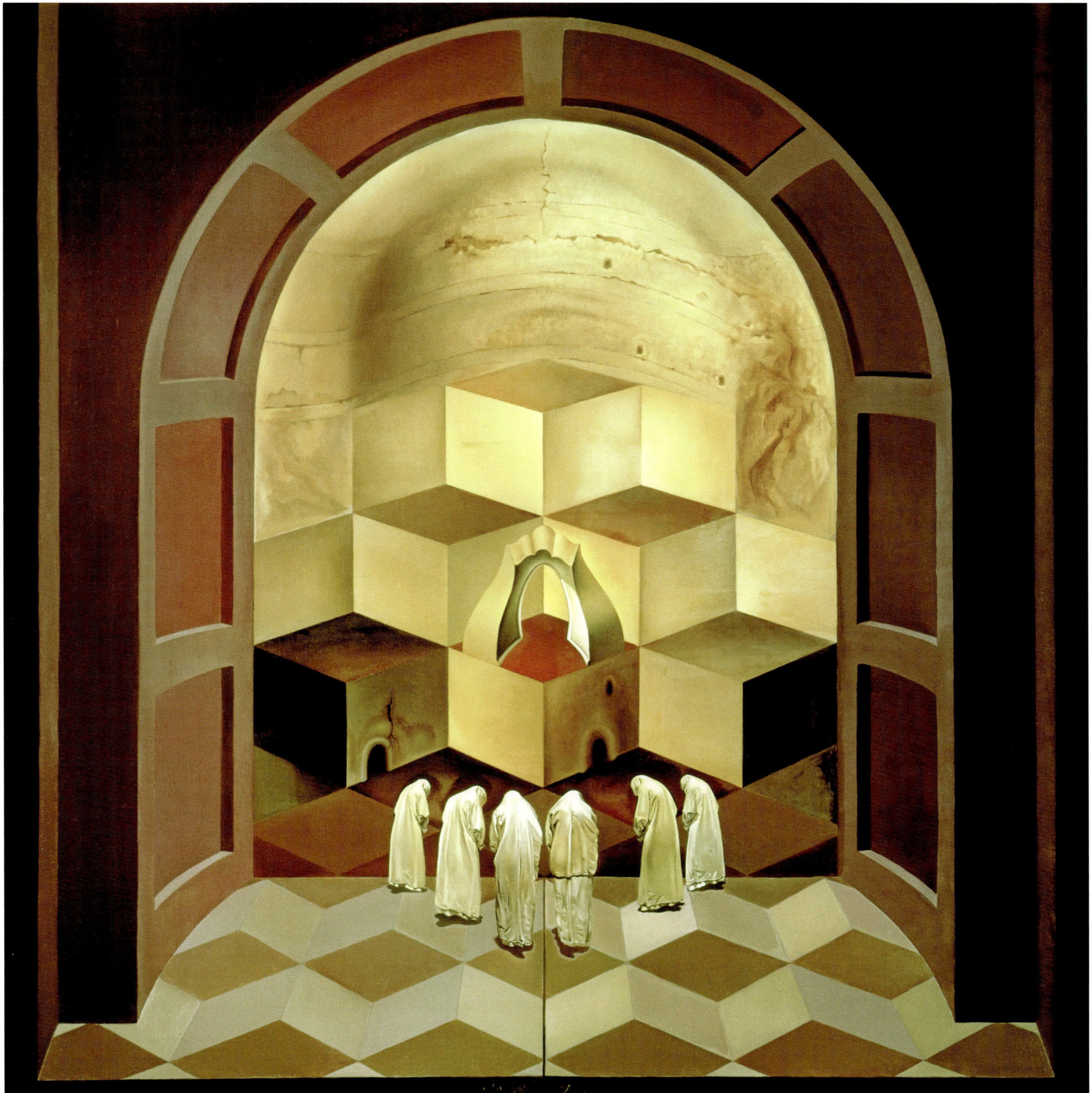

***Skull of Zurbarán*, 1956** | Medium: Oil on canvas | Dimensions: 100.3 x 100.3 cm (39½ x 39½ in) | Location: Hirshhorn Museum and Sculpture Garden, Washington D.C.

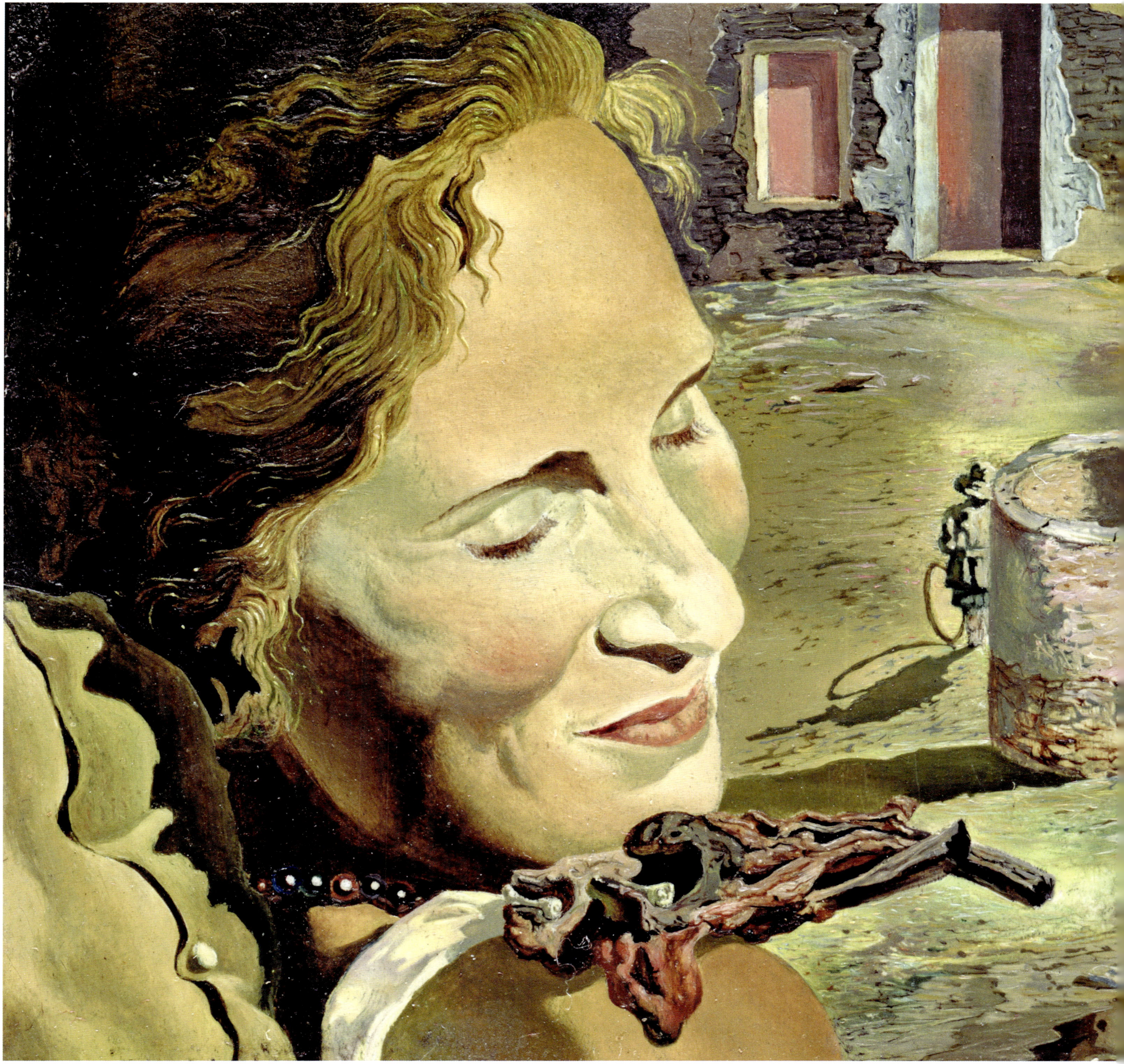

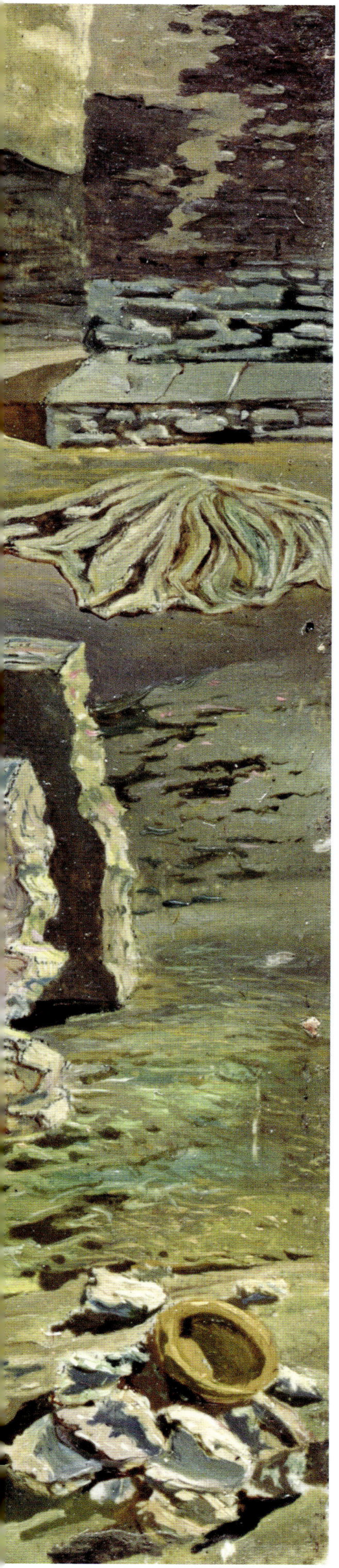

'Every good painter who aspires to the creation of genuine masterpieces should first of all marry my wife.'

(Left)

Portrait of Gala Balancing Two Lamb Chops on Her Shoulder, c. 1934

Medium: Oil on canvas
Dimensions: 6.9 x 8.8 cm (2¾ x 3½ in)
Location: Fundació Gala-Salvador Dalí, Figueres

The Empordà

This landscape of sea stretching to the horizon, framed by imposing headlands of rock, would form a consistent backdrop to Dalí's most famous works, along with the Empordà, the wide plain from which the town of Figueres rises up, 'whose unique geology with its utter vigour was later to fashion the entire aesthetic of the Dalinian landscape', as he describes it in his autobiography, *The Secret Life*. It is just such a notional plain as the Empordà, 'the most concrete and most objective piece of landscape that exists in the world', that appears in *Atavistic Vestiges After the Rain* (1934, *see* page 33) and other works that are now considered icons of Surrealism (albeit looking rather more parched than the lusher countryside to be seen around his childhood hometown). Dalí's opinion of this 'objective piece of landscape' is of course an entirely subjective judgement from someone who, by his own later admission, had little desire to see the world. But the absolute conviction of this statement reinforces the psychological truism he took to heart: that the experiences of childhood remain the most powerful we ever have and, in Dalí's case, were the inescapable raw material for his lifelong artistic obsessions.

Catalunya was then, as it always had been and as it remains today, a region with a strong identity of its own, not to mention a separate language, which had at different times been or belonged to a separate kingdom from the rest of Spain. This innate sense of difference was reinforced by the economic strength of the former principality, especially Barcelona, the largest city, which from the mid-nineteenth century onwards had built an industrial sector that was far in advance of anything that existed elsewhere in the country. As a result, resentment against rule from Madrid was always high, even among the prosperous middle class, and Dalí's father was not unusual in being an atheist, a Republican and a supporter of Catalan separatism, betraying a streak of defiance and rebellious independence that would quickly manifest in his son. Dalí's mother, however, was a Catholic whose humble piety was made more pronounced by the tragedy that befell the family – the death of Dalí's elder brother – before the future self-declared genius was even born, and that would cast a long shadow across his life.

The Other Salvador

In fact, Dalí's account, which describes his brother as having died at the age of seven and as bearing 'the unmistakable facial morphology of a genius' is a greatly distorted, even mythical version of what was still a terrible truth. His brother, also called Salvador, was born in 1901, less than three years before Dalí, but died at the age of 21 months, possibly of meningitis, as Dalí describes, although the death certificate gives the cause as 'catarrh with gastroenteritic infection'. In their grief, the parents nevertheless succeeded in replacing him just nine months later with a second son to whom his father had no qualms about giving the same name, his own, and who was never allowed to forget the boy he had replaced. It didn't help matters that the new child bore an uncanny resemblance to the one who preceded him, which the parents only accentuated by dressing the young Salvador in his dead brother's clothes and giving him the same toys to play with. Indeed, although this went against Catholic doctrine, his parents were convinced that Dalí was the reincarnation of his dead brother, and the young boy grew up believing the same.

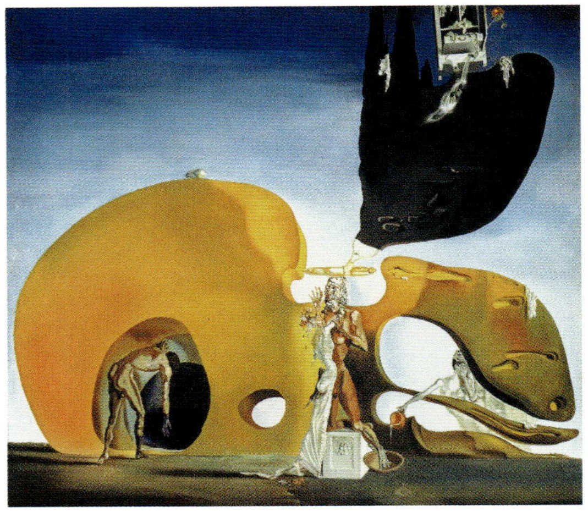

(Above)

The Birth of Liquid Desires, 1932

Medium: Oil on canvas
Dimensions: 95 x 112 cm (37⅖ x 44⅑ in)
Location: Peggy Guggenheim Foundation, Venice

Little Napoleon

The unreality of this belief, and the damage it did to young Salvador's sense of self was something of which he was always acutely aware. He later described his father's love as being like a laser beam which ceaselessly scanned his soul, 'looking for the other who no longer existed', and referred to a bloody wound which he carried in his side 'that my father, unmoved, unfeeling, ignorant of my anguished feelings, scoured incessantly with a love that battered me like a bludgeon'. The parents kept a photograph of the dead son in their bedroom, and indeed the young Salvador, the saviour of his parents' hopes, the redeemer of their grief, was taken regularly by his mother to visit his brother's grave. As a child, his imagination always haunted by his phantom sibling, he would fall asleep at night comforted by the fantasy that he himself was dead, picturing his own corpse lying inside a coffin. The thought of his brother, whom he later imagined as a young man in *Portrait of My Dead Brother* (1963, *see* page 168), remained a cause of anguish throughout his life.

Ever fearful of some new calamity that might befall their eldest living child, the parents wrapped the young Dalí in cotton wool and ceded to his every whim, thus encouraging the manipulative rages that

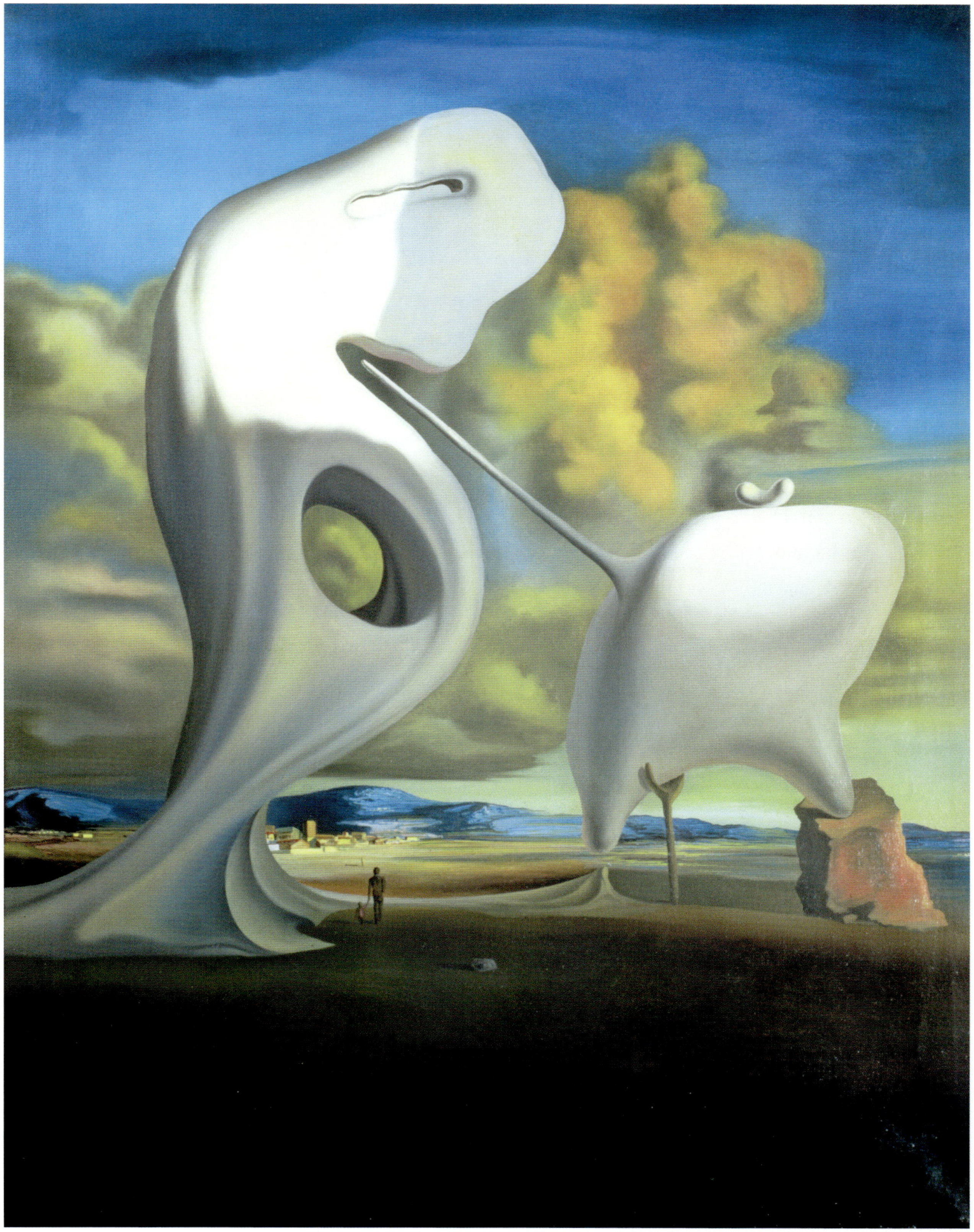

(Right)

The Architectonic Angelus of Millet, 1933

Medium: Oil on canvas
Dimensions: 73 x 60 cm (28¾ x 23⅝ in)
Location: Perls Galleries, New York

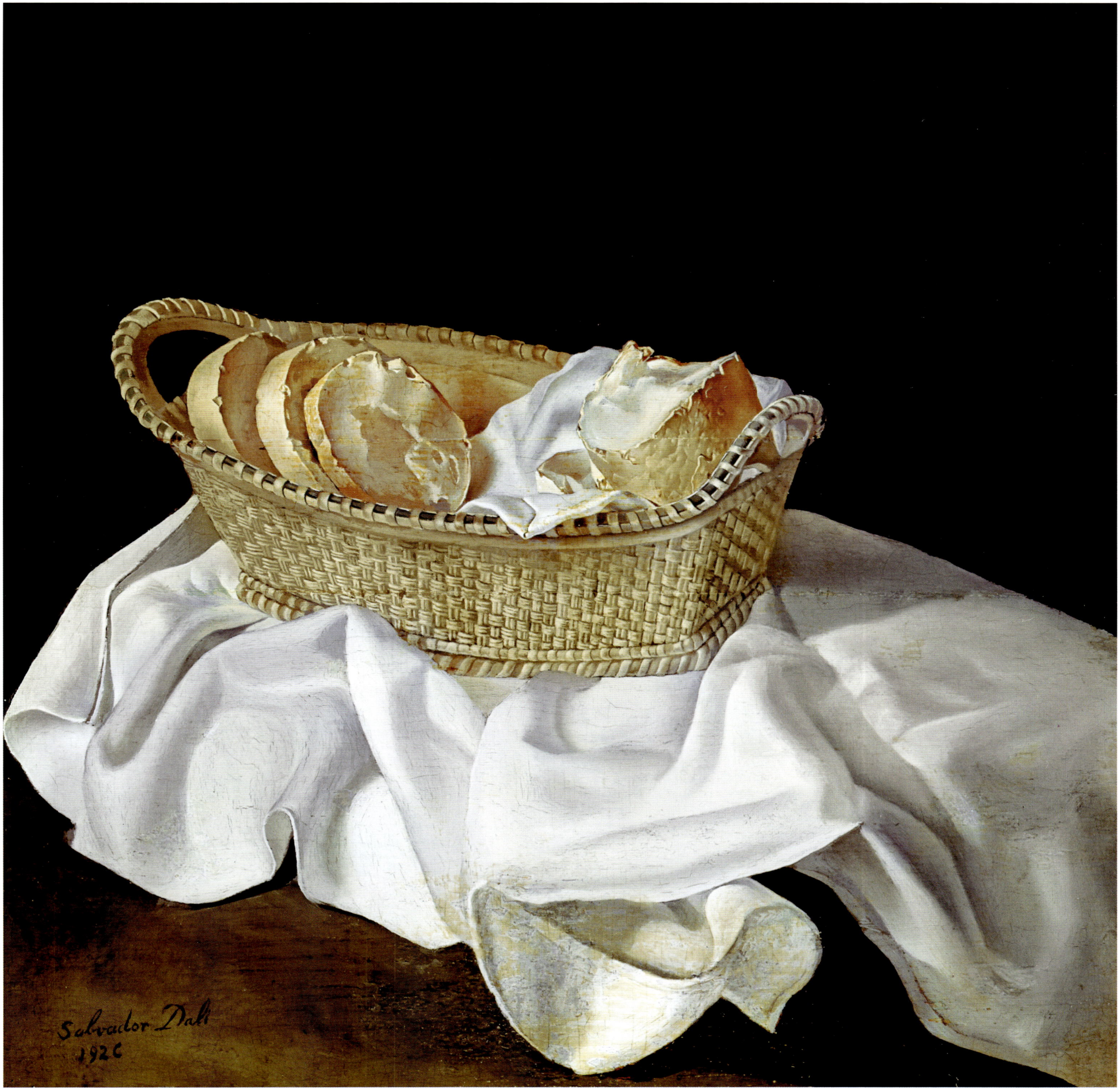
Salvador Dali
1926

became a lifelong pattern of behaviour when things did not go his way. 'I was the absolute monarch of the house. Nothing was good enough for me. My father and mother worshipped me.' A monarch indeed, Dalí routinely wore a child-size crown and cape that befitted such a status, betraying an egotistical sense of entitlement which he played on for the rest of his life. As he famously puts it at the beginning of *The Secret Life*: 'At the age of six I wanted to be a cook. At seven I wanted to be Napoleon. And my ambition has been growing ever since.'

The Optical Theatre of Esteban Trayter Colomer

Despite being well off, the notary was determined to send his son to the local school, where this cossetted little boy, protected from life's ordinary developmental hurdles by his anxious parents, was a strange anomaly among the working-class children who attended the institution. His teacher, a man named Esteban Trayter Colomer, was hopelessly idle and spent long hours asleep in his chair while mayhem ensued in the classroom. But he also sometimes took the impressionable boy to his private apartment where, in a room that Dalí later described as 'the most mysterious of all the places that still crowd my memory', the indolent teacher had, among other treasures, an optical theatre that provided young Salvador 'with the greatest measure of illusion of my childhood'. He continues: 'It was in this marvellous theatre of Señor Traite that I saw the images which were to stir me most deeply, for the rest of my life; the image of a little Russian girl especially … appeared to me swathed in white furs and deeply ensconced in a sled.' He was convinced when he wrote this account that the girl in the picture in the optical theatre was a vision of Gala, his future wife.

'At the age of six I wanted to be a cook. At seven I wanted to be Napoleon.'

As Dalí remembers it, the following day in Figueres it snowed for the first time in his life, which in a classic piece of magical thinking confirmed to him the power of his own imagination. 'When I awoke, Figueres and the whole countryside appeared before me covered by that ideal shroud, under which everyday reality was buried, and it was as though this were due to the sole and unique autocratic magic of my will.'

(Left)

Basket of Bread, 1926

Medium: Oil on wood panel
Dimensions: 31.5 x 31.5 cm (12⅜ x 12⅜ in)
Location: Salvador Dalí Museum, St Petersburg, Florida

The *Angelus* of Millet

Nevertheless, for all the extracurricular benefits of Trayter's chamber of treasures, which would indeed bear rich fruit in later life, as a place of learning the school was a disaster. Salvador, who had begun his time there at least knowing how to spell his name, had forgotten everything by the time his father swallowed his atheist ideals and installed him in the private school run by the Christian Brothers, which catered to the town's professional class. But the habit of daydreaming that the young boy had already fallen into continued at the new institution. Every day he would stare out of the window at the cypress trees, noting the way their colour changed as the day advanced through its rituals of learning and prayer.

Even when he was moved away from the window so that he could no longer gaze distractedly at the same view, Salvador would follow in his mind the same shifts of colour, which by now he knew by heart, or else he would stare at a reproduction of Millet's *Angelus* that hung in the corridor, a hugely popular image among pious Catholics across Europe in the late nineteenth and early twentieth centuries – one, as we have seen, that would haunt Dalí's imagination throughout his life and would reappear in different forms in numerous works.

Cherries and Wormholes

Around the age of six or seven Salvador began to show a talent for drawing and received encouragement from Ramon Pichot (1871–1925), a friend of the family and also a local Impressionist painter who was friends with Picasso. Salvador loved the time he spent with this cultured family at their house, the Moli de la Torre, close to Figueres, where according to *The Secret Life* he would later have an erotic encounter with a peasant girl he refers to as Dullita, which would play a part in shaping his imaginative world. It was here at the Pichot house that one day he decided to paint a bunch of cherries hanging on the back of an old door. When Ramon saw it he was impressed but he also pointed out to the young artist that the cherries depicted had no stalks. Salvador immediately addressed the problem by sticking stalks from the real cherries he had been painting directly on to the image, so that they stood out in relief against his work. But he had not finished. Seeing the wormholes in the

'I began to be a subject of intriguing controversy.'

(Right)

Atavistic Vestiges After the Rain, 1934

Medium: Oil on canvas
Dimensions: 65 x 54 cm (25⅗ x 21¼ in)
Location: Perls Galleries, New York

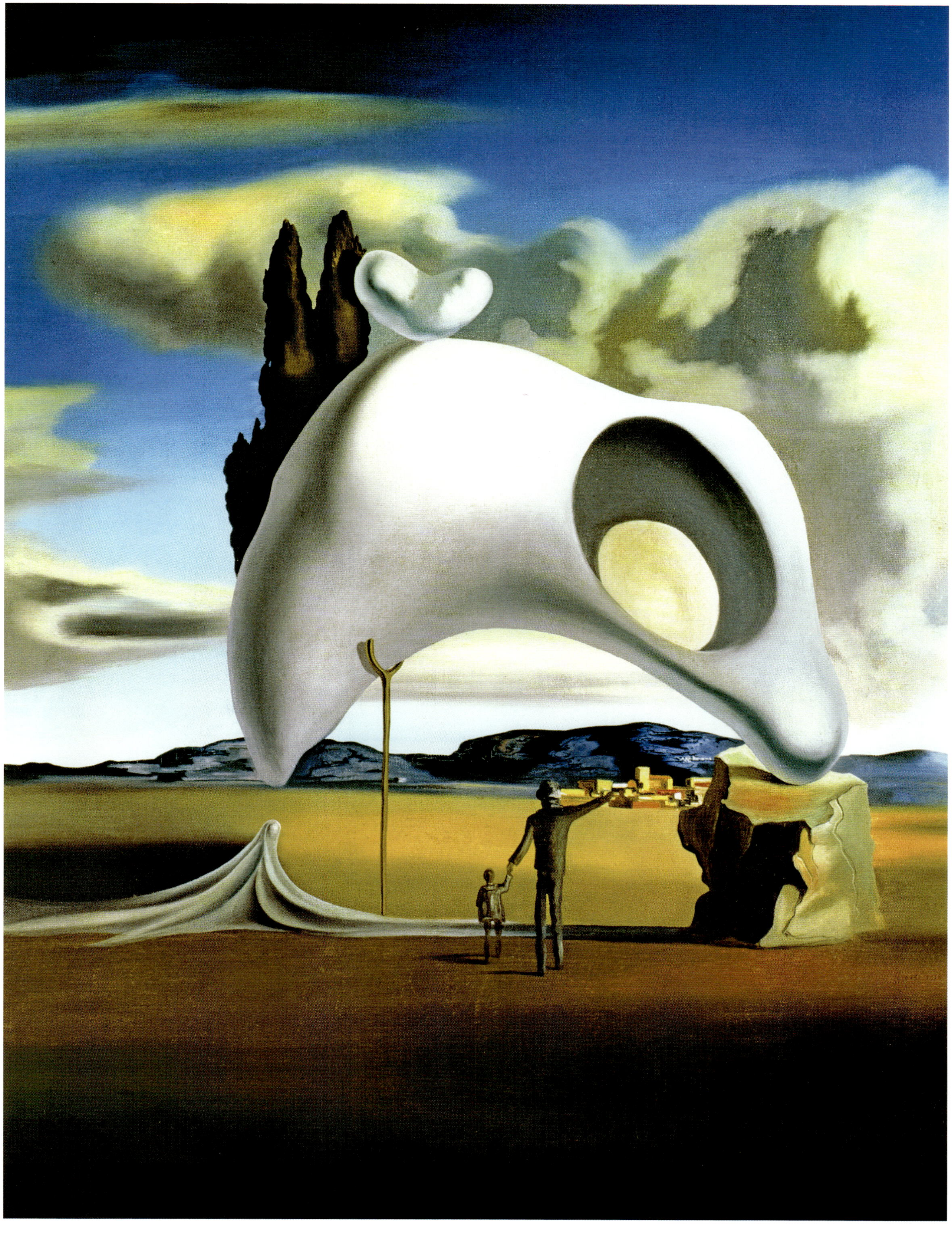

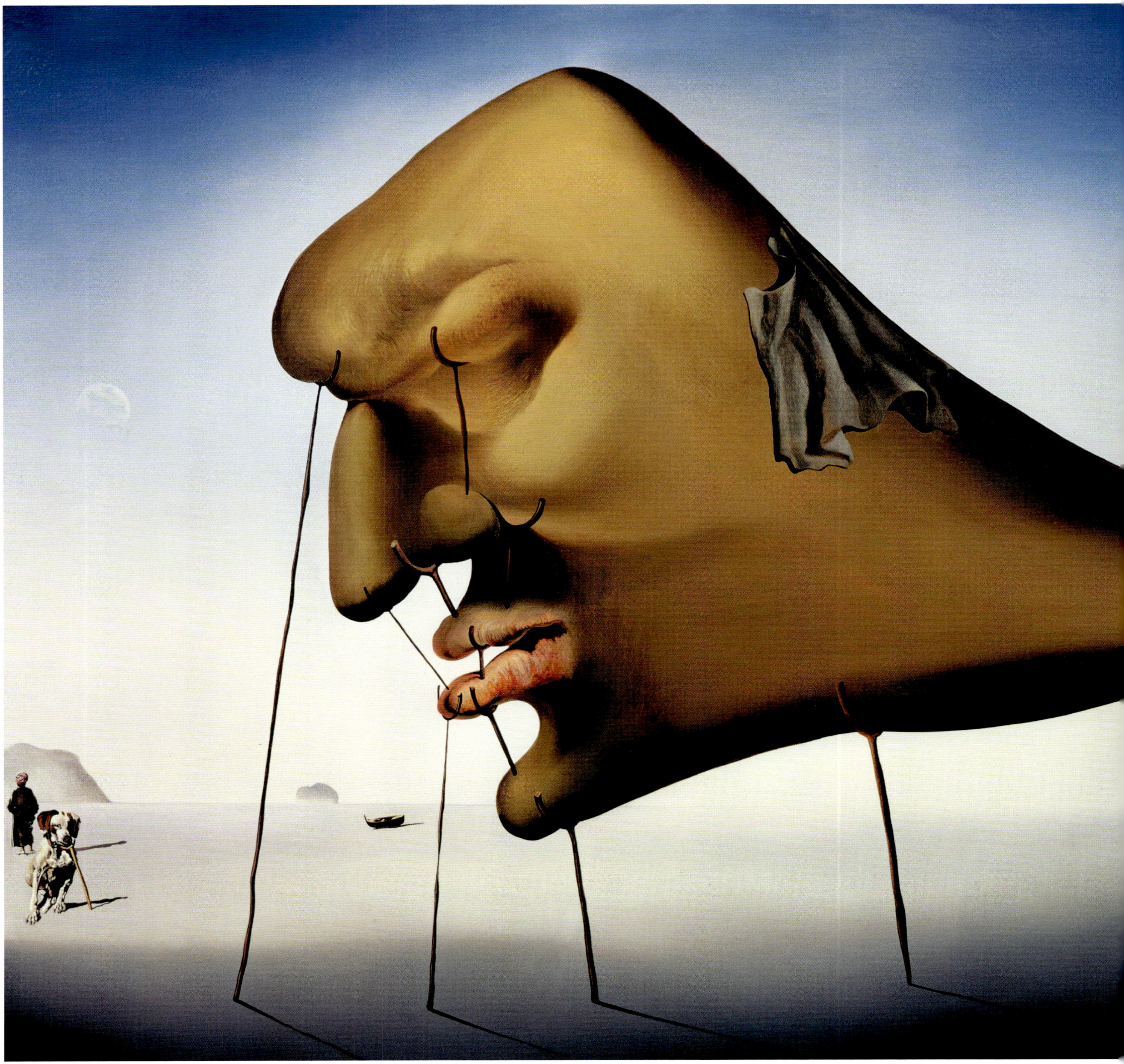

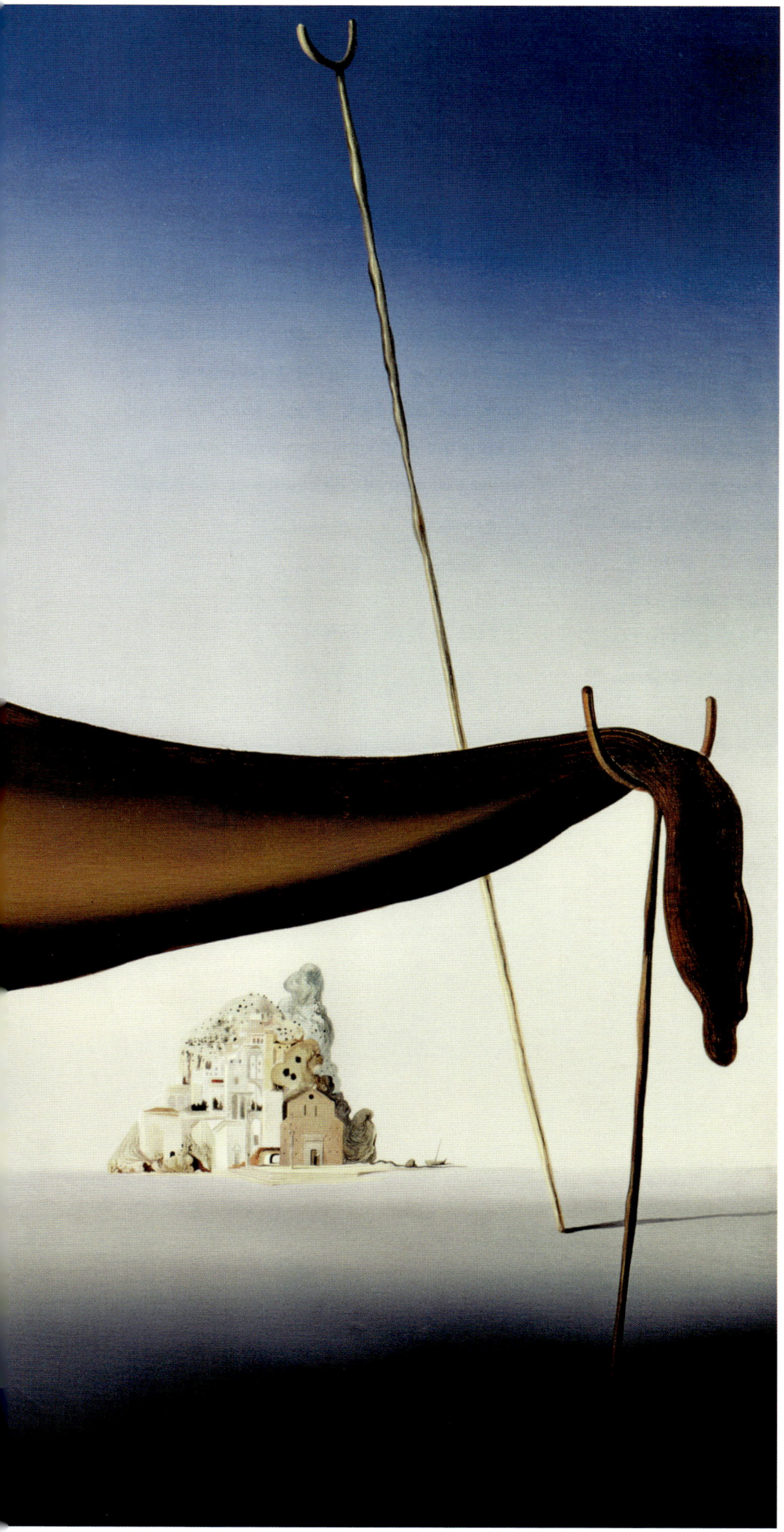

wood of the door, which pockmarked the painted cherries, he extracted tiny worms, placing them in the holes in the real cherries that had been ravaged in a similar way while still hanging from the tree. If there was a clear line between reality and its representation, then the future Surrealist either did not see it, or else regarded the urge to blur such clear distinctions as a perfectly natural impulse.

A Precocious Intellect

Dalí's artistic tastes were still in their infancy, but his first passion was for Spanish nineteenth-century academic painting, which in some artists would be something to outgrow with increased exposure to more contemporary models, but in his case would remain a touchstone of his aesthetic tastes. Dalí was also influenced around the age of 10 by a series of monographs on the great artists that his father had given him; some of these figures – for instance Diego Velázquez (1599–1660) and Johannes Vermeer (1632–75) – would remain paragons to whom he would return throughout his life. By this time, too, according to his own account, the precocious child had read most of his father's extensive library, which featured books by the great philosophers – among them Voltaire (1694–1778), Immanuel Kant (1724–1804) and Friedrich Nietzsche (1844–1900) – that would plant the seed of intellectual seriousness which underscores even Dalí's most apparently trivial later works.

(Left)

Sleep, c. 1937

Medium: Oil on canvas
Dimensions: 51 x 78 cm (20 x 30¾ in)
Location: Private Collection

Nevertheless, Dalí's penchant for the fantastical was also given licence to express itself when as a teenager he designed a huge carnival carriage topped by gigantic dragons with phosphorescent eyes for the Cabalgata de los Reyes, the Epiphany procession in Figueres. By then Dalí had had his first exhibition when, aged 14, he was given the honour of showing his work in the theatre of Figueres, next to the church of Sant Pere in which he had been baptized. What a coincidence that the same building some 50 years later would offer him the site for his own museum!

The Little Sadist

By this point his ever-indulgent parents, increasingly keen to encourage their child's clear vocation, had furnished him with a studio in an unused laundry room on the roof of their apartment in Figueres. But such constructive help had never done anything to discourage the young Dalí's contrarian tendencies – as he put it, 'the desire constantly, systematically and at any cost to do just the opposite of what everybody else did'. Perhaps out of that same desire to flout the accepted rules of behaviour among the bourgeoisie he habitually despised, in *The Secret Life* he seems to take pleasure in documenting the apparently random acts of cruelty, whether true or not, which he remembers committing as a child. Dalí gleefully confesses that on one occasion, aged five, he pushed another boy off a bridge for no reason at all. As he writes in a spirit of calm reminiscence: 'I don't recall having experienced the slightest feeling of guilt over the incident. That evening while taking my usual solitary walk I remember having savoured the beauty of each blade of grass.'

'The superb crutch! ... the height of authority and solemnity.'

The Discovery of a Crutch

In another, even more bizarre incident, Dalí introduces the reader to one of many fetishes that developed in childhood, in this case a crutch that would become a literal prop in many of his most famous works, a symbol which he later admitted 'propped up my weak notion of reality'. Taking possession of the object, which he found in an attic at the Pichot house, 'I felt that I should never again in my life be able to separate myself from it, such was the fetishistic fanaticism which seized me at

(Right)

Self-Portrait with the Neck of Raphael, 1921

Medium: Oil on canvas
Dimensions: 41.5 x 53 cm (16 x 21 in)
Location: Fundació Gala-Salvador Dalí, Figueres

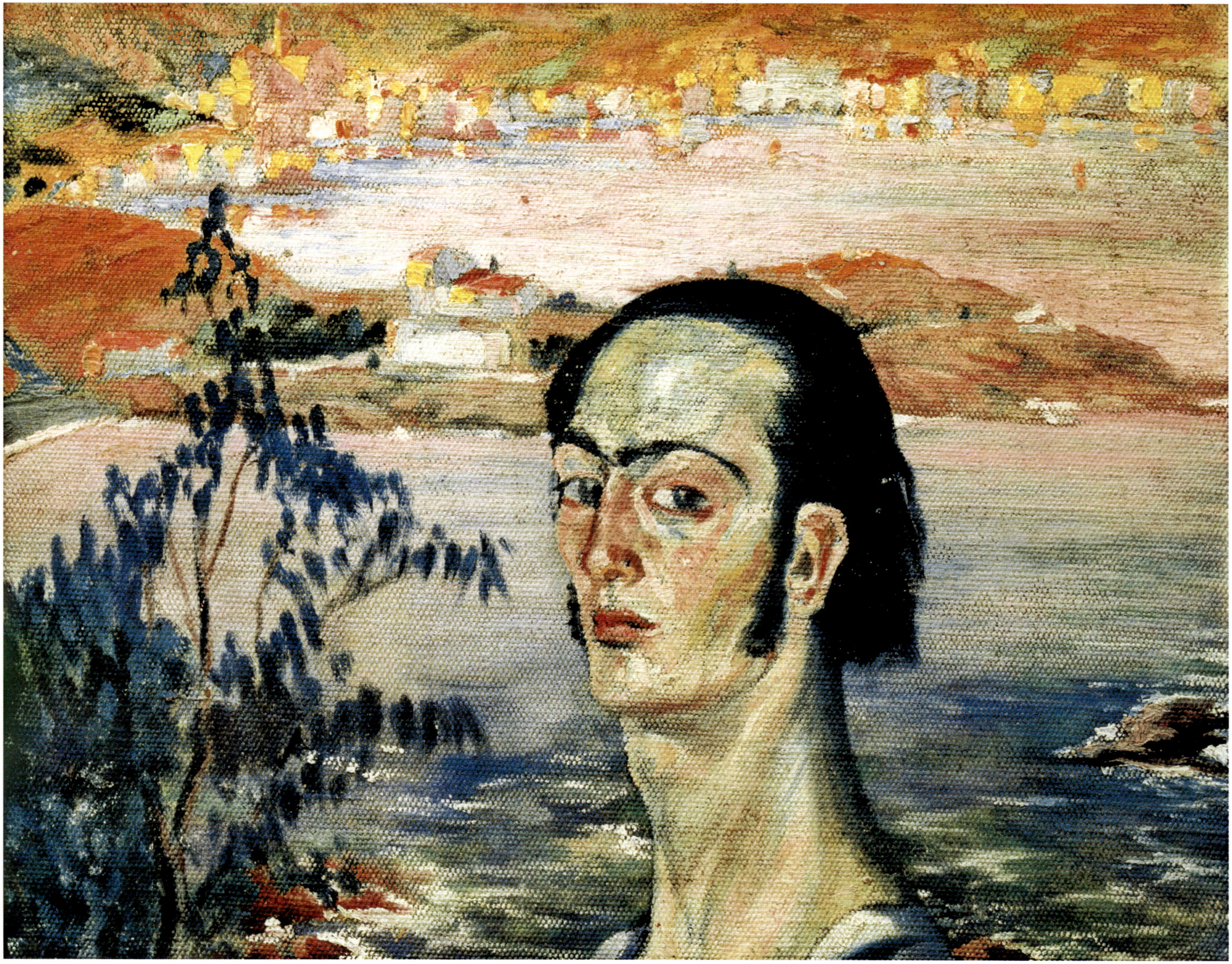

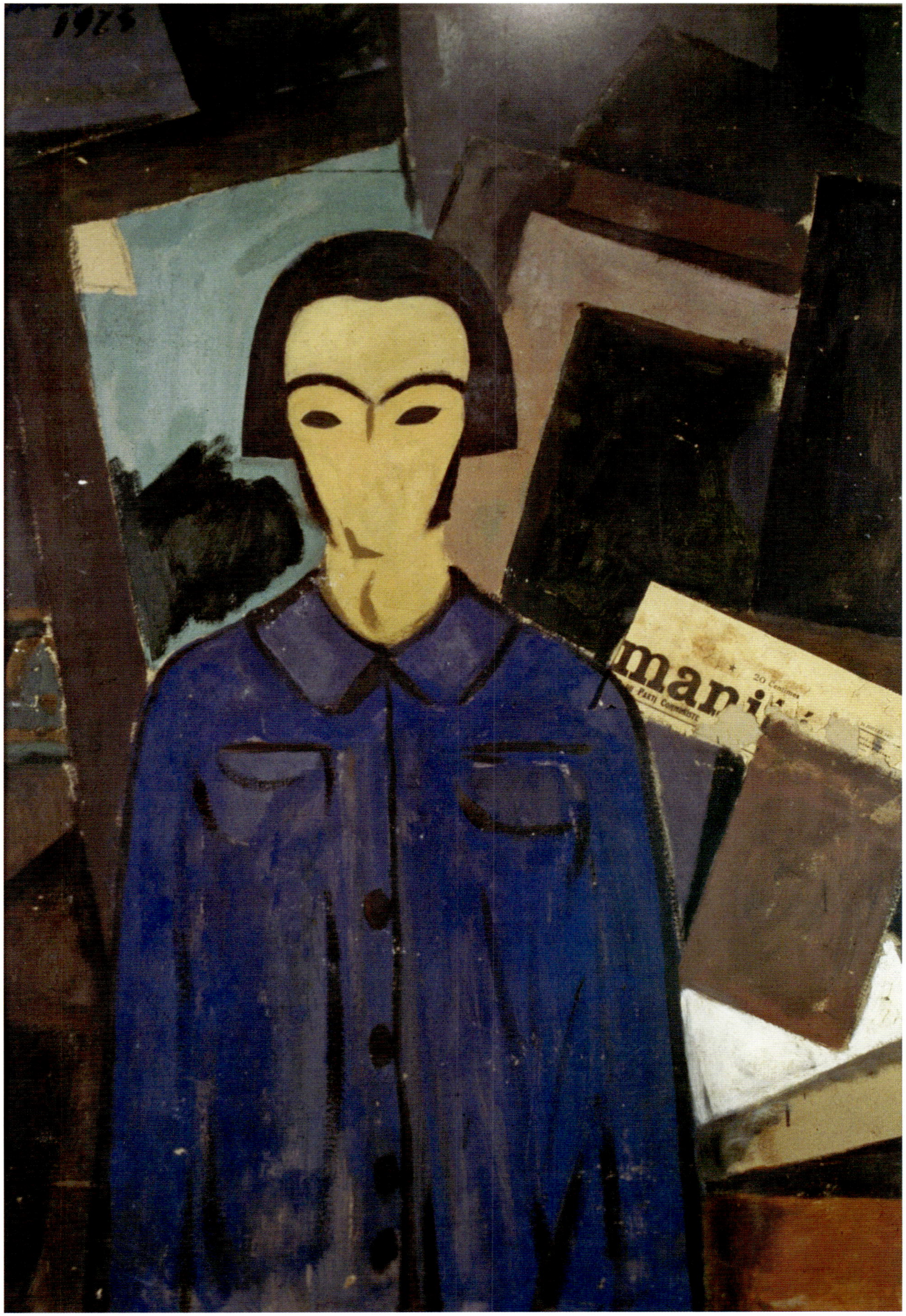

the very first without my being able to explain it. The superb crutch! Already it appeared to me as the object possessing the height of authority and solemnity.... I vicariously descended into the garden, hobbling solemnly with my crutch in one hand. The object communicated to me an assurance, an arrogance even, which I had never been capable of until then.'

Of course, no symbol is unambiguous in Dalí's complex imagination, and the beloved crutch soon became a contaminated object when days later he discovered the rotting carcass of a hedgehog in the back of a barn. Simultaneously infatuated with the peasant girl Dullita, whom he had met that summer, he found himself rushing back and forth between 'the rustic and timid angel's face' of Dullita, whom he longed to embrace 'with all my might', and the putrefied hedgehog crawling with 'gesticulating worms', an object of equal fascination that eventually he could

(Left)

Self-Portrait with L'Humanité, 1923

Medium: Temper, oil and collage on cardboard
Dimensions: 105 x 75 cm (41.34 x 29.53 in)
Location: Town Hall of Figueres, on permanent deposit at the Fundació Gala-Salvador Dalí, Figueres

not stop himself from probing with his crutch, recalling that 'I stirred this nightmare-bristling pile with such terrifying intensity and such morbid voluptuousness that for a moment I thought I was going to faint.' The crutch, 'contaminated as it now was by the gluey contact of the hedgehog's mass of worms, from being a favourable fetish … had become transformed into a frightful object synonymous with death'. Fetish and phobia, sex and death entwined – it is the classic disturbing Dalinian cocktail of the fundamental forces of existence, whose primal energy informs his greatest works. As he later put it in an interview with his friend, Alain Bosquet (1919–98), 'I value death greatly. After eroticism, it's the subject that interests me most.'

Making a Spectacle of Himself

Anna Maria, Dalí's sister, could not possibly have known the intimate details of his inner life or even those formative experiences – private moments unique to her brother as they are to every child – which led him to the fractured, unstable sense of who he was. Anna Maria's memoir, *Salvador Dalí as Seen by His Sister*, published in 1949, some seven years after *The Secret Life*, downplays his weirdness and avowed sadism, and indeed in support of her account his own teenage diaries paint a picture of a conscientious boy concerned for the welfare of others, a lad who for a time described himself as a Communist.

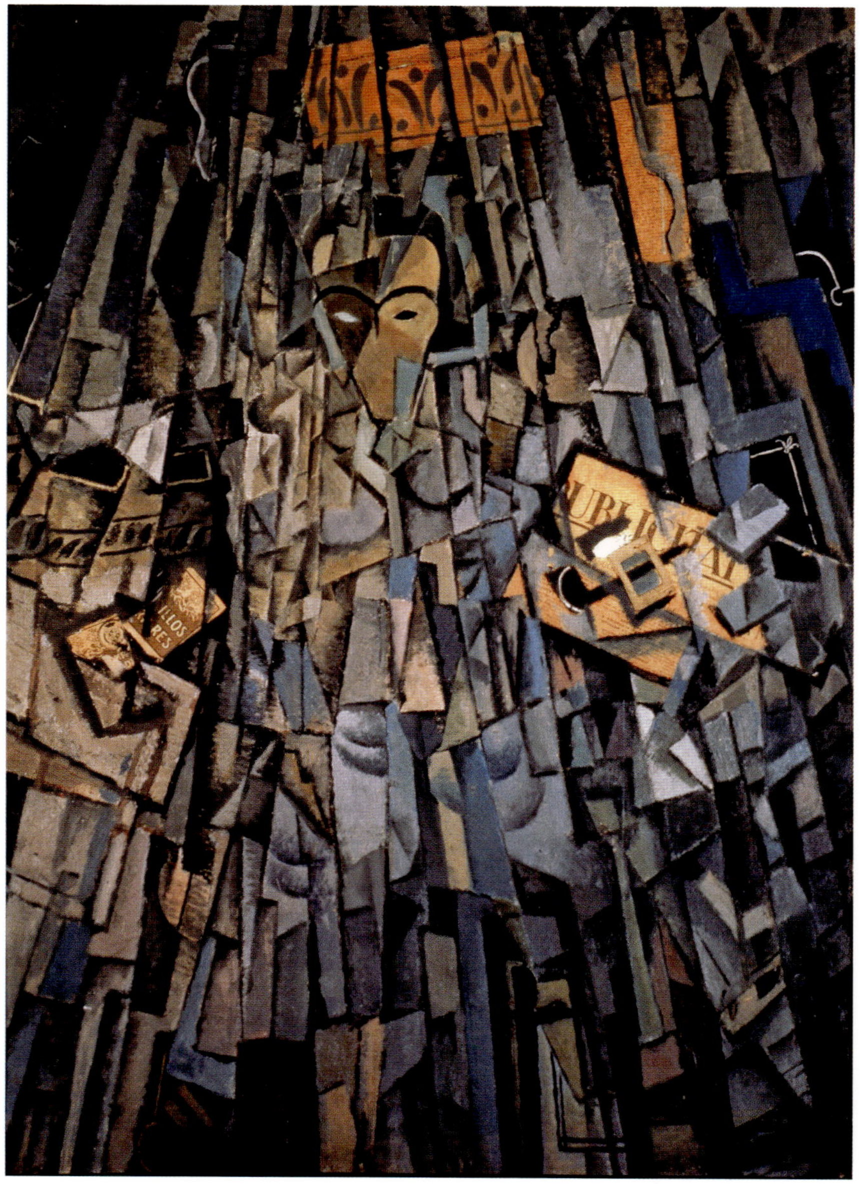

(Above)

Cubist Self-Portrait, 1923

Medium: Oil and collage on cardboard on wood
Dimensions: 104 x 75 cm (41 x 29½ in)
Location: Museo Nacional Centro de Arte Reina Sofia, Madrid

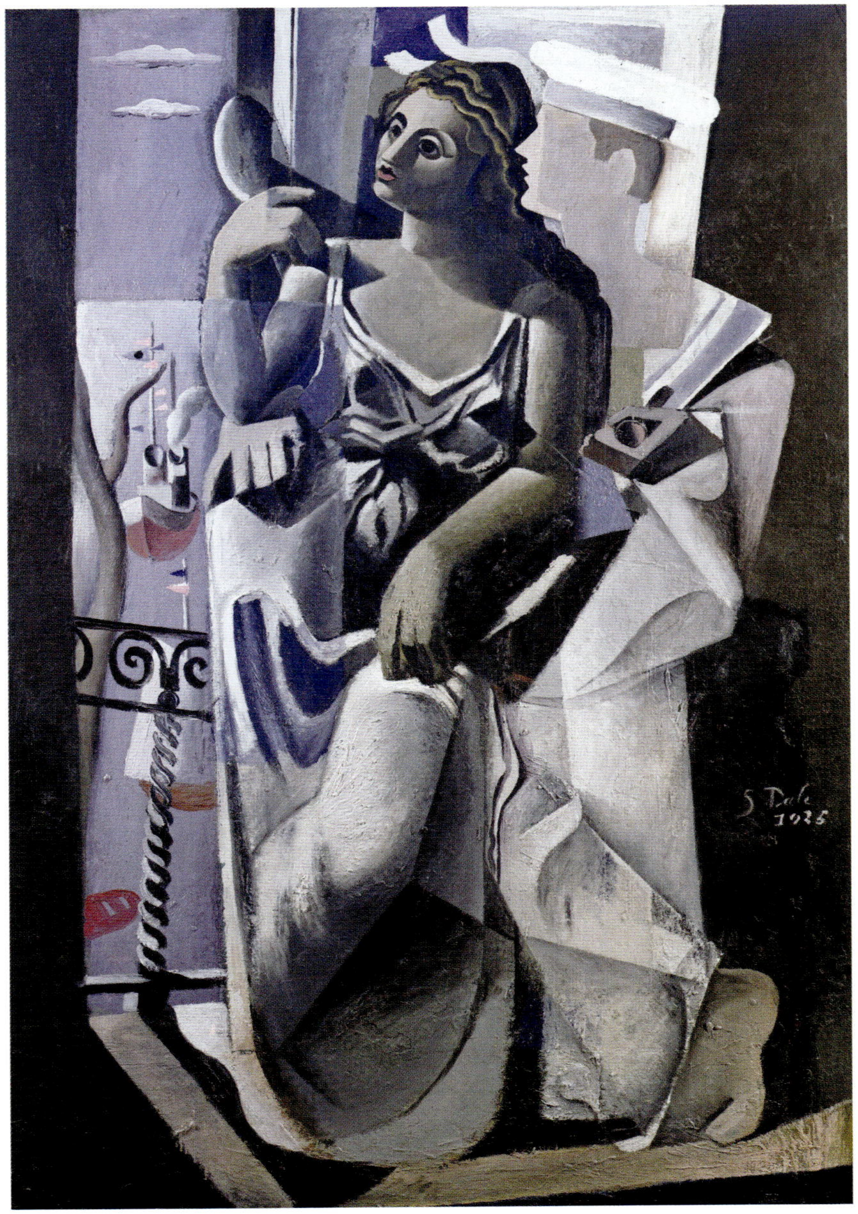

But even then 'the tragical sequence of exhibitionism', which in later years came to define his public image, was manifesting in increasingly bizarre behaviour that garnered the attention he so craved.

As a teenager, by now at the school run by the Marist Brothers in Figueres, Dalí had the idea one day of throwing himself down the stairs simply to get a reaction from the other boys and the members of staff. He was lucky not to emerge with worse than the bruises he sustained, but – as he recalled in *The Secret Life* – any injury, even death, would have been worth it for the rapt astonishment of those who witnessed his reckless leap. And having repeated the gesture a few days later, he now had his schoolmates in a state of horrified suspense over when he might next risk his life in this extraordinary manner. Dalí found their attention intoxicating and still clearly cherished the memory when recalling it in *The Secret Life*: 'I descended the stairway step by step. With a slow deliberation of blind ecstasy so moving that suddenly a great silence fell upon ... the play-yard. I would not at that moment have changed places with a god.'

The Question of Madness

This startling exhibitionism was born partly from a desire to shock, but also from a need to overcome his otherwise crippling timidity.

(Above)

Venus and Sailor – Homage to Salvat-Papasseit, 1925

Medium: Oil on canvas
Dimensions: 215 x 147.5 cm (84⅔ x 58 in)
Location: Ikeda Museum of 20th Century Art, Shizuoka

(Right)

View of Cadaqués from the Creus Tower, c. 1923

Medium: Oil on canvas
Dimensions: 98 x 100 cm (38⅗ x 39⅗ in)
Location: Fundació Gala-Salvador Dalí, Figueres

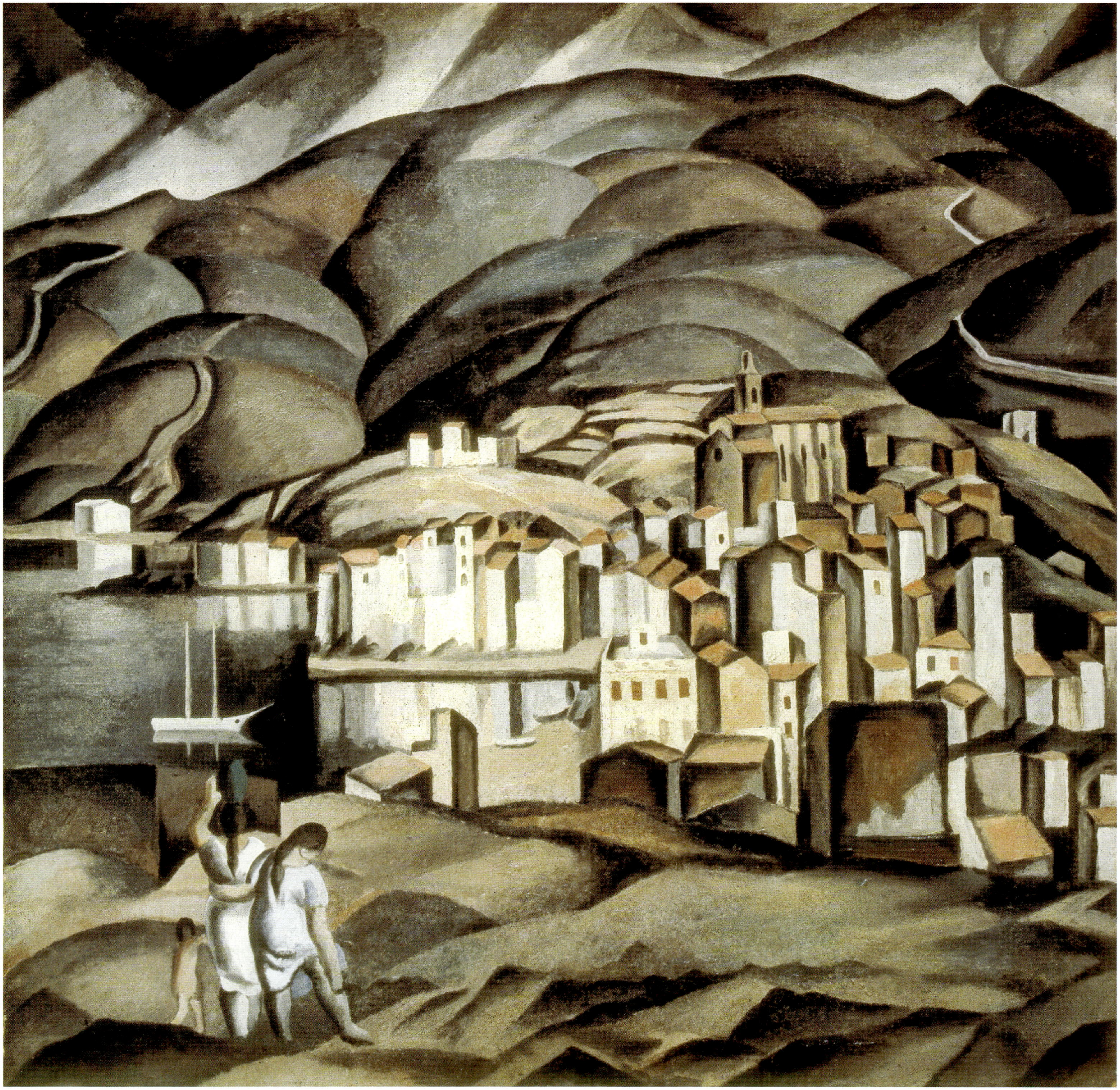

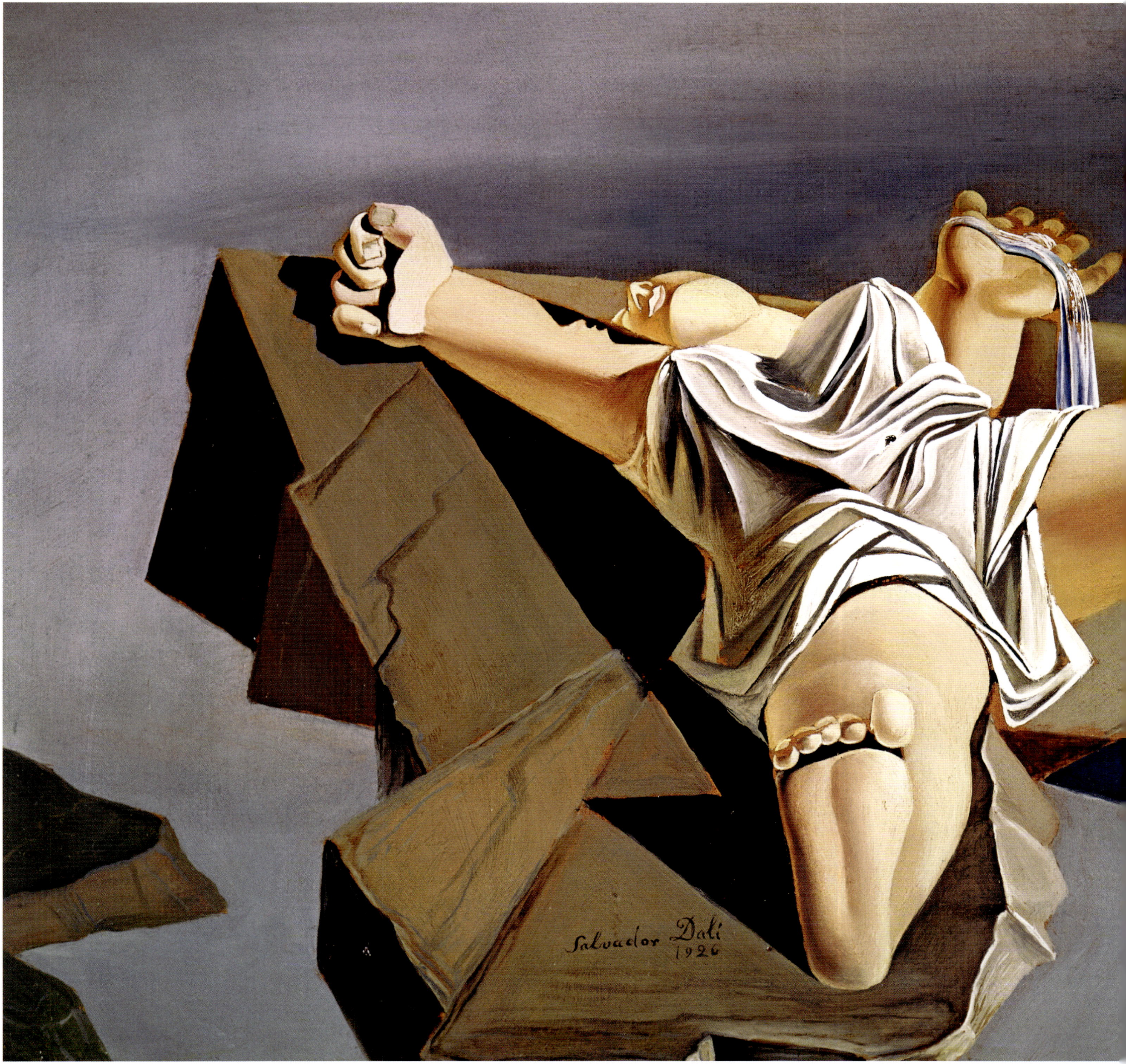
Salvador Dalí
1926

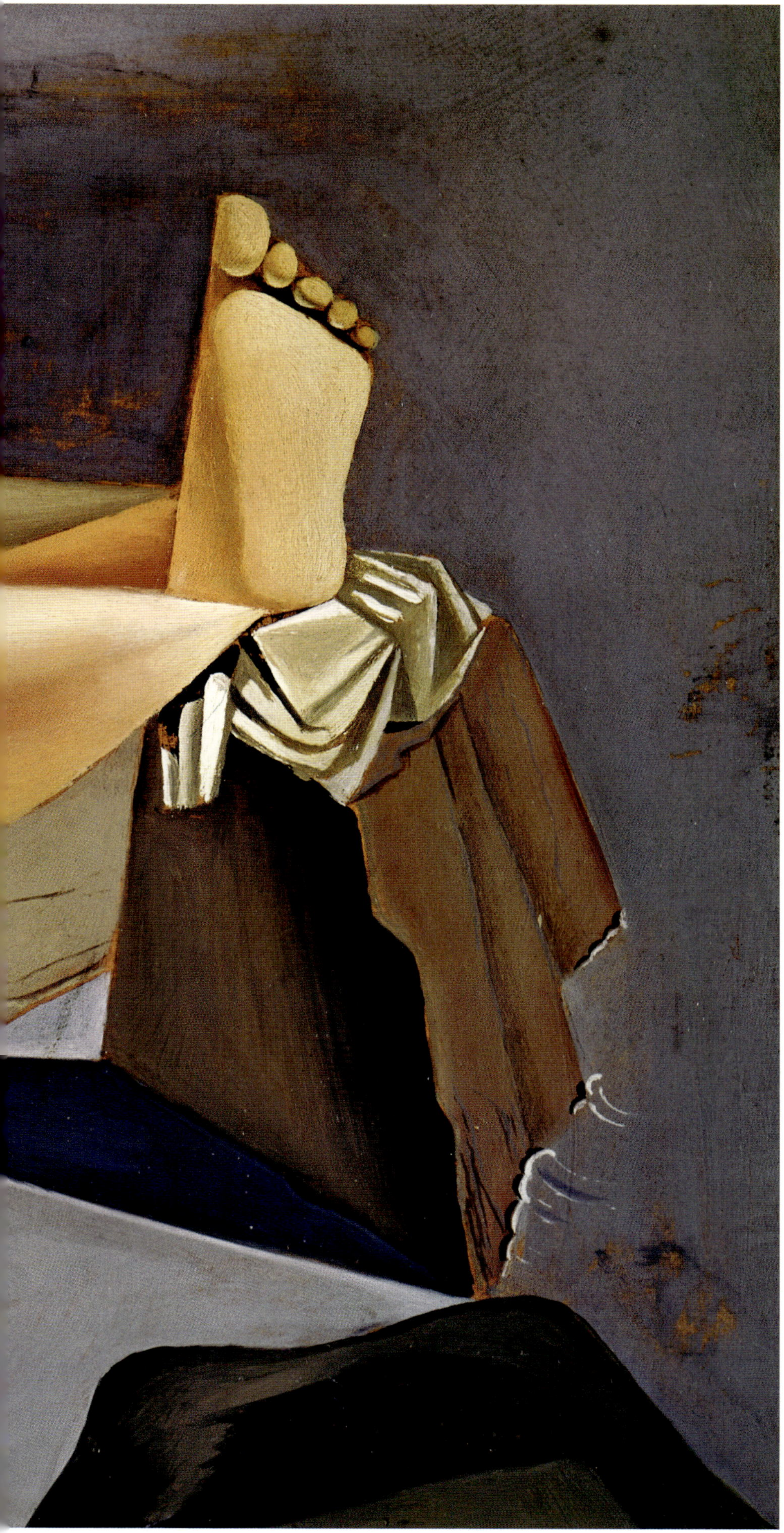

Dali insisted in *The Secret Life* that any speculation over his sanity among his peers only added to the pleasure such gratuitous acts afforded him. 'I began to be a subject of intriguing controversy. Is he mad? Is he not mad? Does he show the beginnings of an extraordinary but abnormal personality?... One thing at any rate was ... certain: everything abnormal or phenomenal that occurred was automatically attributed to me: and as I became more "alone" and "unique", I became by that fact each day more "visible".'

Mad, not mad. Even to entertain the question, let alone the antic disposition that would provoke those around him to ask it, indicates a mind in underlying turmoil. Perhaps he was protesting too much when later he famously declared that 'The only difference between me and a madman is I am not mad.' Reading Dali's own various accounts of his life, it is not unreasonable to ask whether he himself was absolutely sure.

The Death of His Mother

In 1921, on the cusp of his leaving school, Dali's beloved mother, who doted on him to an extent that infantilized the young man, died of cancer. He described this as 'the greatest blow I had experienced in my life', and it seems evident from his account that her death provided Dali with a moral structure within which his exhibitionism and egomania seemed not only justifiable but necessary. Describing his

(Left)

Figure on the Rocks, 1926

Medium: Oil on panel
Dimensions: 27 x 41 cm (10⅝ x 16 in)
Location: Salvador Dali Museum, St Petersburg, Florida

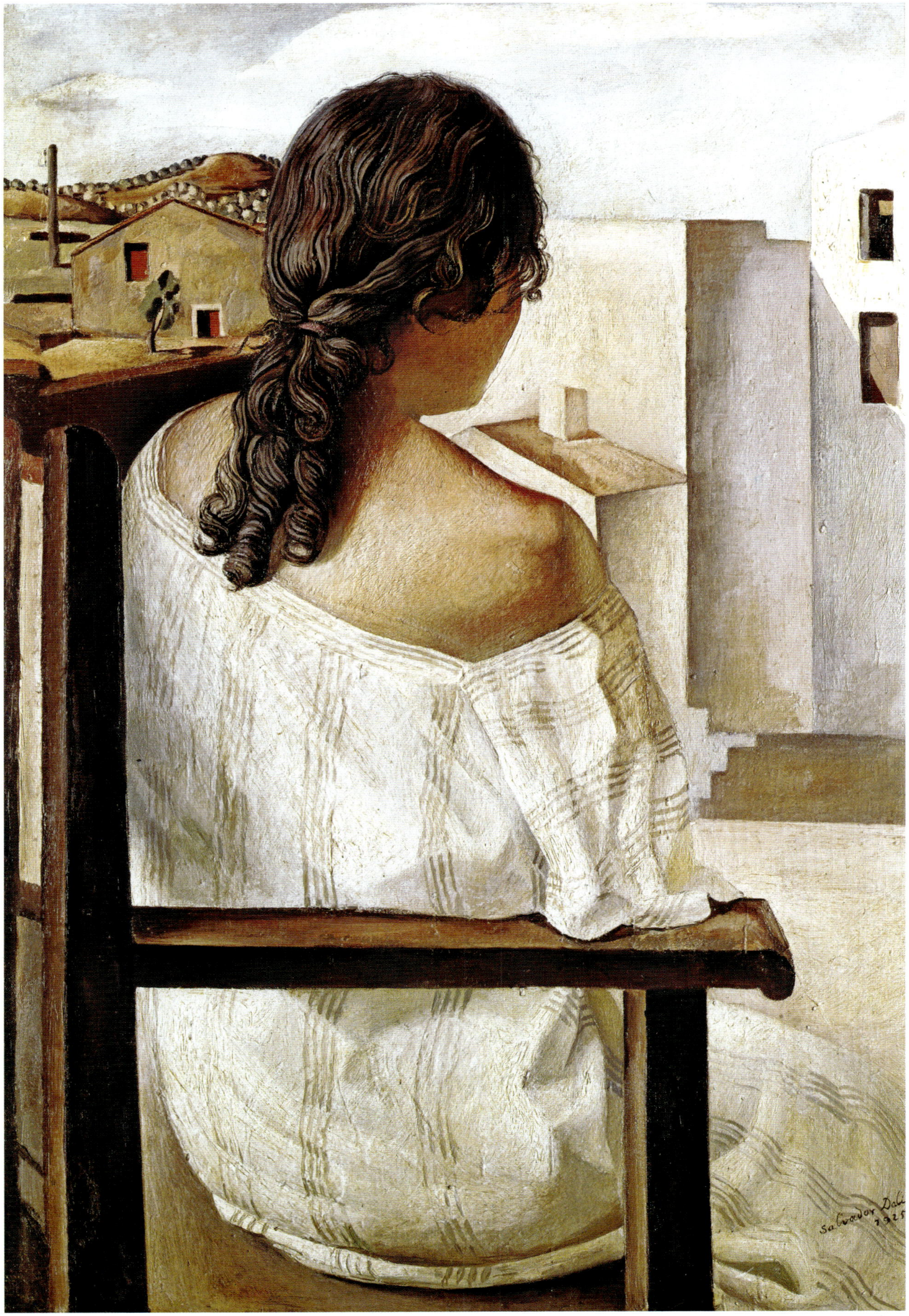

mother as 'a being on whom I counted to make invisible the unavowable blemishes of my soul' – how frightening then to lose such a redemptive presence – he continued, 'I swore to myself that I would snatch my mother from death and destiny with the swords of light that some day would savagely gleam around my glorious name!'

A painting from the same year, *Self-Portrait with the Neck of Raphael* (1921, *see* page 37) shows us that he was consciously cultivating the look of a Bohemian dandy but also one with an awareness of the classical past, an epoch and a worldview which he would always regard as a model of artistic perfection. Not that Dalí was not already aware of some of the most experimental trends in modern art. By the early 1920s he had absorbed and passed through the impressionism of Ramon Pichot and the painters of Spanish *tipicísmo* – as he refers to it rather contemptuously in *The Secret Life* – and was now clearly

(Left)

Seated Girl Seen from the Back, 1925

Medium: Oil on canvas
Dimensions: 104 x 74 cm (41 x 29 in)
Location: Museo Nacional Centro de Arte Reina Sofía, Madrid

mastering the Post-Impressionist idiom of the next generation. It was good progress for a 17-year-old, though these were still very much apprentice works.

Madrid and Meeting Lorca

The young Dalí had talent and also – unlike so many with equal ability – an enormous appetite for hard work and the acquisition of knowledge. He was admitted to the San Fernando Academy of Fine Arts in Madrid, but remained aloof from his fellow students, cooped up in his room at the Residencia, the halls where a large number of students from a range of disciplines intermingled in what for the time was a far-sighted attempt to have them learn from each other. During the first year, Dalí was always painting, and he still dressed in what to the sophisticated crowd of students known as the 'Ultraists', who were also billeted at the Residencia, seemed like an old-fashioned, pre-war style. These Young Turks, all of them scions of wealthy families, included several figures who, like Dalí, would soon become leading players in the arts in Spain. Two men in particular were to form a special bond with the painter that would leave its mark on his work and on his life. One was Luis Buñuel, his future collaborator on *Un Chien Andalou*; the other, the most important of all, was the poet Federico García Lorca (1898–1936), who personally impressed everyone who met him throughout his short life, and who seems on at least one occasion to have sought to consummate his sexual love for Dalí. If we are to believe the painter's own account, Dalí would not reciprocate, though this did not stop them from forming a deep friendship that saw Lorca spend successive summers in the mid-1920s at the Dalí summer home in Cadaqués, and which was only interrupted when a few years later Dalí wrote some typically insulting and unnecessary remarks in a review of Lorca's work.

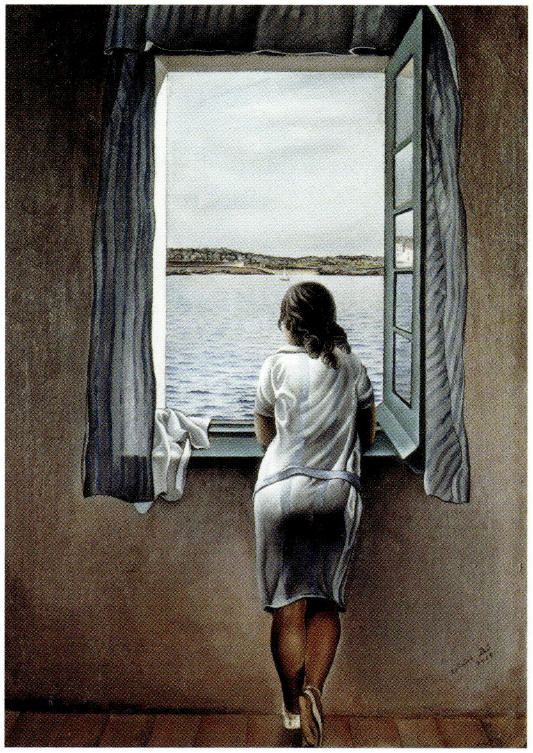

(Above)

Girl at a Window, 1925

Medium: Oil on cardboard (masonite)
Dimensions: 105 x 74.5 cm (41⅓ x 29⅓ in)
Location: Museo Nacional Centro de Arte Reina Sofía, Madrid

The Autodidact

Under the influence of these new friends Dalí modernized his outlook and his image. He cut his Bohemian hair and sideburns and dressed in the typically English suits they favoured, although Dalí exaggerated the dandyism of the style so as to strike an unmistakable figure. He also learned how to drink and in later life, by which point his habits were decidedly abstemious, he recalls these wild nights and wretched days with a certain degree of horror. Nonetheless, these lessons in hedonism proved far more valuable than anything he could learn from his teachers at the school, whom he found to be limited and full of excuses for not thinking deeply about the medium of painting. 'I immediately understood that those old professors covered with honours and decorations could teach me nothing. This was not due to their academicism or to their philistine spirit but on the contrary to their progressive spirit, hospitable to every novelty. I was expecting to find limits, rigour, science. I was offered liberty, laziness, approximations!'

These august professors had only recently absorbed Impressionism and slavishly followed the received wisdom associated with the style, advocating temperament over technique, even when Dalí pressed them to be more concrete. Madrid was, in fact, a less advanced centre for art than Barcelona, and the young Catalan painter had already outgrown his teachers. He was now painting Cubist portraits and still lifes in imitation of pictures by Picasso, Georges Braque (1882–1963) and Juan Gris (1887–1927), or Purist works in the manner of Amédée Ozenfant (1886–1966) and Charles Edouard Jeanneret (soon to call himself Le Corbusier) (1887–1965), which he had seen in journals of modern art that the professors at the Academy clearly had not read themselves.

'Picasso is doubtless the man I have most often thought about after my father.'

Expulsions

In 1923, Dalí was even suspended for a year for having, in this case, inadvertently started a riot at the school. He took it easily in his stride, went home to Figueres and worked with sedulous discipline according to the pattern of independent learning he had already established. Then in September of that year, General Miguel Primo de Rivera (1870–1930) took over the government of Spain in a coup and introduced punitive measures to suppress resurgent Catalan separatism, banning the use of the language in public institutions

(Right)

Portrait of My Father, 1925

Medium: Oil on canvas
Dimensions: 104.5 x 104.5 cm (41 x 41 in)
Location: Museu Nacional d'Art de Catalunya, Barcelona

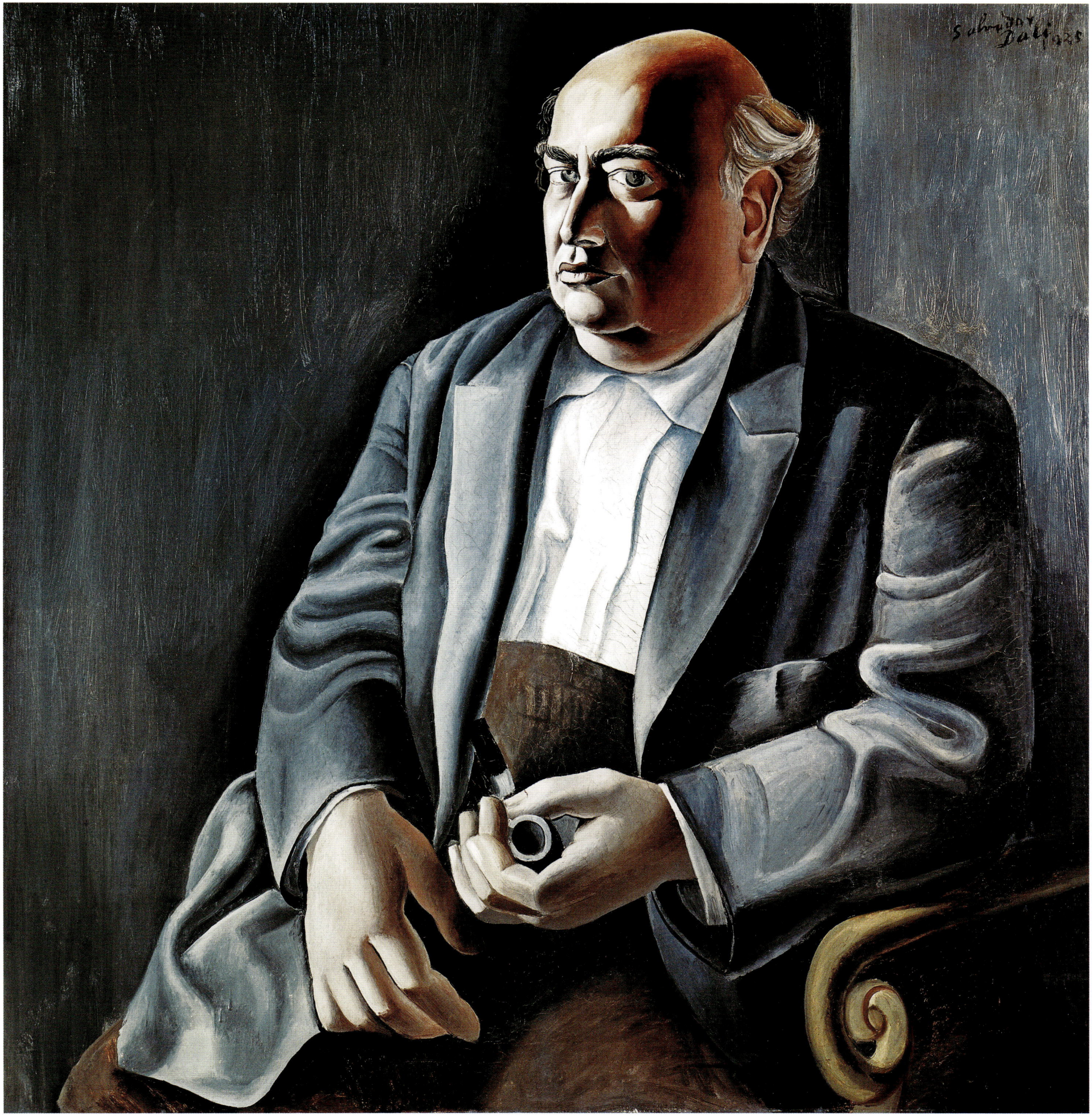
Salvador
Dalí 1925

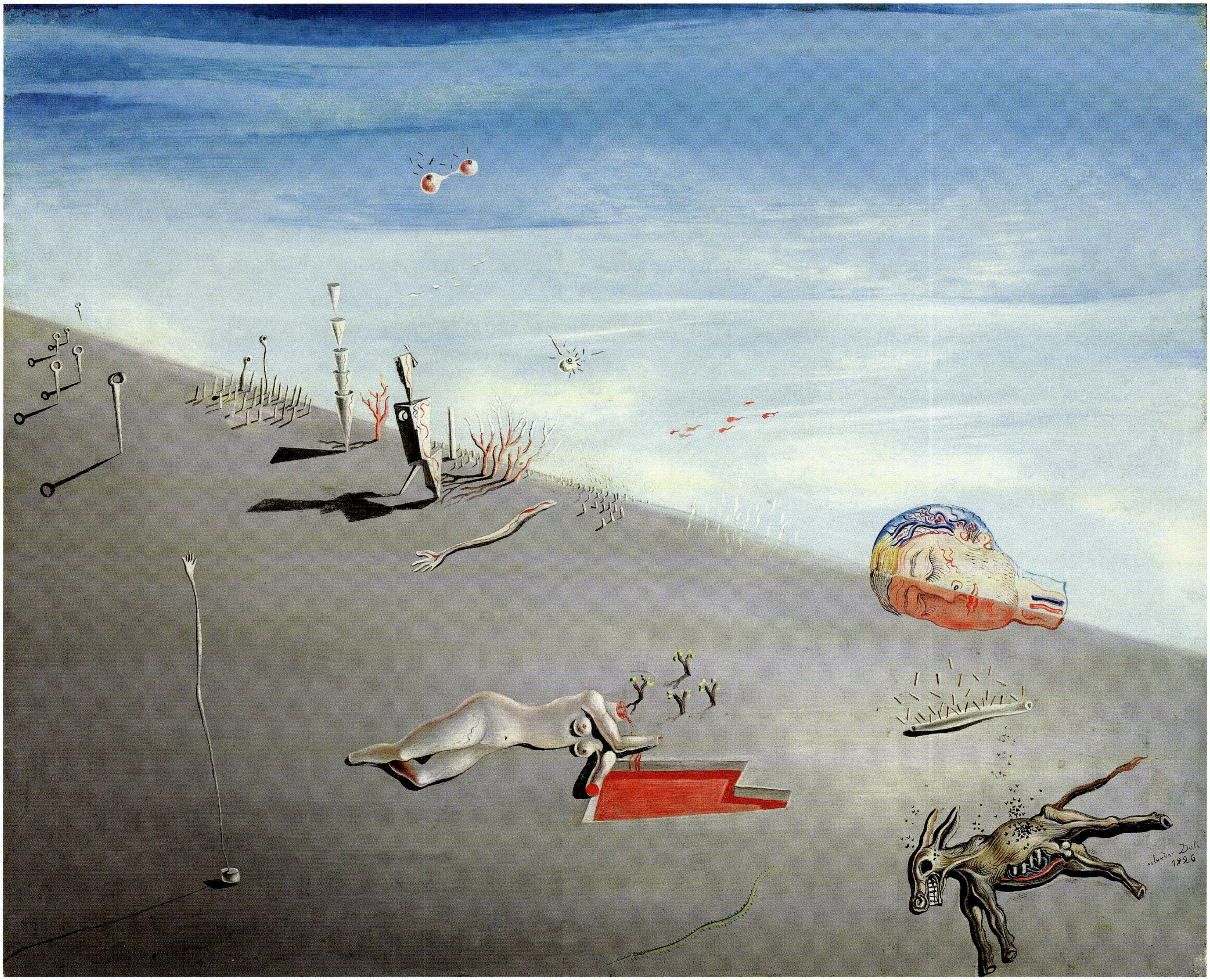

and in the Church, and even prohibiting the *sardana*, the folk dance associated with the region. Somehow Dalí, who had previously thought of himself as an anarchist, got caught the following spring with banned separatist literature that may in fact have belonged to his father. He spent a short period of time in jails in Figueres and Girona, which in fact appealed to the ascetic side of his nature, though this would also be the last time he got mixed up in revolutionary politics.

In the autumn of 1924 he was readmitted to the Academy of San Fernando and resumed his friendships with Lorca and his future collaborator Luis Buñuel. Dalí sometimes considered himself a better writer than painter, and his body of work in each of the two disciplines certainly has the same qualities of vividness of imagery and narrative, and a frequent tendency toward baroque excess. By the later 1920s he was writing all manner of texts – poetry and prose pieces – for publications such as the Catalan review of art and literature, *L'Amic de les Arts*. In these early pieces, we already encounter the radical thinker who would shake up the art world of the 1930s.

In the meantime, in June 1926, Dalí was faced with his final exam at the Madrid Academy. Presenting himself to the committee, he was asked to choose three subjects on which they should examine him, but he declined, telling them bluntly: 'I am very sorry, but I am infinitely more intelligent than these three professors, and I therefore

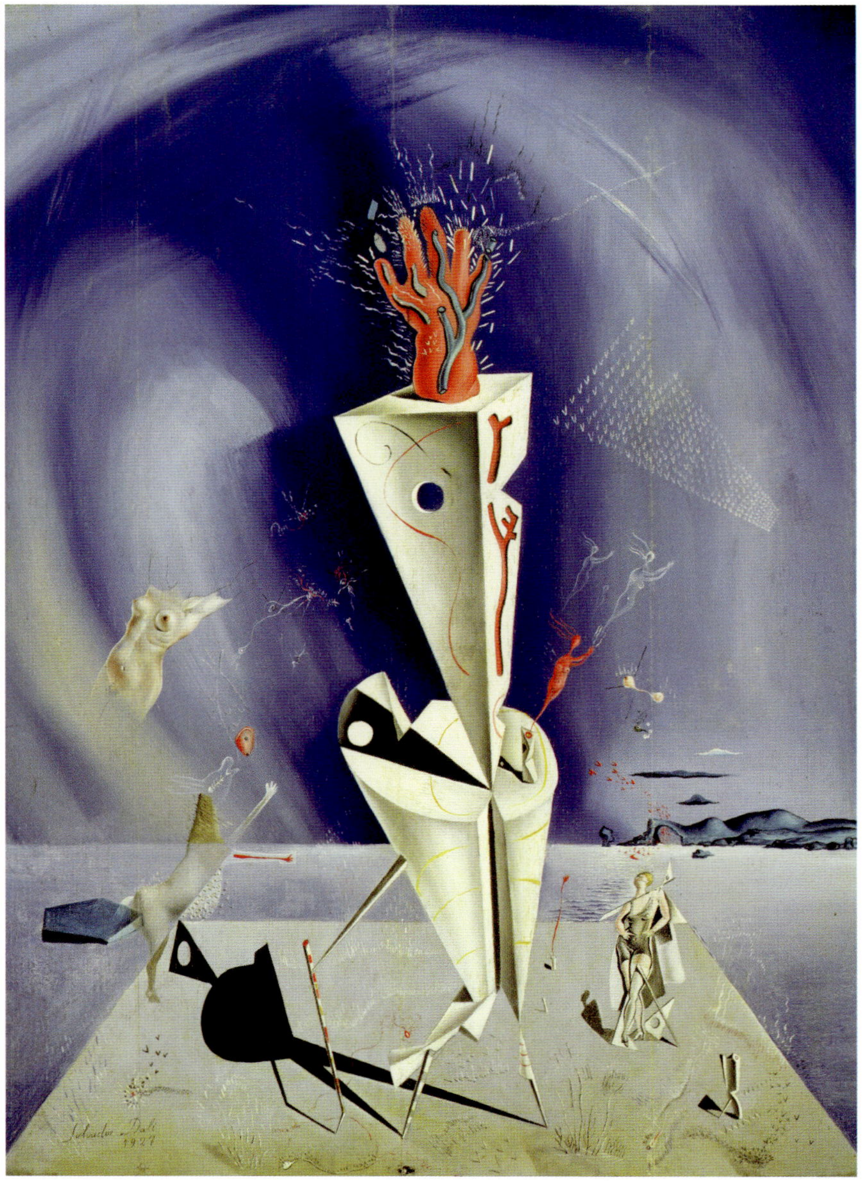

(Left)

Study for 'Honey is Sweeter than Blood', 1926
Medium: Oil on wood panel
Dimensions: 37.8 x 46.2 cm (15 x 18 in)
Location: Fundació Gala-Salvador Dalí, Figueres

(Above)

Apparatus and Hand, 1927
Medium: Oil on wood
Dimensions: 62 x 47.5 cm (24½ x 18¾ in)
Location: Salvador Dalí Museum, St Petersburg, Florida

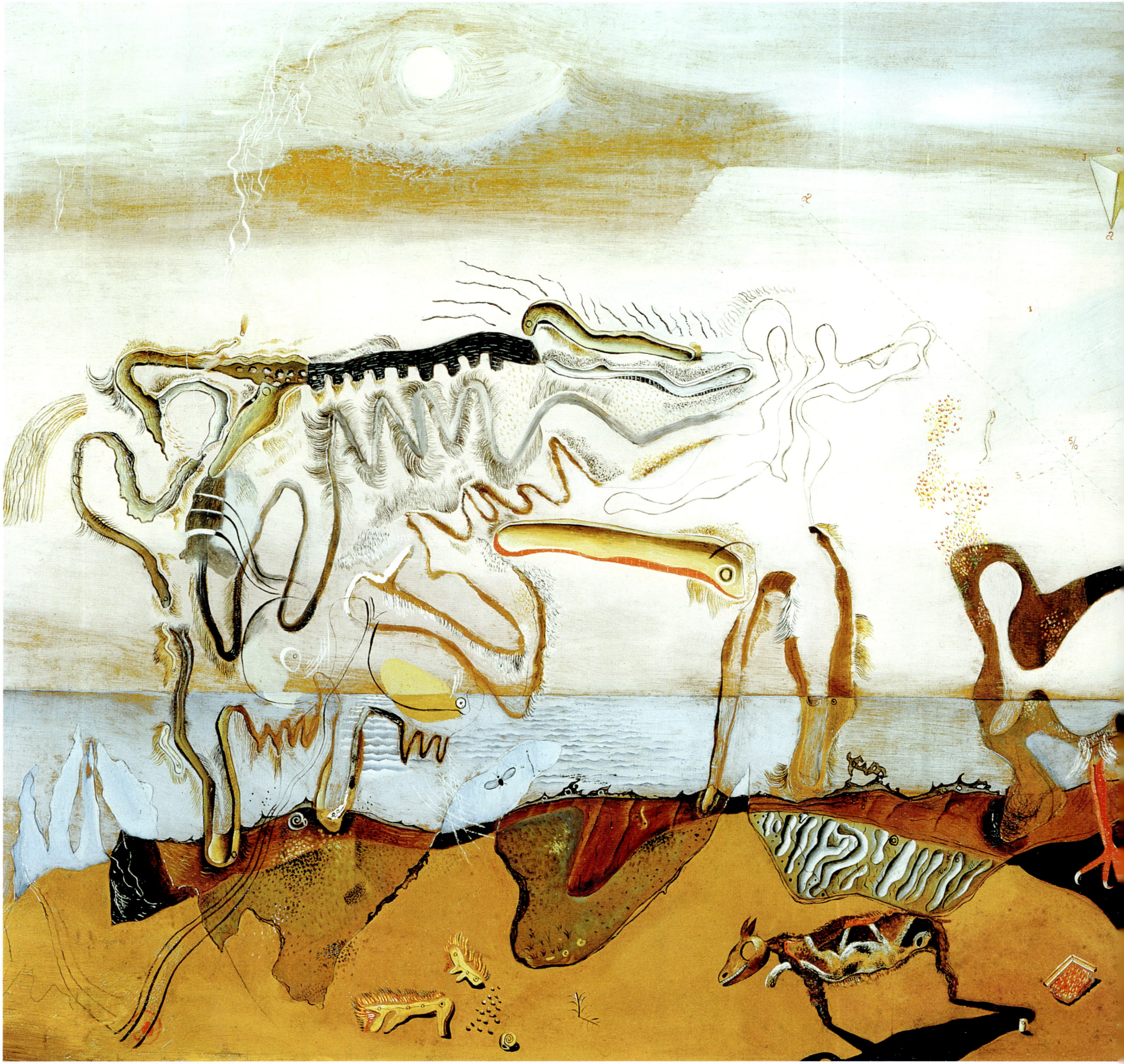

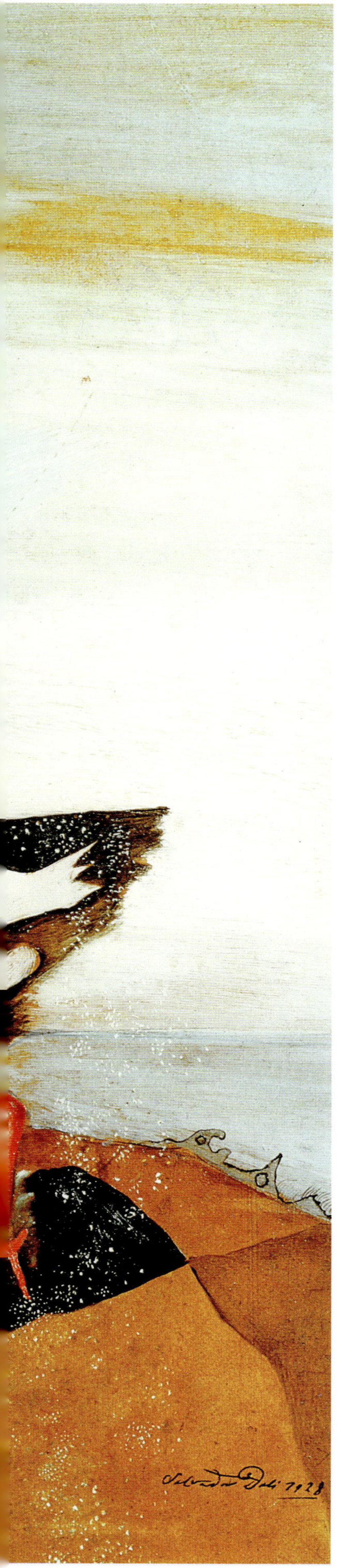

'My life was a constant and furious affirmation of my growing and imperialistic personality.'

refuse to be examined by them.' For this act of supreme, even if justifiable, arrogance he was summarily expelled without receiving his diploma, thus ruling out any possibility of a salaried teaching post, the kind of comfortable sinecure that Dalí clearly saw would have crushed his ambition at birth.

Mastering the Modern

By this time, Dalí had already enjoyed a one-man show the previous year at the Dalmau Gallery, the leading avant-garde gallery in Barcelona (and thus in the whole of Spain). Picasso saw it during a visit to the city and was particularly struck by *Seated Girl Seen from the Back* (1925, *see* page 44), one of a series of modern Neoclassical paintings of his sister, Anna Maria, that Dalí executed that year. It was yet another style of painting then in fashion that the future Surrealist had quickly mastered and would soon discard, though not before he had painted the brooding *Portrait of My Father* (1925, *see* page 47) and then, the following year, the luminous still life, *Basket of Bread* (1926, *see* page 30), whose dark background and photographic clarity of line is strongly reminiscent of Francisco de Zurbarán (1598–1664), another Old Master he greatly admired. Picasso had certainly seen enough to recommend his compatriot to his own Paris dealer, Léonce Rosenberg (1879–1947), and it was to Paris and the heartbeat of the avant-garde that Dalí now set his sights.

(Left)

The Spectral Cow, 1928

Medium: Oil on plywood
Dimensions: 50 x 64.5 cm (19¾ x 25⅓ in)
Location: Musée National d'Art Moderne, Centre Pompidou, Paris

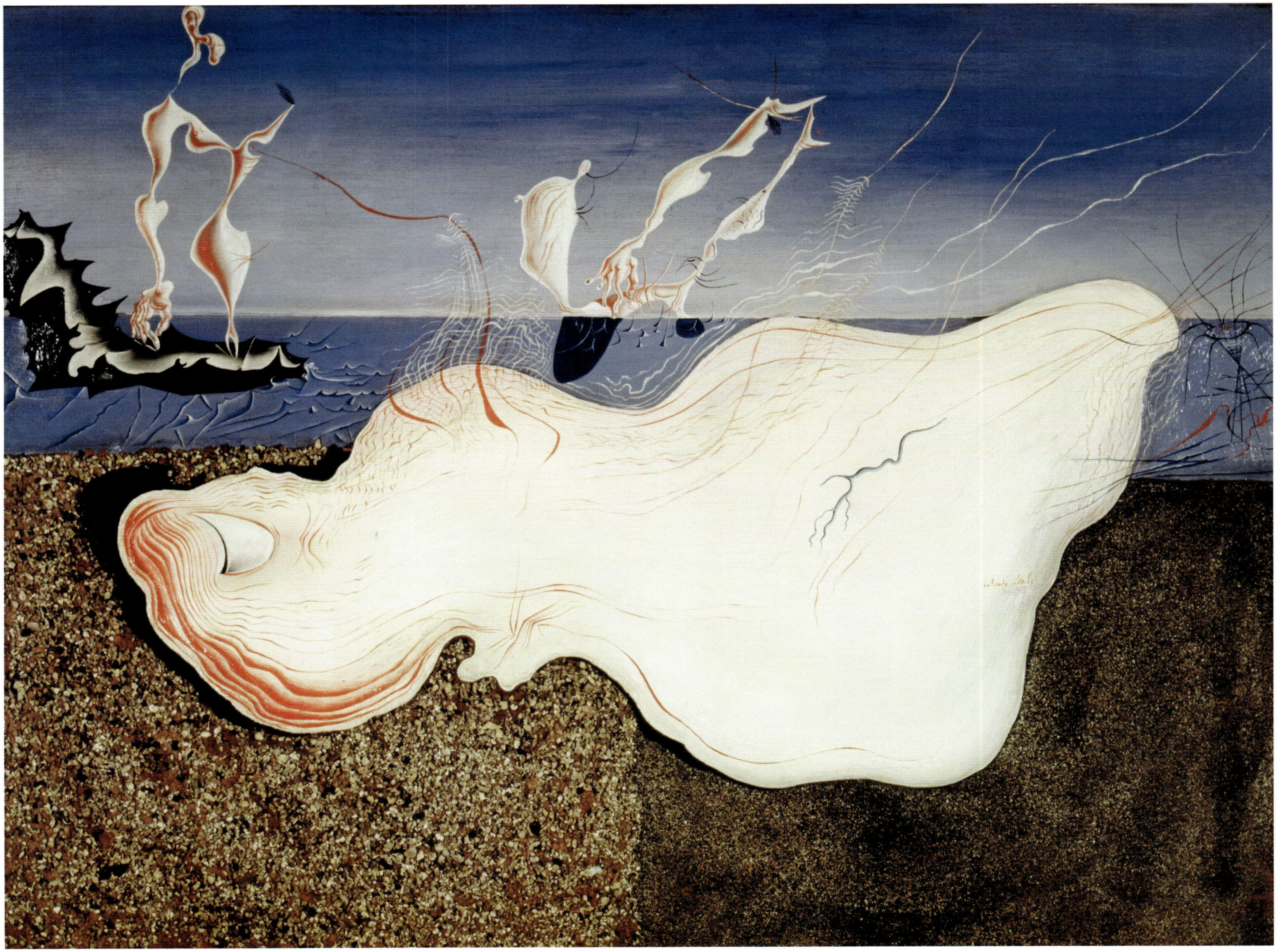

Dalí's father may have despaired previously at his son's expulsion from the San Fernando Academy but he had already had his head turned by the prestigious exhibitions and the accolades in the press that his boy was beginning to attract. On one occasion in early 1926, they received a visit in Figueres from Joan Miró (1893–1983), who affirmed to the notary the great prospects his son could look forward to, putting it to him that the best place for a young painter of such obvious talent was in Paris. By that time, Miró had been in Paris himself for a decade and Salvador senior, always respectful of genuine artistic achievement, took the painter at his word, the more so when it became clear that Miró was prepared to help his young compatriot establish himself in the French capital.

Paris and Picasso

With his father's blessing, Dalí made his first trip to Paris in April 1926, accompanied by his sister and his aunt Tieta, his mother's sister, who had married his father not long after her sister's death. It is hard to know what Dalí made of this marital arrangement as he fails to mention it anywhere in his writings. But in any case the trip seems to have been a happy one, with the trio visiting the sights of Paris, including Millet's studio in Barbizon just to the south. Dalí's most important purpose, however, was to see Picasso in his studio on the Rue La Boétie. It was a momentous occasion, as he recalls in *The Secret Life*:

> 'When I arrived at Picasso's on Rue de la Boétie I was deeply moved.'

'When I arrived at Picasso's on Rue de la Boétie I was deeply moved and as full of respect as though I were having an audience with the Pope.' He brought the titan of modern art a painting of a girl similar to the one Picasso had admired in Barcelona, and then the master took him up to the studio to show his countryman a huge number of paintings. From this encounter, Dalí seems not only to have fully understood the task ahead of him but to also have embraced it.

At the same moment in Paris, another movement that would soon interest Picasso himself was beginning to recalibrate the artistic consciousness of Europe after the First World War. Surrealism had grown out of Dada, the satirical, anti-aesthetic and often performance-based group of artists whose absurdist work had been a direct response to the folly and waste of that conflict. Under the leadership of André Breton (1896–1966), a former prime

(Left)

Bathers, 1928

Medium: Oil and collage on panel
Dimensions: 52 x 71.7 cm ($20\frac{1}{2}$ x $28\frac{1}{4}$ in)
Location: Salvador Dalí Museum, St Petersburg, Florida

mover of the Dada group, the Surrealists had grown into a powerful new collective which, at least to begin with, took its lead from the theories of Sigmund Freud (1856–1939) concerning the influence of the unconscious on apparently rational human behaviour. Dalí had devoured Freud's *The Interpretation of Dreams* (1900) in 1922, as soon as it was published in Spanish, and the influence of leading Surrealists such as André Masson (1896–1987) and Yves Tanguy (1900–55) can be felt in the work he would create over the next couple of years.

Surrealism: A Decisive Encounter

A central tenet of Surrealist doctrine was the liberation of unconscious desires which when communicated through artistic activity could be integrated into a person's consciousness, thus enabling them to become more fully realized human beings; this in turn would lead to a society of better-adjusted men and women who, being satisfied with their lives through greater self-knowledge, would thus be less inclined to propagate catastrophic wars such as the one so recently passed. So went the theory at least, and in pursuit of this aim the Surrealists used certain key techniques to enable the unconscious to emerge from beneath the martial scrutiny of the conscious mind, as they viewed it – in particular, both automatic writing and automatic drawing. The latter was practised most assiduously by Masson, whose pictures using sand and other materials are a clear inspiration behind such works of Dalí's as *The Stinking Ass* (1928).

The influence of Tanguy, in both composition and atmosphere, can be felt in works such as *Apparatus and Hand* (1927, *see* page 49) and *Little Ashes* (1927–28, *see* page 58). In a way that bears resemblance to Tanguy's *He Did What He Wanted* (1927), there is the same deeply recessed dream landscape with a random distribution of seemingly unconnected figures and abstract shapes, though in the case of Dalí's pictures, especially *Little Ashes*, already the

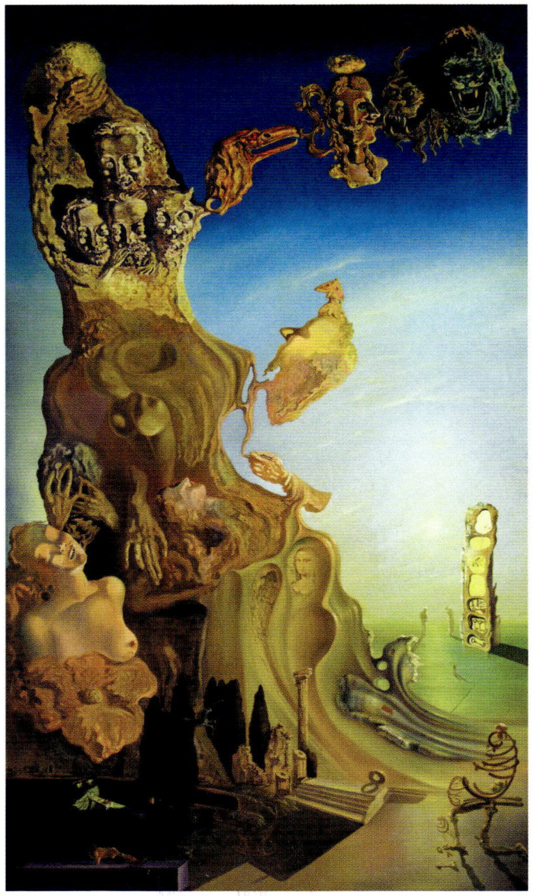

(Above)

The Memory of the Woman-Child, 1929

Medium: Oil and collage on canvas
Dimensions: 140 x 81 cm (55 x 31 in)
Location: Museo Nacional Centro de Arte Reina Sofía, Madrid

menagerie of objects has grown immense, depicting a kind of centrifugal psychic chaos that perhaps points to an incipient crisis. The character of both pictures is archetypal, but again, to the cocktail of dreamlike motifs Dalí added elements of realist representation that were much more concrete than those in the work of other Surrealists. These motifs would crop up again and again in his work: the wide expanse of sea and rocks, the view from Cadaqués, in *Apparatus and Hand*; the voluptuous female torsos in both pictures; and the rotting donkey crawling with ants in *Little Ashes* (as also in the study for *Honey is Sweeter than Blood* of 1926, *see* page 48), which would reappear in *Un Chien Andalou*.

A Hysterical Summer

Given the erotic elements manifest in these pictures, which would only become more pronounced in the years to come, it is worth

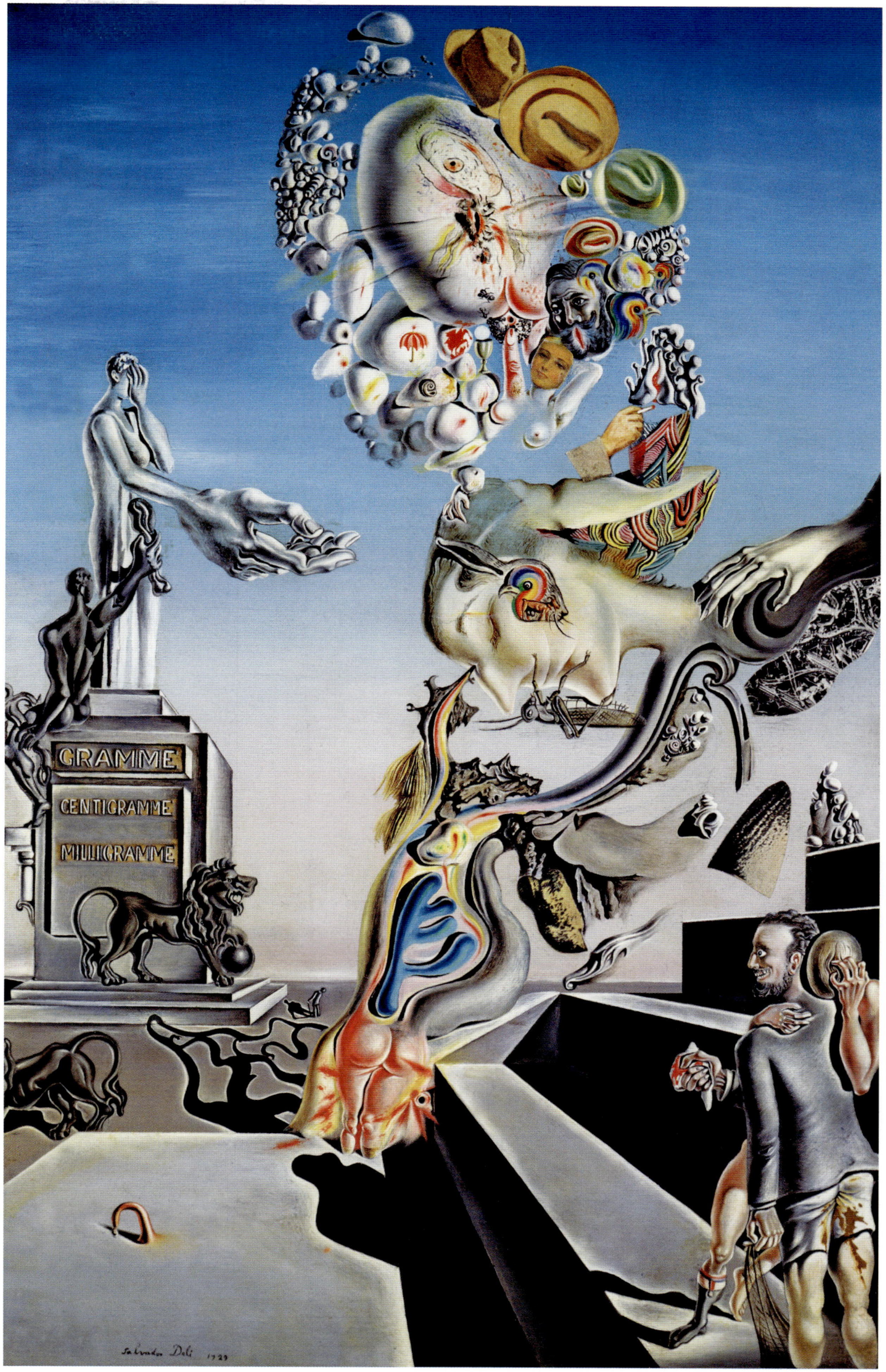

(Right)

The Lugubrious Game, 1929

Medium: Oil and collage on cardboard
Dimensions: 44.4 x 30.3 cm (17½ x 12 in)
Location: Private Collection

noting that Dalí was still a virgin. He seems never to have doubted his heterosexuality – the advances of Lorca were enough to confirm it to him, or so he would have us believe. But his early encounters with the likes of Dullita and other girls such as a fellow student in the philosophy class at school, whom he tells us in *The Secret Life* he strung along for some five years without ever coming close to consummating the relationship, reinforce what he later recognized as being a morbid fear of sex. This forced him back on his own resources, a confirmed habit of masturbation that is also depicted, albeit in the form of a grotesquely distorted female figure performing the act, in *Bather (Feminine Nude)* (1928). By now in his mid-twenties, Dalí's long-deferred sexual needs were being increasingly displaced into his alarmingly disinhibited work.

These disinhibitions emerged most notoriously in *Un Chien Andalou*, completed in the spring of 1929 after Dalí had returned to live in Paris. The premiere of the film would not take place until the autumn and would do more than any of his paintings to announce Dalí's name to the world and promote him to the front rank of the Surrealist movement. But already, as summer approached, the painter felt increasingly overwhelmed by a growing hysteria of the kind that Freud could have diagnosed in his sleep. Dalí was well aware himself of the likely cause, but this did not enable him to control its symptoms. By then he had made the acquaintance of Camille Goemans (1900–60), his future dealer, who introduced him to Paul Éluard (1895–1952), a Surrealist poet and a leading light in the movement. The two of them promised to visit Dalí

'I'm in a constant interrogation: where does the deep and philosophically valid Dalí begin, and where does the looney and preposterous Dalí end?'

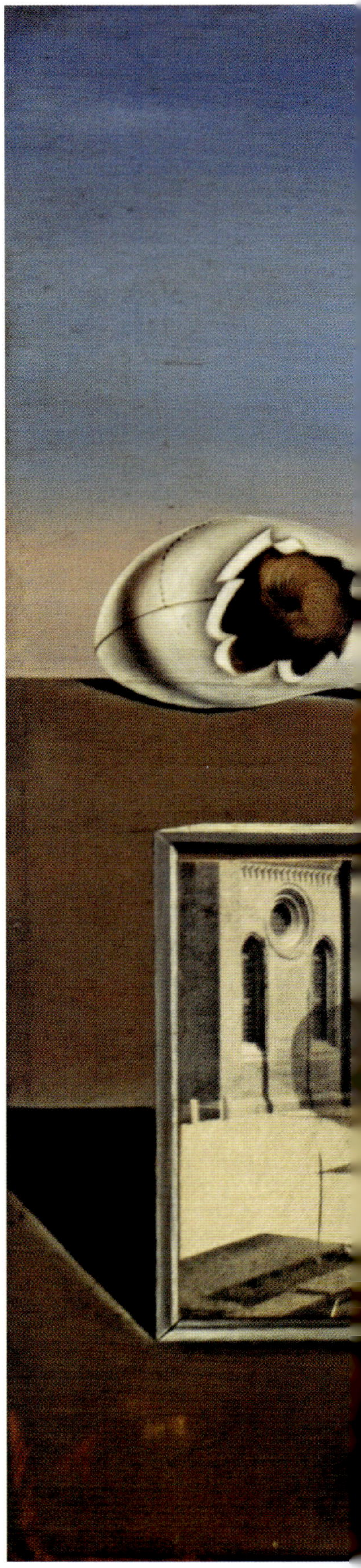

(Right)

Illuminated Pleasures, 1929

Medium: Oil and collage on composite panel
Dimensions: 23.8 x 34.7 cm (9⅖ x 13⅔ in)
Location: Museum of Modern Art, New York

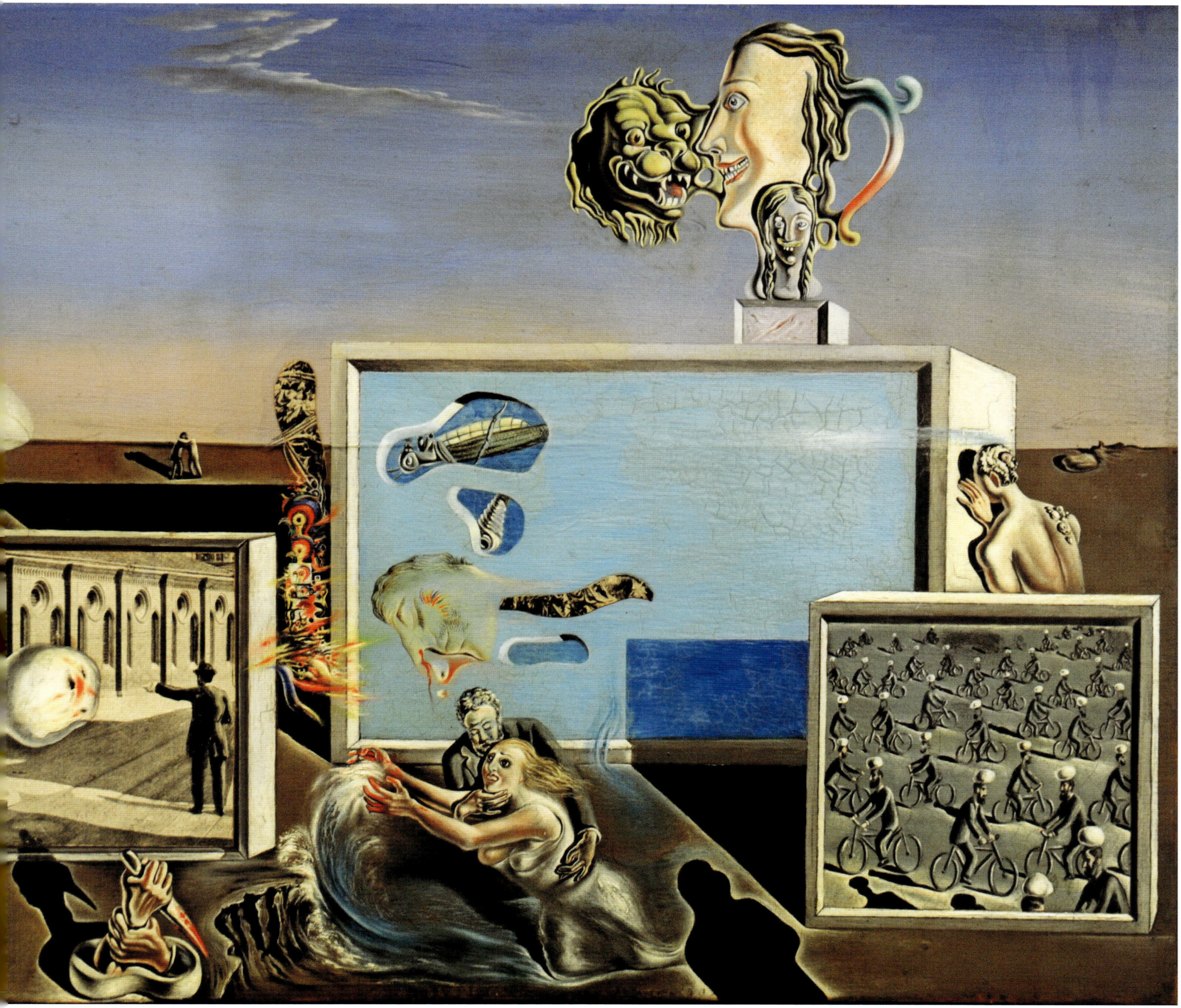

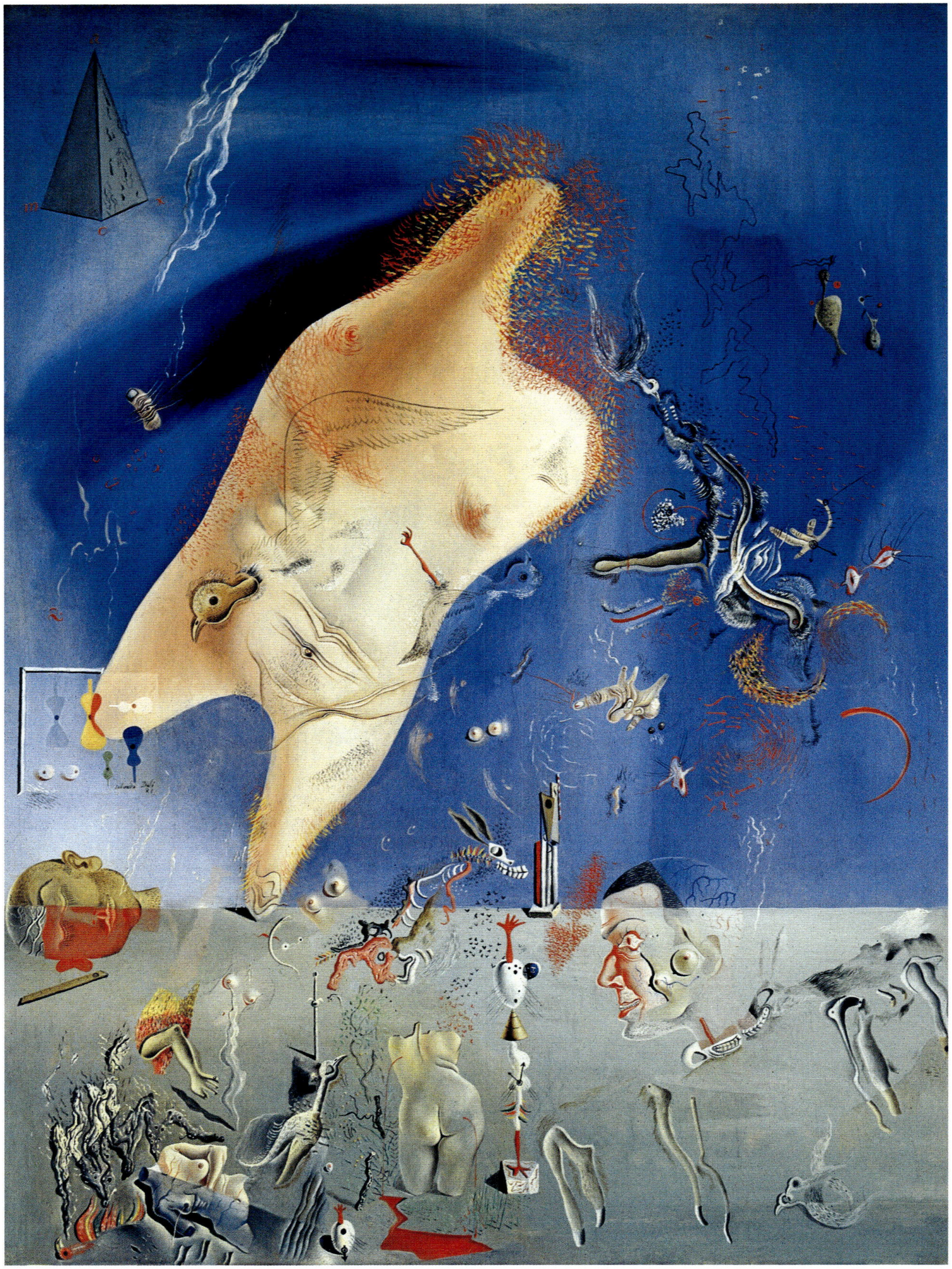

that summer in Cadaqués, and they brought along with them René Magritte (1898–1967) and his wife, Georgette, as well as Buñuel, Dalí's partner in crime in *Un Chien Andalou*. Also accompanying Éluard was his wife, Gala, whom Breton had previously described as *la femme eternelle*, and who gradually became a central figure in the Surrealist movement, mainly for the role of muse she played to some of its most prominent members, above all to Dalí.

La Femme Eternelle

It was Éluard, her first husband, who gave her the name Gala, though in fact her real name was Elena Ivanovna Diakonova. In complete contrast to Dalí, the man whose life and career she would do so much to define, little is known about her childhood, as she closely guarded its secrets. But it seems that she was born in Kazan in Russia in 1894 (or perhaps a few years earlier – again, we cannot be sure) to a Jewish

(Left)

Little Ashes, 1927–28

Medium: Oil on panel
Dimensions: 64 x 48 cm (25¼ x 19 in)
Location: Museo Nacional Centro de Arte Reina Sofía, Madrid

father and a mother who belonged to the Orthodox Church. As a girl, Gala experienced bouts of mental illness and then at the age of 18 fell ill with tuberculosis; it was in a Swiss sanatorium that she met and fell in love with Éluard. Following him to Paris she bore him a daughter, and when Éluard fell in with Breton and the nascent Surrealist movement, she was famously implicated in the break-up of the first marriage of Max Ernst (1891–1976) when Ernst, smitten with Gala, came to live with the Éluards in Paris in a notorious *ménage à trois*. She reminded Ernst's wife, Lou (1893–1944), of a panther, and she clearly possessed a magnetic sexual power.

The Lugubrious Game

Dalí seems to have spent the summer of 1929 at Cadaqués in a kind of shamanistic trance as he plumbed the depths of his unconscious in an attempt to realize a new imaginative vision. The account he gives of this process in *The Secret Life* is worth quoting at length for the crucial insight it gives into his methods: 'I would awake at sunrise, and without washing or dressing sit down before the easel which stood right beside my bed. Thus the first image I saw on awakening was the painting I had begun, as it was the last I saw in the evening when I retired. And I tried to go to sleep while looking at it fixedly, as though by endeavouring to link it to my sleep I could succeed in separating myself from it. Sometimes I would awake in the middle of the night and turn on the light to see my painting again for a moment. At times again between slumbers I would observe it in the solitary gay light of the waxing moon. Thus I spent the whole day seated before my easel, my eyes staring fixedly, trying to "see", like a medium … the images that would spring up in my imagination. Often, I saw these images exactly situated in the painting. Then, at the point commanded by them, I would paint, paint with the hot taste in my mouth that panting hunting dogs must have at the moment when they fasten their teeth into the game killed that very instant by a well-aimed shot.'

The painting in question was *The Lugubrious Game* (1929, *see* page 55), its title and its content – including figures covering their faces in shame – both clear references to the guilt Dalí felt over the masturbation that was still his only sexual outlet. It shocked the normally

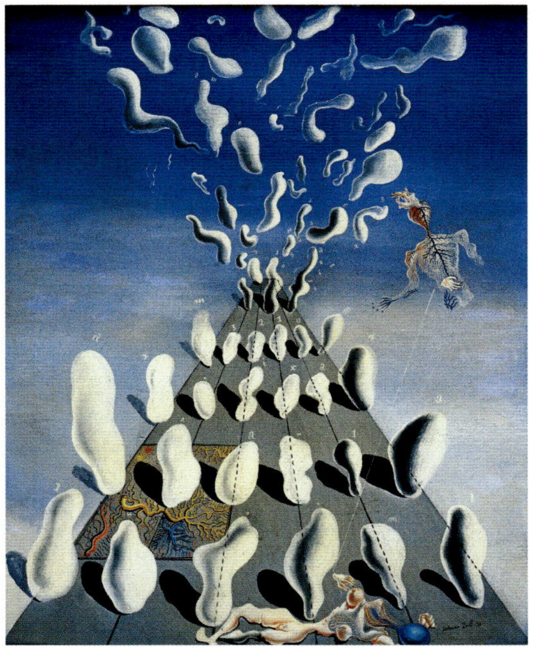

(Above)

Inaugural Gooseflesh, 1928

Medium: Oil on cardboard
Dimensions: 76 x 63.2 cm (30 x 25 in)
Location: Fundació Gala-Salvador Dalí, Figueres

unshockable group of Surrealist friends who arrived in Cadaqués that August. In particular, they were dismayed by the soiled underwear of the bearded man in the painting's lower-right corner, which seemed to stray beyond the breaking of taboos that was approved Surrealist activity into a world of private, personal fetish and disgust.

Gala's Little Boy

By that point Dalí seemed on the verge of a nervous breakdown, breaking out in fits of increasingly hysterical laughter brought on by the continual surge of crazy images erupting in his mind. Gala was selected to have a talk with the painter to discern his motives, and Dalí was able to assure her that he was not 'coprophagic' (by which he meant 'coprophilic'), though in the light of the repeated fascination with his stool and other scatological references in later writings such as *Diary of a Genius* (1964), this assertion has to be

'Take me, I am the drug; take me, I am hallucinogenic.'

questionable at best. And, to be fair to Dalí, excrement should not have been any more off limits in the supposedly irrational world of Surrealism than it is in the world of dreams. As the painter himself critiques it in a footnote in *The Secret Life*: 'Between the excrement and a piece of rock crystal, by the very fact that they both sprang from the common basis of the unconscious, there could and should be no difference in category. And these were the men who denied the hierarchies of tradition!'

In any case, Gala was reassured and, more to the point, her presence had an immediate effect on Dalí, giving him a sudden, compelling focus for the spiralling eroticism that was threatening to overwhelm him. Éluard and the others would soon head back to Paris, leaving Gala, who by that time was in fact living separately from her husband, to stay on with Dalí. She was clearly fascinated by the young Catalan and had the intelligence, moreover, to attempt to see beyond the chaotic surface to the soul of a man who, she may have sensed even then, would worship her for the rest of his life. In *The Secret Life* Dalí describes with fanatical excitement the momentous walk along the cliffs in which their love and mutual need became apparent to them both, despite his outbursts of laughter having reached a pitch of hysteria that he describes as terrifying. Finally, in desperation he threw himself to the ground at her feet. Gala gazed upon him with compassion, with love, and uttered words of absolution that he would never forget: 'My little boy! We shall never leave each other.' Salvador had been saved.

(Right)

The First Days of Spring, 1929

Medium: Oil and collage on panel
Dimensions: 49.5 x 64 cm (19½ x 25⅛ in)
Location: Salvador Dalí Museum, St Petersburg, Florida

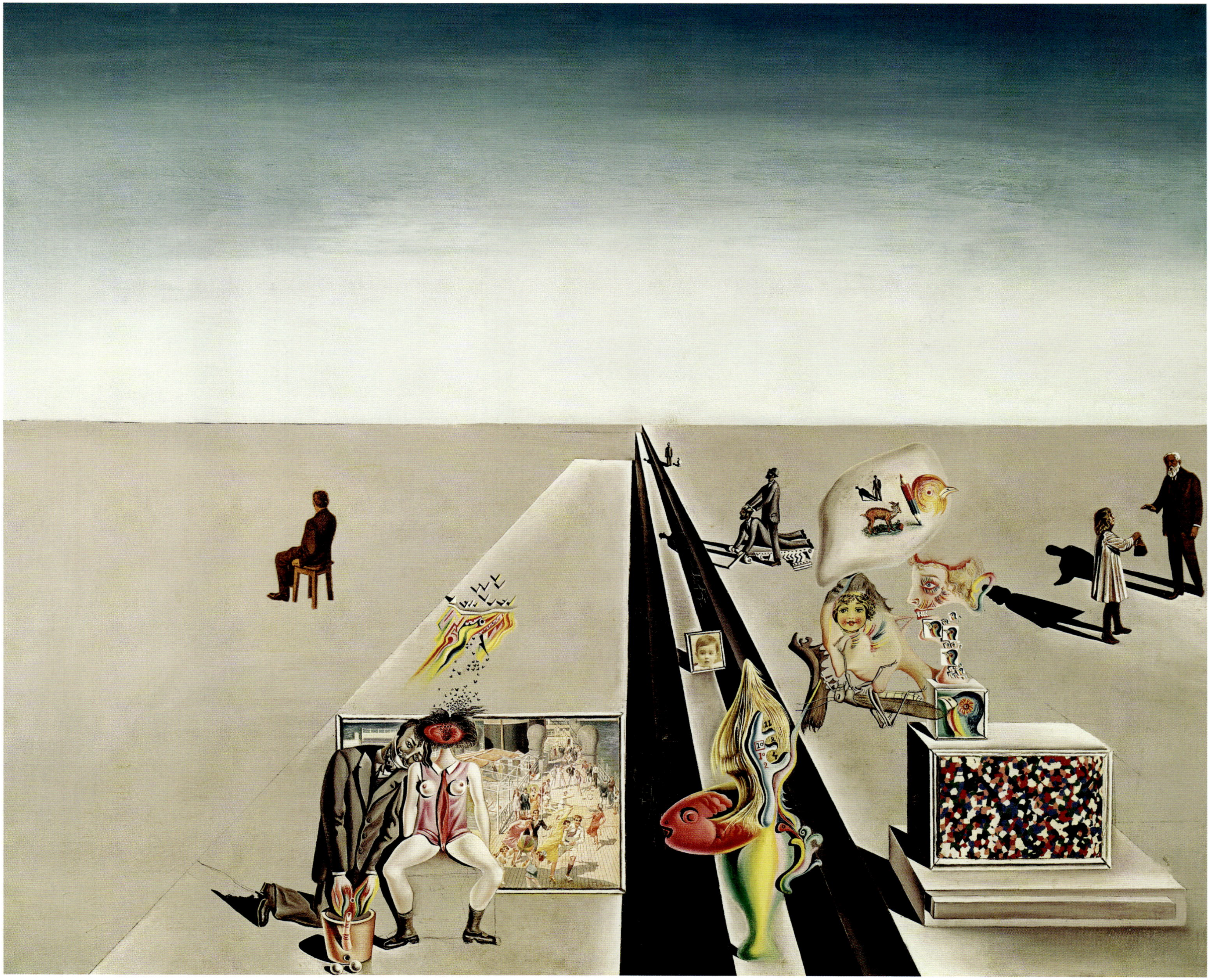

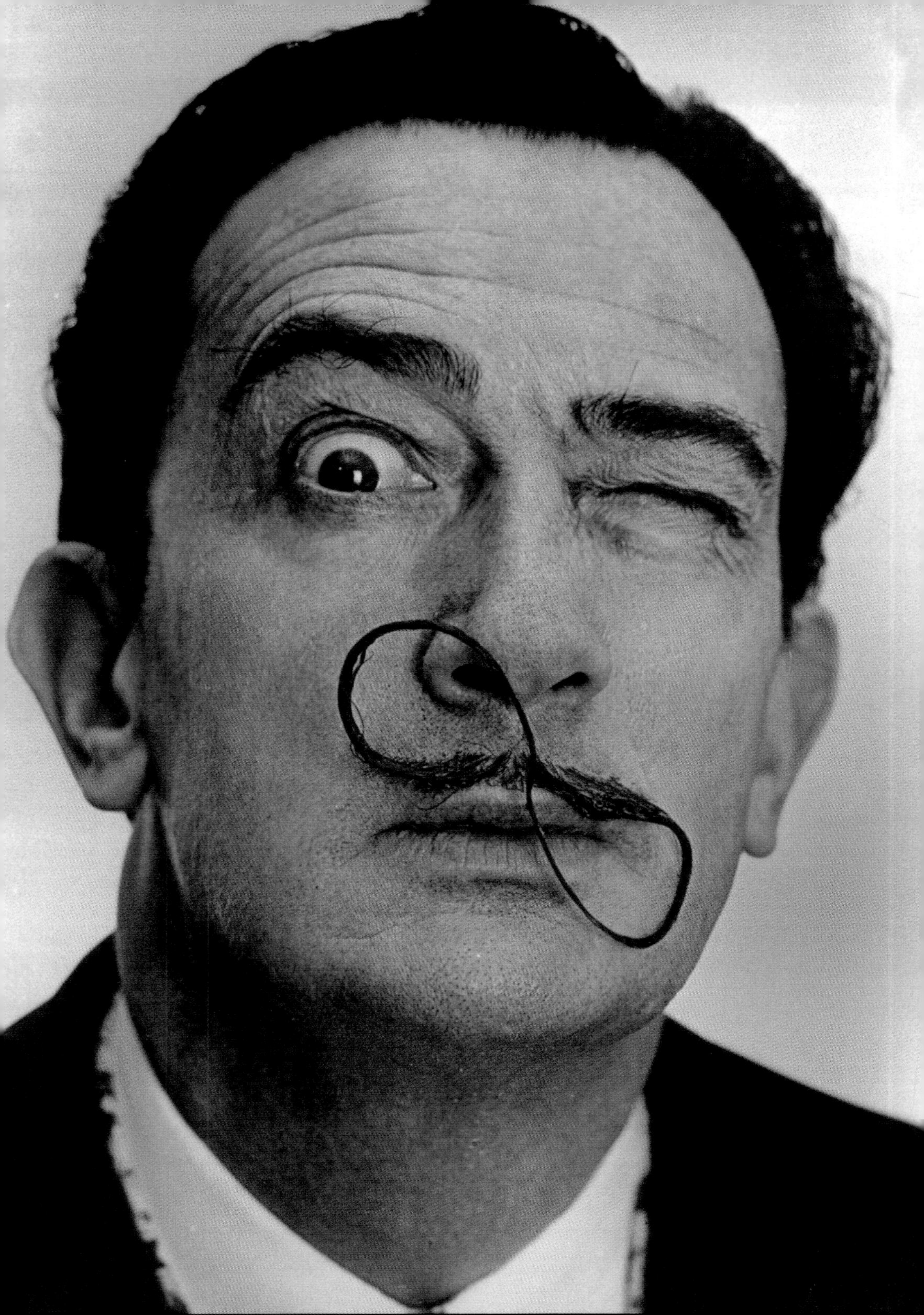

I am the Don Quixote of unreality.

'O, Salvador Dalí! You know it now! If you play at genius you become one!'

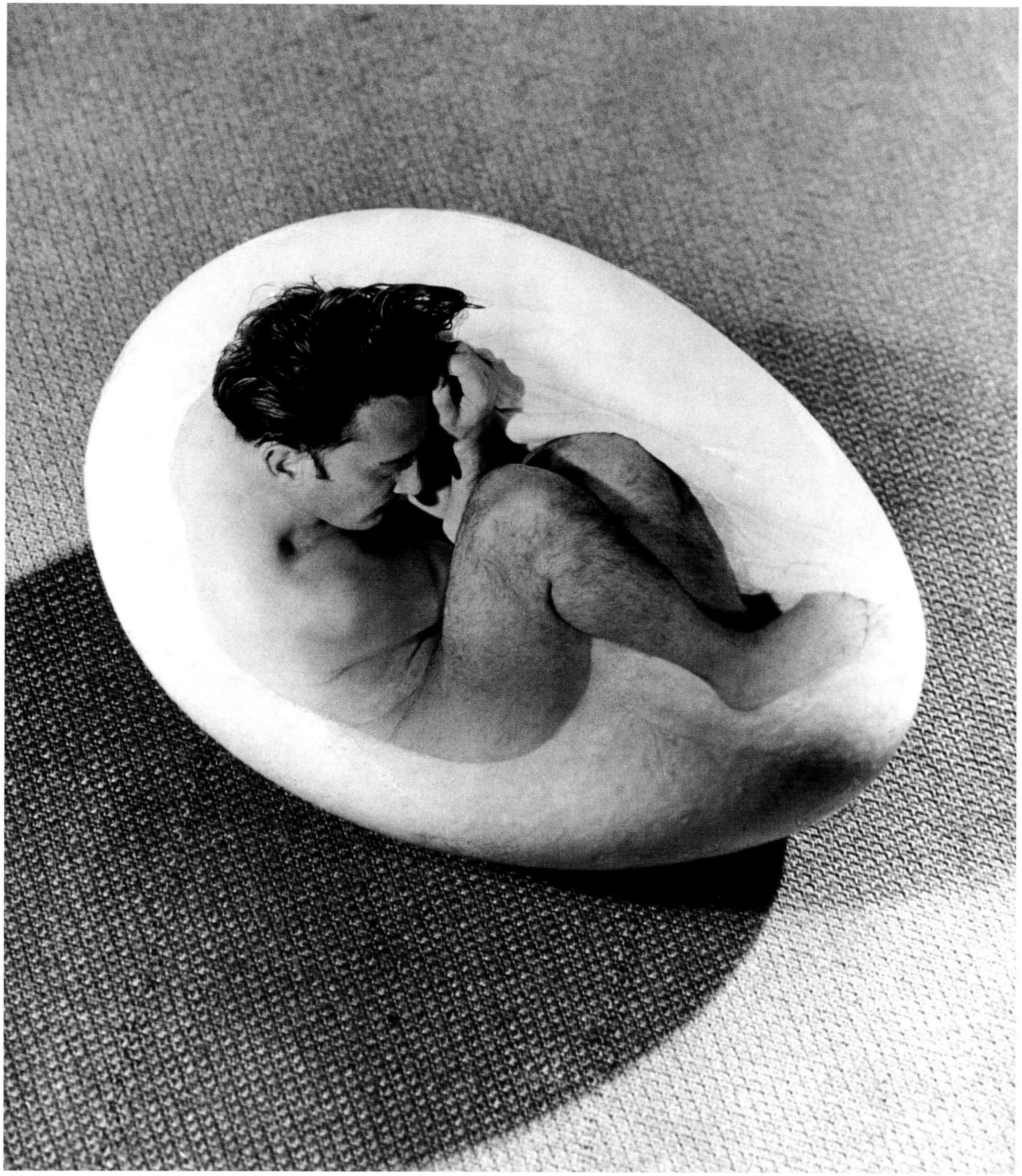

The Great Paranoiac

The relationship with Gala soon dispelled the worst fears Dalí had entertained that sex with a woman would somehow bring about his death. Gala returned to Paris and Dalí settled down to work again in Figueres. He felt that the 'murderous impulses of my childhood had in fact disappeared from my imagination forever', banished by the 'principle of reality' which Gala compelled him to acknowledge; on the other hand, she also represented its opposite in Freudian terms, the 'principle of pleasure', as is clear from the explosion of erotic and in some cases pornographic images that he made from then on, in particular in the early 1930s.

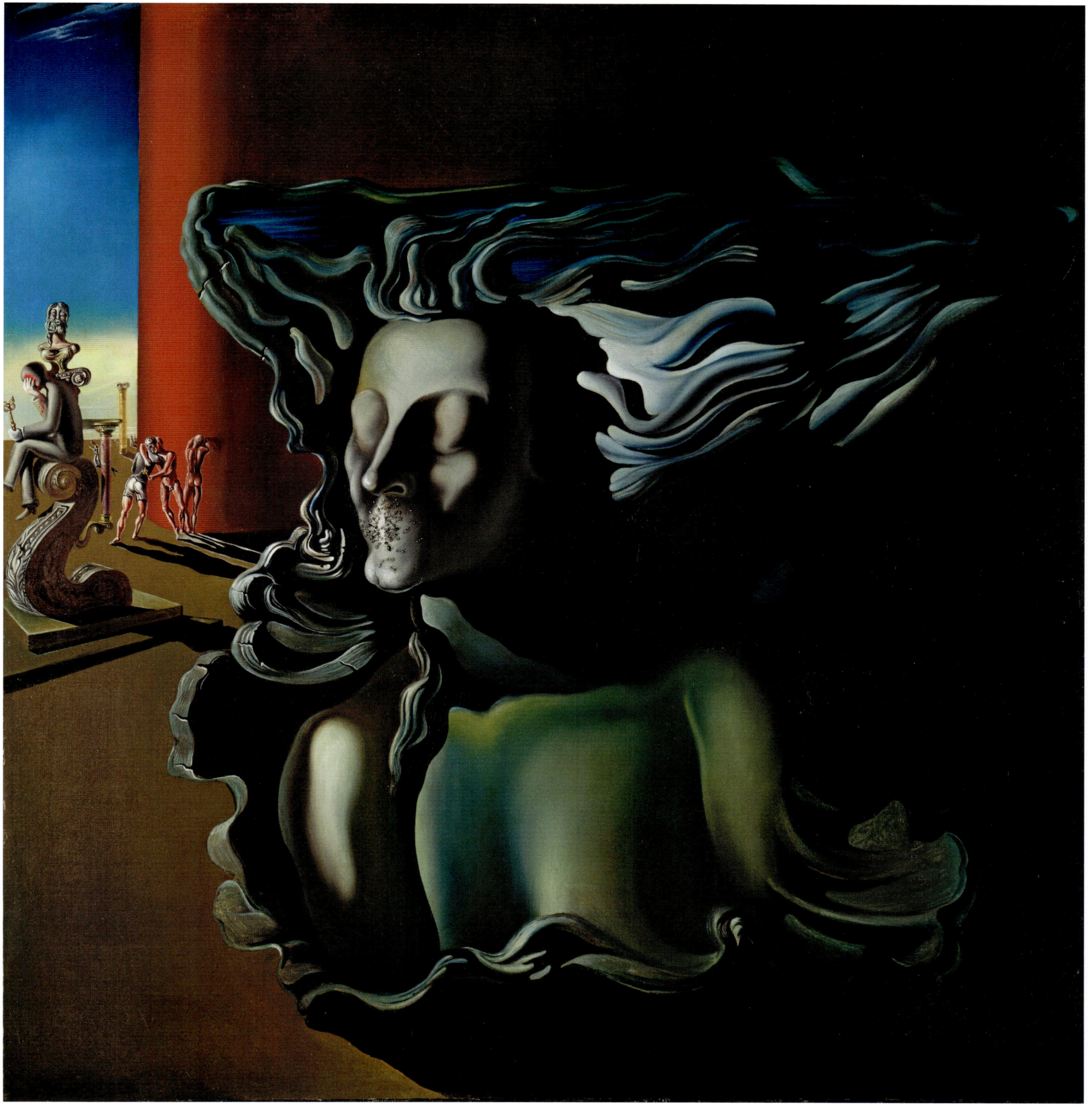

The Dream, *c.* **1930** | Medium: Oil on canvas | Dimensions: 96 x 96 cm (37⁴⁄₅ x 37⁴⁄₅ in) | Location: Cleveland Museum of Art, Ohio

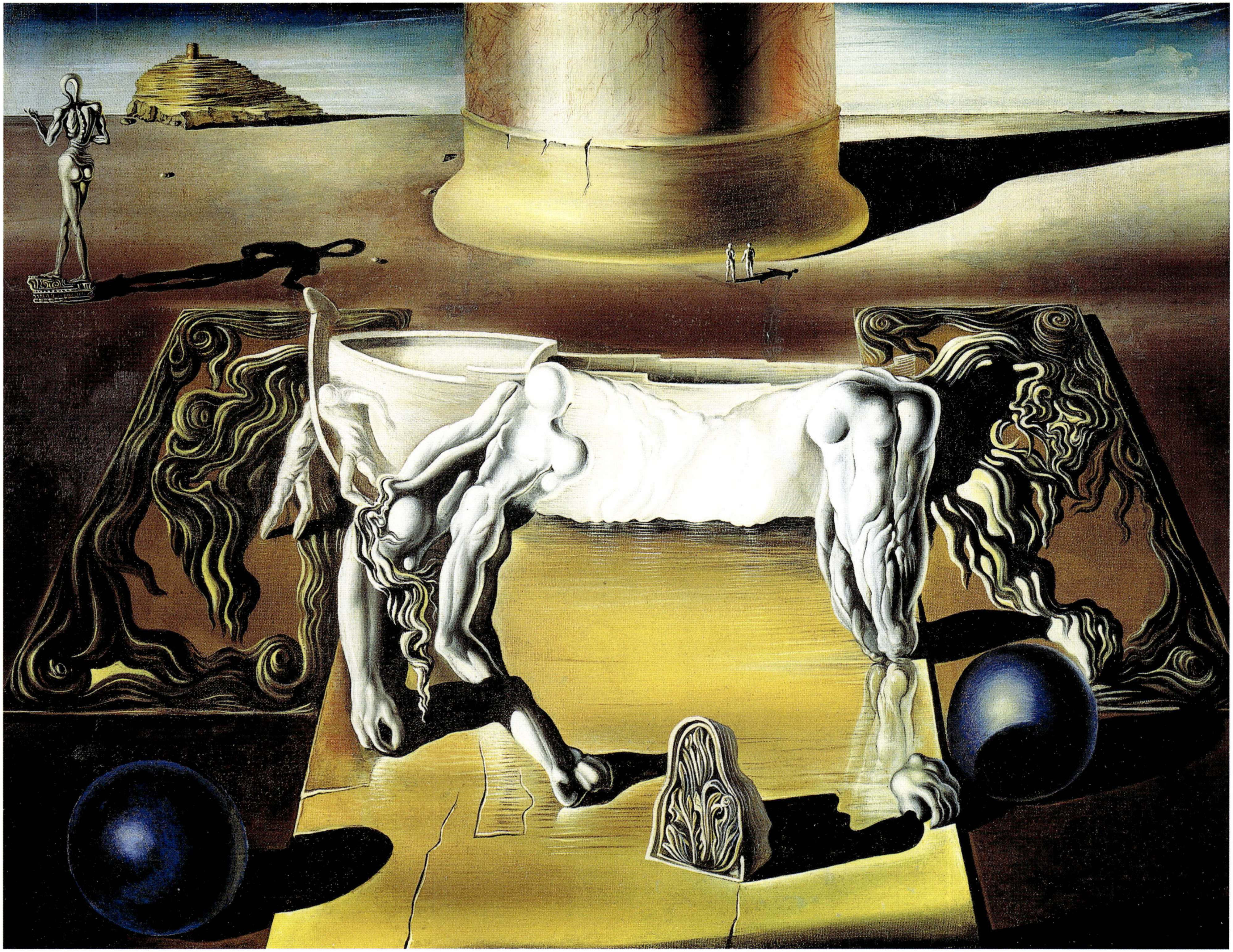

A Grasshopper Phobia

Now anchored by the thought of the woman who would remain the source of his stability for the rest of her life, Dalí seems to have worked on several paintings simultaneously, among them the as yet unfinished *Portrait of Paul Éluard* (1929, *see* page 69), the man he had so recently cuckolded, and a new one he called *The Great Masturbator* (*see* page 20), a clear self-reference. The new erotic concreteness of life with Gala is immediately apparent in both, along with a confident deployment of personal motifs which had already appeared in works of the previous few years and to which he would return time and again. One that appears in both works, as it does in *The Lugubrious Game* (*see* page 55), is the grasshopper, a personal phobia which as Dalí explains in *The Secret Life* dated to a time during his schooldays when his fellow students had mercilessly exploited his fear of the creatures. In the same volume, he also recalls a boyhood memory of discovering a bat which he had tried to nurse back to health, only to find the following day that it had turned putrescent and was being slowly eaten alive by ants. Dalí picked up the animal at the moment when Dullita, the object of his erotic interest that summer, approached through the garden gate. But having decided to kiss the dying animal as she came near – a course of action bizarre enough in itself – instead he found himself biting it and flinging it violently away to continue its agonizing death in some forgotten corner of the yard.

A Double Horror

The grasshopper symbol in the *Portrait of Paul Éluard* is further complicated by the illusionistic doubling of its inverted head as the eye of a fish which in *The Secret Life* Dalí refers to as a 'slobberer'. This was yet another childhood memory, in this case of a fish he had caught whose face disturbingly resembled a grasshopper's and which he

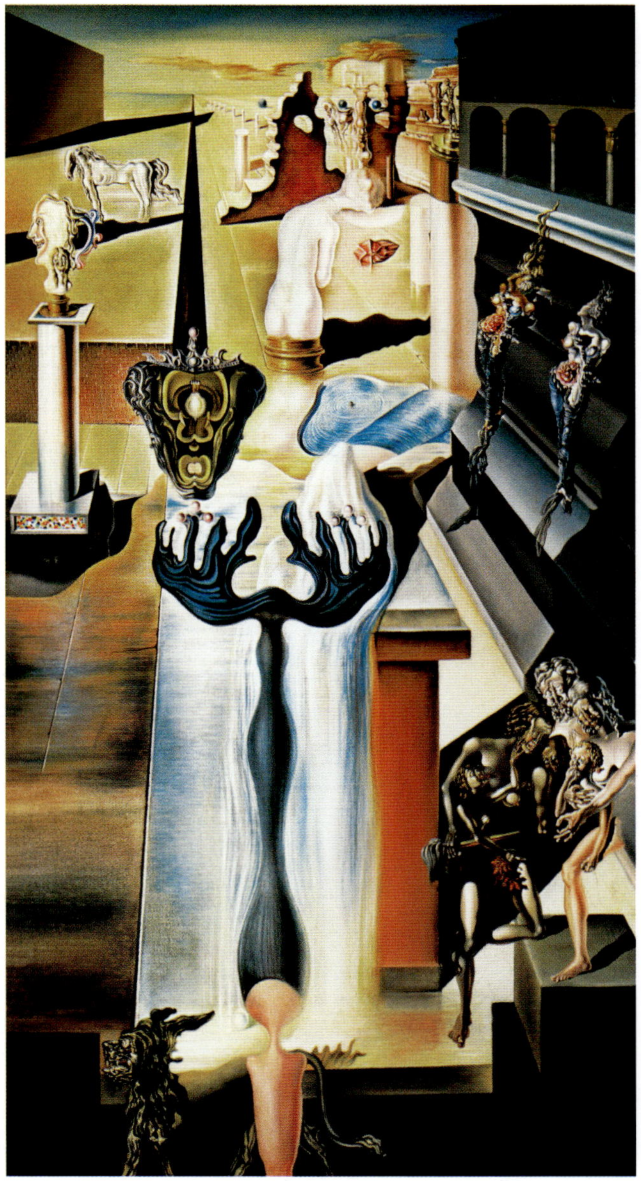

(Left)

Invisible Sleeping Woman, Lion, Horse, 1930

Medium: Oil on canvas
Dimensions: 50 x 65 cm (19¾ x 25⅝ in)
Location: Musée National d'Art Moderne, Centre Pompidou, Paris

(Right)

The Invisible Man, 1929–32

Medium: Oil on canvas
Dimensions: 140 x 81 cm (55 x 32 in)
Location: Museo Nacional Centro de Arte Reina Sofía, Madrid

also found repulsive. This double horror of fish and grasshopper is compounded by the belly of the fish being transformed into the sleeping human face of a figure that would reappear in *The Great Masturbator* – a truly monstrous hybrid. It is an early instance of Dalí's fondness for double images and visual ambiguities, but also of the 'delirium of interpretation' on which his most crucial artistic contribution was based. This he called the 'paranoiac-critical method', which he defined in the essay on Millet's *Angelus* from 1933 as a 'spontaneous method of irrational knowledge based upon the interpretive-critical association of delirious phenomena'; although even then it would be several more years before he fully understood it himself. It is a *modus operandi* that Dalí was temperamentally made for, given his innate paranoid tendency to over-interpret visual phenomena almost as portents or signs – in a manner not dissimilar to that of a traditional shaman or, less deliberately, to someone suffering a genuine paranoid illness.

The Rocks of Cadaqués

But Dalí, most certainly not mad, as he always insisted, applied to these 'voluntary hallucinations', as he called them – fantasies or daydreams which he purposefully invoked in order to exploit them artistically – a pseudo-rational visual critique made compellingly plausible by the lifelike and photographic fidelity of representation that by 1929 he was beginning to master. This paranoiac delirium, based partly on the metamorphic illogic of dreams but also on the waking reverie of persistent, disturbing memory, led Dalí to the unprecedented strangeness and eroticism of images such as *The Great Masturbator* (see page 20). It also signalled a new conception of Surrealism whose mixture of the erotic and the necrotic, of love with death, was the key to its power.

'I like only the landscape of Cadaqués, and I would not even look at any other.'

In this seminal painting, in addition to the grasshopper there is also the shape of the distorted sleeping head hinted at in the *Portrait of Paul Éluard* (see right), here writ large, seemingly that of a giant. Dalí tells us that it was based on one of the distinctive rock formations around the shores of Cadaqués that he knew so well, which reappears in altered form in yet another work of this period, *The Enigma of Desire* or *My Mother, my Mother, my Mother* (1929, see page 70). These rocks, shaped by wind and weather over time, assume different shapes suggestive of animals or inanimate objects, which become transformed as the viewer changes their position, particularly when seen from the sea. For this reason, as Dalí explains in *The Secret Life*, 'the fishermen of the region had since time immemorial baptized each of these imposing conglomerations – the camel, the eagle, the anvil, the monk, the dead woman, the lion's head'.

The Great Masturbator

In the case of the rock that appears in this painting as the sleeping head of the masturbator, out of its cheek grows the bust of a naked woman in the grip of erotic ecstasy, her face turned to within titillating inches of the clothed but clearly discernible penis of a man whose identity is not revealed. These elements alone – the grasshopper, crawling with ants and clinging repulsively to the face of the masturbator, as well as the enraptured

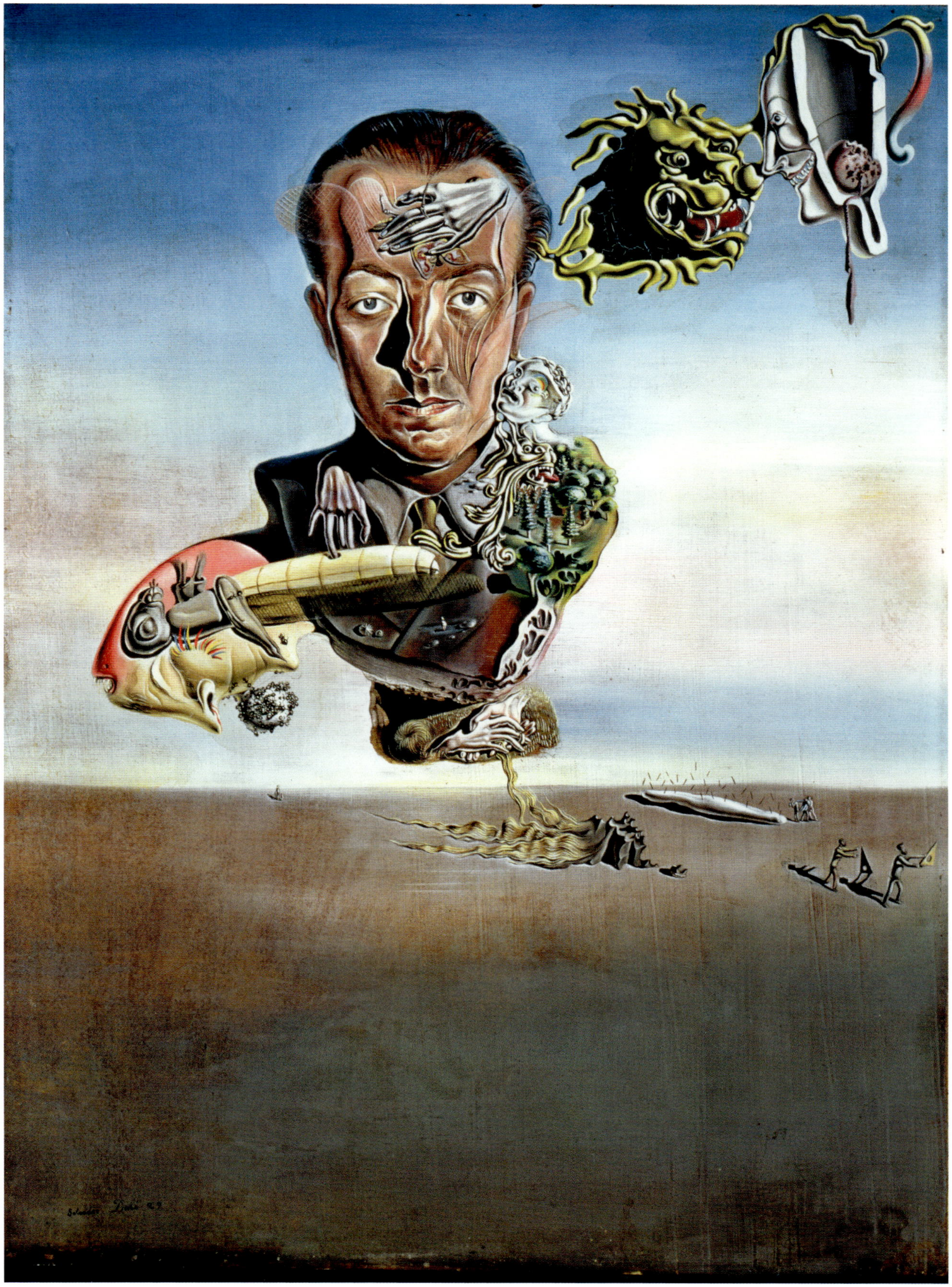

(Right)

Portrait of Paul Éluard, 1929

Medium: Oil on cardboard
Dimensions: 33 x 25 cm (13 x 9⅞ in)
Location: Private Collection

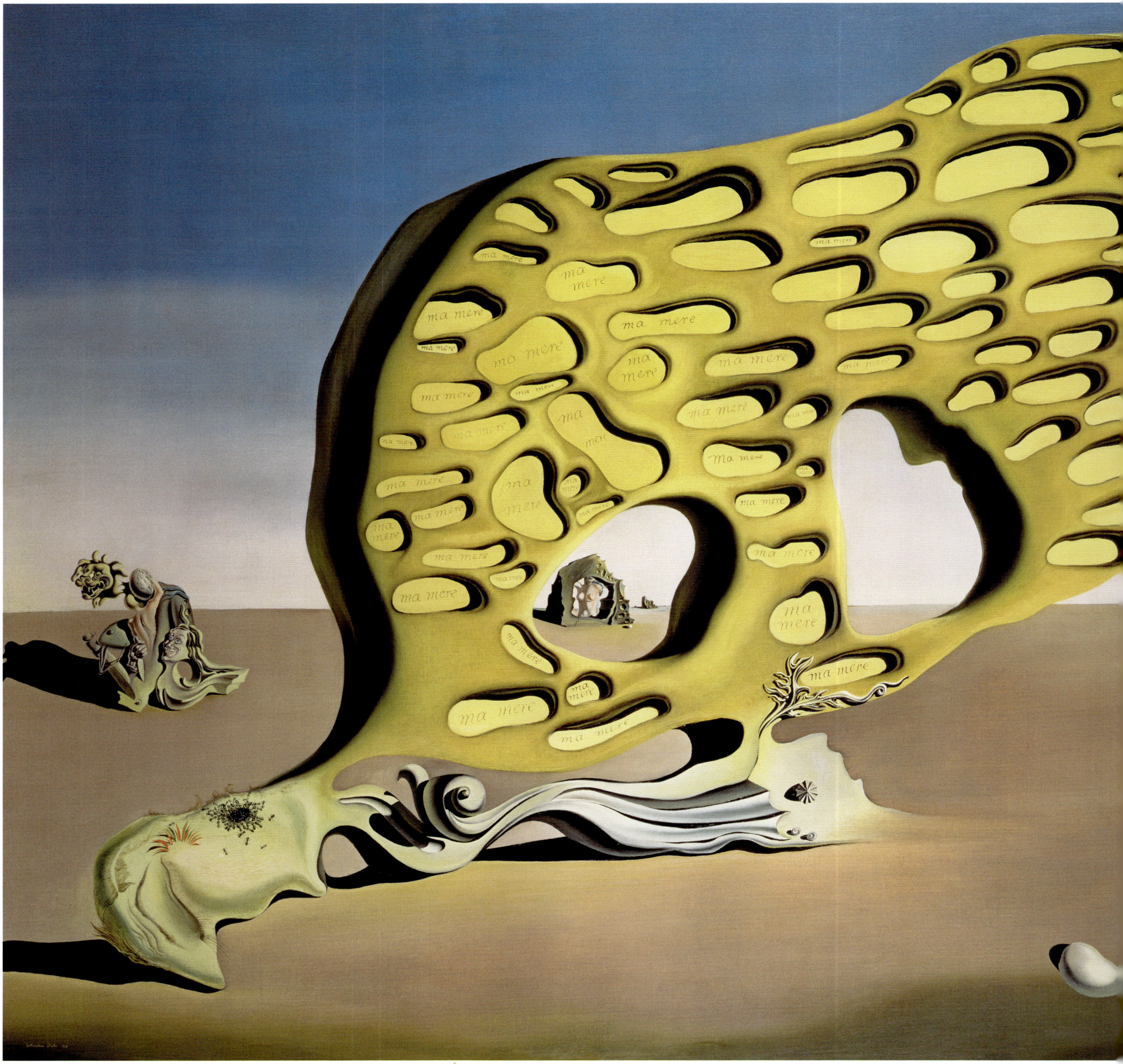
ma mere
ma mere
ma mere
ma mere
ma mere
ma mere
ma mere
ma mere
ma mere
ma mere
ma mere
ma mere
ma mere
ma mere
ma mere
ma mere
ma mere
ma mere
ma mere
ma mere

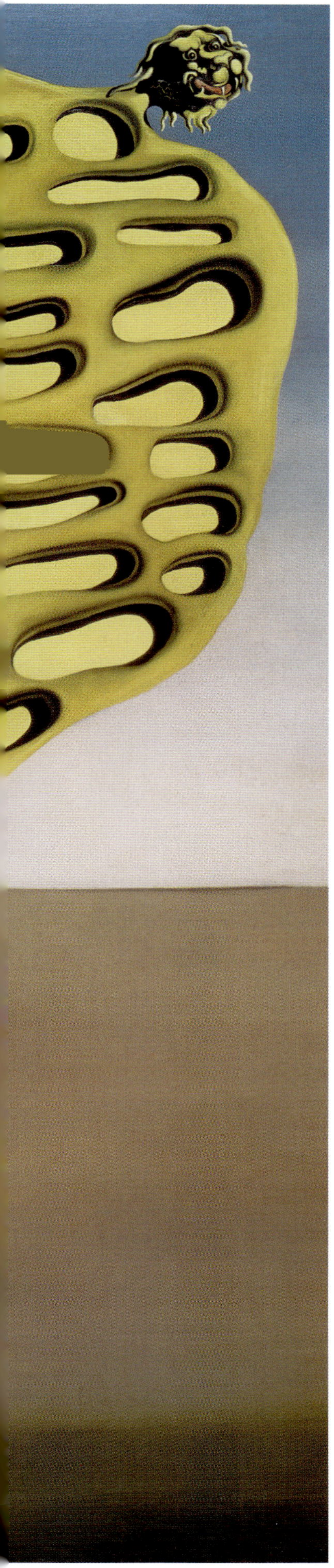

'I would follow only my own pleasure, my most uncontrollably biological desire.'

woman and the sheathed sex organ of the unknown man – make for an image already complex enough even before the smaller figures at large in the landscape below and numerous other small, obscure objects of fear or desire are factored in to any rational analysis.

Any such appraisal, of course, could only limit the meaning of the painting and could not hope to explain its power. The landscape in which this impossible scene is set is a flat and featureless plain, crossed by long, late-afternoon shadows whose source was probably the works of Giorgio de Chirico (1888–1978; widely acknowledged even then as the spiritual father of Surrealist painting), as much as it is the harsh afternoon light of the Empordà. But de Chirico's metaphysical pictures drew on the common architectural heritage of the streets and squares of an unnamed European city, which he furnished with the statues and symbolic bric-a-brac of a collective European history. Dalí's symbolic lexicon, however, is drawn, almost exclusively in these pictures and those that follow over the next few years, from a private world of fetish and phobia which in rational terms ought to render them baffling to any viewer unfamiliar with the painter's intimate personal history. But Dalí, the self-confessed narcissist, found his inner world so compelling that it seemed quite natural to him that everyone should be similarly enthralled. And there is no denying that, despite the idiosyncratic content of these paintings, the strength of his obsessions and the formidable brilliance of his technique instead endow vision after disturbing vision with a mythological power insisting, above all, that we must not look away.

(Left)

The Enigma of Desire or *My Mother, my Mother, my Mother*, 1929

Medium: Oil on canvas
Dimensions: 110 x 150.7 cm (43½ x 59¼ in)
Location: Staatsgalerie Moderner Kunst, Munich

The Banishment

These paintings were exhibited in October 1929 at the gallery of Camille Goemans in Paris, but Dalí did not attend, having taken off with Gala on a boat across the Mediterranean. Before long they had ensconced themselves in a hotel in Sitges, south of Barcelona, as the pair plunged headlong into a tryst that by then had entered its most carnal phase. Meanwhile, word had reached Dalí's father of a scandalous work which on the one hand may have been a brave Surrealist attempt to break a bourgeois taboo and on the other could be seen as evidence of Dalí's age-old need to transgress, to show off, to shock – the compulsive and 'tragical sequence of exhibitionism' that in later life so often overshadowed his art and still colours his posthumous reputation. The piece in question was a cheap holy picture Dalí had bought, a lithograph depicting the Sacred Heart. Across it he had written the words, 'Sometimes I spit with pleasure upon the portrait of my mother', a statement so provocative in itself that it did not matter what the artist's motivation really was in fashioning the image, nor what justifications he came up with after the fact. Upon learning through a newspaper article of this very public dishonour (and also that he had taken up with a married Russian woman), Dalí's father sent him a letter, banishing him from his childhood home in Figueres and the summer house in Cadaqués.

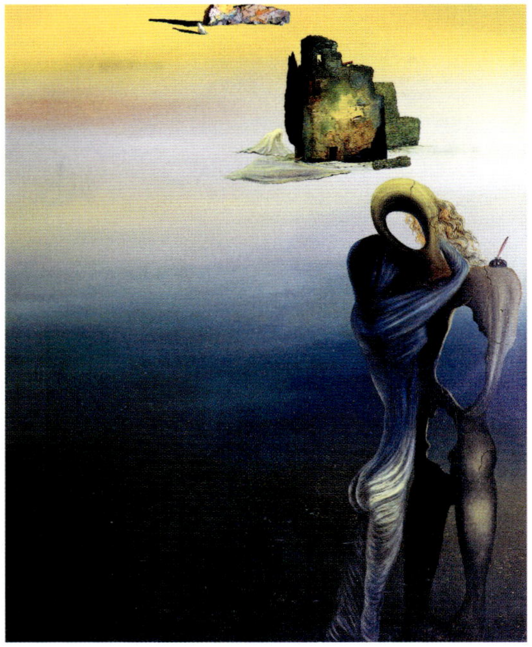

Fathers and Sons

Dalí was distraught and, unable to make amends, cut off all his hair and buried it – no doubt in penitence and pain but also perhaps with a sense of liberation at leaving behind his father's suffocating love. There is a photo of the artist at this moment of crisis and opportunity in which he is standing with his head shaved. On top of it, he has placed a sea urchin, whose flesh was a delicacy loved by both Salvador senior and his aberrant son. Dalí's recall of this moment in *The Secret Life* provokes a flood of typically grandiose mythological and religious examples of fathers killing, or being willing to kill, their sons – Saturn and his son, Abraham and Isaac, God the Father and His Only Begotten Son – as well as the legend of

(Above)

Gradiva Rediscovers the Anthropomorphic Ruins, c. 1931–32

Medium: Oil on canvas
Dimensions: 65 x 54 cm (25½ x 21¼ in)
Location: Museo Thyssen-Bornemisza, Madrid

(Right)

Archaeological Reminiscence of Millet's Angelus, 1933–35

Medium: Oil on canvas
Dimensions: 31.8 x 39.4 cm (12½ x 15⅓ in)
Location: Salvador Dalí Museum, St Petersburg, Florida

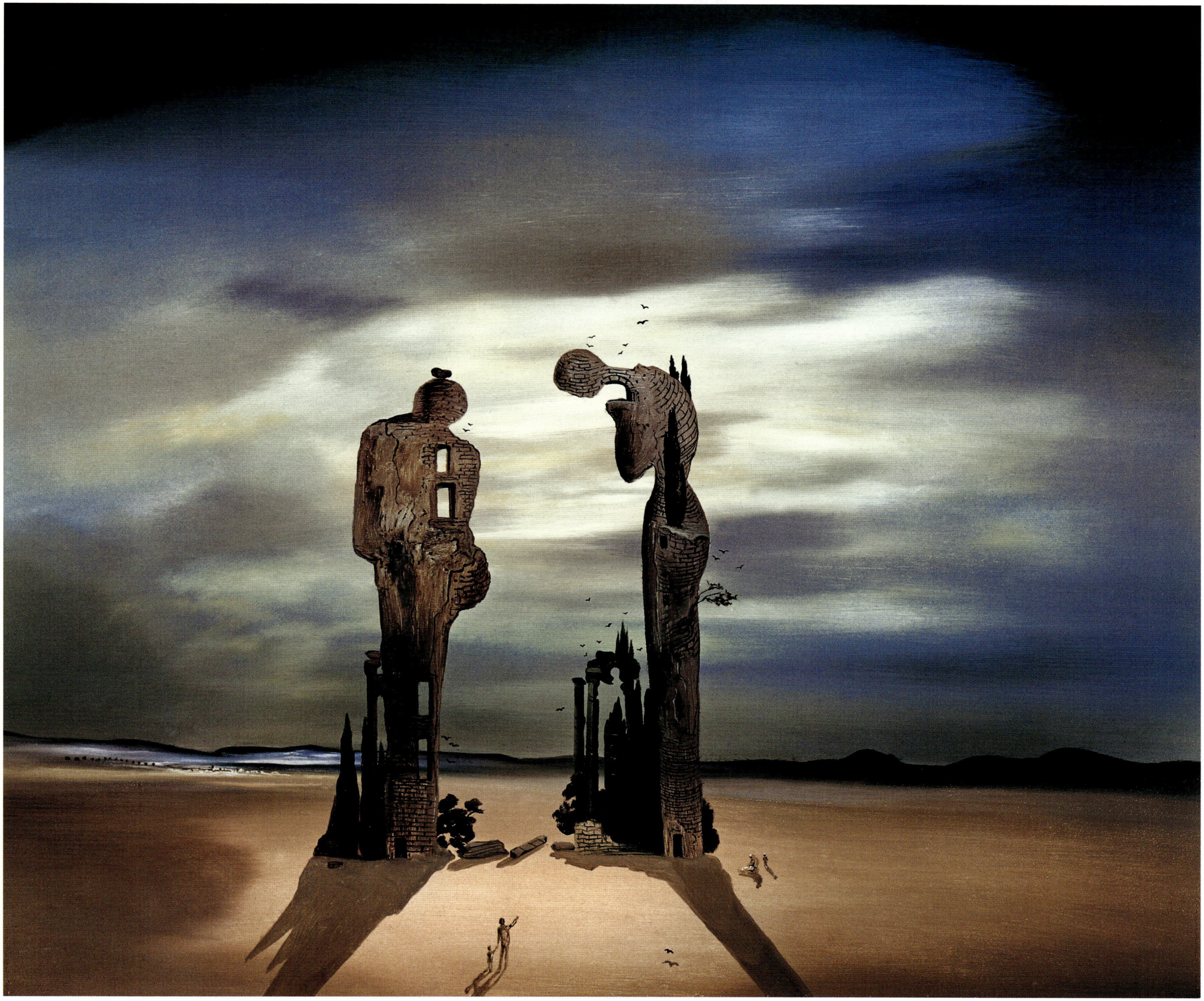

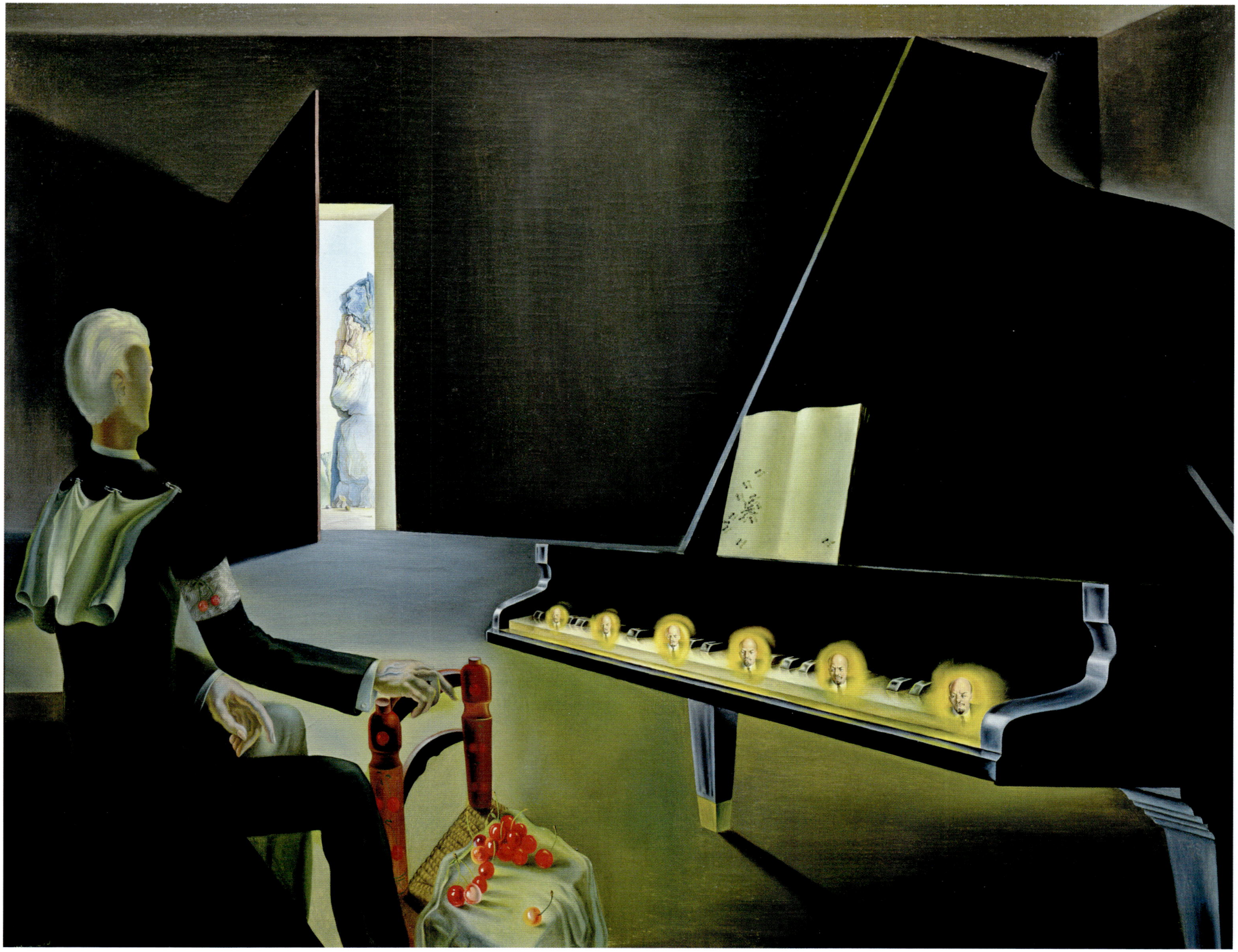

William Tell, the Swiss patriot forced to shoot an apple off his son's head with a crossbow in order to save both their lives. This last comparison, somewhat more prosaic than the others, gave him a new mythic symbolism arising from this recent rupture between father and son, though in the photo the apple is replaced with a sea urchin. But it may also have had roots in the dysfunctional trinity of Salvadors in which he was implicated: father, dead brother and his replacement, the 'Holy Ghost of Dalí', a phrase he does indeed use to describe himself at one point in *The Secret Life*.

William Tell

Whatever it stood for or stemmed from, the story figures in various works of the early 1930s: from the pornographic aggression of *William Tell and Gradiva* (1930) to the rather candid narrative of sexual shame in *The Old Age of William Tell* (1931), and from the troubling sexual enigmas of *The Birth of Liquid Desires* (1932, *see* page 28) to the ambiguous political provocations of *The Enigma of William Tell* (1933, *see* pages 78–79). In fact, Dalí did later provide the following explanation for the last of these listed: 'William Tell is my father and the little child in his arms is myself; instead of an apple I have a raw cutlet on my head. He is planning to eat me. A tiny nut by his foot contains a tiny child, the image of my wife Gala. She is under constant threat from this foot. Because if the foot

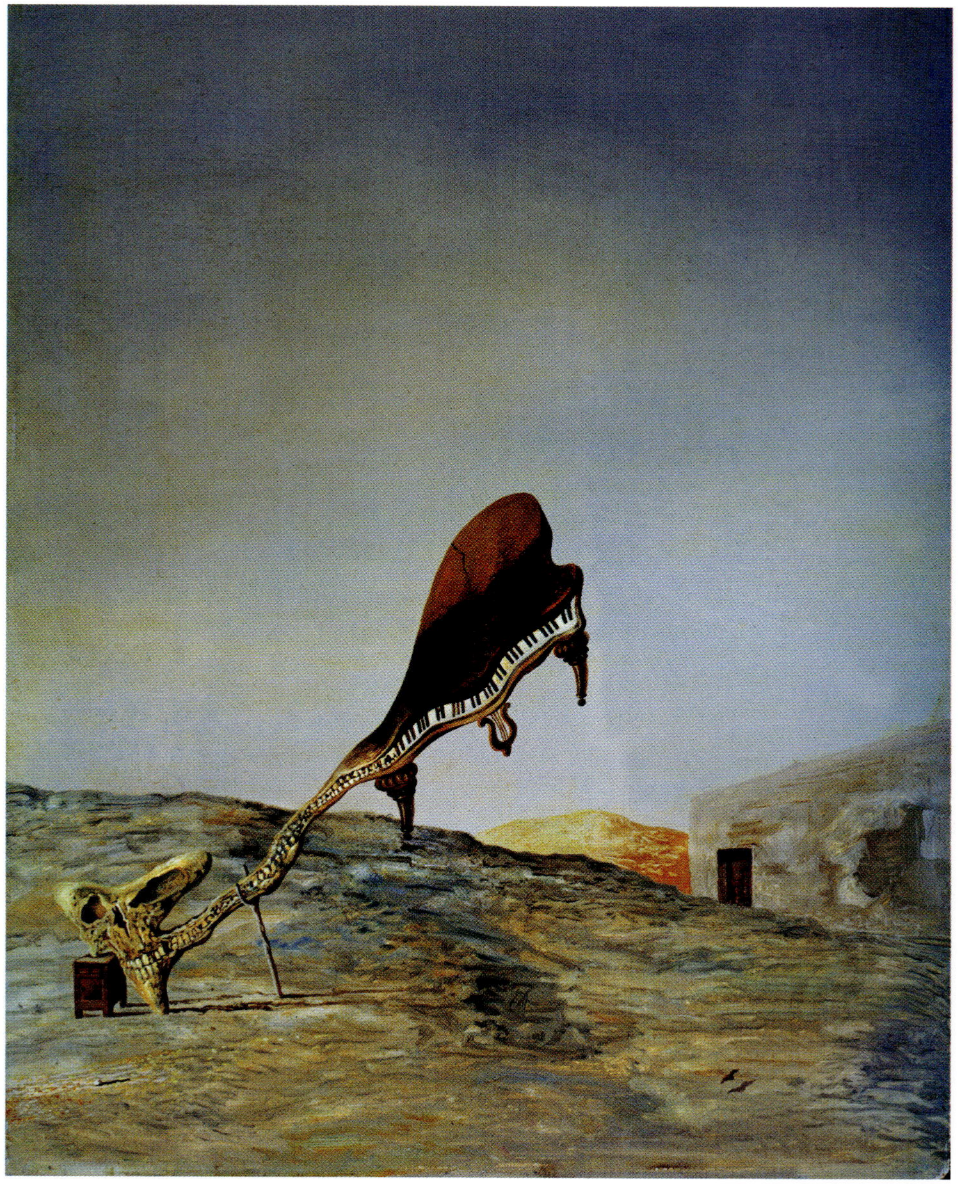

(Left)

Partial Hallucinations: Six Apparitions of Lenin on a Piano, 1931

Medium: Oil on canvas
Dimensions: 114 x 146 cm (45 x 57½ in)
Location: Musée National d'Art Moderne, Centre Pompidou, Paris

(Above)

Skull and its Lyric Appendage Leaning on a Bedside Table which should have the Exact Temperature of a Cardinal's Nest, 1934

Medium: Oil on panel
Dimensions: 24 x 19 cm (9½ x 7½ in)
Location: Salvador Dalí Museum, St Petersburg, Florida

moves only very slightly, it can crush the nut.' This may well have been what went through the artist's mind when he painted it, though the psychological scenario he puts forward does sound rather contrived. But in any case, it does little to convey the irrational power of the realized image.

Insulting the Fathers

It is certainly clear that the various William Tell images from the early 1930s use their common inspiration as a dramatic scenario on which Dalí could project a private psychological reality rather than the truth of events. But this psychology was also beginning to be foisted on the wider circle of his acquaintances and, as such, his obsession with the father figure began to be displaced on to the surrogate father he had found in André Breton. This impression is confirmed in *The Enigma of William Tell* by the apparent subject of the picture, a man naked from the waist down whose grotesquely hyperextended buttock is supported by a crutch, being given the face of Vladimir Ilyich Lenin (1870–1924). Dalí had already made ambiguous use of this dead hero of the radical left in his painting, *Partial Hallucinations: Six Apparitions of Lenin on a Piano* (1931, see page 74), in which the father of Soviet Communism appears as a series of miniature icons distributed at intervals along the keyboard of a piano; although an ambiguous image, it is not especially transgressive. In *The Enigma of William Tell*, however, not content with exploiting his own individual father complex, Dalí here is also trying to provoke his Surrealist comrades by taking possession of another, the Communist doctrine that was increasingly popular among intellectual circles in Paris in the early 1930s, and especially among the Surrealist group of which by then he was a leading member.

'Give me two hours a day of activity, and I'll take the other twenty-two in dreams.'

To Conquer the Irrational

In fact it had been obvious to Breton and the others right from the start, even in 1929, that Dalí offered the injection of intellectual and creative energy the movement needed to re-establish itself at the forefront of the Parisian avant-garde. Dalí, despite his outward timidity, had the ambition 'to ruin systematically the logical meaning of all the

(Right)

Invention of the Monsters, 1937

Medium: Oil on canvas
Dimensions: 51.4 x 78.1 cm (20¼ x 30¾ in)
Location: Art Institute of Chicago, Illinois

mechanisms of the rational practical world', an aim at least superficially in keeping with the Surrealist mission. But in *The Secret Life* he also tells us he wanted nothing less than to usurp Breton himself, a clear father figure, and in that regard he soon became not only one of the movement's leading painters but one of its principal theorists, too, the role in which Breton was pre-eminent. Dalí had quickly dismissed traditional Surrealist methods, writing that 'Nothing now appeared more boring, more out of place and

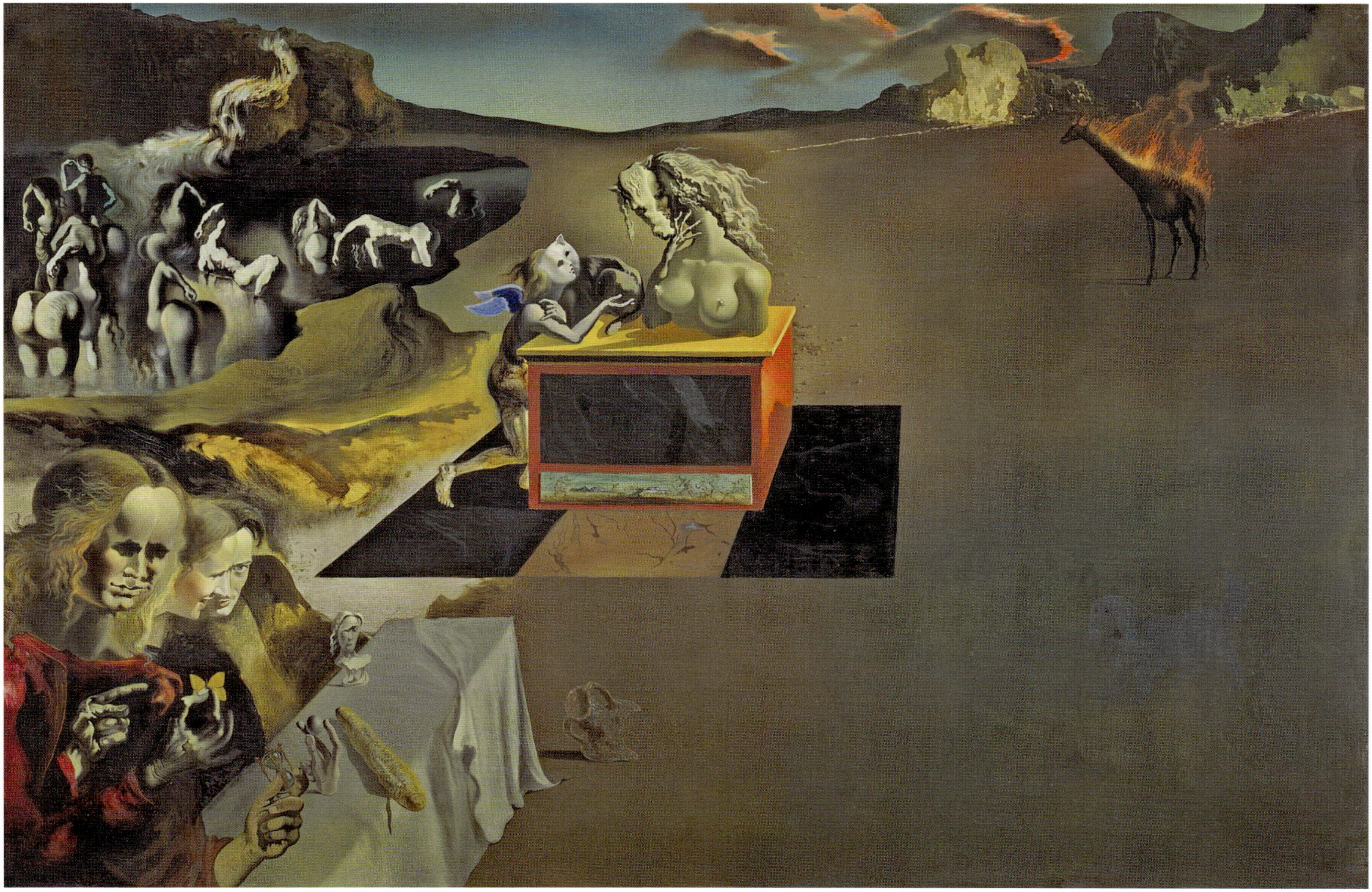

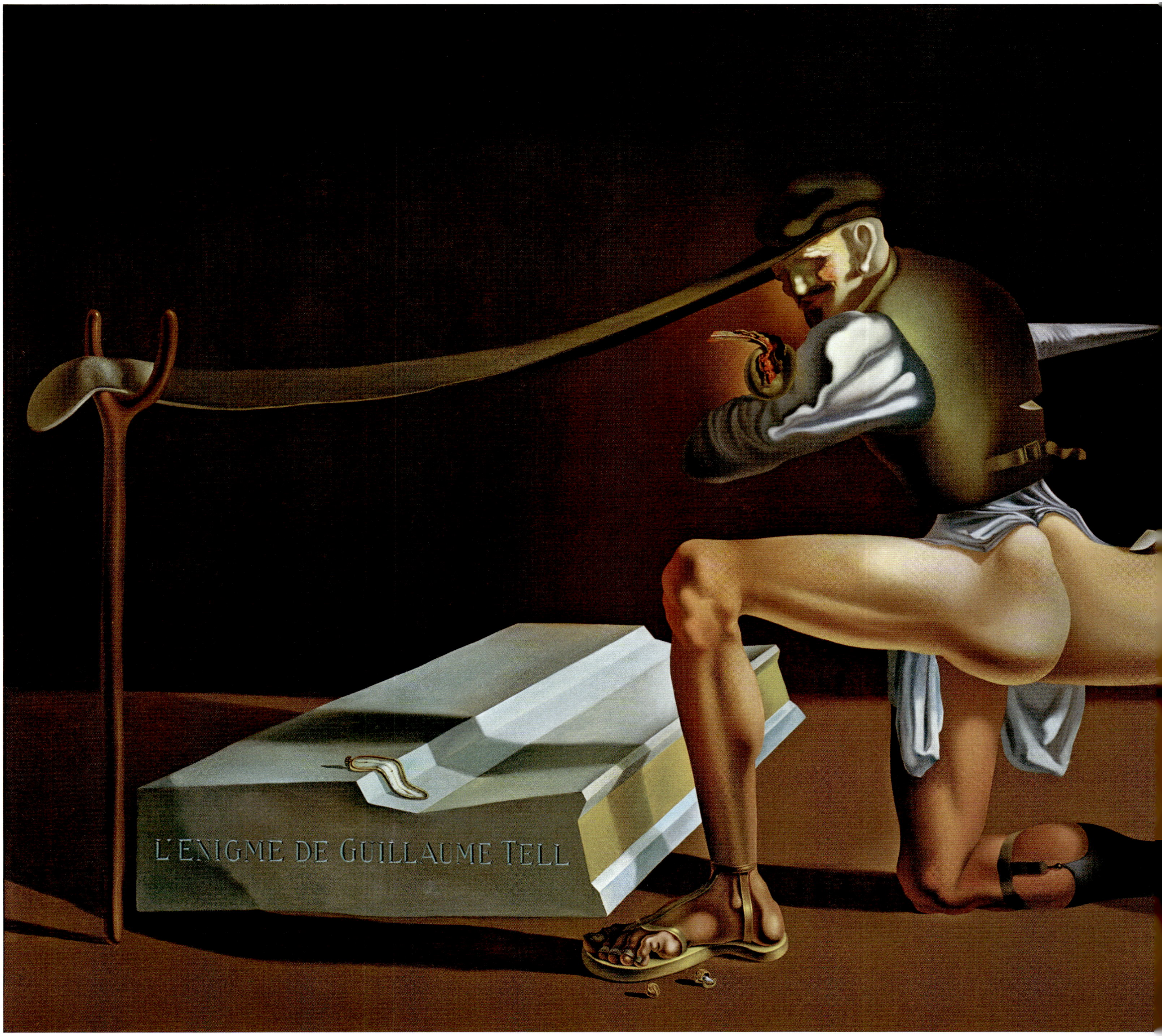
L'ENIGME DE GUILLAUME TELL

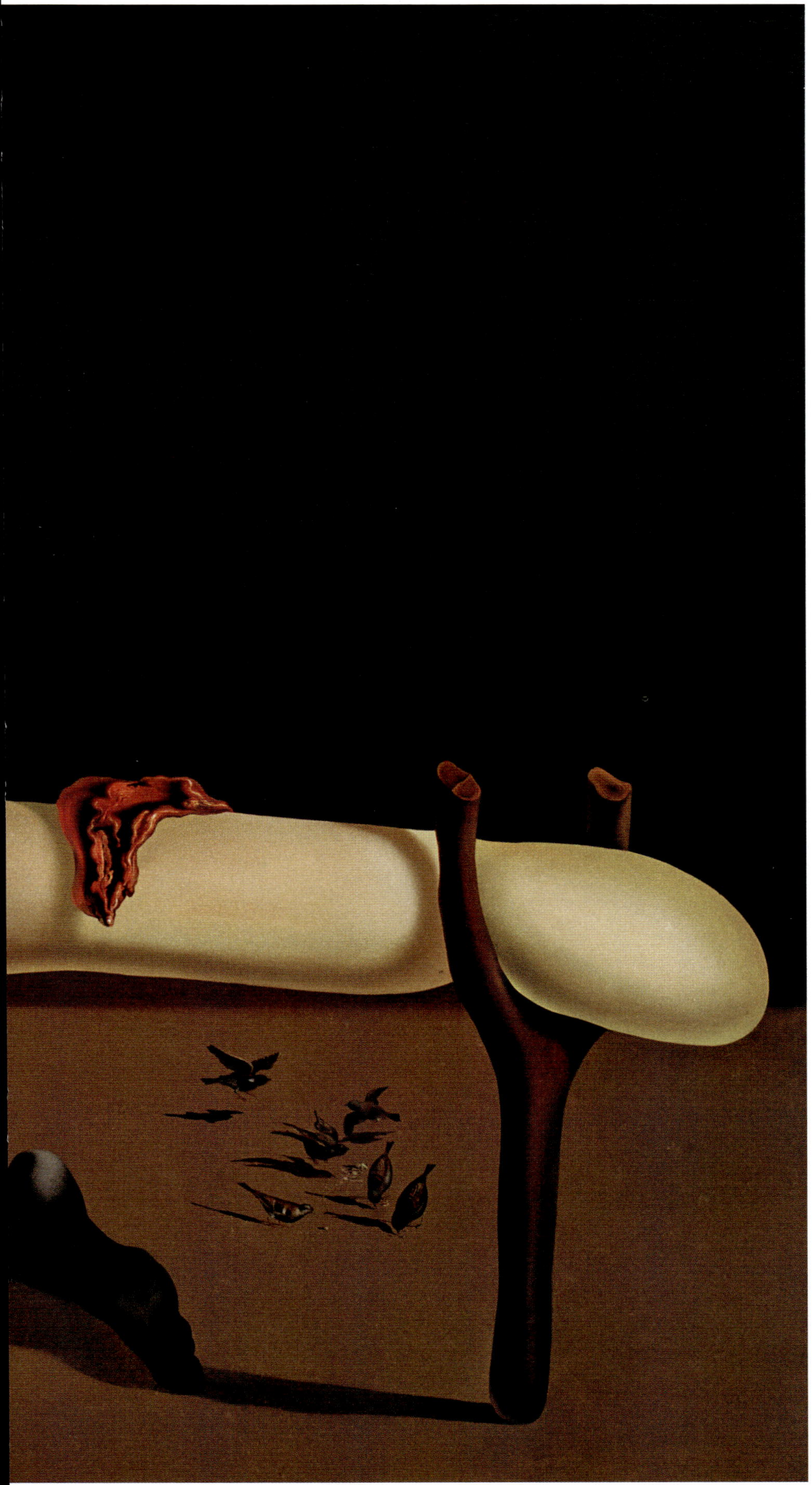

anachronistic, than to relate one's dreams or to write fantastic and incongruous tales at the automatic dictate of the unconscious.' On the contrary, he wanted consciously to make use of the unconscious, to make a 'conquest of the irrational', to be its master not its slave.

As Dali continually acknowledged throughout his life, of critical importance in achieving that goal was Gala, not only for the emotional and sexual crutch she represented but also for her tireless efforts in promoting his work and negotiating sales. Cut off from his father's support, Dali moved in with his muse and for several years they managed to live on what was a very meagre income, despite increasing attention from the critics and the occasional sales of pictures to society people and his fellow Surrealists. Gala went out every day to try to sell the copious produce of his ceaseless creativity – ideas for everything from false fingernails to bathtubs with odd new shapes to streamlined motorcars. All were rejected by the firms that might have made them, though as Dali writes in *The Secret Life*, each would become a reality in the years that followed as lesser talents made mediocre versions of his original plans.

A Dagger in the Heart of Paris

In late 1929, Dali's career had been launched with the show at the Goemans gallery but especially with the showing of

(Left)

The Enigma of William Tell, 1933

Medium: Oil on canvas
Dimensions: 201 x 346 cm (79¼ x 136⅛ in)
Location: Moderna Museet, Stockholm

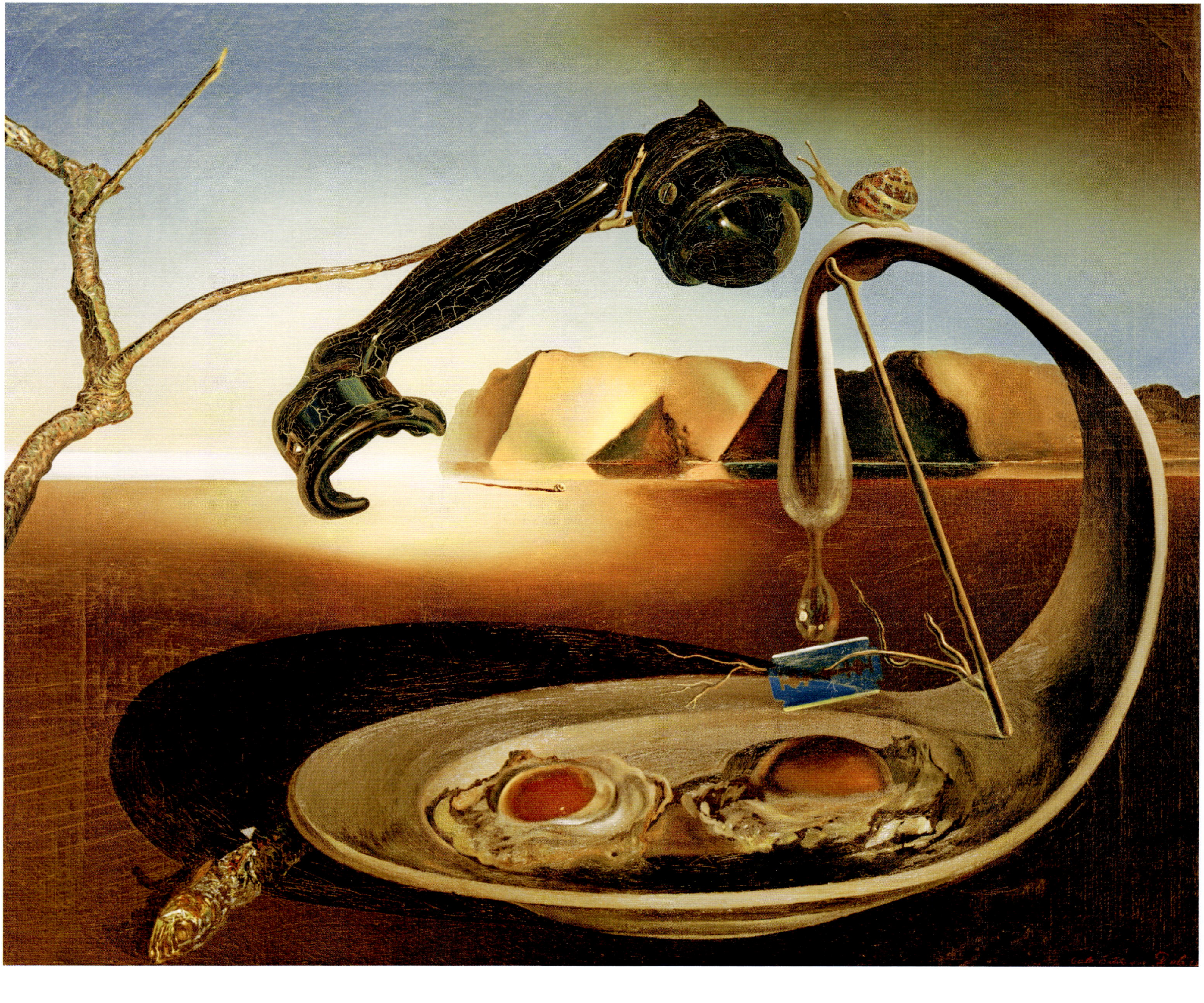

Un Chien Andalou, the film he had scripted with Buñuel and in whose production he was involved as both technician and bit-part actor. It was a *succès de scandale* from the moment in the opening scene when a razor blade appears to slice through a young woman's eyeball – still a horrifying spectacle today, even when we know how it was done. As he wrote in *The Secret Life*, 'The film produced the effect I wanted, and it plunged like a dagger into the heart of Paris … [ruining] in a single evening ten years of pseudo-intellectual post-war advance-guardism…. There was no longer room in Europe for the little maniacal lozenges of Monsieur Mondrian.' It is a bragging and typically spiteful reminiscence from someone who regarded himself, as he had as a child in his cape and crown, as 'an absolute king'. But it does not underestimate by much the effect the film had on the intellectual elite in what was then the most important city in world art.

The Buying of a Shack

The Goemans show was also a success but the money was slow in coming, as the dealer was in fact in the throes of going bankrupt. Luckily, among Dalí's most enthusiastic patrons was the Vicomte de Noailles (1891–1981), an important champion of Surrealism and already the owner of *The Lugubrious Game* (*see* page 55), in whose mansion the painting was hung between a Cranach and a Watteau, to the painter's great satisfaction. Knowing of the failure of the Goemans gallery and the difficulties Dalí was facing, the Vicomte now paid 29,000 francs up front for *The Old Age of William Tell*. Dalí and Gala agreed that they should use the money to buy a house. But despite his father having banished him, Dalí could not conceive of living anywhere else than the landscape of his beloved coastal village of Cadaqués, so that is where they went. But his influential father had already made sure his son would get short shrift from everyone who lived there that might have helped him, so they turned to Port Lligat, just over the headland, which at the time was not so much a settlement as a cluster of shacks in which the fishermen kept their equipment. Dalí bought one of these tiny dwellings from the sons of Lydia Nogues, the only local prepared to help him, and paid a local carpenter to make it habitable; in years to come they would add a labyrinth of connecting rooms

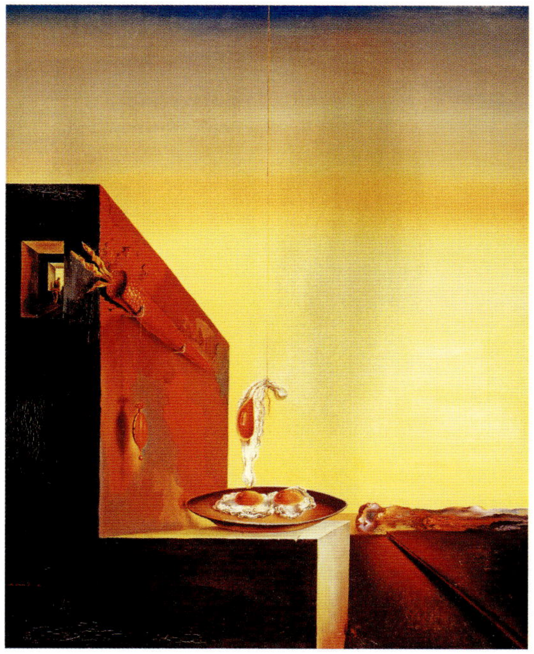

(Left)

The Sublime Moment, 1938

Medium: Oil on canvas
Dimensions: 38 x 47 cm (15 x 18½ in)
Location: Staatsgalerie, Stuttgart

(Above)

Eggs on the Plate (Without the Plate), 1932

Medium: Oil on canvas
Dimensions: 60 x 41.9 cm (23⅔ x 16½ in)
Location: Salvador Dalí Museum, St Petersburg, Florida

that sprawled across the hillside. It was the house the couple always returned to after their frequent trips abroad, where Dalí could practise the private, ascetic side of his nature and, most importantly, get on with his work.

Uncharacteristic Sympathies

In fact, although he seemed to take great pleasure in stirring up hostility and controversy among the public and especially among the artistic community – so as to 'cretinize' them, as he was callously accustomed to putting it – Dalí was not altogether devoid of sympathy for his fellow human beings. In *The Secret Life* he tells us he always preferred the company of very poor people, such as the fishermen of Port Lligat, or the aristocracy or society people – social extremes which he felt reflected his own nature: 'I remained always the Catalonian peasant, naïve and cunning, with a king in my body.' *The Secret Life* is often tiresome in its habitual boasting and self-obsession, but there are also moments when Dalí focuses his attention almost wholly on other people, viewing his fellow creatures with a compassionate interest in human particularity that is not usually associated with the painter.

One such character is Lydia Nogues, an eccentric fantasist whom he refers to as 'the godmother to my madness'. But the aristocracy of

'I am here to confuse and cloud the issue, you to put matters straight.'

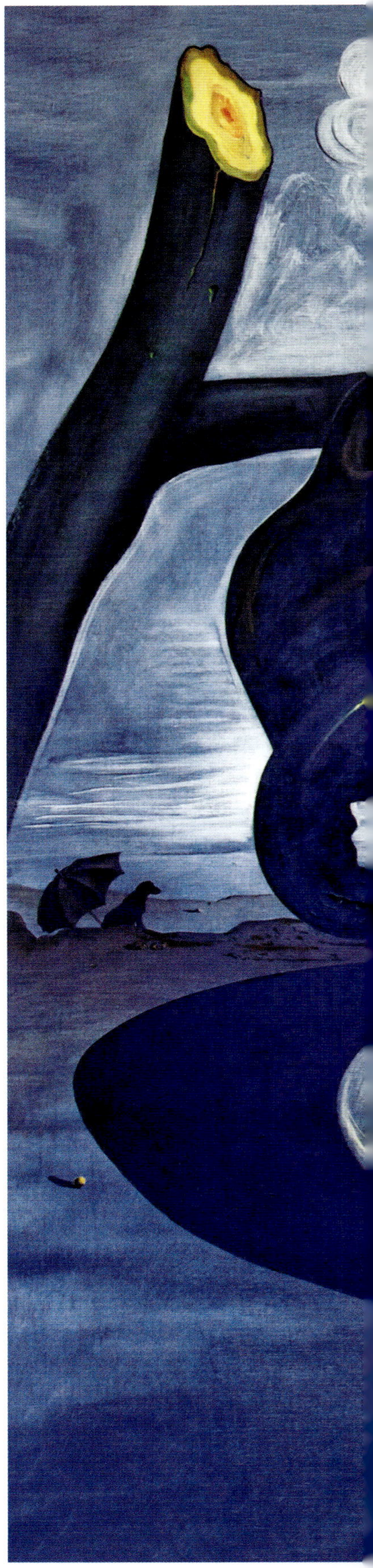

(Right)

The Enigma of Hitler, **1939**

Medium: Oil on canvas
Dimensions: 95 x 141 cm (37²⁄₅ x 55½ in)
Location: Museo Nacional Centro de Arte Reina Sofía, Madrid

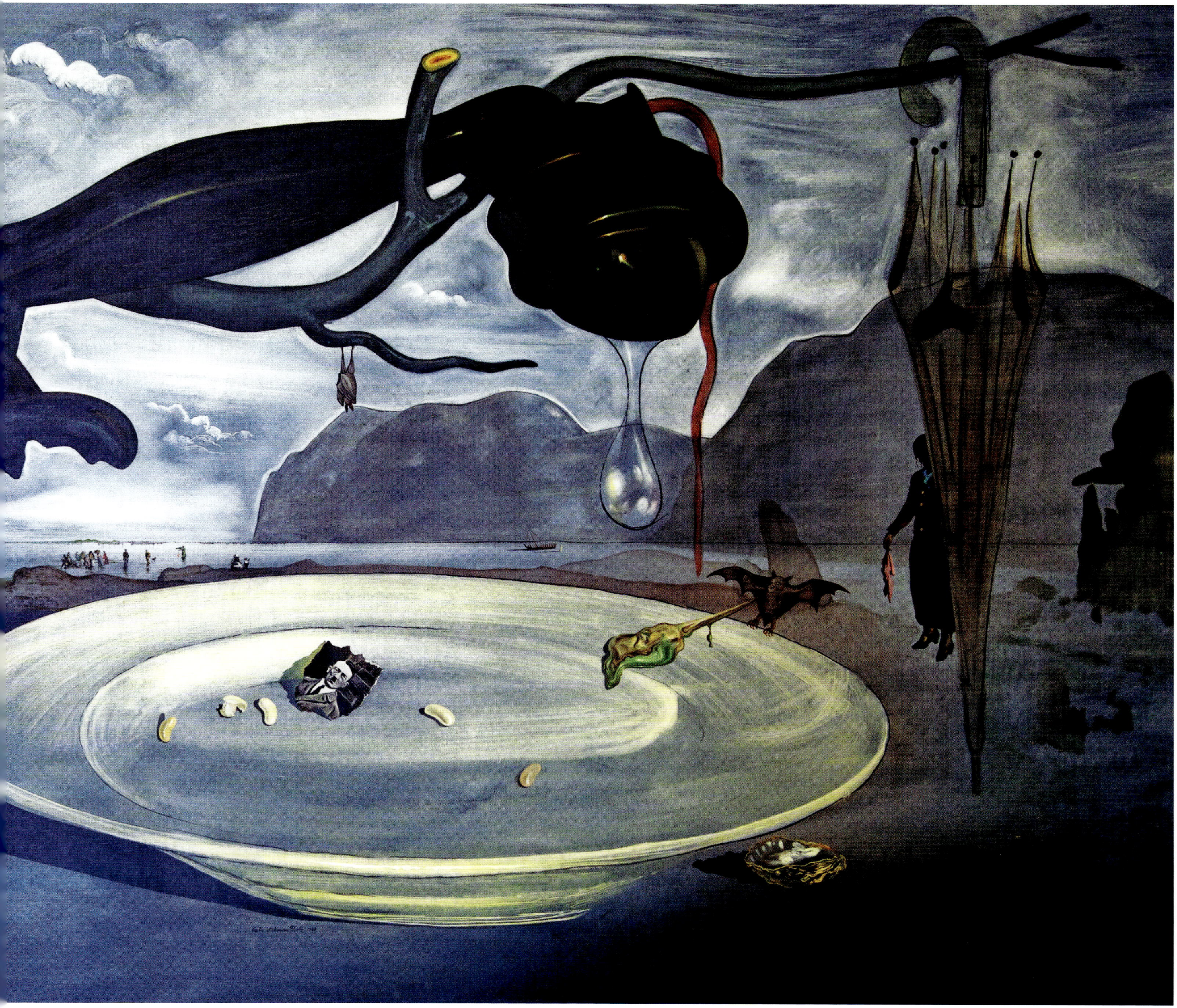

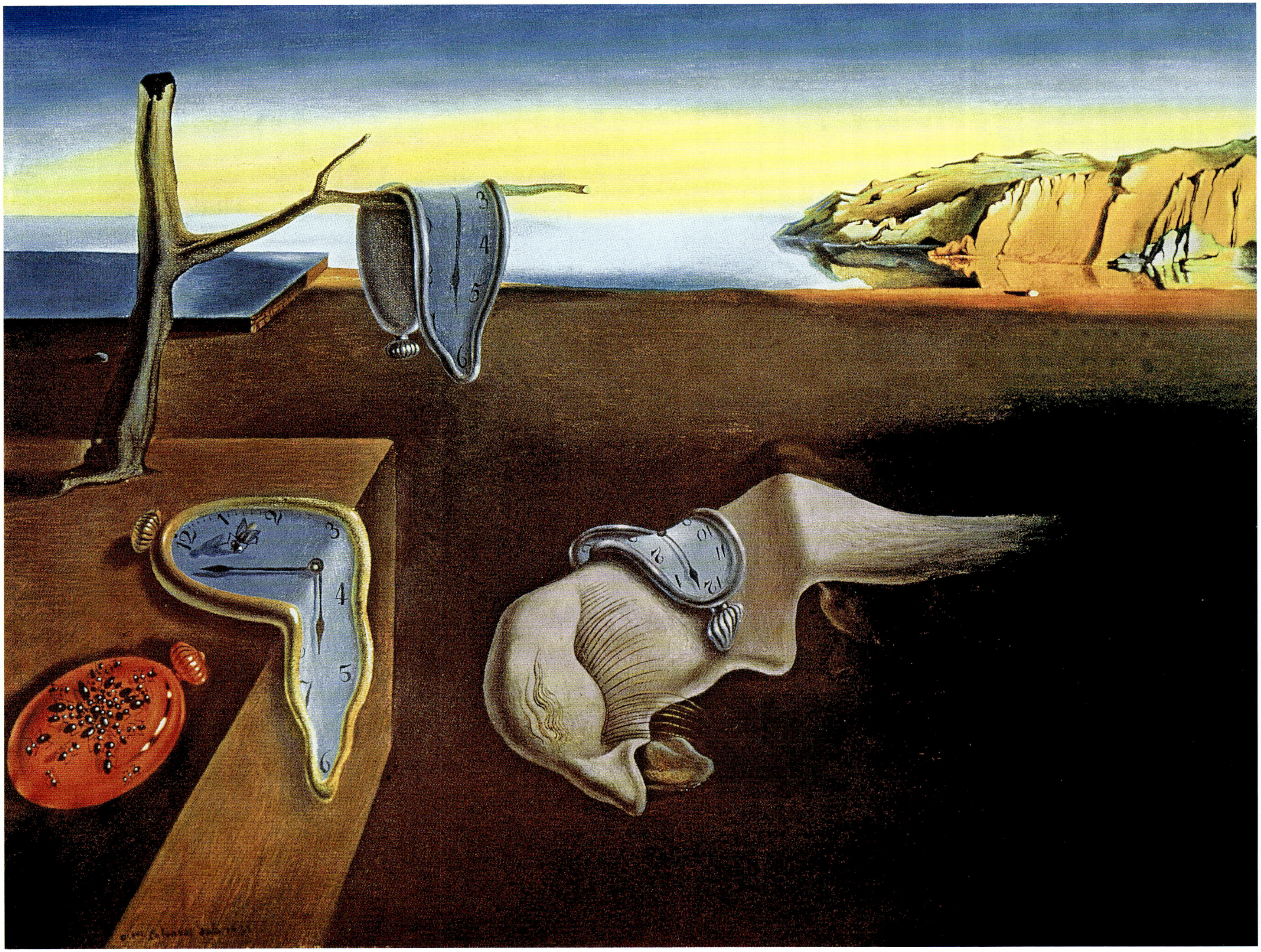

artistic Paris in the mid-1930s also inspire a fond admiration for that rarefied world, made all the more poignant (as Dalí acknowledged when writing *The Secret Life* in 1942) in that this *haut monde* would soon disappear amid the savagery of the next world war. This tender interest in other beings, albeit in the context of a typically paranoiac transformation, even finds its way on occasions into paintings of the period, such as *The Weaning of Furniture Nutrition* (1934), whose subject is his beloved childhood nurse Llúcia. Dalí had vivid memories of leaning against her broad back as a child, so the crutch in this image may well be a symbol for the artist himself.

The Persistence of Memory

It was the more familiar sleeping head that stood in for him in what is probably Dalí's most famous image of all, *The Persistence of Memory* of 1931 (see left), which by his own account was ostensibly painted in a single session at his and Gala's Paris apartment. In *The Secret Life*, Dalí describes the story of its creation with compelling vividness. He relates that he was tired, with a slight headache. Gala had gone out to the cinema with some friends, Dalí having decided to stay home with the intention of going to bed early. He goes on: 'We had topped off our meal with a very strong Camembert, and after everyone had gone I remained for a long time seated at the table meditating on the philosophic problems of the "super-soft" which the cheese presented to my mind. I got up and went into my studio, where I lit the light in order to cast a final glance, as is my habit, at the picture I was in the midst of painting. This picture represented a landscape near Port Lligat, whose rocks were lighted by a transparent and melancholy twilight; in the foreground an olive tree with its branches cut, and without leaves. I knew that the atmosphere which I had succeeded in creating with this landscape was to serve as a setting for some idea, for some surprising image, but I did not in the least know what it was going to be. I was about to turn out the light, when instantaneously I "saw" the solution.

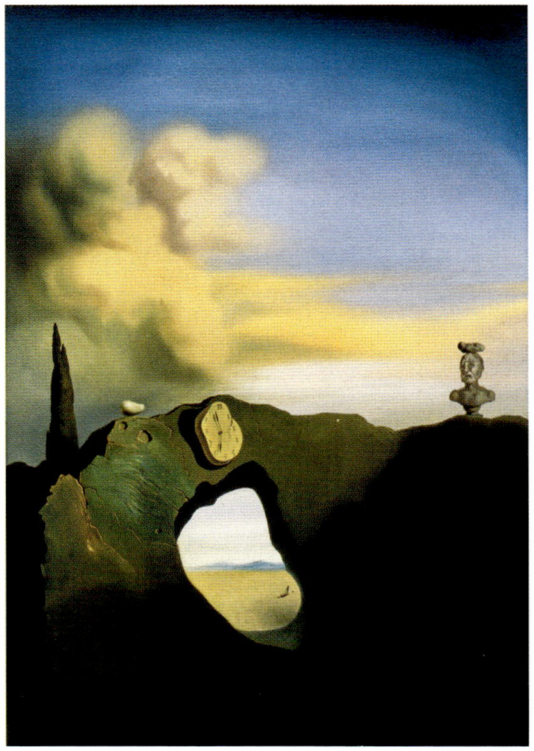

(Left)

The Persistence of Memory, 1931

Medium: Oil on canvas
Dimensions: 24 x 33 cm (9½ x 13 in)
Location: Museum of Modern Art, New York

(Above)

The Triangular Hour, 1933

Medium: Oil on canvas
Dimensions: 62.3 x 47.9 cm (24½ x 18⅞ in)
Location: Kagoshima City Museum of Art, Kagoshima

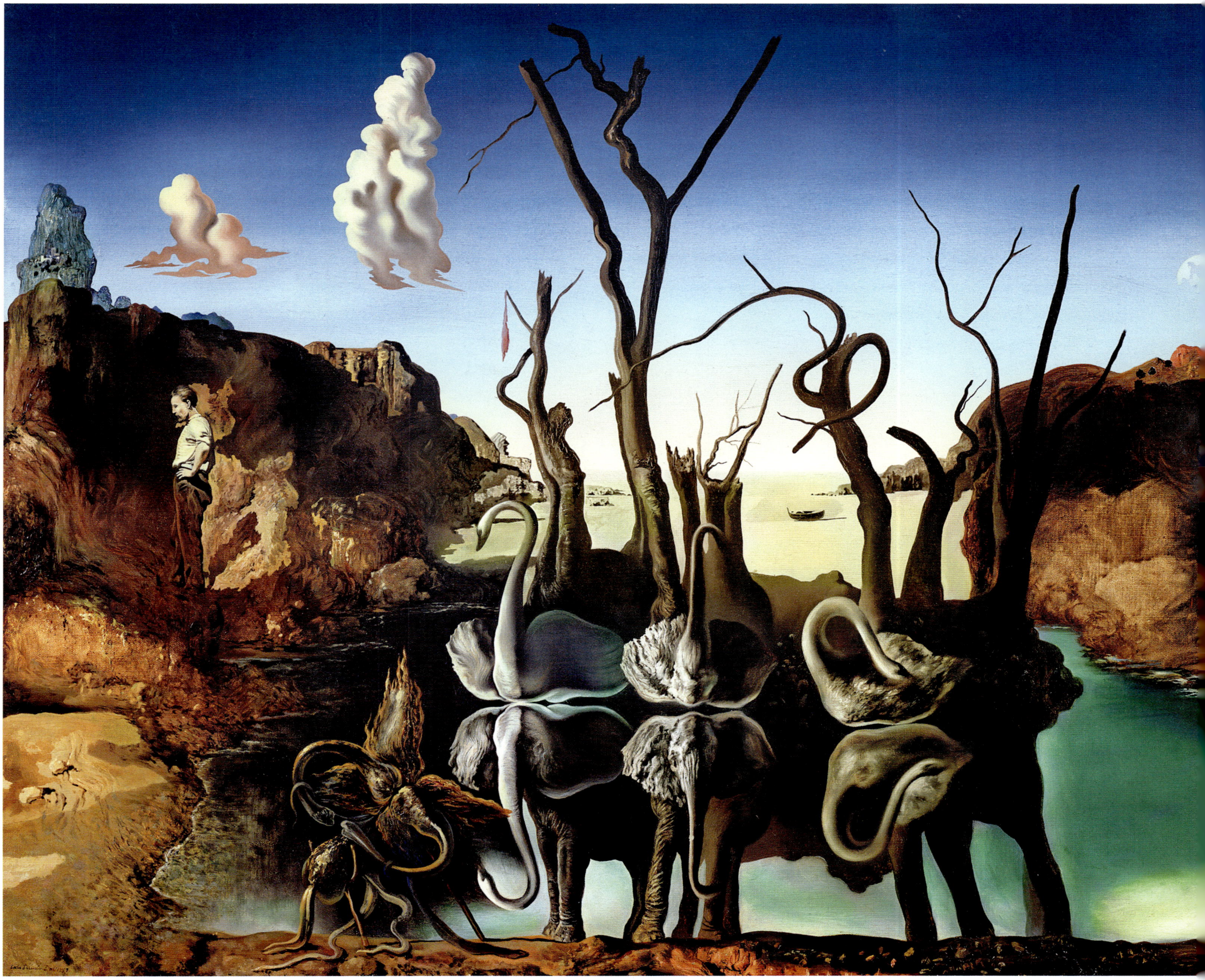

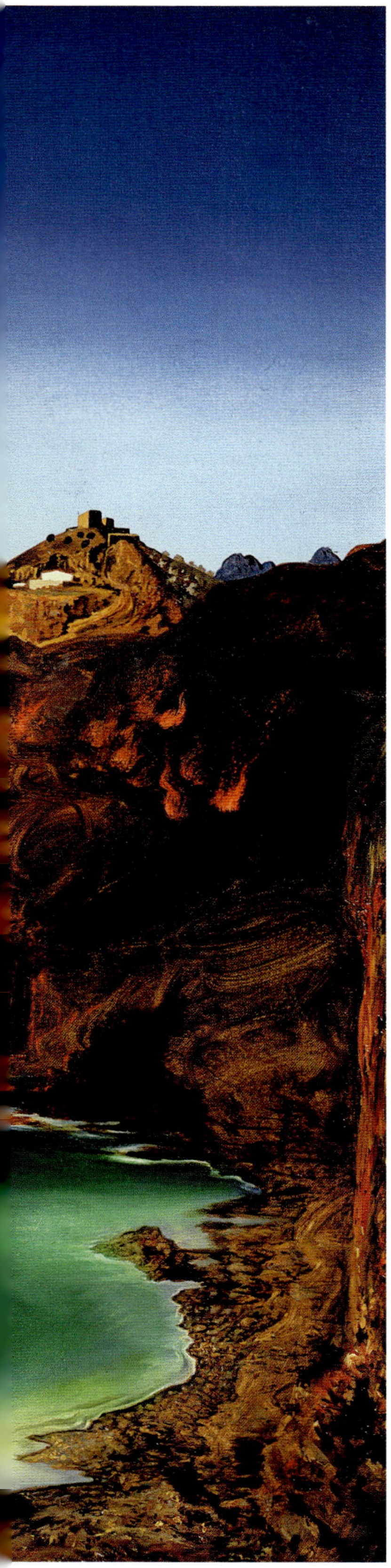

'Paranoiac-critical activity… makes the world of delirium pass on to the plane of reality.'

I saw two soft watches, one of them hanging lamentably on the branch of the olive tree. In spite of the fact that my headache had increased to the point of becoming very painful, I avidly prepared my palette and set to work. When Gala returned from the theatre two hours later the picture, which was to be one of my most famous, was completed. I made her sit down in front of it with her eyes shut: "One, two, three, open your eyes!" I looked intently at Gala's face, and I saw upon it the unmistakable contraction of wonder and astonishment. I asked her, "Do you think that in three years you will have forgotten this image?" To which Gala replied, as would anyone, "No one can forget it once he has seen it.'"

Americans in Paris

A few days later, the New York dealer Julien Levy (1906–81), newly arrived in Paris, came to Dali's studio and bought the painting on the spot. It would become the stand-out piece in the Surrealist exhibition he put on in Manhattan early in 1932, and would eventually become a popular addition to the collection of New York's Museum of Modern Art. The director of the museum, Alfred H. Barr (1902–81), was also visiting the French capital, and Dali found him to be infinitely more knowledgeable about modern art than his European counterparts; in general he found Americans to

(Left)

Swans Reflecting Elephants, 1937

Medium: Oil on canvas
Dimensions: 51 x 77 cm (20 x 30⅓ in)
Location: Private Collection

be more open-minded and less weighed down by historical baggage. Another person who confirmed this impression was a wealthy widow, Caresse Crosby (1891–1970), whom Dalí met around the same time. She lived in a mansion, Le Moulin du Soleil, in the forest of Ermenonville to the north of Paris, to which he and Gala were frequent visitors; a more accommodating and indulgent patron he could not hope to have found, as events would later prove.

Despite these new contacts and Dalí's increasing notoriety, the couple were still not at all well off. In 1934, now obsessed with getting to America, having seen how popular Surrealism had become after Julien Levy's landmark show two years earlier, Dalí did the rounds of his Parisian acquaintances to borrow the money to make the trip, eventually getting the sum he needed from Picasso, although he declines to tell us the identity of the donor in *The Secret Life*. In fact, from the 1940s onwards Dalí became rather obsessed with Picasso's reputation as the greatest living artist, taking any opportunity he could to denigrate the painter who had been so helpful early on, even executing a typically monstrous caricature of his great compatriot, now in the Theatre-Museum in Figueres. It was yet another example of the father complex, the filial ingratitude, which supplied some of the rocket fuel for Dalí's extraordinary creative endeavours of the 1930s.

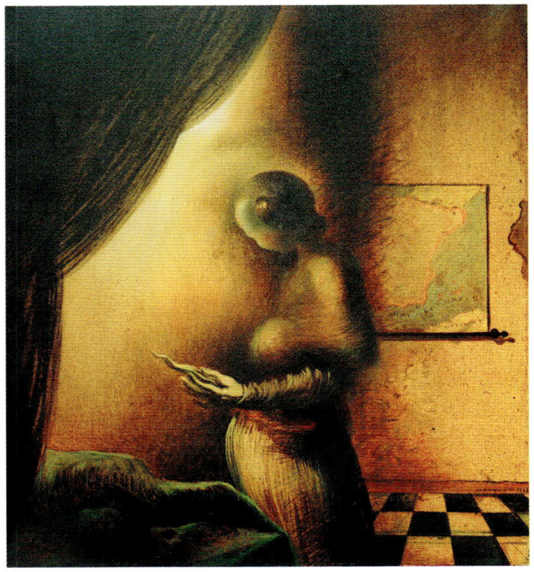

A Master Manipulator

In any case, Dalí, the court jester who dreamt of becoming king, was always looking for some new stunt with which to 'cretinize' the public. As he put it with the chilling callousness he revels in throughout *The Secret Life*, 'I have always had the gift of manipulating and of dominating with ease the slightest reaction of people who surround me, and it is always a voluptuous pleasure to feel at constant "attention" to my capricious orders all those who in obeying me to the letter, will most likely go down into their own purgatory, without even suspecting their faithful and involuntary submission.' In the light of such a monstrous admission, it certainly seems a blessing to humanity that Dalí was such a good artist and could exercise his sadistic urges mostly in his art. And in any case, the fantasies he entertained of being 'an absolute king' were surely compensation for the deficiencies of his upbringing and the general cowardliness engendered by his parents' overprotective attitude.

(Above)

The Image Disappears, 1938

Medium: Oil on canvas
Dimensions: 56.5 x 50.5 cm (22¼ x 20 in)
Location: Fundació Gala-Salvador Dalí, Figueres

(Right)

Paranoiac Face, 1935

Medium: Oil on wood
Dimensions: 18.5 x 22.5 cm (7⅓ x 8⅞ in)
Location: Private Collection

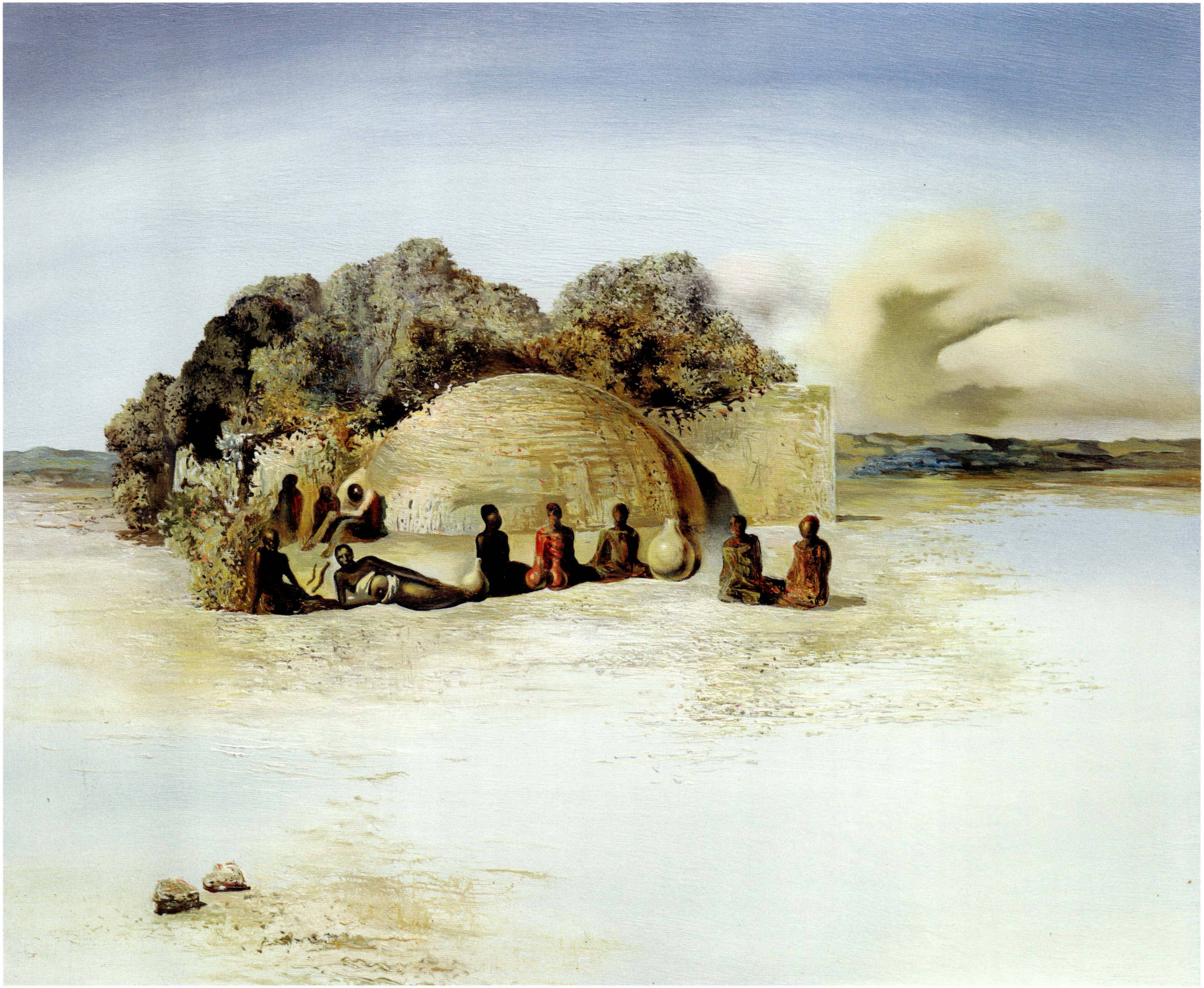

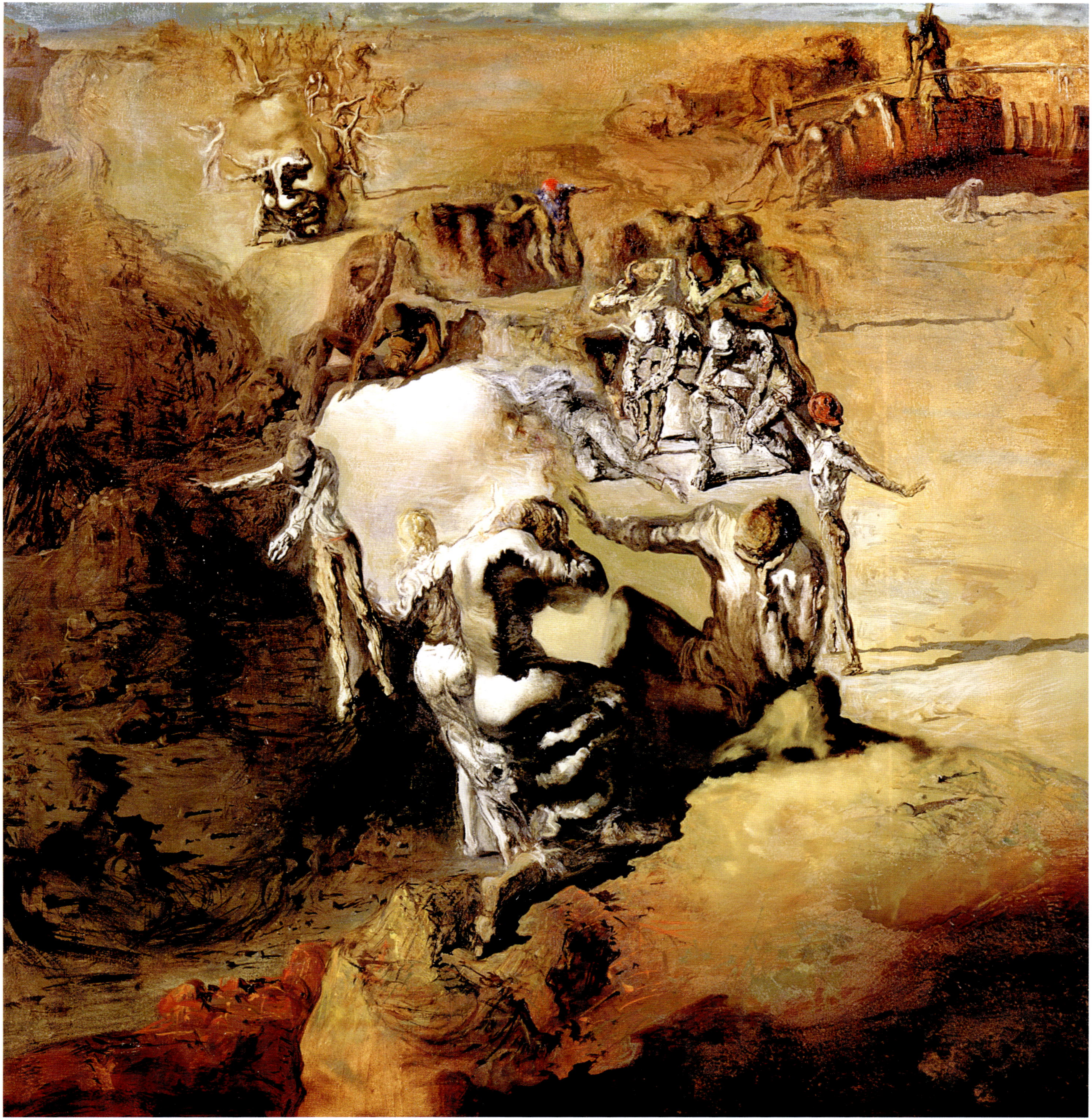

Indeed, while crossing the Atlantic, Dalí was so terrified that he never took off his lifebelt, though that did not stop the flow of ideas. Caresse Crosby travelled with them and, at Dalí's request, arranged for the ship's baker to make an 8-foot-long baguette, which the artist promptly held as a prop when they docked in Manhattan, though in the event none of the assembled press pack was remotely fazed by its intended absurdity. In fact, Dalí described American newswriters as 'far superior to European reporters. They had an acute sense of "non-sense".' And where Port Lligat became a refuge for the ascetic, increasingly abstemious painter, he at once recognized the United States as the spiritual home of the showman, the exhibitionist, the clown. Indeed, unlike the wealthy clientele on board the SS *Champlain*, who he said affected a horror of reporters, Dalí was characteristically frank in admitting that 'I love getting publicity, and if I am lucky enough to have the reporters know who I am, I will give them some of my own bread to eat just as Saint Francis did with his birds.' In the event, not one of the reporters asked him about the excessively long loaf he was holding, but at least they all knew who he was.

'My genius resides in that double reality of my personality...'

New York

Dalí regarded New York City with wonder, describing it as 'an Egypt turned inside out', an 'Atlantis of the subconscious'. Above all, with the enthusiasm of a true Surrealist (the only true Surrealist, as he saw it) and with an absence of artistic snobbery that anticipates our own age, he saluted American popular culture, admiring in particular the 'anti-artistic' qualities of Hollywood movies, which gave the audience stories and images that fed the people's basic psychological needs. This love affair with the US, which also brought with it a new playfulness and sense of fun, began appearing in his pictures almost immediately, in works such as *Mae West's Face Which May Be Used as a Surrealist Apartment*, another example of his double paintings, his lifelong fascination with hallucination and *trompe l'oeil*.

Above all, in New York Dalí saw an example of the phenomenon that informs so many of his paintings of the 1930s, describing the poetry of the city as being 'not serene aesthetics' but 'seething biology'. This is fundamental to the anti-aesthetic, anti-sentimental art that Dalí was developing,

(Left)

The Great Paranoiac, 1936

Medium: Oil on canvas
Dimensions: 62 x 62 cm (24⅜ x 24⅜ in)
Location: Museum Boijmans van Beuningen, Rotterdam

whose component elements, whether animal, vegetable or mineral, have the vitality of living forms. This astonishing gift for imparting three-dimensional modelling of compelling plausibility – as if he was working from photographs – to what were frequently implausible and certainly imaginary forms is all the more disturbing, too, in that these forms so often directly confront us with the polymorphous perversity of sexual desire. If art had always tended to aestheticize sex – and for Dalí this was as true of modernist art as it was of earlier painting – the discoverer of critical paranoia was bringing it all to the surface again, making the biological origins of his subject matter utterly explicit. If the results were often grotesque, then so be it. As he wrote in *The Secret Life*, 'For me, then, the erotic must always be ugly'.

Scandals and Suicides

The paintings Dalí exhibited at the Julien Levy Gallery in 1934 caused the splash he had hoped for, with critics praising his imaginative and pictorial gifts. Most of them were sold, establishing the US as the incredibly lucrative market for his art that it quickly became. At the end of their New York trip, a Surrealist ball was given in Dalí and Gala's honour at the Coq Rouge on East 56th Street. The great and the good of New York society turned up in wildly eccentric costumes inspired by what by then was a Surrealist craze. But the biggest scandal was caused by Gala, who arrived with the lifelike model of a

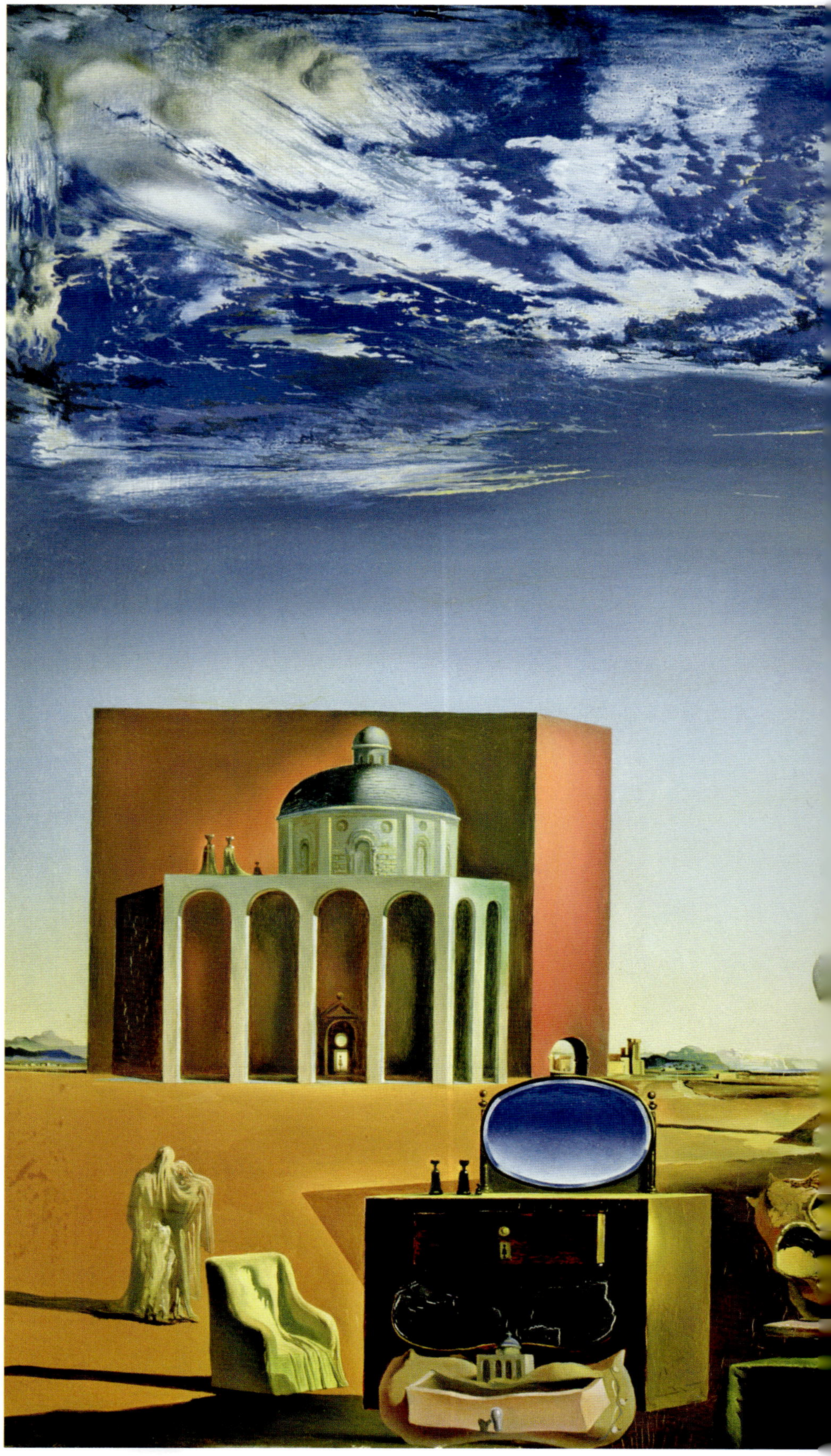

(Right)

Suburbs of a Paranoiac-Critical Town: Afternoon on the Outskirts of European History, **1936**

Medium: Oil on panel
Dimensions: 46 x 66 cm (18 x 26 in)
Location: Museum Boijmans van Beuningen, Rotterdam

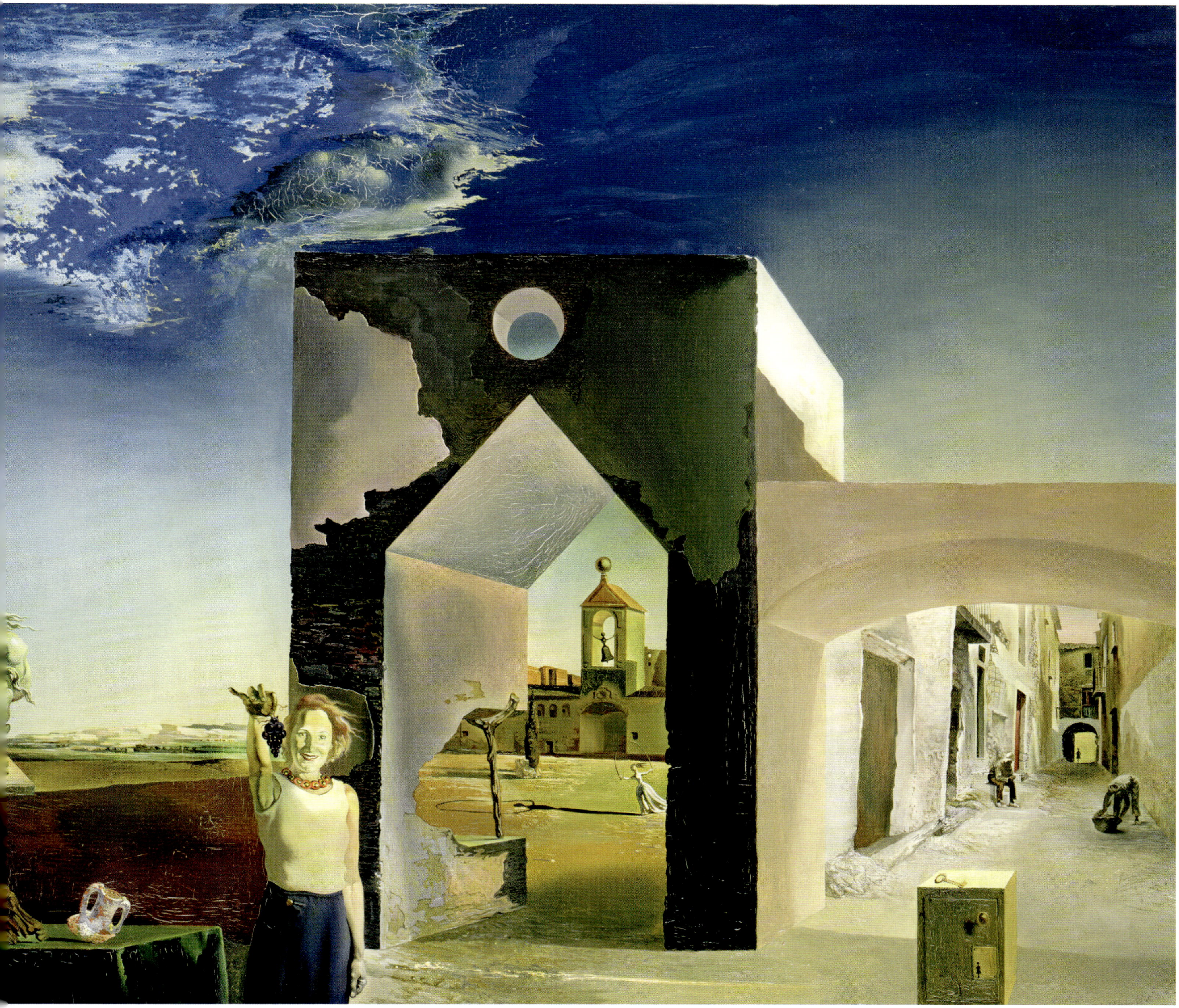

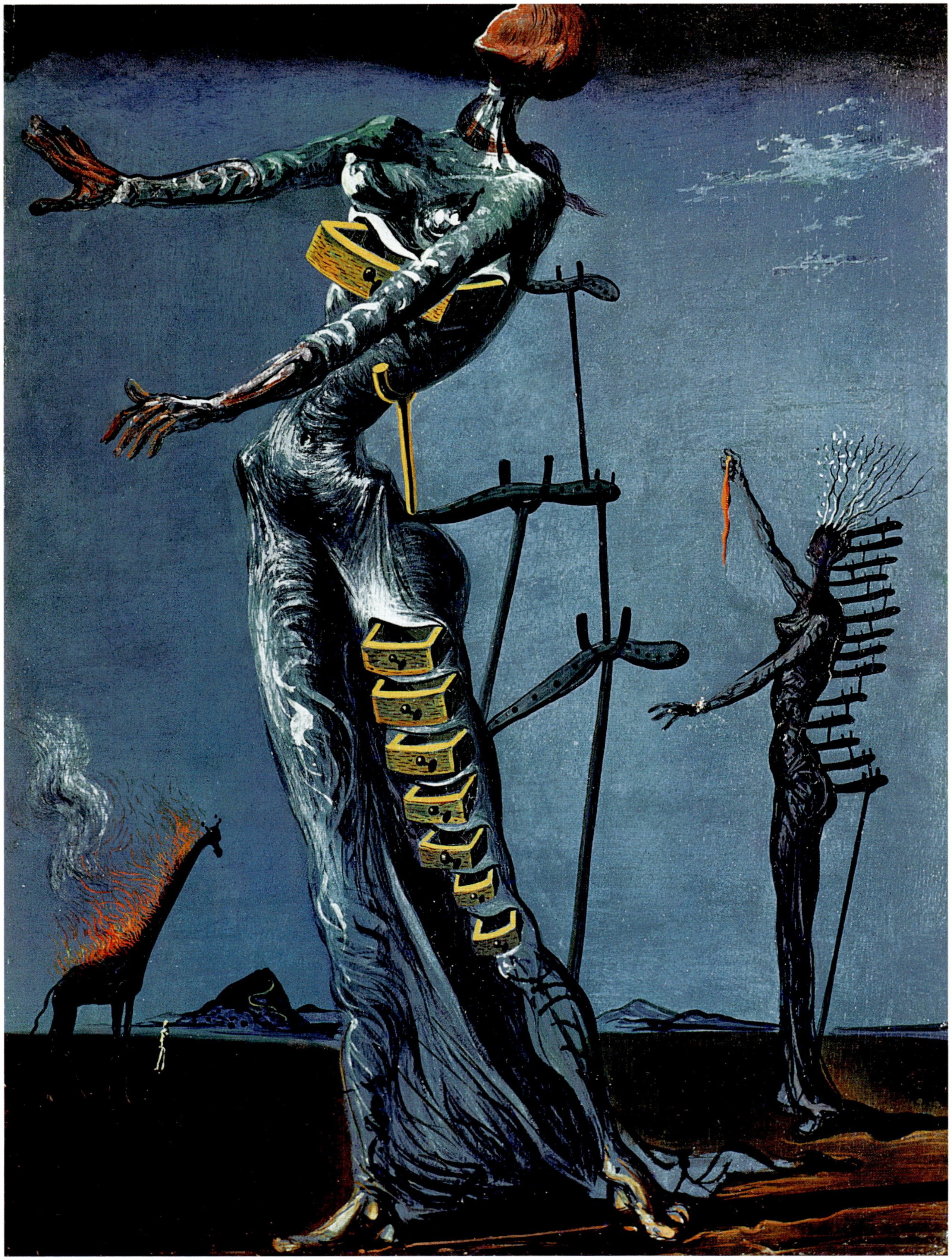

dead baby on her head, made by Dalí, a get-up which in the wake of the killing of the Lindbergh baby some two years earlier was roundly attacked as offensive in the European press when the feted couple returned home to France a week later.

A similar level of turmoil now existed among the Surrealists in Paris, with one faction, urged on by another of the group's founder members, Louis Aragon (1897–1982), turning increasingly toward Communism as the turbulent events of the 1930s hardened political attitudes on all sides. Dalí, the arch-individualist, soon fell foul of Aragon's hardline stance, but Breton expelled the Aragonese faction from the group rather than succumb to their extremism. Dalí's friend, the poet René Crevel (1900–35), then committed suicide, but as Dalí describes it, 'The remaining Surrealists were in the process of committing suicide gradually, sinking into the growing obscurity of the lethargic and political tittle-tattle of the collective café terraces.'

(Left)

The Burning Giraffe, *c.* 1937

Medium: Oil on panel
Dimensions: 35 x 27 cm (13¾ x 10⅔ in)
Location: Kunstmuseum, Basel

A Fetish for Hitler

It did not matter to Dali, as he had always embraced an individual fate and, in any case, his exhibitionist high jinks continued no matter whom they offended. In 1934, shortly before going to America, he had been summoned to a Surrealist tribunal at which he was asked to explain himself, this time because in the minds of the intelligentsia he had developed an unhealthy interest in Hitler, seeing him as a fascinating figure with rich potential as a Surrealist subject. Dali made a mockery of this attempt to censor his imaginative freedom, even suggesting to the committee a series of homoerotic works featuring the two of them – Breton and Dali – performing sex acts on each other, echoing an earlier fantasy in which he tells us quite matter-of-factly that he dreamed of sodomizing his own father.

Indeed, the more they reacted like infuriated parents, the more infantile and defiant Dali's resistance became. A born contrarian, always drawn to whatever was taboo, his interest in the Nazi dictator continued, as can be seen in *The Enigma of Hitler* (1939, *see* pages 82–83), a still highly ambivalent painting done in the months after the ultimately unsuccessful diplomacy of British Prime Minister Neville Chamberlain (1869–1940) in Munich, even as war threatened the Continent. Dali explained it in the following passage from *The Secret Life*: 'It constituted a condensed reportage of a series of dreams

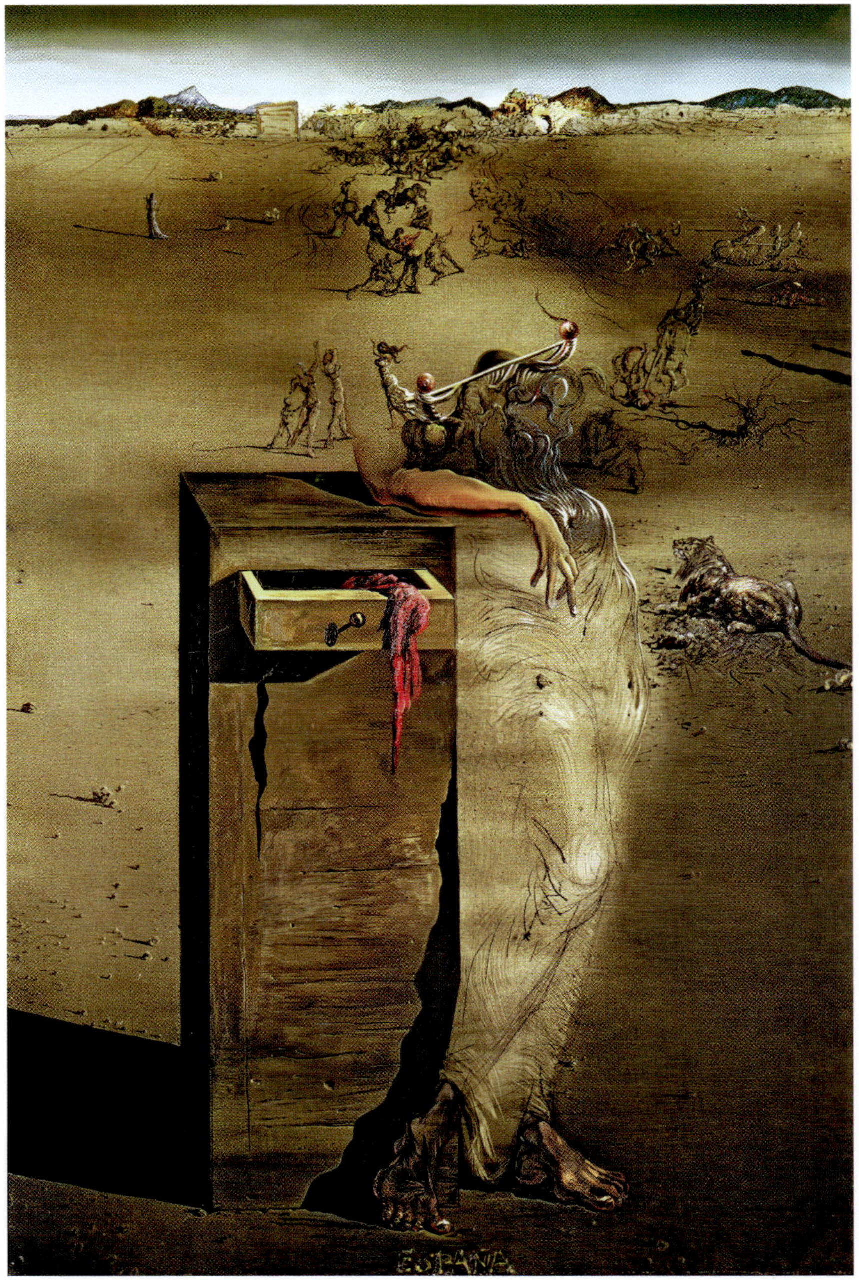

(Above)

Spain, 1938

Medium: Oil on canvas
Dimensions: 91.8 x 60.2 cm (36¼ x 23⅝ in)
Location: Museum Boijmans van Beuningen, Rotterdam

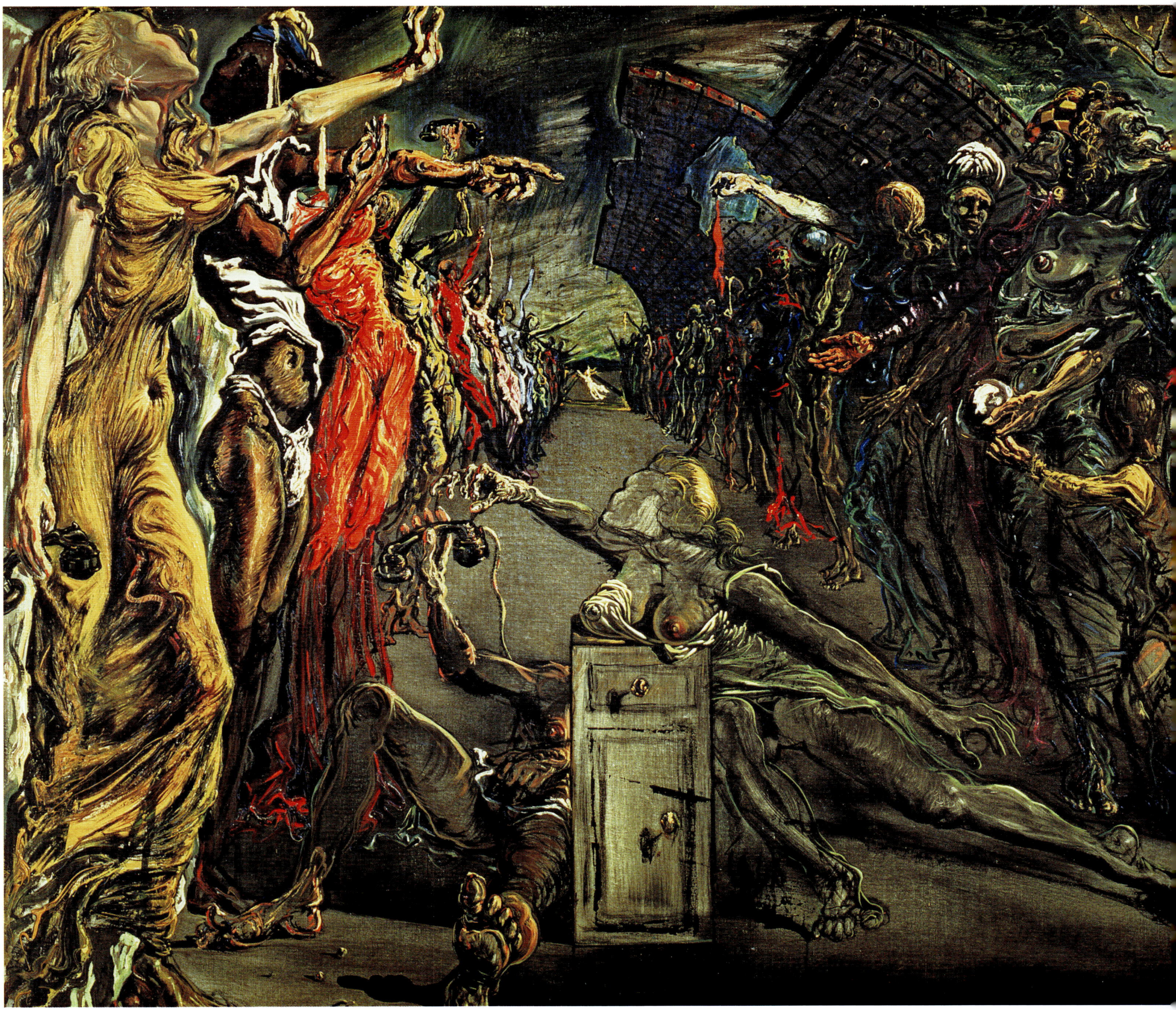

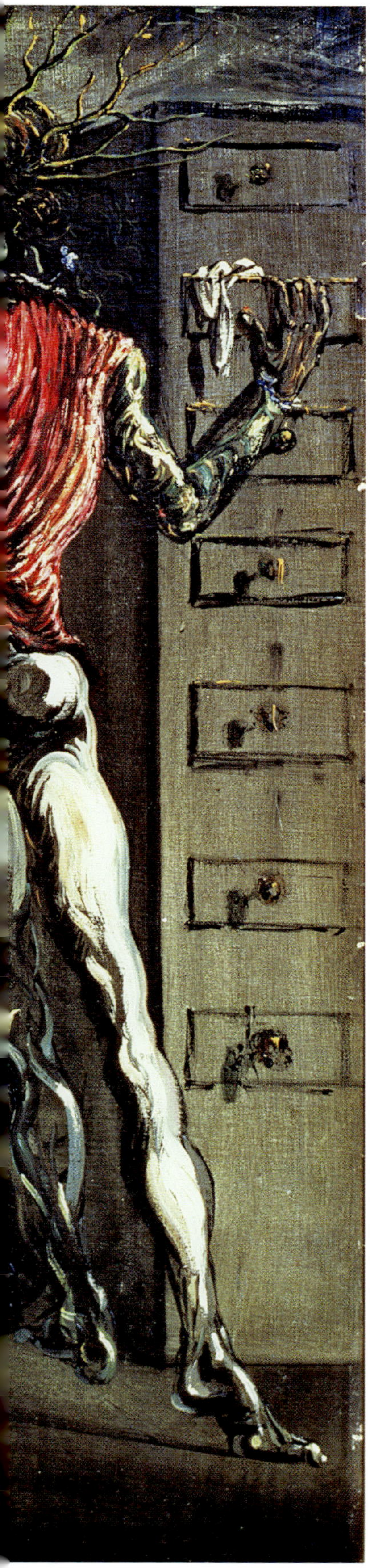

'The difference between me and the Surrealists is that I am a Surrealist.'

obviously occasioned by the events in Munich. The picture appeared to me to be charged with a prophetic value, as announcing the medieval period which was going to spread over Europe. Chamberlain's umbrella appeared in this painting in a sinister aspect with the bat, and affected me as extremely anguishing at the very time I was painting it.' Of course, by this point in the decade it was clearly apparent that despite the Munich Agreement, Europe was heading into war, but the fact that Dali was still seeing Hitler as an enigma, even in 1939, tells us much about the moral universe he inhabited.

TIME magazine

Three years earlier, feeling the pressure to conform, the painter had begun to distance himself from the Surrealists. But they found they could not do without him, as by now Dali's name was synonymous with the movement, and his own contributions to the shows in which he participated inevitably upstaged those of everyone else involved. Dali's fame grew so rapidly, indeed, that on 14 December 1936, by then feted in America where the others were still virtually unknown, his face appeared on the cover of *TIME* magazine, gold-plated publicity that brought him 'great quantities of flabbergasting letters' and 'a shower of extravagant offers, each more unexpected than the last'. It was also these kinds of supposedly compromised commercial activities which aroused the displeasure of the Surrealist

(Left)

Palladio's Corridor of Dramatic Surprise, 1938

Medium: Oil on canvas
Dimensions: 73 x 104 cm (28¾ x 41 in)
Location: Private Collection

apparatchiks – although in this respect he was also a trailblazer – but Dalí had now outgrown the movement, as he had always intended. Even so, he was still happy to lend his magnetic presence to their activities where this might also advance his own interests.

'...I felt myself essentially anti-historic and a-political.'

Dalí in a Diving Suit

In this regard, earlier that year, Dalí had given a now infamous lecture at the First International Surrealist Exhibition at the New Burlington Galleries in London. With typically absurdist showmanship, he decided that this would best be done from inside a diving suit. Dalí relates that 'Lord Berners was in charge of renting the diving suit in question, and over the telephone they asked him to specify exactly to what depth Mr Dalí wished to descend. Lord Berners replied that I was going to descend to the subconscious, after which I would immediately come up again. With equal seriousness the voice answered that in this case they would replace the helmet with a special one.' Thus attired, Dalí staggered onto the stage, holding two Afghan hounds by leads but barely able to walk in the suit's leaden boots. The effort must have been exhausting, as despite the special helmet he was sweating profusely behind its glass face by the time he reached the lectern. He may have been speaking French to an English audience, but their confusion was in any case increased by the helmet, which muffled his words so that they could barely be made out at all. Dalí, by now gesturing frantically, was clearly on the point of fainting, and hurried efforts were made to locate a spanner with which to unlock the helmet so that he could finish his talk. And as if to emphasize that by now he could not put a foot wrong with the public, the little melodrama of the diving suit was taken by the audience to be all part of the act.

A Narrow Escape

By now, Surrealism's star attraction was mixing comfortably with the aristocracy he so admired, and he regularly attended the famous salon of the Princesse de Polignac (1865–1943). It was also at this point that he met Edward James (1907–84), a member of the English aristocracy who until the outbreak of the Second World War would be Dalí's sometime collaborator and sole patron, an exclusive financial arrangement which paid Dalí a decent stipend and enabled James to amass a superb collection of some of the painter's greatest works.

(Right)

Soft Construction with Boiled Beans (Premonition of Civil War), 1936

Medium: Oil on panel
Dimensions: 99.9 x 100 cm (39⅓ x 39⅓ in)
Location: Philadelphia Museum of Art, Pennsylvania

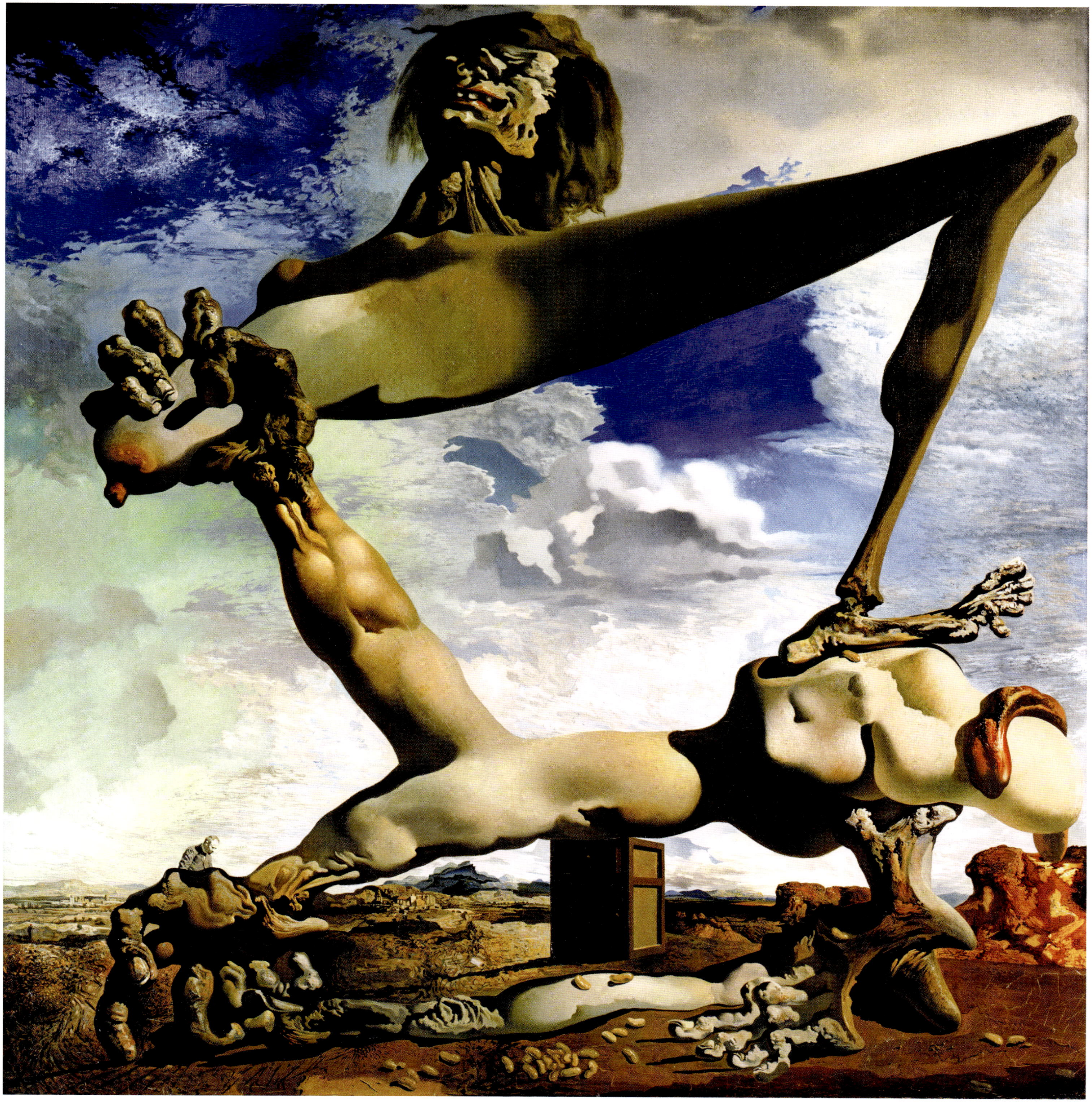

By this time, Dalí had achieved some kind of reconciliation with his father after Gala and he had returned to Figueres in the summer of 1934. This visit coincided with a brief separatist uprising in Barcelona, as strikes paralyzed the ordinary functioning of daily life and the city began to be shelled by government forces, who quickly regained control. The couple found a driver prepared to take them to the border with France, but at a stop en route they overheard a group of men discussing whether or not they should be killed on the spot. These were dangerous times indeed, but the pair managed to get away and, by the skin of their teeth, made it across the border.

Running from History

Dalí vowed to himself from then on that he would never again get mixed up in politics, describing himself in *The Secret Life* as 'definitely not a historic man. On the contrary, I felt myself essentially anti-historic and a-political'. This could be retrospective justification of something which by another name and another standard of behaviour would be called cowardice. Looking at his art, so profoundly caught up in his own dramas, its universal basis in psychology and myth rather than history, we may be unlikely to suspect anything else. However, as we shall see, Dalí's view of what constituted a political stance and what did not was as subjective as anything he ever put into his art. Certainly, his habitual reaction to

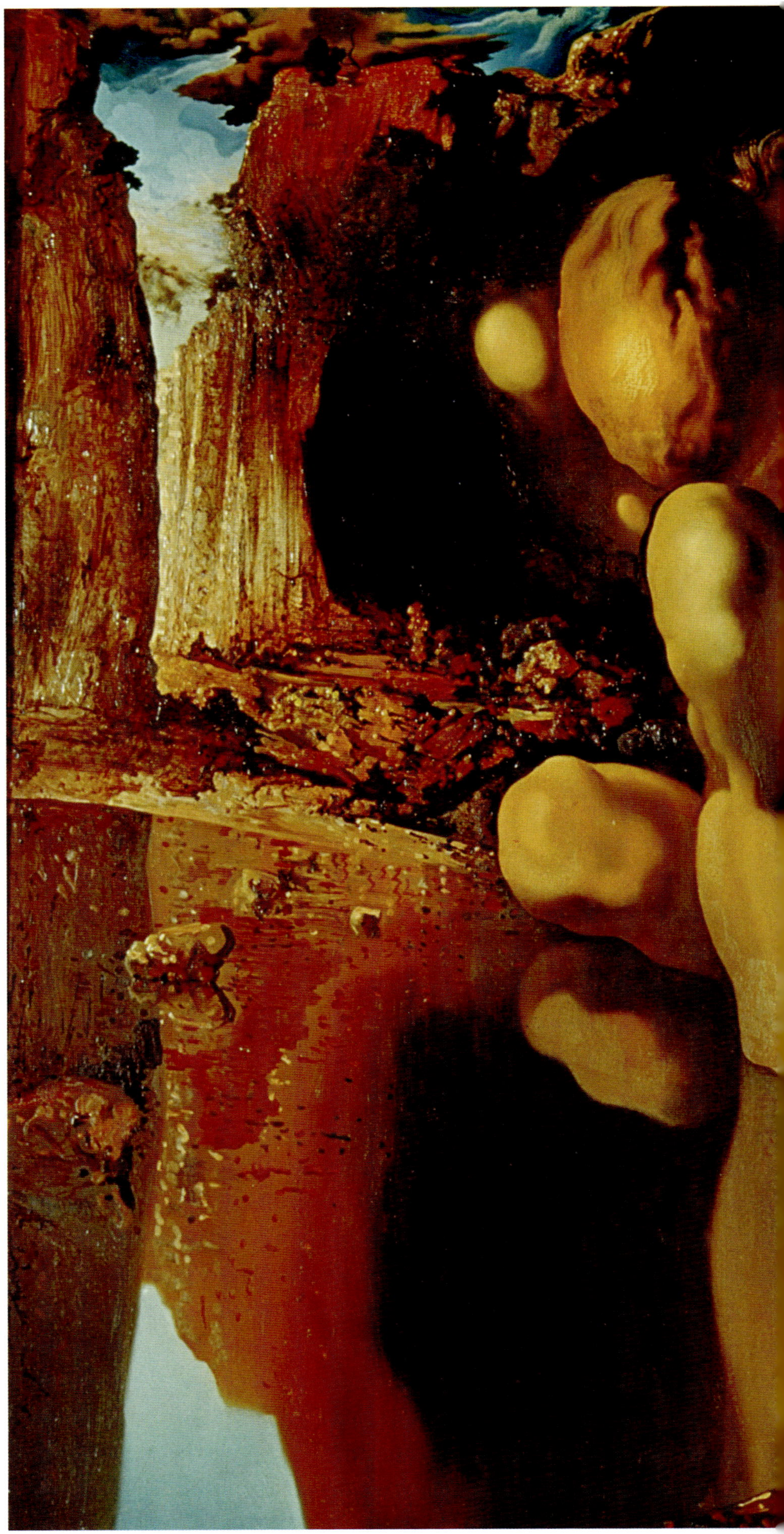

(Right)

Metamorphosis of Narcissus, 1937

Medium: Oil on canvas
Dimensions: 51.1 x 78.1 cm (20 x 30¾ in)
Location: Tate Modern, London

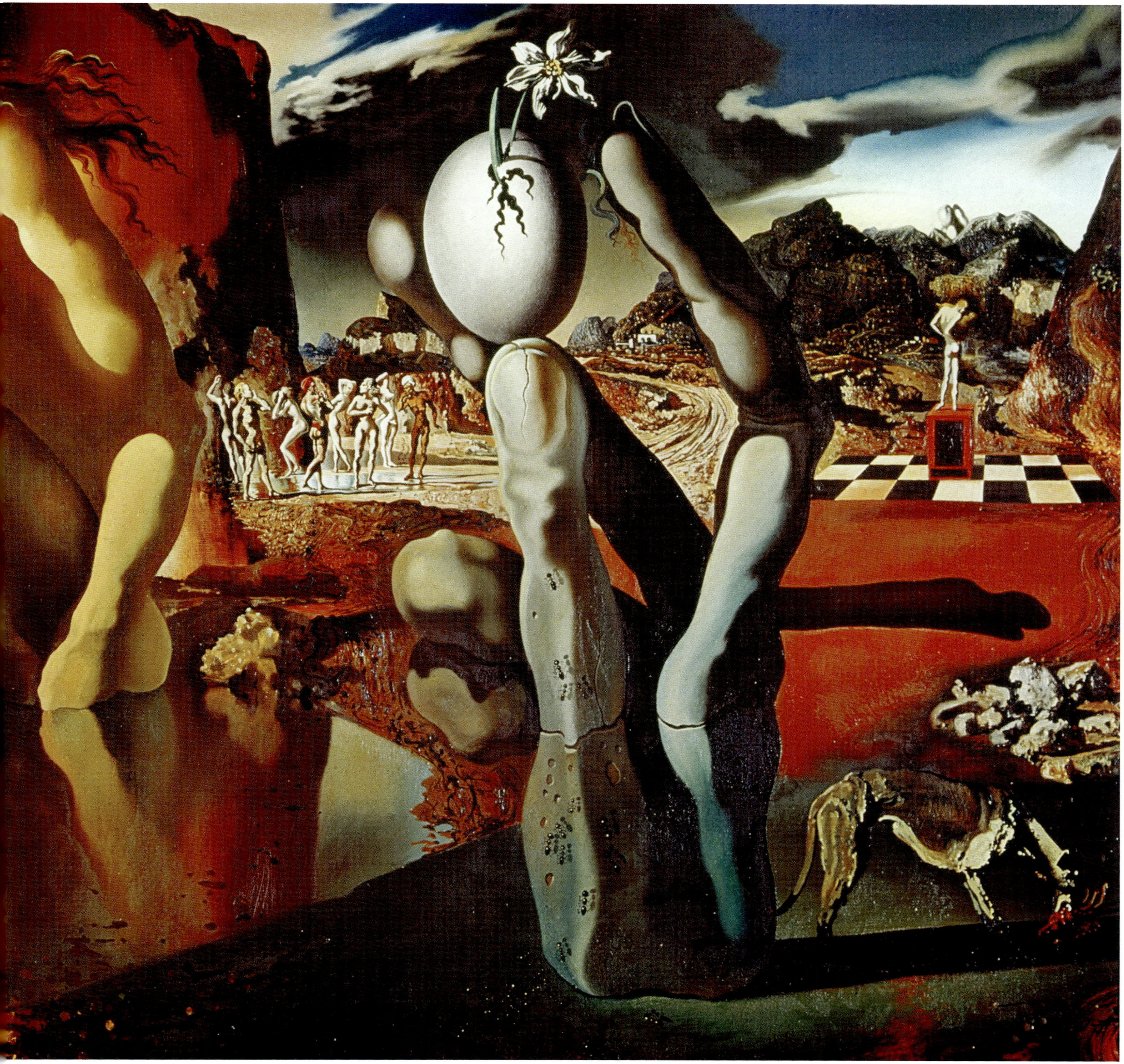

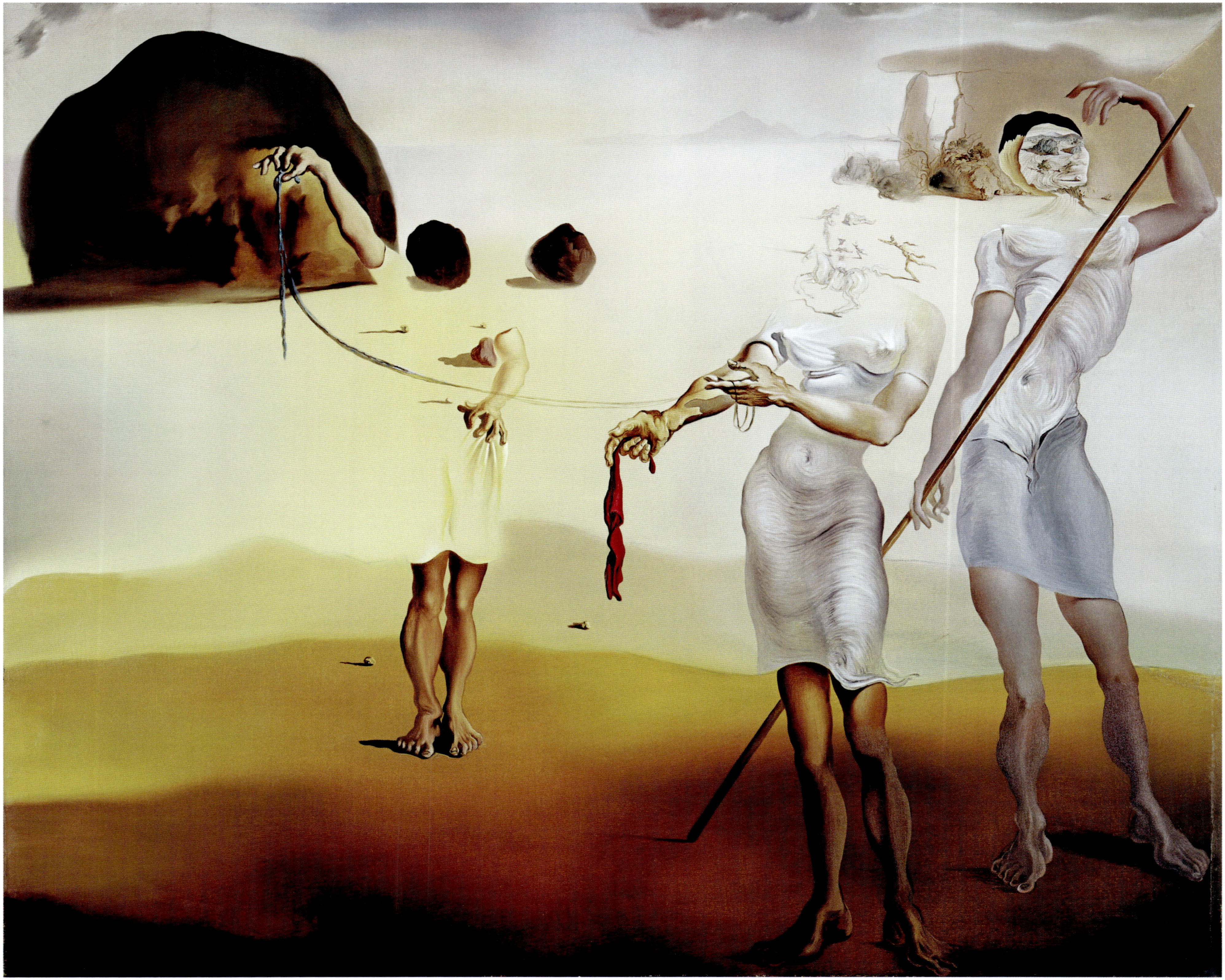

conflict was to run away – first from the Civil War in his own land, then from war in Europe – though he was hardly alone among artists and intellectuals in that impulse. But Dalí also felt justified in his support for the Nationalist victors of the Civil War and later lent public legitimacy to the dictatorial regime of General Francisco Franco (1892–1975). Even as early as 1939, in a letter to Luis Buñuel he not only refused with a callous and unapologetic egoism to lend the money his friend had asked for, but offered a prophetic glimpse of his future reactionary sympathies as a supporter of both Franco and the Catholic Church.

Typically, Dalí's regrets, such as they were, did not concern the collective suffering of ordinary people which Picasso so famously memorialized in *Guernica* (1937). As we might expect, Dalí despised the collective sentiment or the collective consciousness represented, as he saw it, by the 'isms' of his childhood and youth. 'Each claims the truth,' he writes, 'but the sole "truth" which they have demonstrated is that once these "isms" are forgotten (and how quickly they are forgotten!) there remains among their anachronistic ruins only the reality of a few authentic individuals.' It is not quite the 'Great Man' theory of history of the nineteenth century, whose shadow looms large over the whole interwar period and its rash of despots and demagogues; but it is not far off. And Dalí certainly saw himself as a man alone, a kind of Superman in the mould of Nietzsche, by whose thinking he was influenced, writing in *The Secret Life* that 'All alliance depersonalizes; everything that tends to the collective is your death.'

'...everything that tends to the collective is your death...'

The Death of Lorca

Indeed, the only regrets Dalí had over his conduct in respect to the Civil War related not to the country he abandoned, or its people in any general sense, but to a loved individual he believed he might have saved. In June 1936, with war looming in Spain, Dalí and Gala decided to take up an invitation that Edward James had extended to the pair of them and also to Lorca, with whom Dalí had recently been reconciled, to stay at James's home near Amalfi, in southern Italy, for as long as they wished. Dalí needed no second invitation, but Lorca postponed joining them until he had seen his father, whom he believed was gravely ill in his apartment in Granada, Andalusia. The father survived, but Lorca was rounded up by Franco's Nationalists soon after he

(Left)

Enchanted Beach with Three Fluid Graces, 1938

Medium: Oil on canvas
Dimensions: 65 x 81.28 cm (25½ x 32 in)
Location: Salvador Dalí Museum, St Petersburg, Florida

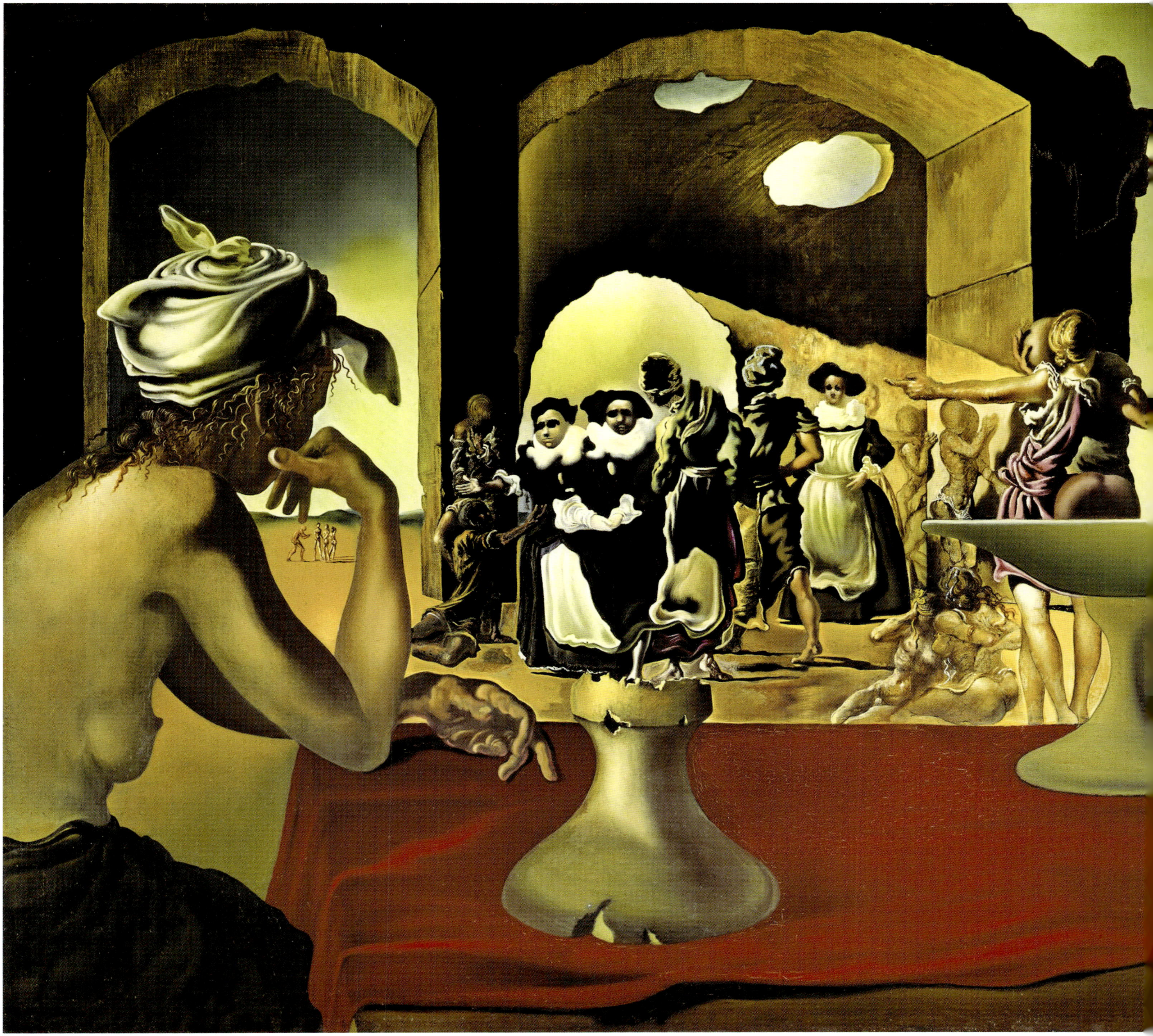

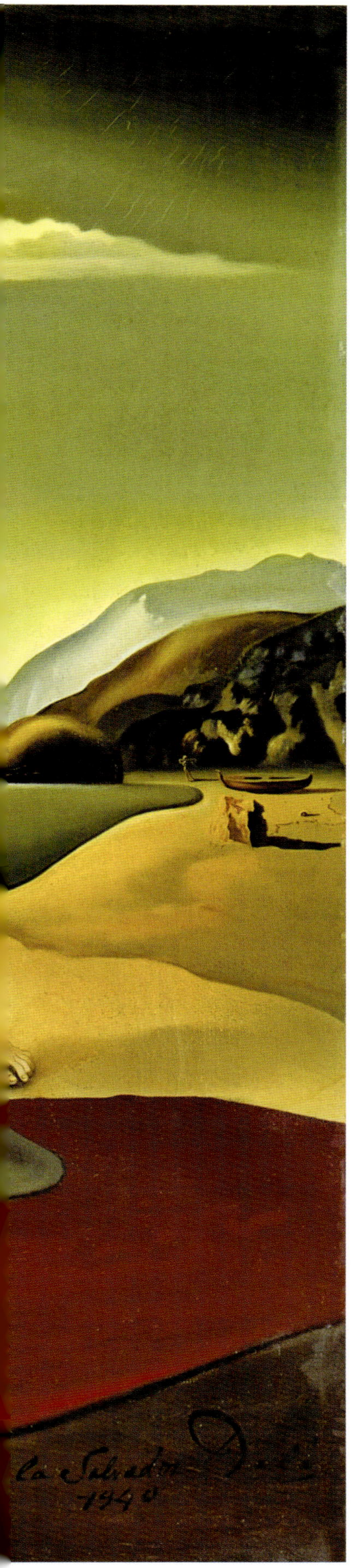

'I must incorporate Surrealism in tradition. My imagination must become classic again.'

got there and summarily executed. Dalí, it seems, could not forgive himself for not trying harder to persuade Lorca to leave with them. He was also moved by reports that, as an example of the savagery that became so routine, the body of his great hero of Catalan Art Nouveau, Antoni Gaudí (1852–1926), was apparently disinterred and dragged through the streets of Barcelona by a group of children; a surreal vision that might have come from the mind of Dalí himself. Certainly, he was defiant in his opinions about the conflict, which he set out with clear frankness in *The Secret Life*: 'The Spanish Civil War changed none of my ideas. On the contrary it endowed their evolution with a decisive rigour. Horror and aversion for every kind of revolution assumed in me an almost pathological form.'

Nevertheless, for all his apparent indifference to the suffering of nameless others (as opposed to specific individuals), let alone his hostility towards their hopes for change, two of Dalí's greatest paintings, *Soft Construction with Boiled Beans (Premonition of Civil War*, 1936, *see* page 99) and *Autumn Cannibalism* (1936), owe their emotional power to the collective horror over the struggle that took place on the Iberian Peninsula in the late 1930s. Moreover, as is clear from statements Dalí made later on, no matter how much he tried to shut it out he was still aware of what was happening in Spain during these years. 'I closed eyes and ears so as to know nothing about it, but the stories of the most terrifying atrocities still reached me and haunted me like nightmares.'

(Left)

Slave Market with the Disappearing Bust of Voltaire, 1940

Medium: Oil on canvas
Dimensions: 46.5 x 65.5 cm (18⅓ x 25⅘ in)
Location: Salvador Dalí Museum, St Petersburg, Florida

The Spanish Civil War

Once again probing the unconscious, although now transforming his own neurotic vocabulary of personal motifs into atavistic metaphors that hideously illustrate the barbarism of war, in *Soft Construction with Boiled Beans* and *Autumn Cannibalism* Dalí made two images that convey a defilement and corruption of life, a base wretchedness, that seem to defy explanation. Some observers see these pictures not so much as an indictment of war itself as practised by conscious actors, but as an almost amoral depiction of its savagery as an unconscious, biological process of destruction. Certainly, in his writings he dodges the question of blame. In writing of *Autumn Cannibalism*, Dalí described the Civil War in terms of impersonal forces, 'as a phenomenon of natural history as opposed to Picasso who considered it as a political phenomenon'; and *Soft Construction*, whose central feature is a gargantuan mutant organism reminiscent of the giant headless amputee in *The Spectre of Sex Appeal* (1934, *see* page 175), he viewed as 'a vast human body breaking out into monstrous excrescences of arms and legs tearing at one another in a delirium of autostrangulation'.

Dalí continued, 'As a background to this architecture of frenzied flesh devoured by a narcissistic and biological cataclysm, I painted a geological landscape that had been uselessly revolutionized for thousands of years, congealed in its "normal course".' It is not quite the argument Franco himself might have made, but of course implicit in his desire for a return to tradition is a resistance to the change for which the Republican cause had stood. It was not for Dalí to speculate on how this tradition, the 'normal course' he refers to, might be reinstated nor who would suffer in achieving it. That was politics, and Dalí, solipsistic and self-deluding, insisted on having nothing to do with it.

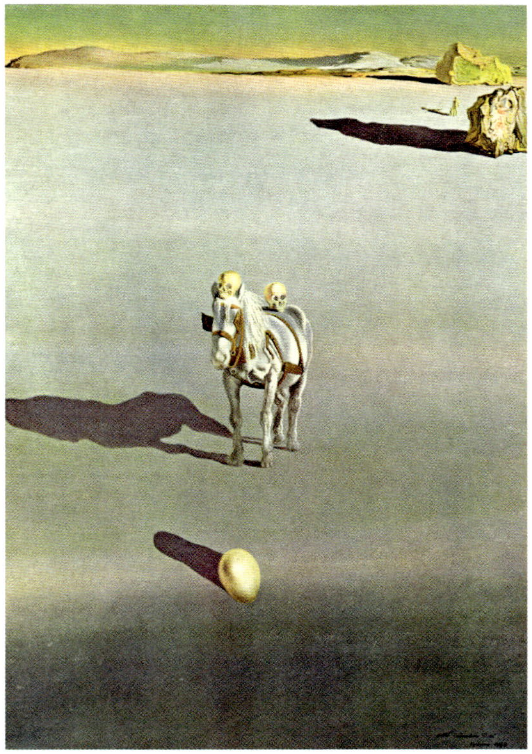

Metamorphosis of Narcissus

Dalí's sojourn in Italy did, however, exert a profound artistic effect through both the country's painting and its architecture. Above all, he encountered Raphael (1483–1520), whom he came to regard as a painter of peerless perfection. The physical

(Above)

Geological Destiny, 1933

Medium: Oil on wood panel
Dimensions: 21 x 16 cm (8¼ x 6⅓ in)
Location: Private Collection

(Right)

The Face of War, 1940–41

Medium: Oil on canvas
Dimensions: 64 x 79 cm (25⅔ x 31 in)
Location: Museum Boijmans van Beuningen, Rotterdam

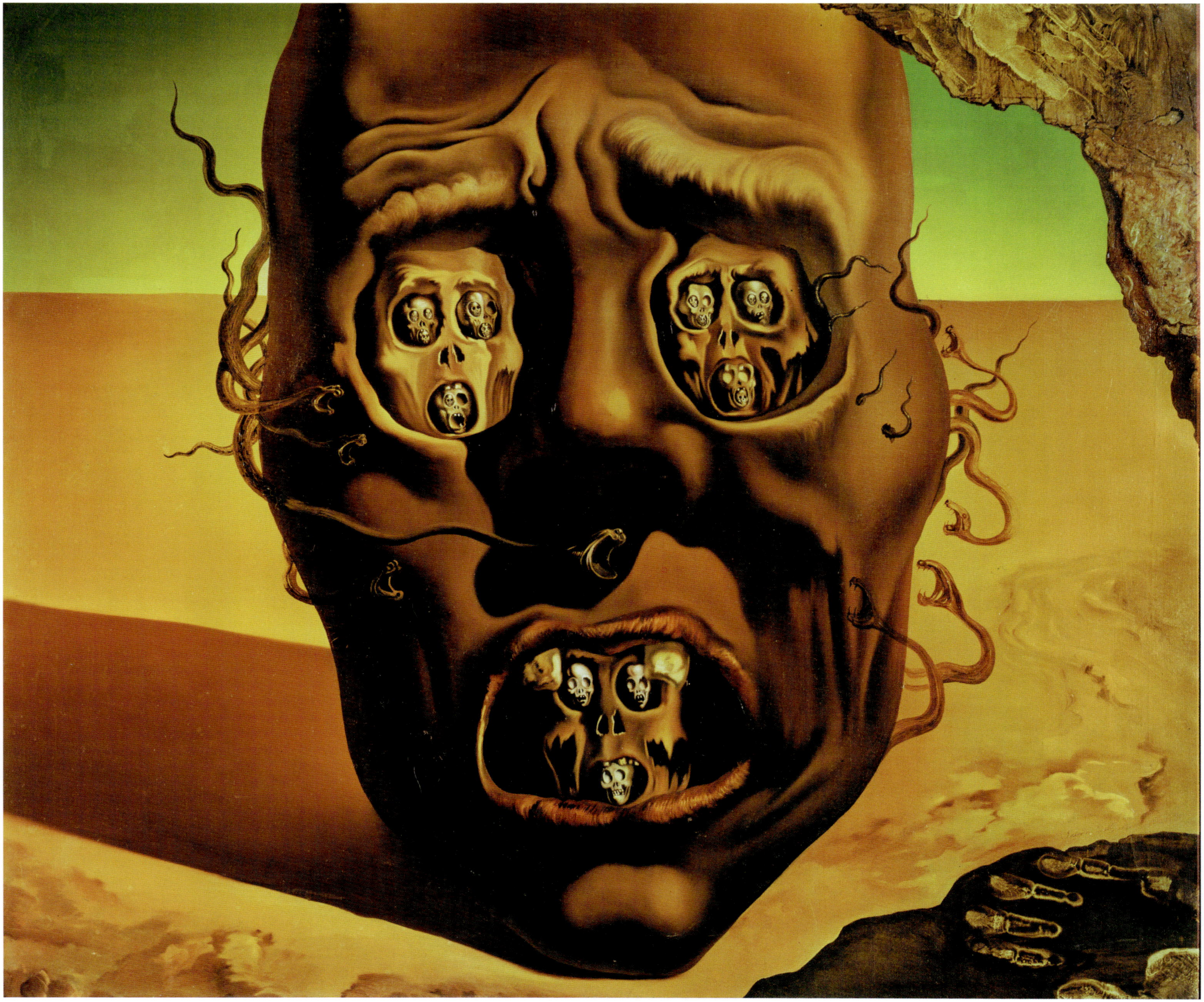

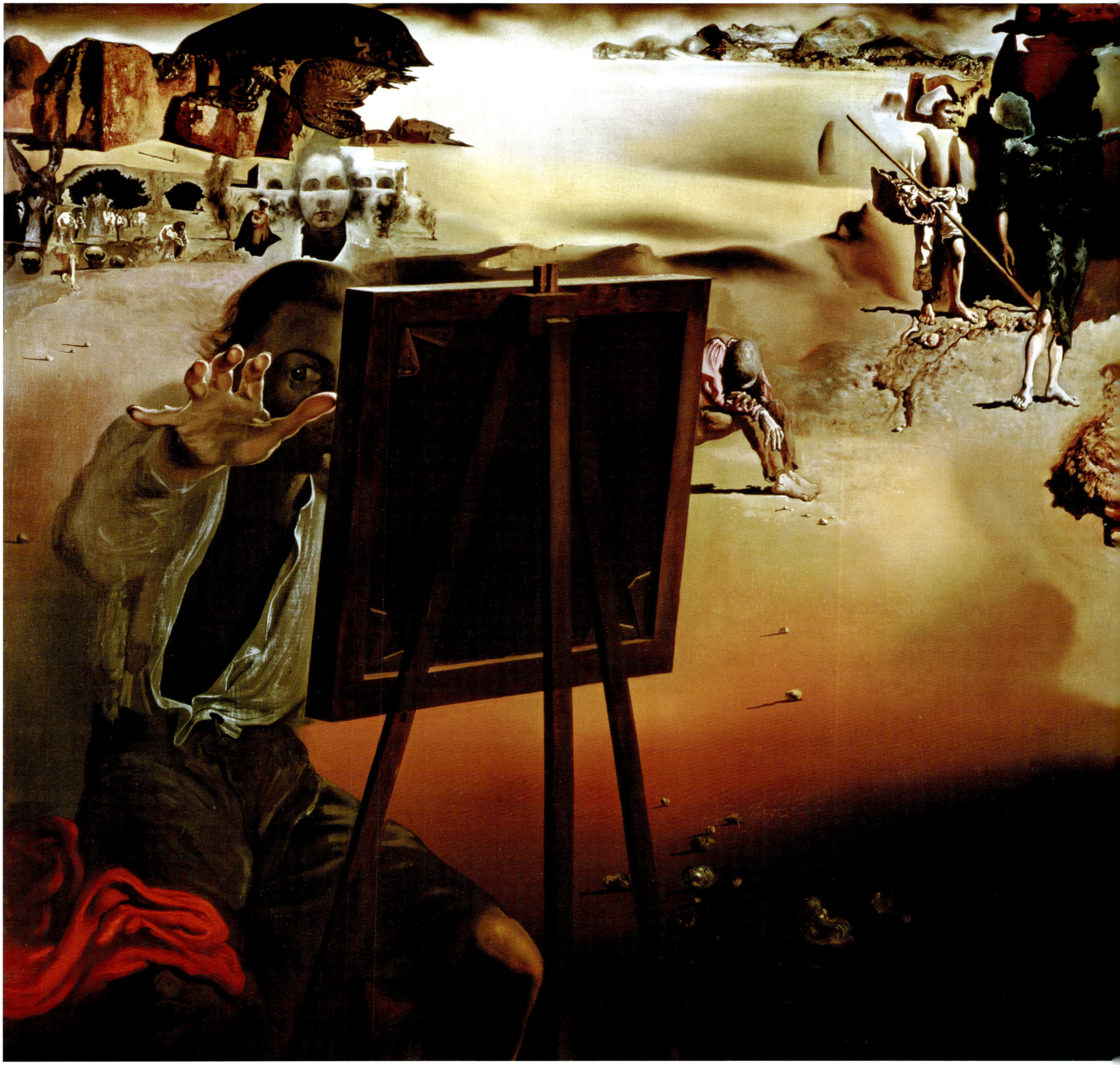

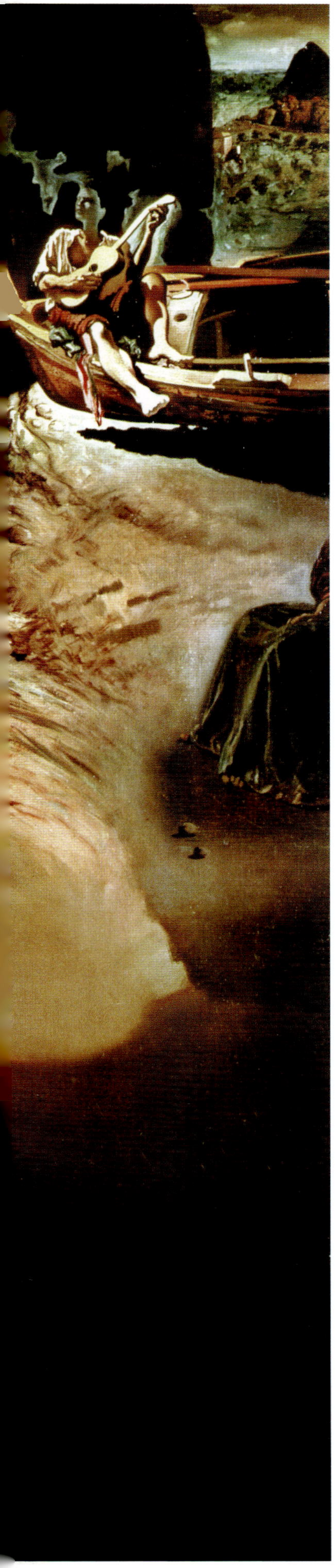

'Thus I spent the whole day seated before my easel, my eyes staring fixedly, trying to "see", like a medium.'

and pictorial architecture of the Renaissance now became a strong presence in paintings such as *Suburbs of a Paranoiac-Critical Town: Afternoon on the Outskirts of European History* (1936, see pages 92–93) and *Palladio's Corridor of Dramatic Surprise* (1938, see pages 96–97). Above all, there was *Metamorphosis of Narcissus* (1937, see pages 100–01), an image for which Dalí wrote a companion poem by way of mirroring interpretation, like the reflection of himself in the water with which the giant Narcissus to the left of the painting is preoccupied. Aside from the extraordinary invention and execution in this remarkable picture, according to Dalí it was also the first (as was the poem) to be 'obtained entirely through the integral application of the paranoiac-critical method', as he tells us in the subtitle to his essay on the subject. Whether or not that is strictly accurate, Dalí continues that 'For the first time, a Surrealist painting and poem objectively allow the coherent interpretation of a developed irrational subject,' and that 'The lyricism of poetic images is philosophically important only when it has attained in its operation, the same exactness as mathematics do in their operation,' adding that 'The poet must, before anyone, prove what he says'.

A Bulb in the Head

The nature of that 'proof' in this painting is both poetic and pictorial. To the left, the giant mythical figure of Narcissus sitting in the water

(Left)

Impression of Africa, 1938

Medium: Oil on canvas
Dimensions: 91.5 x 117.5 cm (36 x 46¼ in)
Location: Museum Boijmans van Beuningen, Rotterdam

seems to peer down at his reflection in the pool. But, Dalí tells us, 'The metamorphosis of the myth takes place at that precise moment, for the image of Narcissus is suddenly transformed into the image of a hand which rises out of his own reflection. At the tip of his fingers, the hand is holding an egg, a seed, a bulb from which will be born the new narcissus – the flower. Beside it can be seen the limestone sculpture of the hand – the fossil hand of the water holding the blown flower.' As if the metamorphosis, the double image of Narcissus and hand, and the sculptural double of the hand and figure (in the form of the flower) were not enough, Dalí adds yet another layer of meaning when further on in the essay he tells us that "'A bulb in the head", in Catalan, corresponds exactly with the psychoanalytic notion of "complex",' and that 'If a man has a bulb in the head, it might break into flower at any moment, Narcissus!'

'...the ideas of Surrealism will work only when they are painted to perfection...'

It does not take much imagination to see this painting as a reference to himself. But by forgoing his habitual neurotic vocabulary of fetishized childhood props in favour of his own form of Classical myth, Dalí has in this instance created a paranoiac-critical self-portrait of profound objectivity, a timeless depiction of the burden of selfhood at the heart of the human condition. Whether it achieves 'the same exactness as mathematics' is an imponderable question, but it is certainly one of the most complex – yet fully integrated – works he ever painted.

Double Images

It also provides further evidence of his fondness for and ingenuity in creating double images, relying on optical hallucinations that arise from combining two separate pictures in a single canvas to undermine the otherwise realistic images of either one. In Dalí's work of the late 1930s, these plausible illusions range from the almost biblical depiction of both individual and collective suffering in *The Great Paranoiac* (1936, *see* page 90) – surely another presentiment of conflict – to the enigmatic contemplation of *Slave Market with the Disappearing Bust of Voltaire* (1940, *see* pages 104–05), in which the features of Voltaire are composed from the figures of two nuns, an irony that the great Enlightenment writer would surely have appreciated. In between them, Dalí created the complex drama of sex and death we find in *Spain* (1938, *see* page 95), a painting that arose from his studies of the notebooks of Leonardo da Vinci (1452–1519), in which the detailed elements of a large figure of a woman with bared breasts are revealed on closer inspection to be various groups of men locked in mortal combat, without whose definition she would simply merge with the landscape. For instance, central to the painting are the woman's breasts, whose contours are in fact the convulsing outlines of two horses and their riders; her very red nipples double as the riders' heads; and the tautened string of her loosened corset becomes a kind of lance on which both combatants seem to be impaled. Clearly, though he may have cloistered himself away from trouble in Italy, Dalí had not forgotten the tumultuous events taking place across the Iberian Sea, though it is not at all clear how he felt about them in this clever but emotionless allegory of war.

But no sooner had one war come to an end than another even more threatening conflict had risen up behind it, like the repeating nightmare depicted in *The Face of War* (1940–41, *see* page 107). Dalí and Gala, having returned to Paris after a further successful trip to New York in the spring of 1939, decided to sequester themselves in what seemed like safer surroundings in southern France. But the German invasion of the country in May 1940 made up their minds for good. They packed in a hurry and made their way to Lisbon, from where, along with thousands of others, including many of the most creative minds in Europe, they set sail for America. They would not return for another eight years.

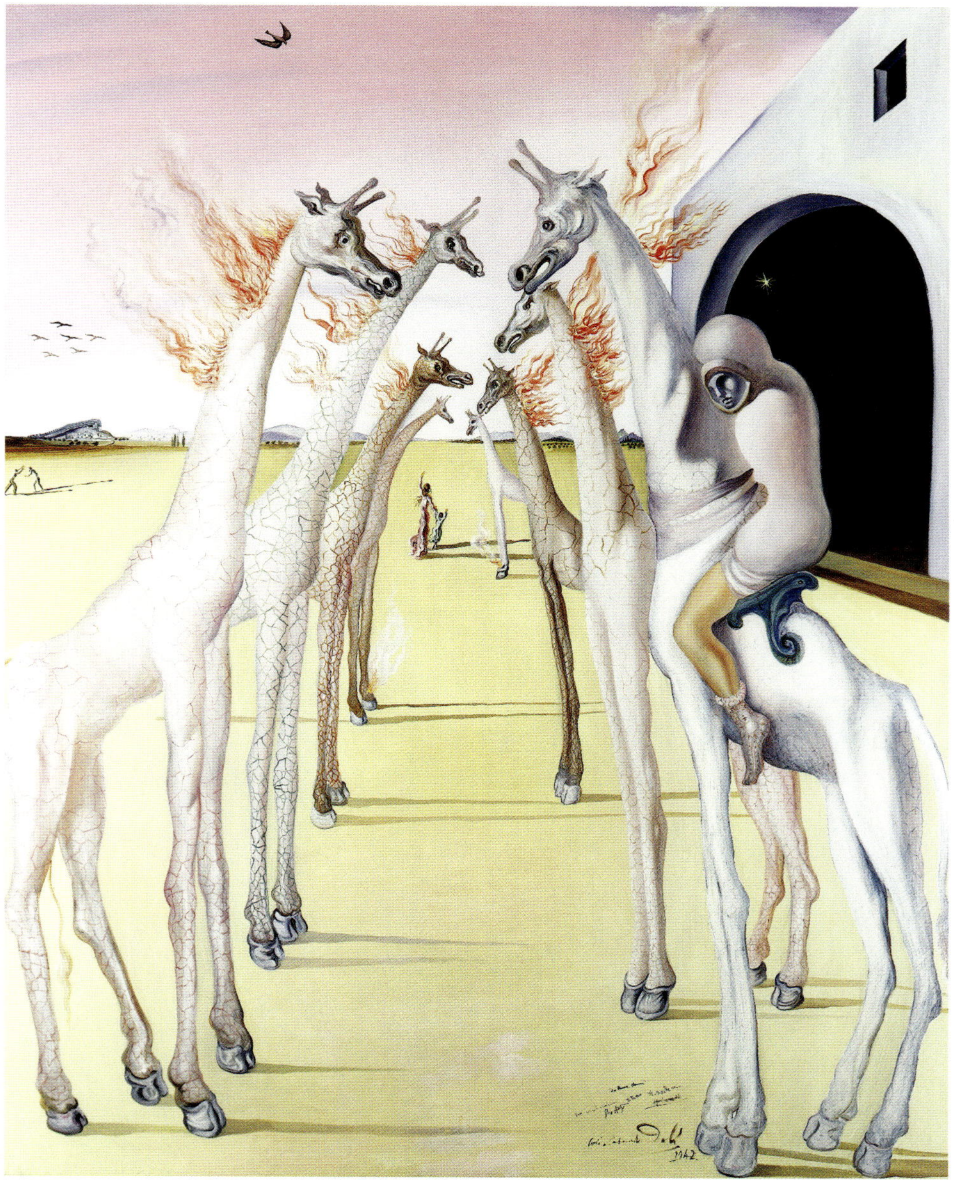

(Right)

The Flames, They Call, 1942

Medium: Oil on canvas
Dimensions: 145 x 123 cm (57 x 48⅜ in)
Location: Nahmad Collection, Switzerland

'Surrealism is destructive, but it destroys only what it considers to be shackles limiting our vision.'

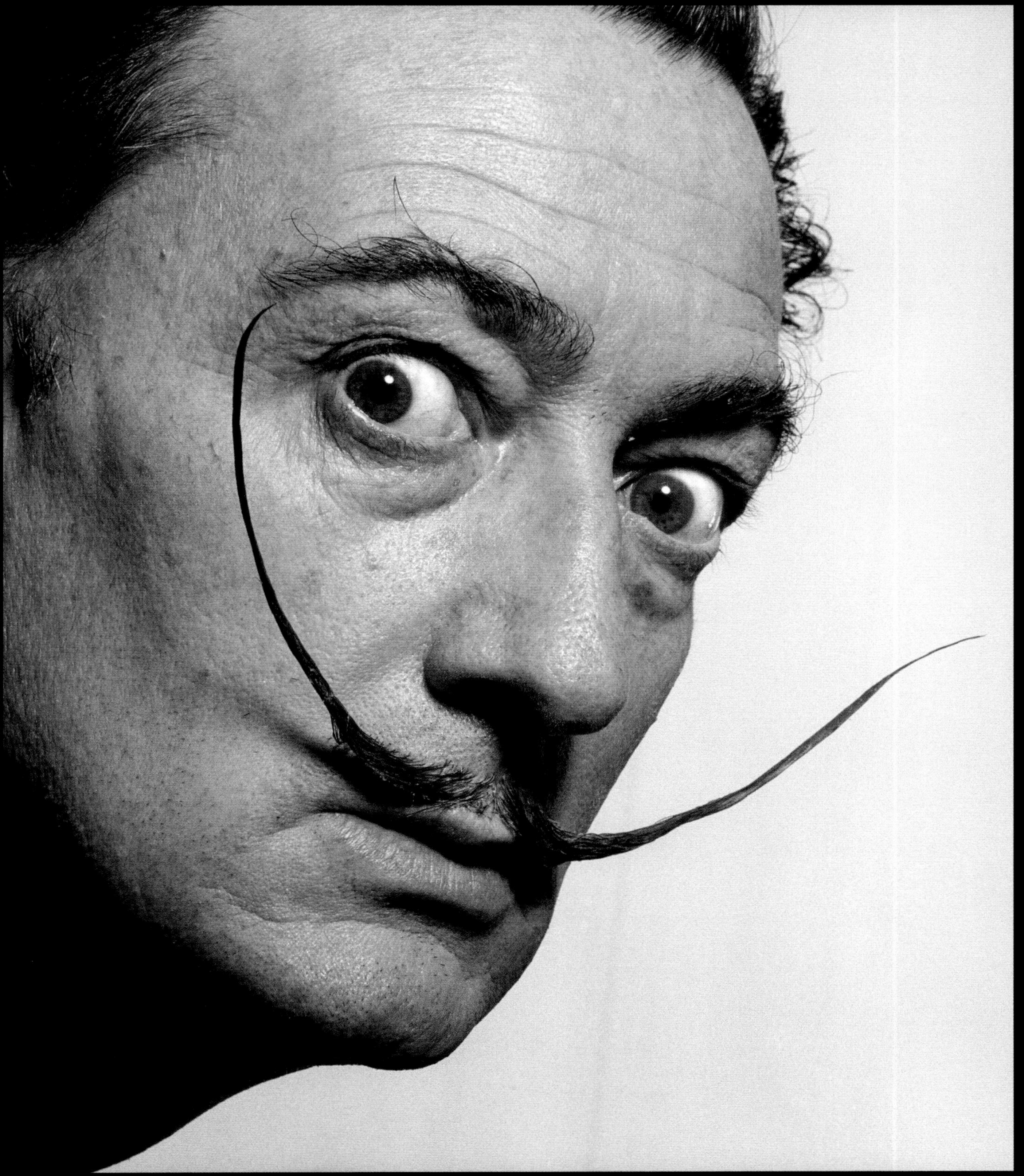

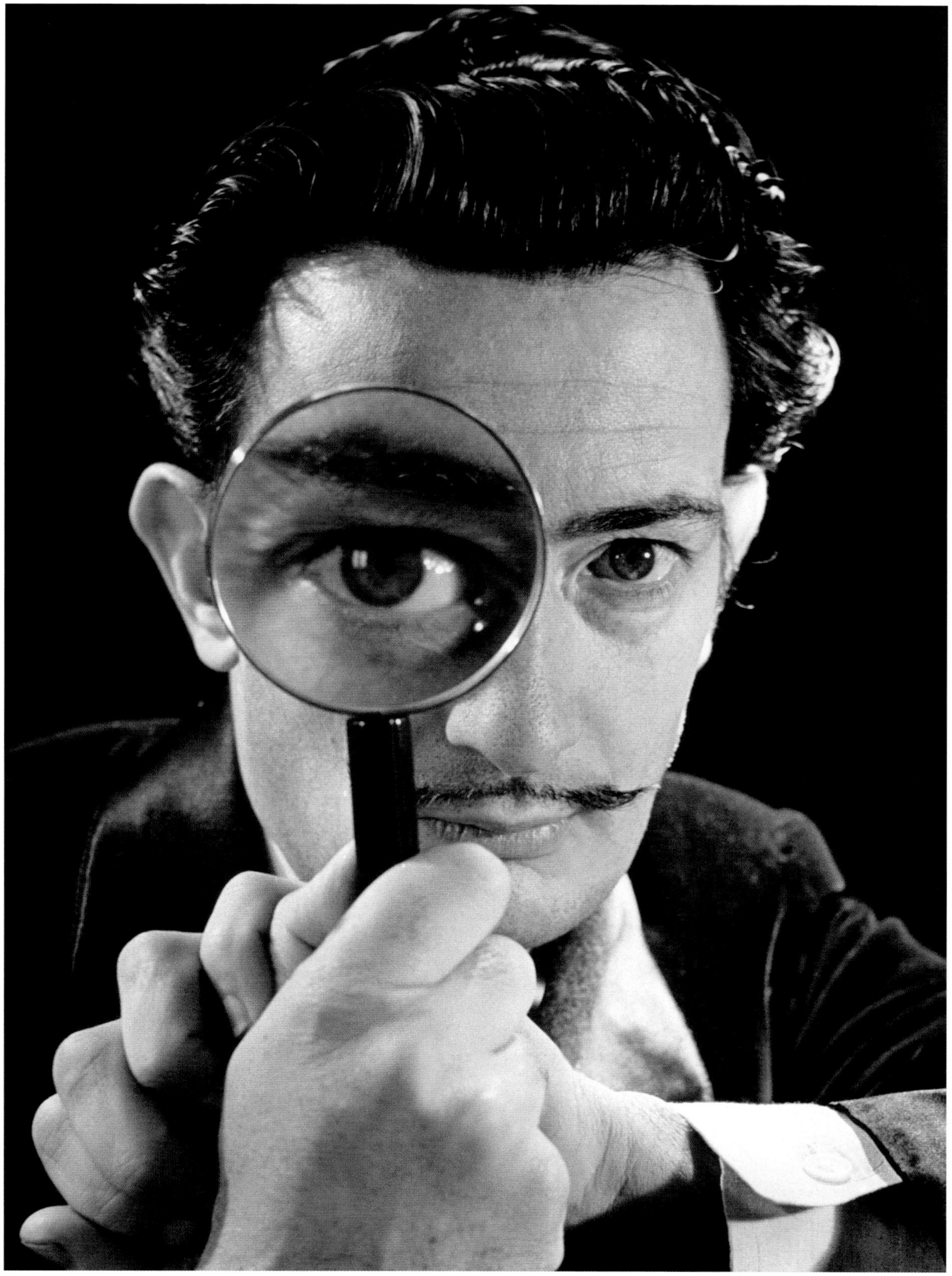

'The only difference between me and a madman is I am not mad.'

The Nuclear Mystic

If emigrating had not been forced upon him, a move to the United States might in any case have seemed like a perfectly natural step at this point in Dalí's career. From his early triumph there in 1934, his reputation had continued to climb no matter what transpired, whether good or bad, to put him in the public eye. On his most recent visit, in early 1939, he had accepted an offer to dress the shop windows of Bonwit Teller, a department store on New York's Fifth Avenue, with the work to be done the night before Dalí's latest one-man show was due to open just a few blocks away. Given two windows to work with, and with Gala acting as assistant, he divided them into 'Day' and 'Night', the two of them working long into the evening before retiring to their hotel in the small hours. On returning to look at their handiwork the following morning, they were shocked to see that their carefully crafted absurdities had been altered, toned down and prettified, following complaints made to the store overnight.

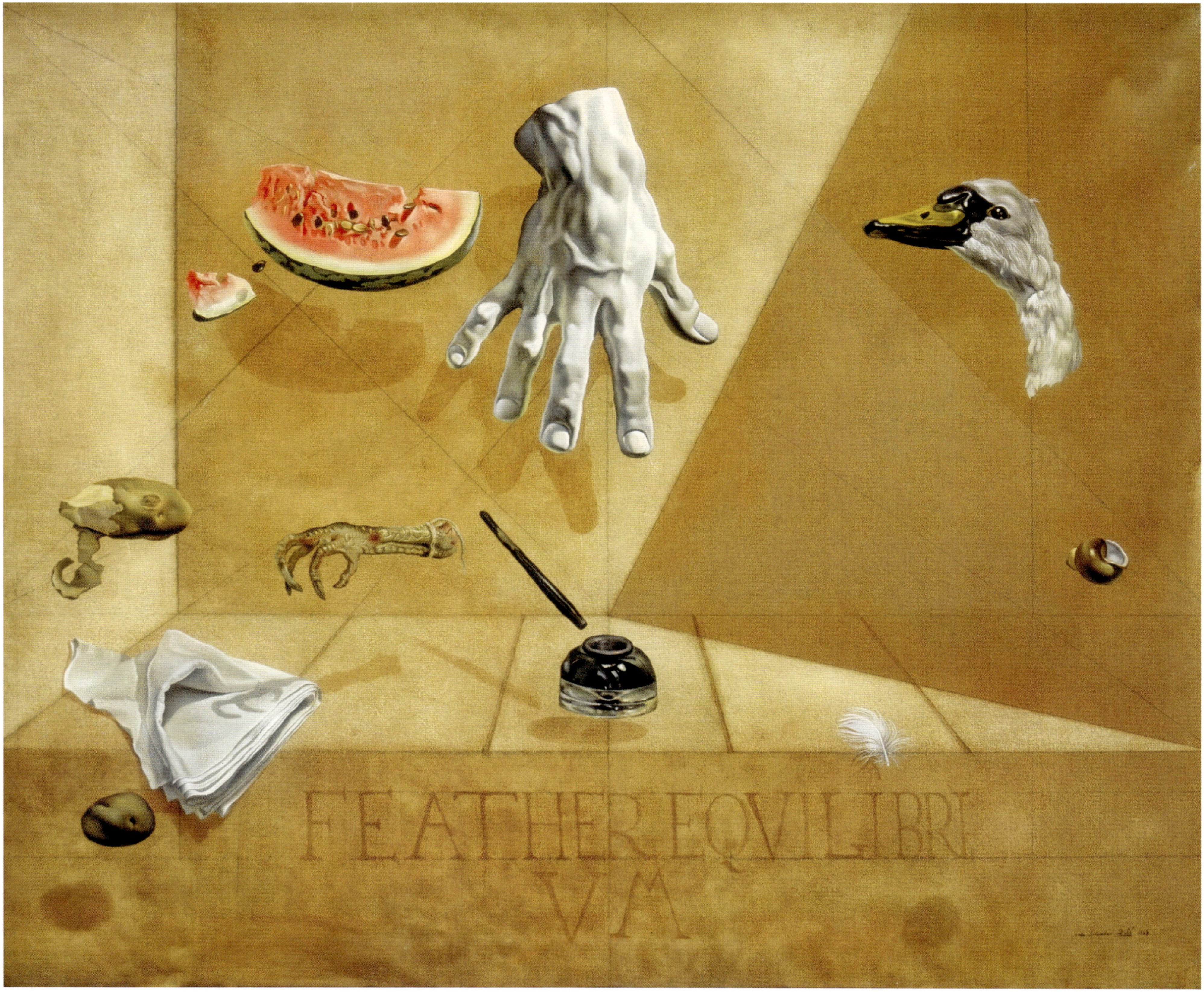

Intra-atomic Equilibrium of a Swan's Feather, 1947 | Medium: Oil on canvas | Dimensions: 78 x 97 cm (30¾ x 38⅖ in) | Location: Fundació Gala-Salvador Dalí, Figueres

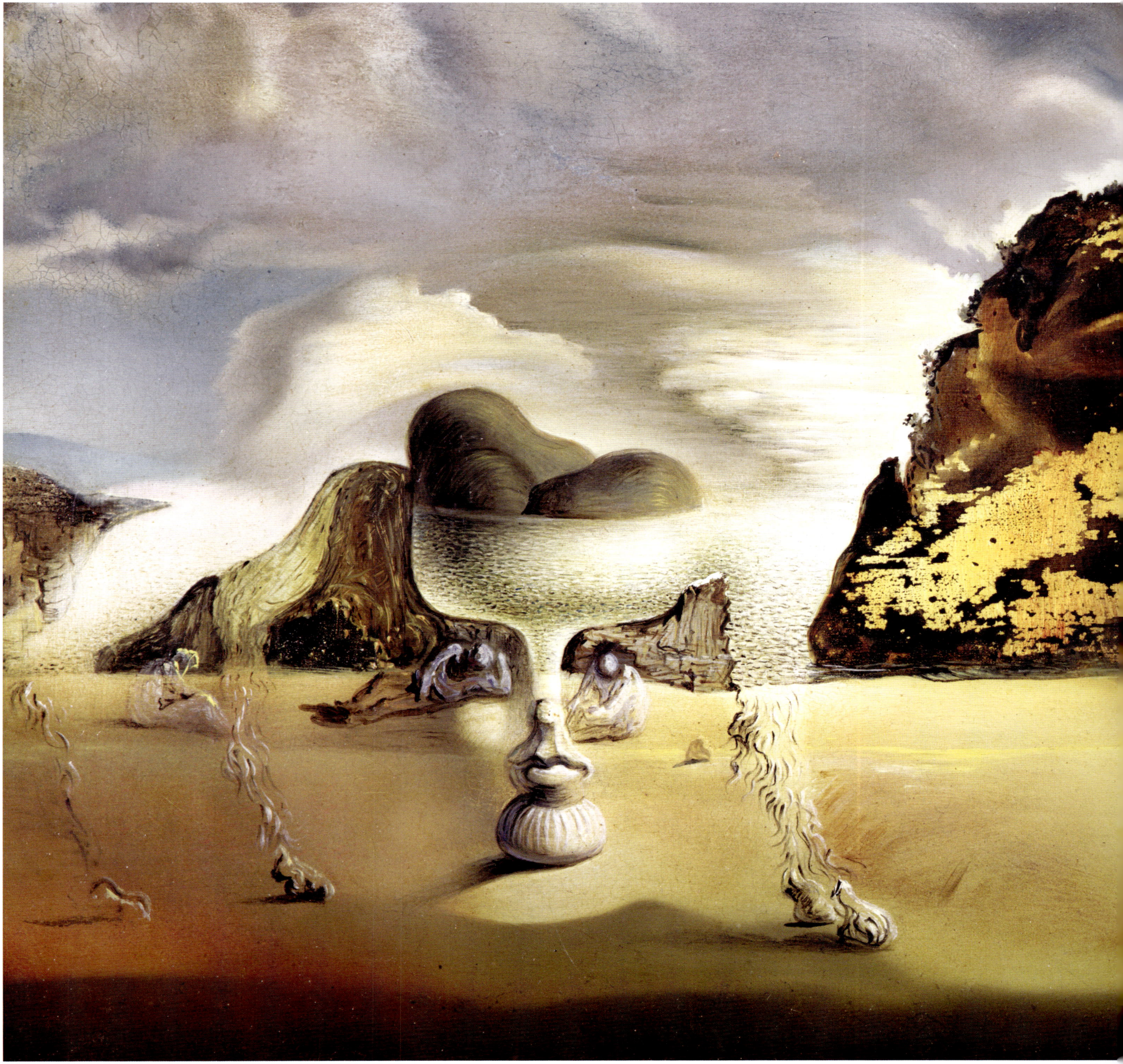

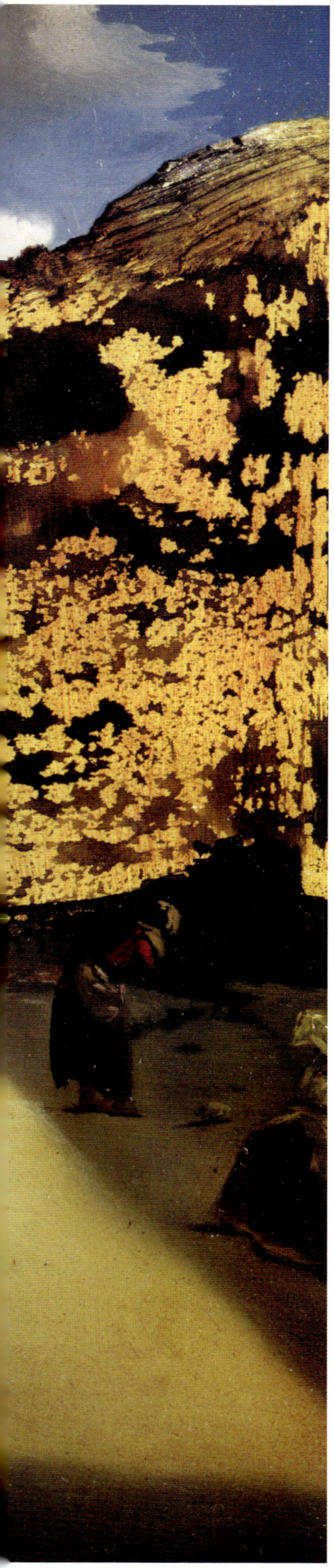

'When I paint, the ocean roars. Others merely paddle in their bath.'

Broken Windows

Dalí marched into the store in a royal rage, and when the management would neither restore his originals nor remove his name from the display, he made up his mind that vandalism was the best course of action. In the 'Day' window he had placed a bathtub lined with black astrakhan and filled to the brim with water; this he now proceeded to overturn, believing that flooding the window would be the most effective form of sabotage. But the filled bathtub proved so heavy that in the process of upsetting it he lost control, sending the tub crashing through the window into the street outside. It was lucky that none of the curious New Yorkers who had gathered to watch were hurt by the shattering glass; nor was Dalí himself, having narrowly avoided a large falling shard as he stepped through the opening onto the pavement. Apprehended by a passing policeman, he received a suspended sentence, but the publicity he gained from this defence of his artistic integrity did him no harm at all, as close to two dozen of the works in the exhibition were sold over the next fortnight.

The Secret Life of Salvador Dalí

Dalí and Gala had sailed for the US knowing they could stay for an extended visit with Caresse Crosby at her mansion, Hampton Manor,

(Left)

Invisible Afghan with Apparition, on the Beach, of the Face of Garcia Lorca in the Form of a Fruit Dish with Three Figs, 1938

Medium: Oil on panel
Dimensions: 19.2 x 24.1 cm (7½ x 9½ in)
Location: Private Collection

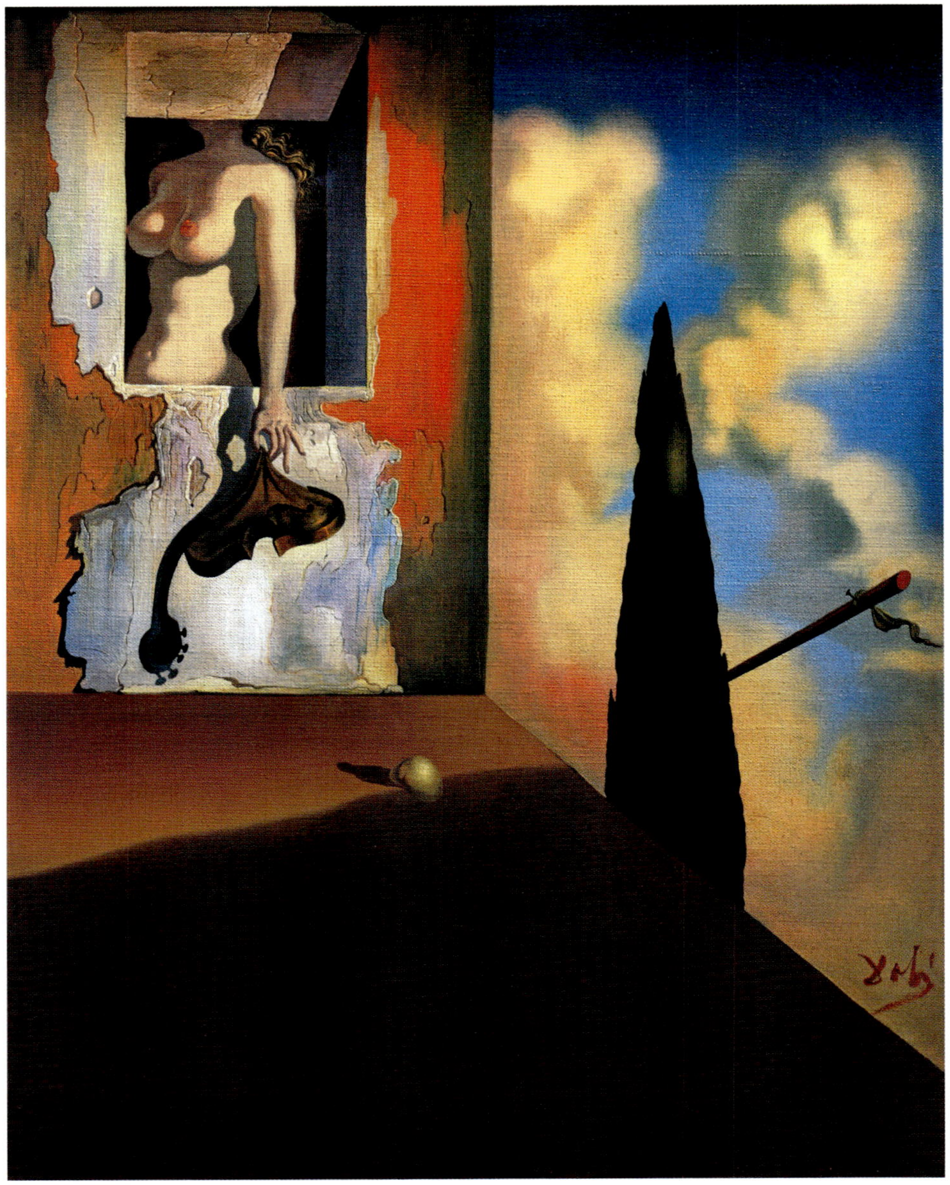

in Virginia. There were other house guests when they arrived – among them Henry Miller (1891–1980) and Anaïs Nin (1903–77) – but Gala had soon reorganized the running of the house to accommodate Dalí's needs, with Crosby's apparent acquiescence. Gala was not much liked by the other guests, but then in the eyes of some she was very well-matched to Dalí in both cruelty and selfishness. It was here, at Crosby's considerable indulgence, that Dalí wrote *The Secret Life of Salvador Dalí*. Its immediate success persuaded him to write his only novel, *Hidden Faces* (1944), a baroque tale featuring a group of aristocrats – the kind of people he had rubbed shoulders with in Paris before the war. His father had once told Dalí he would be a better writer than painter, but having read the novel most critics seemed to disagree, decrying the absence of the discipline and well-defined form that he brought to his painting. In a similar way, in *The Secret Life* the flamboyant subjectivity of his prose, while often funny and sometimes insightful, is also often tediously and sometimes tastelessly self-absorbed.

Indeed, while in response to the fiasco of *The Dream of Venus* Dalí was justified in issuing his 'Declaration of the Independence of the Imagination and the Rights of Man to His Own Madness', his critics were equally well-grounded in excoriating his egomania in the context of the wars he had fled – the habitual narcissism he was only able to continue indulging by virtue of being in the US and which put off many critics who read *The Secret Life*. Perhaps the

(Above)

Masochistic Instrument, c. 1934

Medium: Oil on canvas
Dimensions: 62 x 47 cm (24⅜ x 18½ in)
Location: Private Collection

(Right)

Daddy Long-Legs of the Evening – Hope!, 1940

Medium: Oil on canvas
Dimensions: 40.5 x 50.8 cm (16 x 20 in)
Location: Salvador Dalí Museum, St Petersburg, Florida

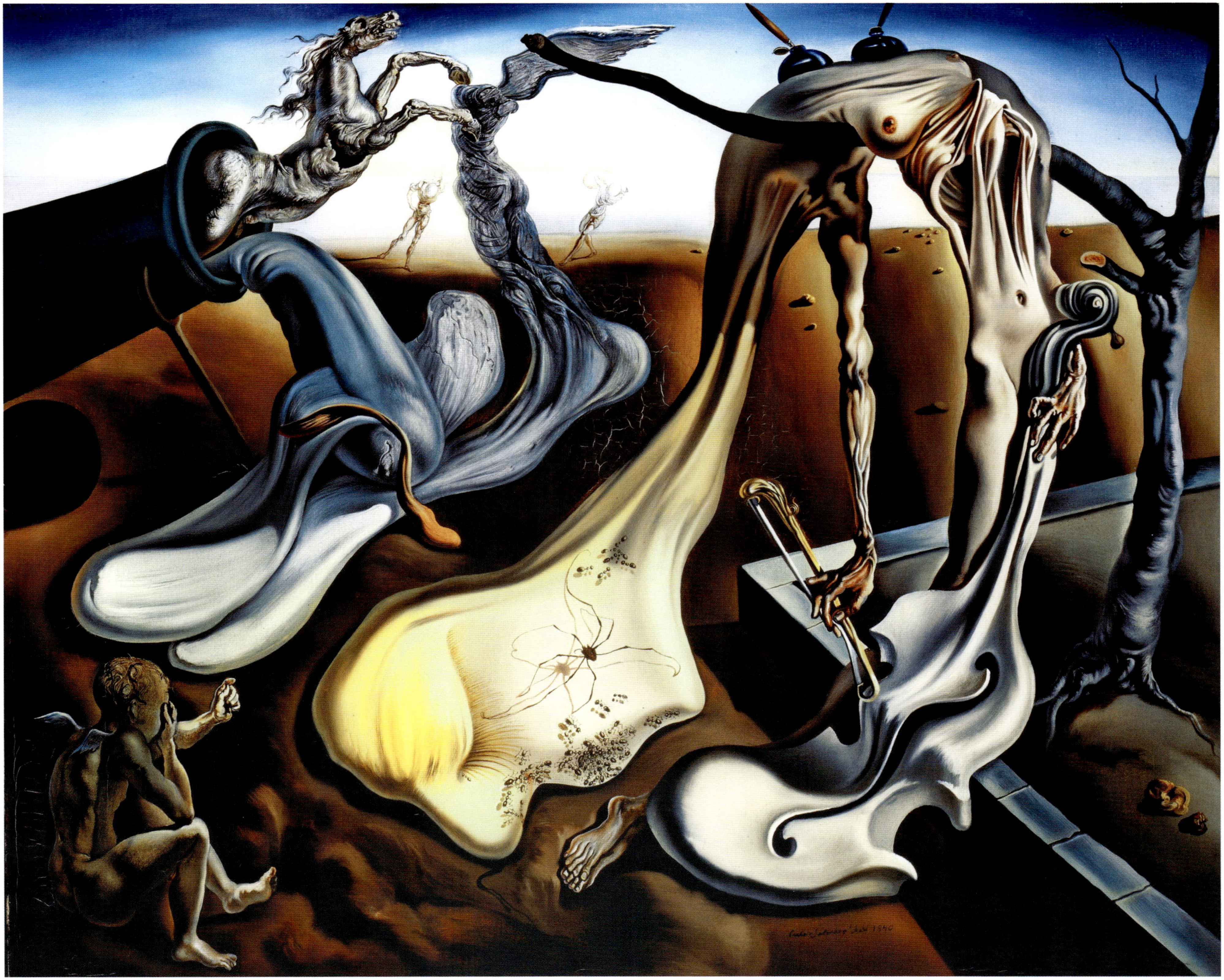

best-known of these reviews is the essay by George Orwell (1903–50), 'Benefit of Clergy: Some Notes on Salvador Dalí' (1944), in which he describes *The Secret Life* as 'a book that stinks' and, famously, the man who wrote it as 'a good draughtsman and a disgusting human being'. Indeed, Orwell called Dalí's paintings 'an unmistakable assault on sanity and decency' – a point which the painter of the 1930s no doubt would have gleefully conceded – before continuing that a society in which people like Dalí can flourish 'has something wrong with it'.

New World, New Patrons

Dalí flourished in the United States like never before, and as American society would be the blueprint of the post-war West, then for better or worse Dalí – 'a symptom of the world's illness', according to Orwell – may well have been the prophet he often claimed he was. Even in the early 1940s, he found countless admirers and could pick and choose his favourite projects to pursue. One of these was his ballet *Labyrinth* (1941), based on the legend of Theseus and Ariadne, choreographed by Léonide Massine (1896–1979) for the Ballets Russes and staged at the Metropolitan Opera in New York. The reconstructed backcloth from that production now hangs impressively in the Dalí Theatre-Museum in Figueres (*see* page 179), although the ballet itself was not a success.

'The Surrealist object is one that is absolutely useless from the practical and rational point of view.'

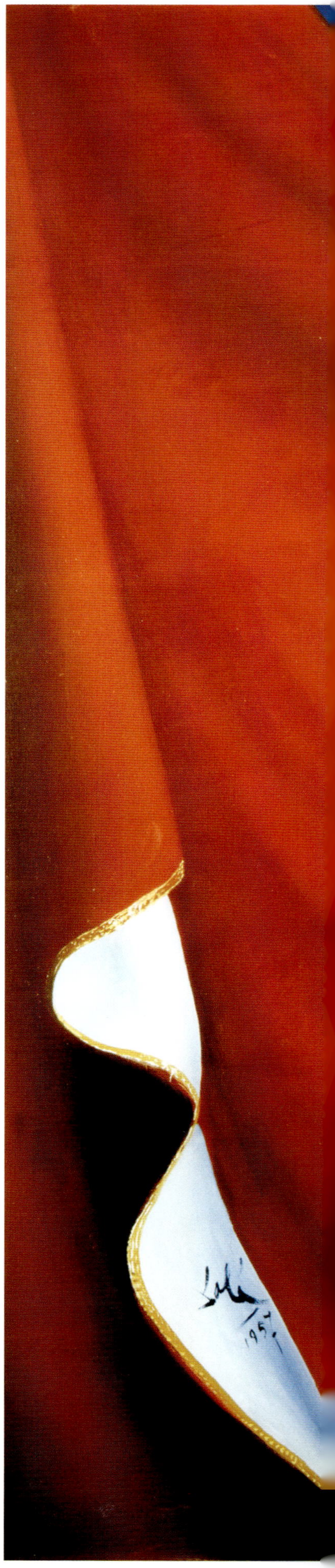

(Right)

Red Orchestra, 1957

Medium: Oil on canvas
Dimensions: 84 x 115.5 cm (33 x 45½ in)
Location: Nahmad Collection, Switzerland

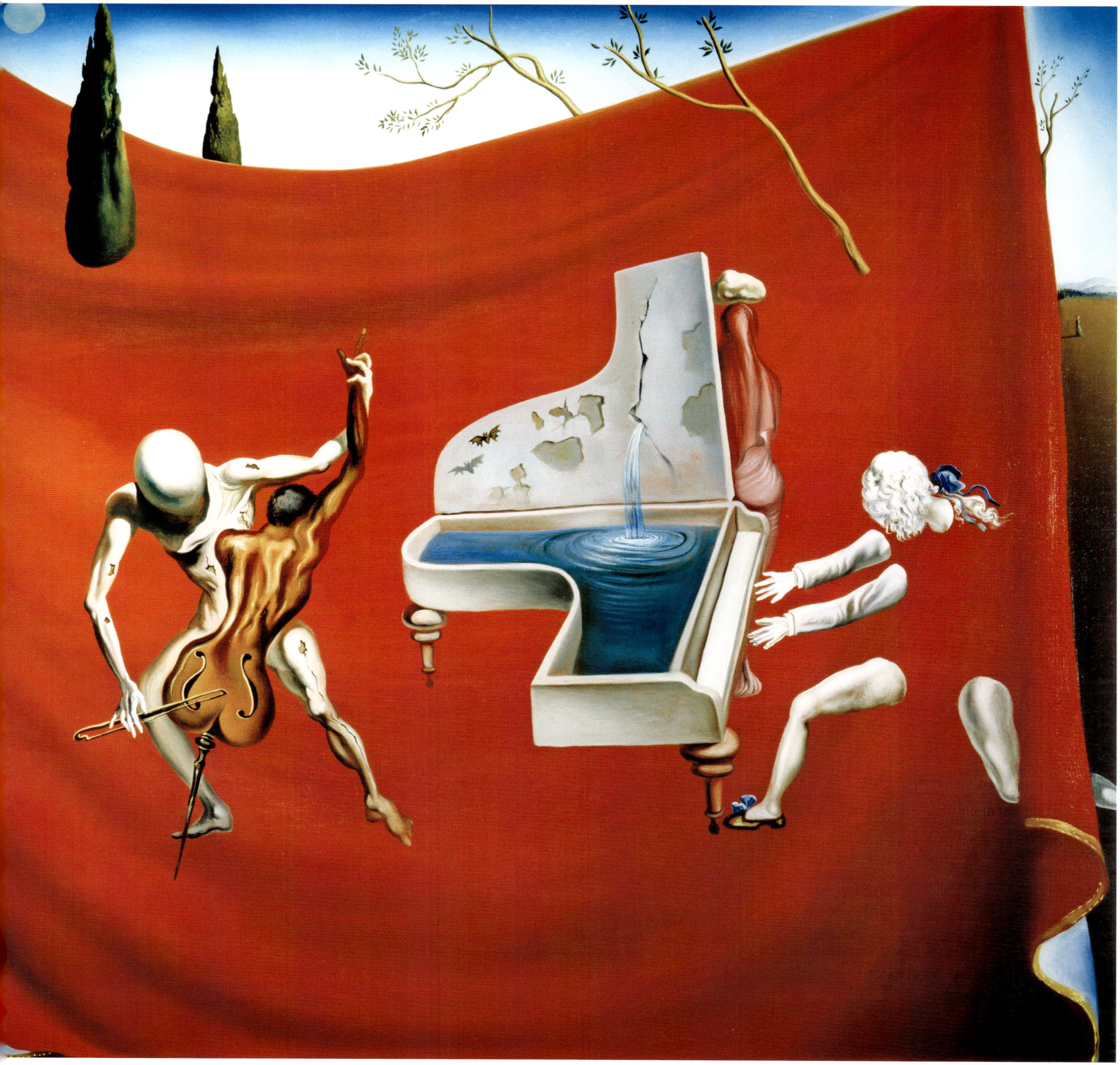

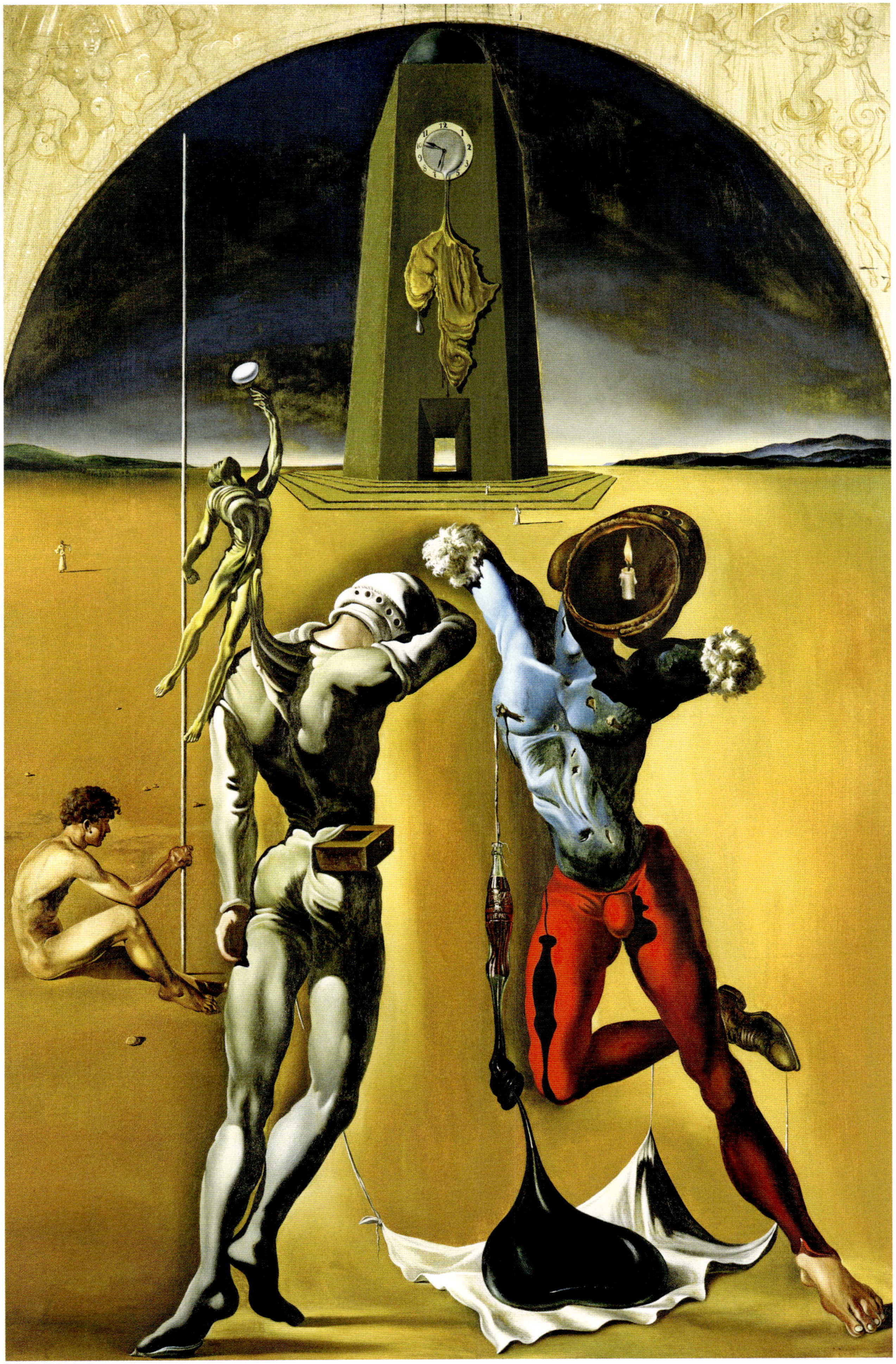

This was due partly to the times. Although not at war until the attack on Pearl Harbor at the end of the year, the US was already feeling the economic effects of the conflict in Europe, and sales of paintings had diminished. So the retrospective of Dalí's work, along with that of his fellow Catalan and Surrealist Joan Miró at the Museum of Modern Art, which opened in November 1941, as well as being notable recognition of the status the 37-year-old artist already enjoyed in the US was also a timely reminder of his talent to potential buyers. After New York, the exhibition toured various cities across America, and it was in Cleveland that a young couple named Reynolds (1914–2000) and Eleanor Morse (1912–2010) came across it. They were duly bowled over and by 1942 had acquired their first Dalí, *Daddy Long-Legs of the Evening – Hope!* (1940, *see* page 119). Over the following four decades the Morses would amass perhaps the greatest collection of Dalí's paintings anywhere in the world, now

(Left)

Poetry of America, 1943

Medium: Oil on canvas
Dimensions: 116 x 79 cm ($45\frac{2}{3}$ x 31 in)
Location: Town Hall of Figueres, on permanent deposit at the Fundació Gala-Salvador Dalí, Figueres

housed in the Salvador Dalí Museum in St Petersburg, Florida. But even in wartime, Dalí, abetted by the dogged business acumen of his wife, could count on multiple sources of income in his temporary home.

Portraits and *Pompiers*

Among the most lucrative kind of work was painting society portraits of some of America's leading industrialists and their spouses – works to which Dalí's formidable representational technique very often contributes a slickness that reminds us why the modernist revolution came about in the first place. In fact, Dalí had already declared his aim, 'TO BECOME CLASSIC!', as he put it in his essay, 'The Last Scandal of Salvador Dalí' (1941), to give the public, 'which was beginning to grow weary of the continuous cult of strangeness, [the] reality and classicism' he felt it was crying out for. In pursuit of this aim he turned increasingly for inspiration to several mid- and late nineteenth-century French academic painters such as William-Adolphe Bouguereau (1825–1905) and, above all, Jean-Louis-Ernest Meissonier (1815–91). The style of these *pompier* painters, as they had derisively come to be known, was being eclipsed by Impressionism even during their own lifetimes, and by 1940 they were almost totally forgotten. But Dalí was apparently sincere in his admiration, and indeed works he owned by Bouguereau and Meissonier, among others from that generation who had painted in a similar style, were treasured items in Dalí's personal collection and can still be seen today at the Theatre-Museum in Figueres.

'America ... threw dollars at my head like handfuls of confetti.'

Added to this apparent retreat into aesthetic conservatism, Dalí's continuing dalliance with the world of advertising and entertainment aroused the ire and perhaps the envy of other artists. As well as more sets and costumes for ballet productions, he also produced ad campaigns for stockings, cosmetics and other consumer products, featuring the arsenal of motifs the public were already aware of from his paintings. There were also a number of commissions for book illustrations, a very lucrative source of income with mixed results but which at their best do show a lyrical and poetic side to Dalí. And then there were the afore-mentioned collaborations with Hitchcock and Disney, which ultimately came to disappoint him.

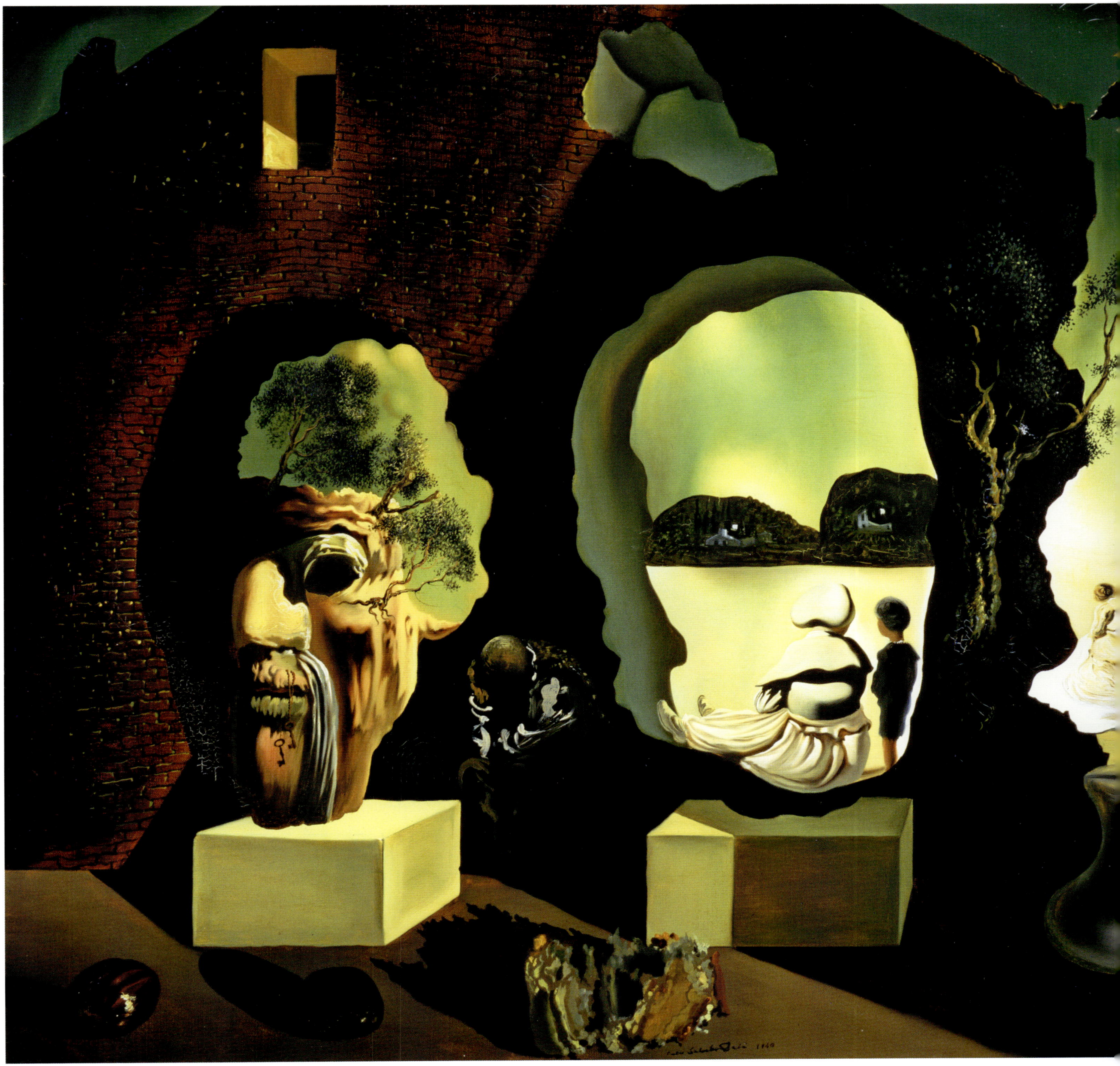

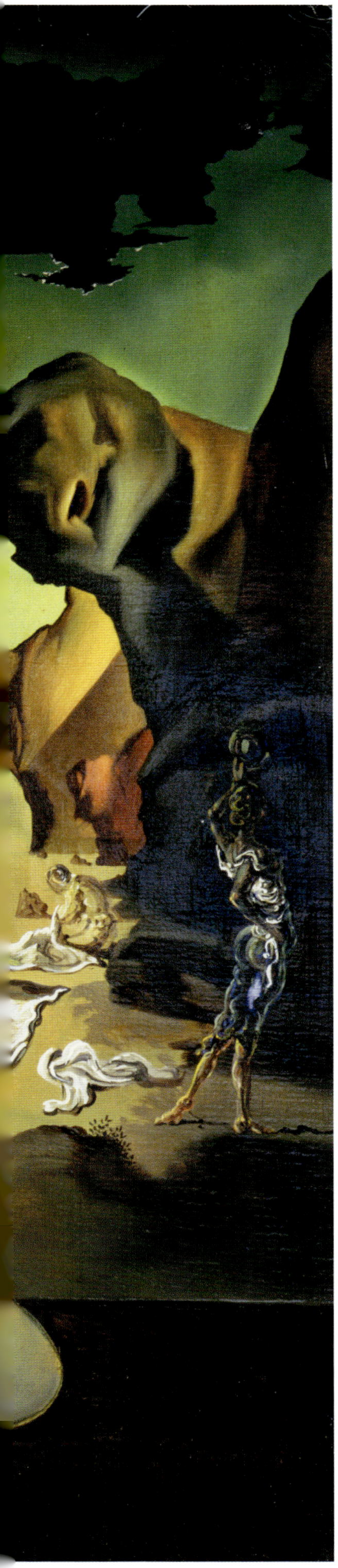

'I have always had the gift of manipulating and of dominating with ease the slightest reaction of people who surround me.'

Surrealist for Hire

There is no doubt that Dalí enjoyed the chance to impose his talent in different spheres of activity, especially if that meant an opportunity to show off to the press, but there was also a fairly naked desire on his part, driven by the avaricious Gala, to make as much money as possible in a country where such an ambition was seen as a virtue. Dalí was particularly struck by Helena Rubinstein (1872–1965), the cosmetics magnate who boasted constantly about her wealth, whom in a portrait he depicted emerging like a Mount Rushmore Madonna from the rocks of Cadaqués. That he set his sitters so often in one of his childhood landscapes no doubt speaks of his homesickness, though the subjects themselves were not universally pleased with the results.

At the same time as all these money-spinning ventures, Dalí also continued to paint more serious works, such as *Poetry of America* (1943, *see* page 122), which with its flaccid continent of Africa dangling, almost lynched, from the clock tower, and a Coca-Cola bottle that metamorphoses into a telephone, which in turn bleeds into a black pool on the ground, seems to offer a commentary on the human cost of America's wealth and on race relations in the country in an era when the Jim Crow laws were still in force. Equally, *Geopolitical Child Watching the Birth of the New Man* (1943, *see* page 127) is clearly a commentary on the struggle then taking place

(Left)

Old Age, Adolescence, Infancy (The Three Ages), 1940

Medium: Oil on canvas
Dimensions: 49.8 x 65 cm (19¾ x 25⅝ in)
Location: Salvador Dalí Museum, St Petersburg, Florida

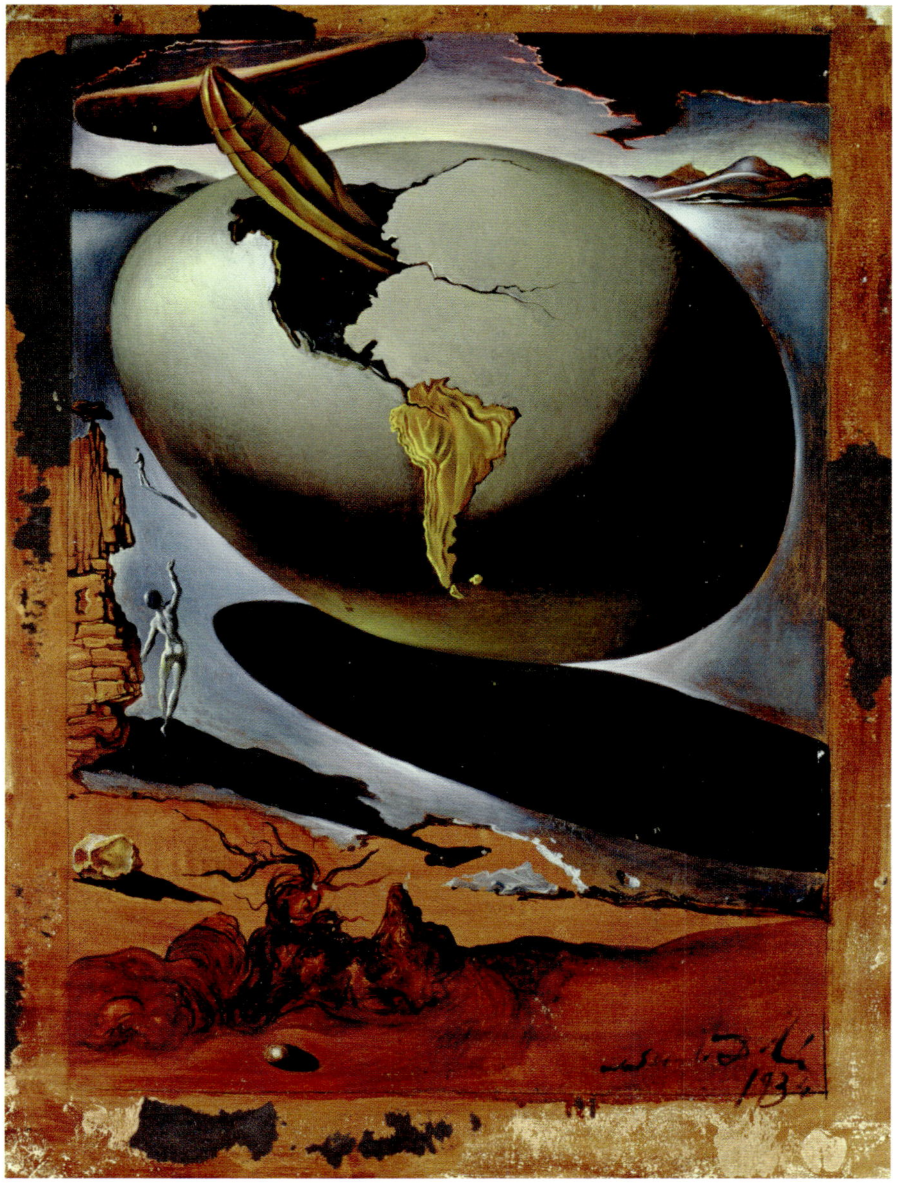

in Europe, though who or what he thought the 'New Man' emerging from the egg was likely to be is hard to say.

New Directions

These were paintings betraying new concerns and the glimmers of a social conscience that was so manifestly missing from Dalí's public statements. In doing so, they also introduced new motifs into his visual lexicon, a trend that continued with *Dream Caused by the Flight of a Bee Around a Pomegranate One Second Before Awakening* (1944, *see* page 128). One of his most popular works, and one which signalled the first inkling of a wholly new direction, Dalí described it thus: 'For the first time, Freud's discovery that a typical narrative dream is prompted by something that wakes us was illustrated in a picture. If a bar falls on a sleeper's neck, it both wakes him and prompts a long dream that ends with the falling of the guillotine; similarly, the buzzing of the bee in the painting prompts the bayonet prick that wakens Gala. The burst pomegranate gives birth to the entirety of biological creation. Bernini's elephant in the background bears an obelisk with the papal insignia.' It is a typical Dalínian cocktail of different ideas thrust together with Surrealist illogic. But, in fact, the sheer variety of concerns reveals it as a pivotal work in his intellectual journey, looking both backwards and forwards at once.

(Above)

Allegory of an American Christmas, 1934

Medium: Oil on cardboard
Dimensions: 40.5 x 30.5 cm (26 x 22 in)
Location: Private Collection

(Right)

Geopolitical Child Watching the Birth of the New Man, 1943

Medium: Oil on canvas
Dimensions: 45.5 x 50 cm (18 x 20½ in)
Location: Salvador Dalí Museum, St Petersburg, Florida

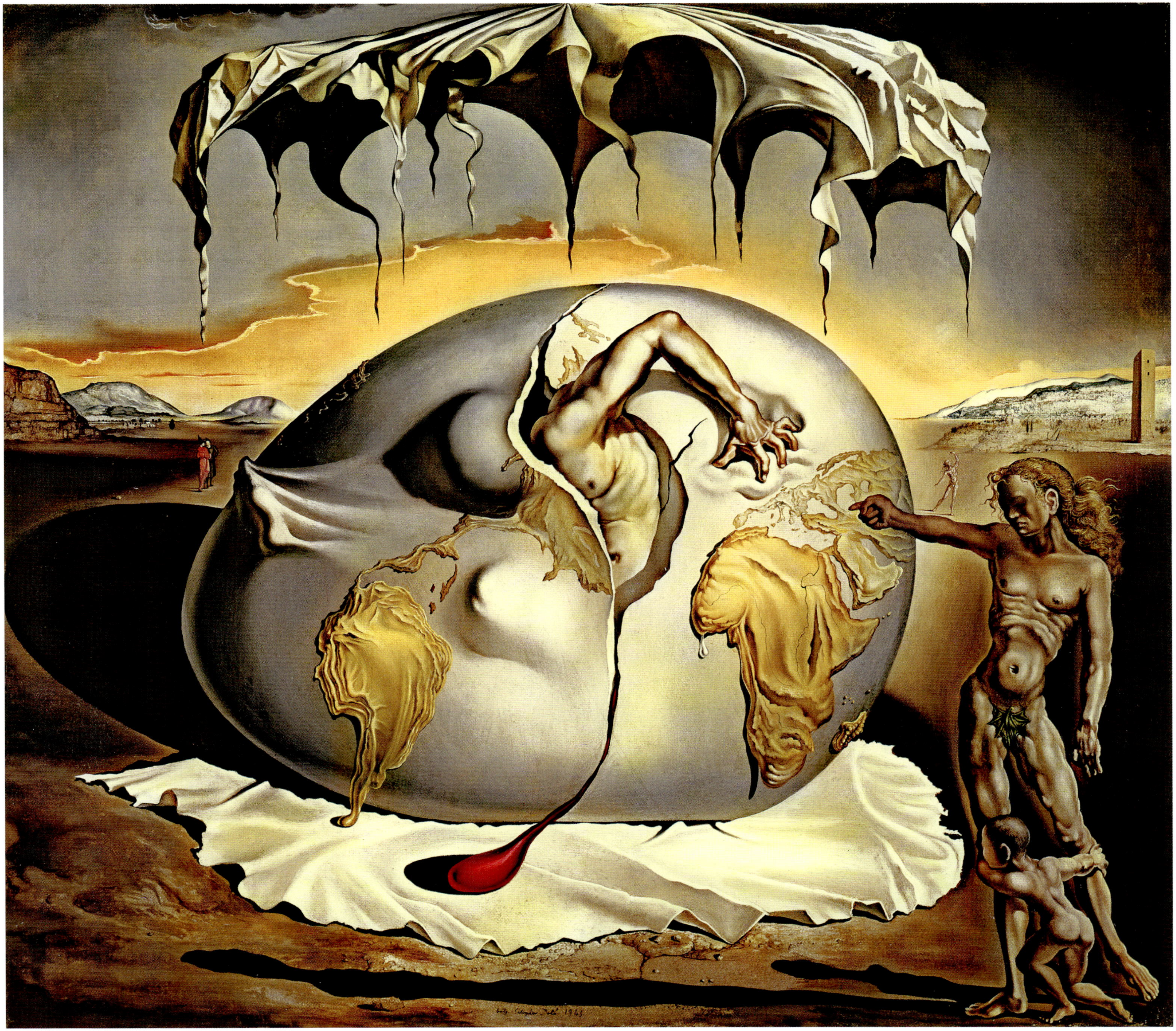

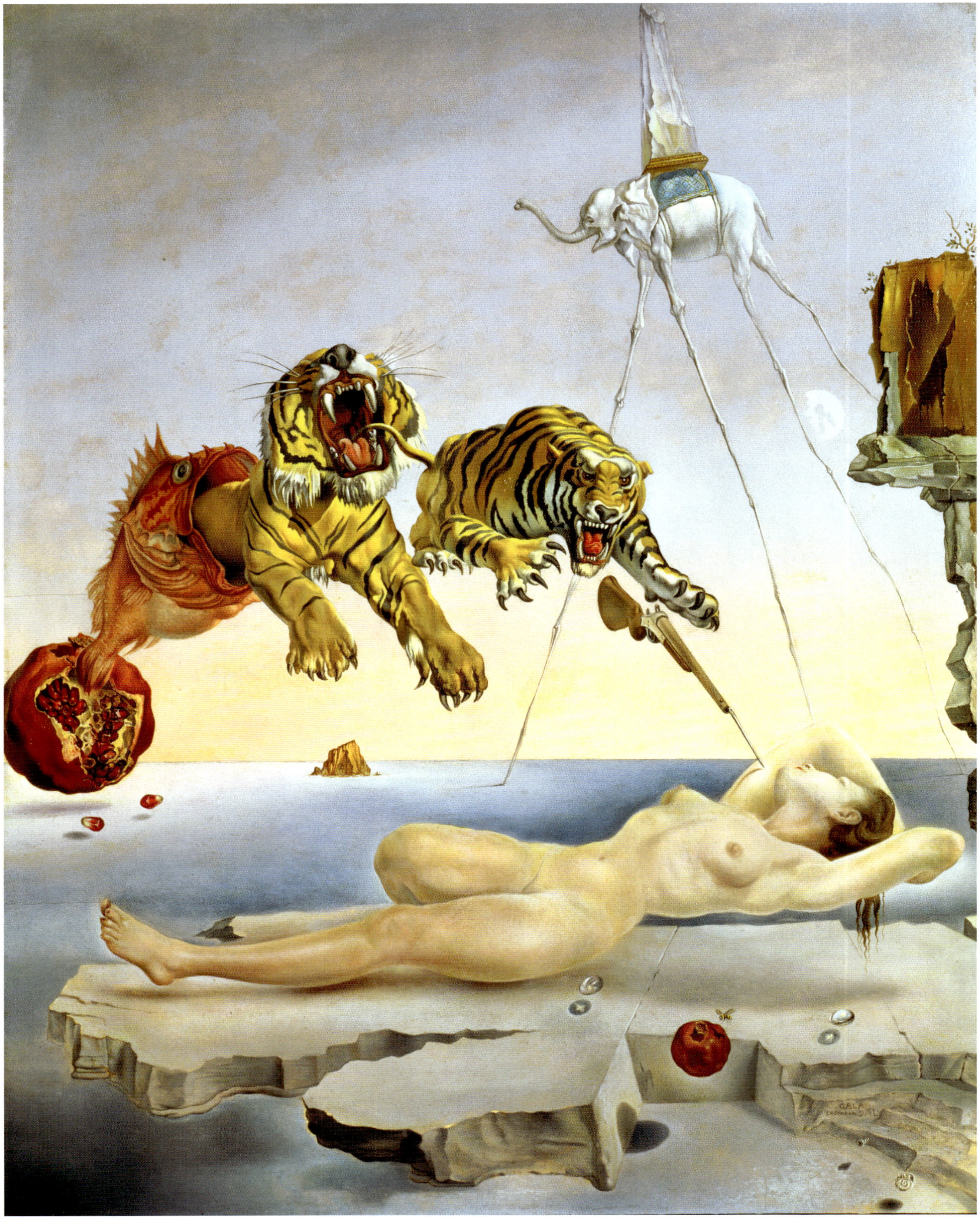

Meeting with Freud

Freud had been central to Dalí's methods for nigh on two decades, with the unresolved fetishes gradually giving way to the more conscious symbolism of *Metamorphosis of Narcissus* in 1937 (*see* pages 100–01). It was this work that Dalí had taken with him to London the following year on the one occasion he met the father of psychoanalysis through the persistent agency of the writer, Stefan Zweig (1881–1942). Zweig had insisted to Freud that Dalí was 'the only painter of genius of our epoch, and the only one who will survive'. The Surrealists in general acknowledged a debt to Freud, although this had become less important in the political 1930s, but the elderly Viennese told Zweig afterwards in a letter that he had always regarded them as '100 per cent fools'. Dalí, however, was a different proposition, with Freud conceding that the 'young Spaniard, with his ingenuous fanatical eyes, and his undoubtedly technically perfect mastership, has suggested to me a different estimate'.

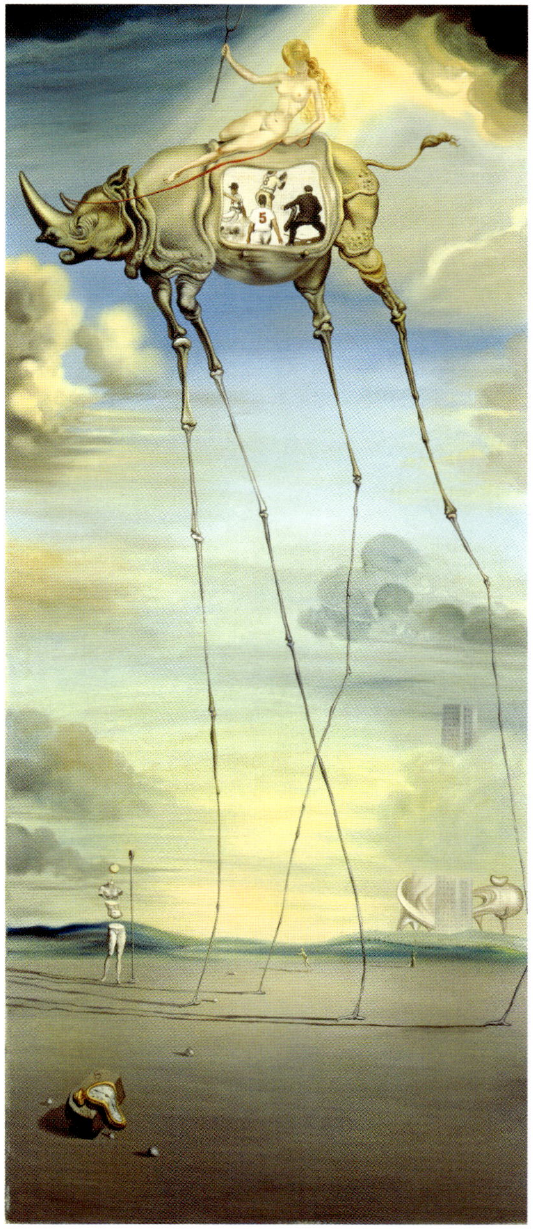

Dalí had sketched the great psychoanalyst as they sat together with Zweig and Edward James, who had also come along. Freud looked at the painting, which seemed to draw so closely on his own ideas, pronouncing after some deliberation that 'in classic painting I look for the sub-conscious – in a Surrealist painting, for the conscious'.

It was a sharp distinction that even then had chimed with the way Dalí was thinking. A few years later, in *The Secret Life*, he is confirmed in his new course, steering away from his 'Surrealist glory', which by then he viewed as 'worthless', convinced by the destructiveness of war that all revolutions were futile and that only a return to tradition could restore the order that was lost. Moreover, in Dalí's mind the tradition was one that only he, 'the most representative incarnation of post-war Europe', could achieve, according to his newfound priorities. These priorities he described as 'The conquest of all, the systematic interpretation of all metaphysics, of all philosophy, and of all science,

(Left)

Dream Caused by the Flight of a Bee Around a Pomegranate One Second Before Awakening, 1944

Medium: Oil on panel
Dimensions: 51 x 41 cm (20 x 16 in)
Location: Thyssen-Bornemisza Collection, Madrid

(Above)

Celestial Ride, 1957

Medium: Oil on canvas
Dimensions: 188 x 84 cm (74 x 33 in)
Location: Private Collection

according to the fund of Catholic tradition which alone the rigour of the critical-paranoiac method would be capable of reviving.'

Dream Caused by the Flight of a Bee

It was a typically immodest undertaking, but in *Dream Caused by the Flight of a Bee* (see page 128) we see a full range of Dalí's major intellectual concerns from both the interwar years (the 'post-war' period he refers to in *The Secret Life*) and the years after the Second World War. To the Freudian dream and its irrational symbolic content is added the reference to the Catholic Counter-Reformation in the form of the elephant with the Egyptian obelisk of Bernini, which he had seen in the Piazza della Minerva in Rome, although in the painting (as in the similar piece of jewellery he made a decade later) the poor pachyderm is given spiders' legs, which the painter once referred to as 'multijointed, almost invisible legs of desire'. But there is also a further element that would become as important as that of religion over the coming years, which can be seen not only in the reclining nude but also in the variety of smaller objects that surround her, as well as the giant pomegranate that hovers above the sea. Nothing is touching; not only these objects but the girl and even the rock beneath her seem suspended in mid-air. Although Dalí had not yet declared his interest, the atomic revolution was already a presence in this work. But the most pivotal element of all was

'The atomic explosion of 6 August 1945 shook me seismically.'

the change in mood it represents, away from the nightmarish, still hallucinatory images of even the previous year, towards a whimsical fantasy world, bleached of any paranoiac element, in which tigers are mere pussycats and the predominant colouring is a celestial, Marian blue.

Leda Atomica

In part this was due to Dalí's shift towards Classicism and 'the unique splendour of the Catholic faith'. He had already declared as much in *The Secret Life*, but in addition he seems to have intuited the coming of a new understanding of the world, which may have seemed theoretical at best in 1944 but would soon become horribly real with the dropping of the atom bomb on Hiroshima in August the following year. It was an event which he claimed 'shook me seismically', but beyond explicit references to the destructiveness of nuclear power, such as

(Right)

Leda Atomica, 1949

Medium: Oil on canvas
Dimensions: 61 x 46 cm (24 x 18 in)
Location: Fundació Gala-Salvador Dalí, Figueres

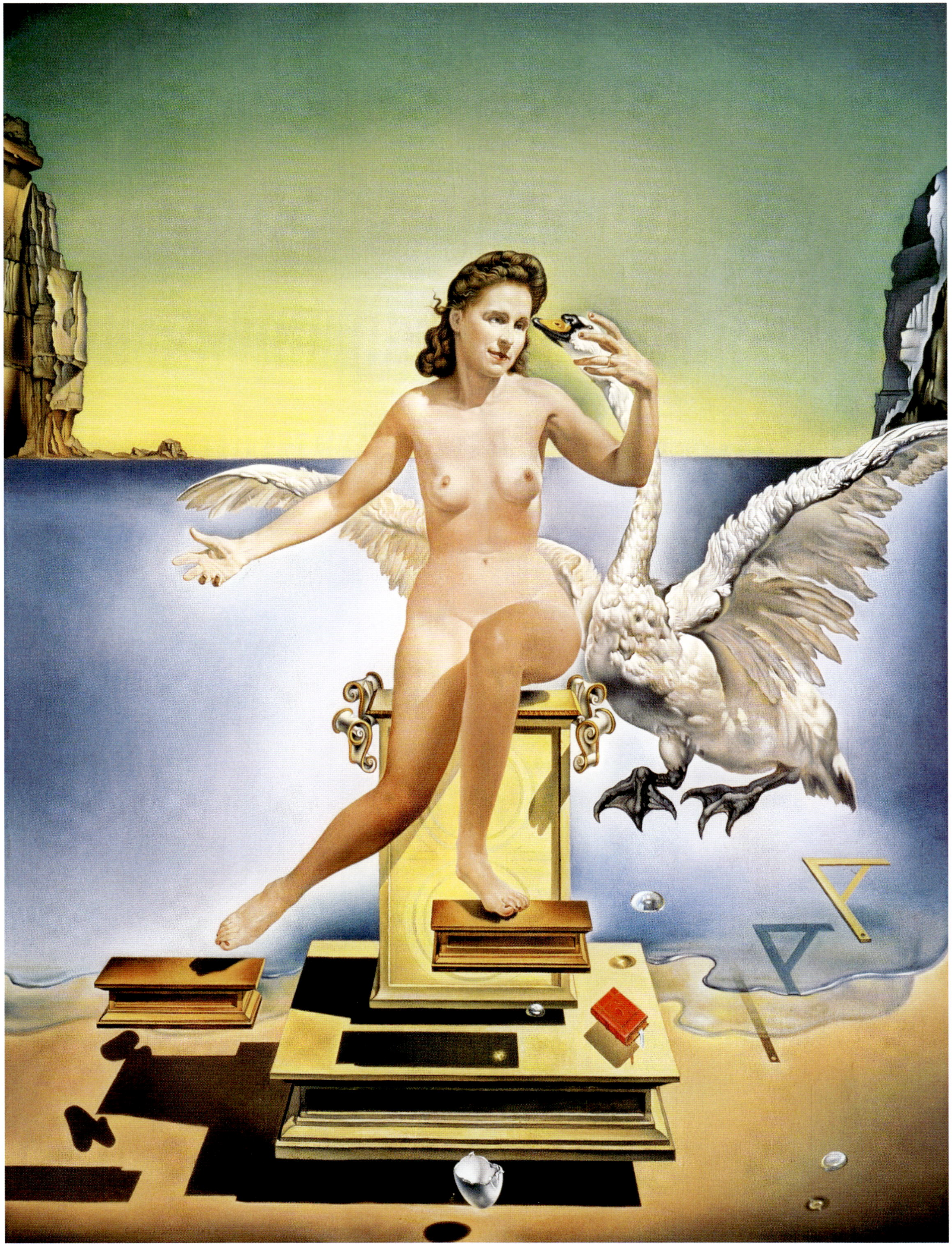

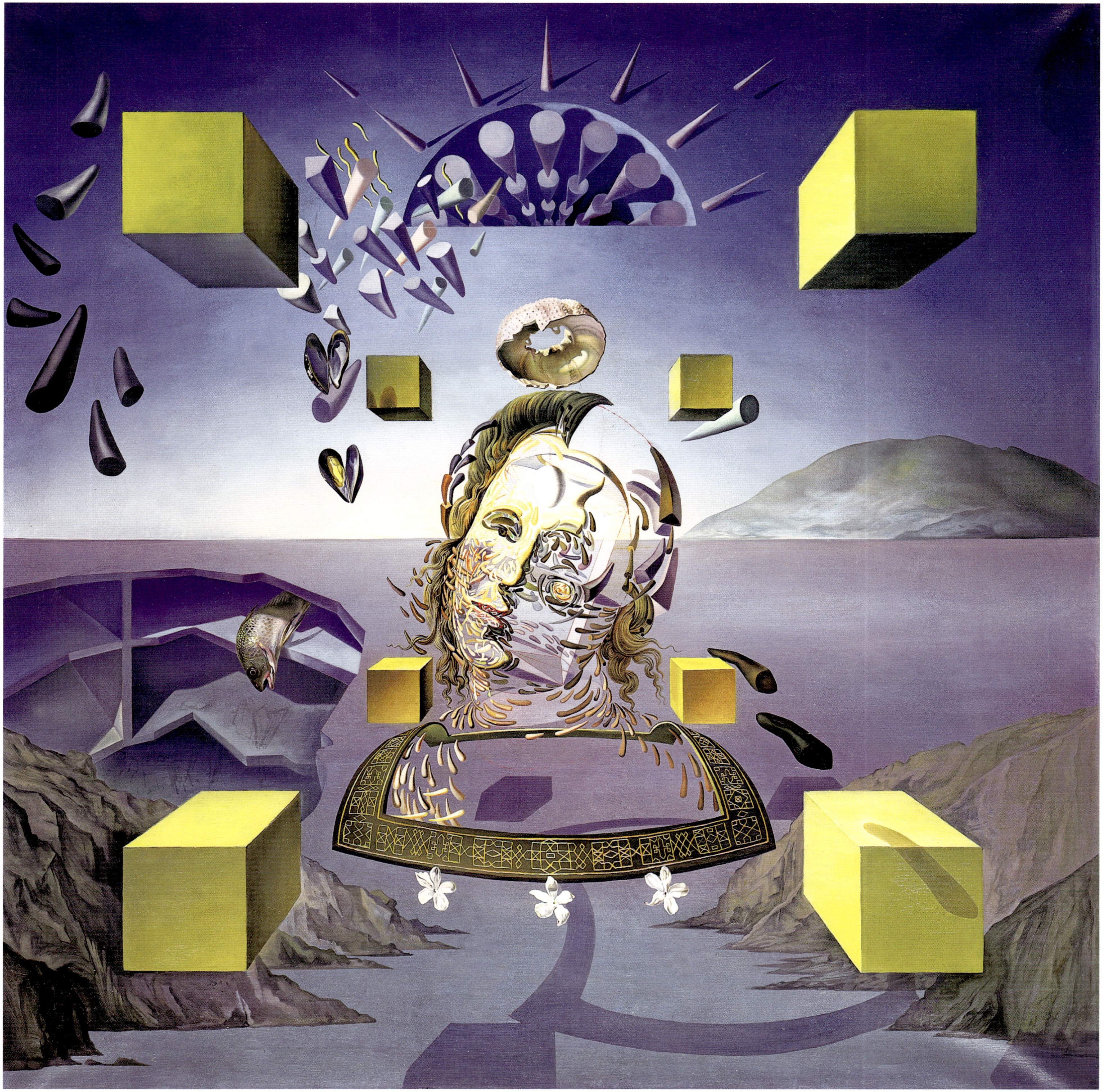

The Three Sphinxes of Bikini (1947), Dalí developed a more subtle, optimistic understanding of the new view of the fundamental forces of the universe already manifest in *Dream Caused by the Flight of a Bee*. This is made explicit in a work, *Leda Atomica* (1949, *see* page 131), whose first version he painted in 1947, for which he wrote the following detailed explanation: 'The sea is for the first time represented as not touching the earth; that is, one could easily put one's arm between the sea and the shore without getting wet. Therein resides, I believe, the imaginative quality which has determined the treatment of one of the most mysterious and eternal of those myths in which the "human and the divine" have crystallized through animality.

'Instead of the confusion of feathers and flesh to which we have been accustomed by the traditional iconography on this subject, with its insistence on the entanglement of the swan's neck and the arms of Leda, Dalí shows us the hierarchized libidinous emotion, suspended and as though hanging in mid-air, in accordance with the modern "nothing touches" theory of intra-atomic physics.

'Leda does not touch the swan; Leda does not touch the pedestal; the pedestal does not touch the base; the base does not touch the sea; the sea does not touch the shore. Herein resides, I believe, the separation of the elements earth and water, which is at the root of the creative mystery of animality.'

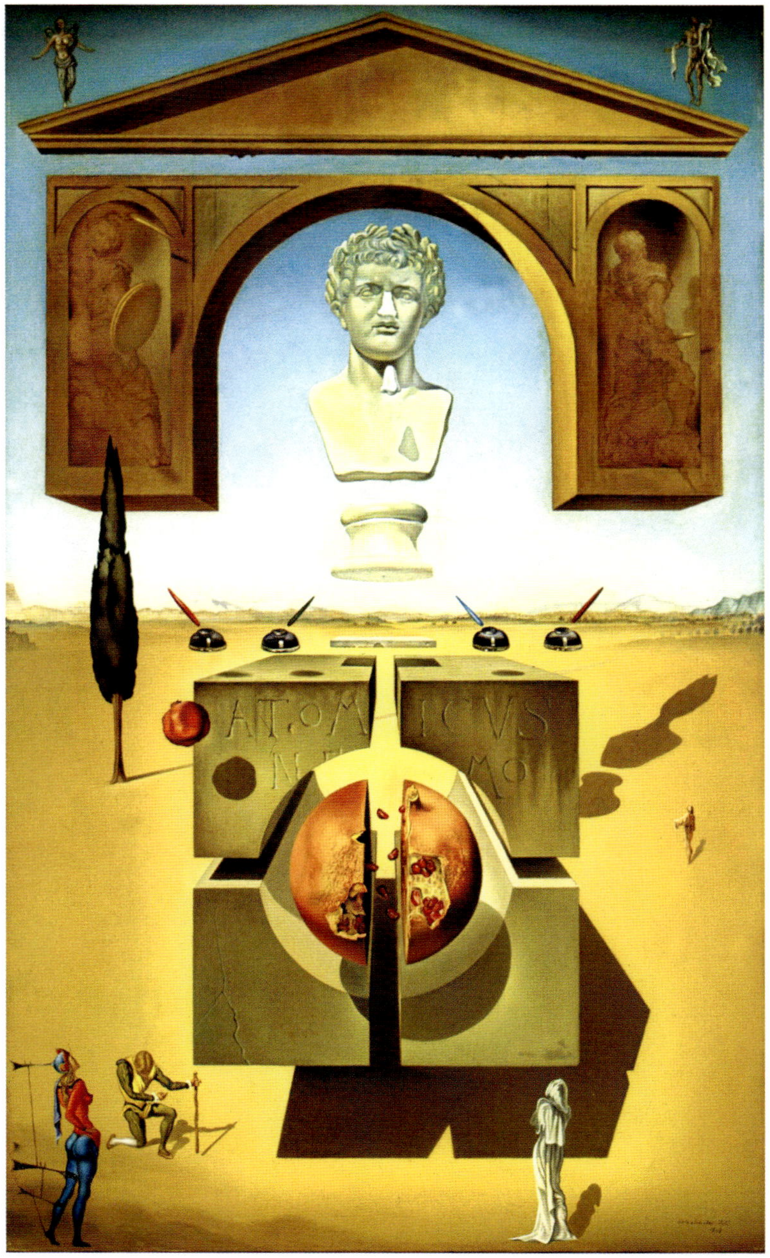

(Left)

Galatea, *c.* 1954

Medium: Oil on canvas
Dimensions: 100.6 x 101 cm (39⅝ x 39¾ in)
Location: Private Collection

(Above)

Dematerialization Near the Nose of Nero, 1947

Medium: Oil on canvas
Dimensions: 76.5 x 46 cm (30 x 18 in)
Location: Fundació Gala-Salvador Dalí, Figueres

A Mystical Manifesto

Although Gala as Leda is nude in this painting, the sense of 'nothing touches' – a weightlessness whose only approximate models might be the Renaissance examples, especially Raphael, that Dalí was increasingly consulting – drains away the eroticism, the animality, normally associated with paintings of this subject. In that regard, the painting exudes such an air of serenity that atomic physics seems to have been fused with some other influence, perhaps a religious sentiment, lending the whole work a veneer of grace normally associated with the Renaissance; indeed, Dalí insisted that it was in the Renaissance 'that the means of pictorial expression were invented once and for all and with the maximum of perfection and visual effectiveness'. Those words come from his 'Mystical Manifesto' (1951), in which he argues that the 'decadence of modern painting comes from scepticism and lack of belief' (never mind that scepticism is at the heart of the scientific method of whose discoveries he was now so in awe) and that 'if a powerful Renaissance of mystical painting has not yet begun, it is due to the fact that the artists [are] this time very late in relation to today's scientific progress'. Seeing the new physics, in particular the quantum world, as scientific confirmation of the spiritual pieties espoused by the Church, Dalí now sought to unite them in a new philosophy which he called 'nuclear mysticism'.

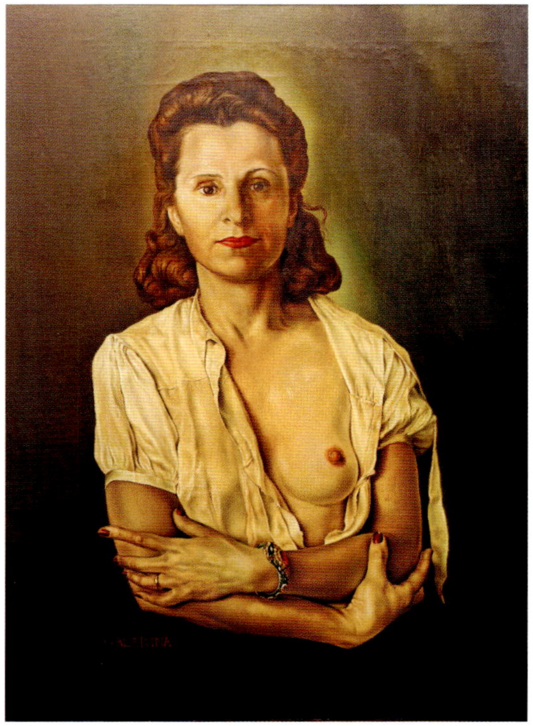

A Need for Order

What are we to make of Dalí's growing religious inclinations? A lifelong atheist, he is not unique in having changed his mind on religion in mid-life, though he did confess that he was only able to aspire to faith, unable to feel it naturally; this is hardly surprising in someone so self-centred. In any case, of more importance to Dalí were order, culture and tradition, which the Church could undoubtedly represent, and which already at the end of *The Secret Life* he was looking to religion to provide, long before he had thought of moving back to Europe. In Franco's Spain, it was unwise to do anything that

(Above)

Galarina, 1945

Medium: Oil on canvas
Dimensions: 64 x 50 cm (25⅕ x 19⅗ in)
Location: Fundació Gala-Salvador Dalí, Figueres

(Right)

My Wife, Nude, Contemplating her own Flesh Becoming Stairs, Three Vertebrae of a Column, Sky and Architecture, 1945

Medium: Oil on panel
Dimensions: 61 x 52 cm (24 x 20½ in)
Location: Private Collection

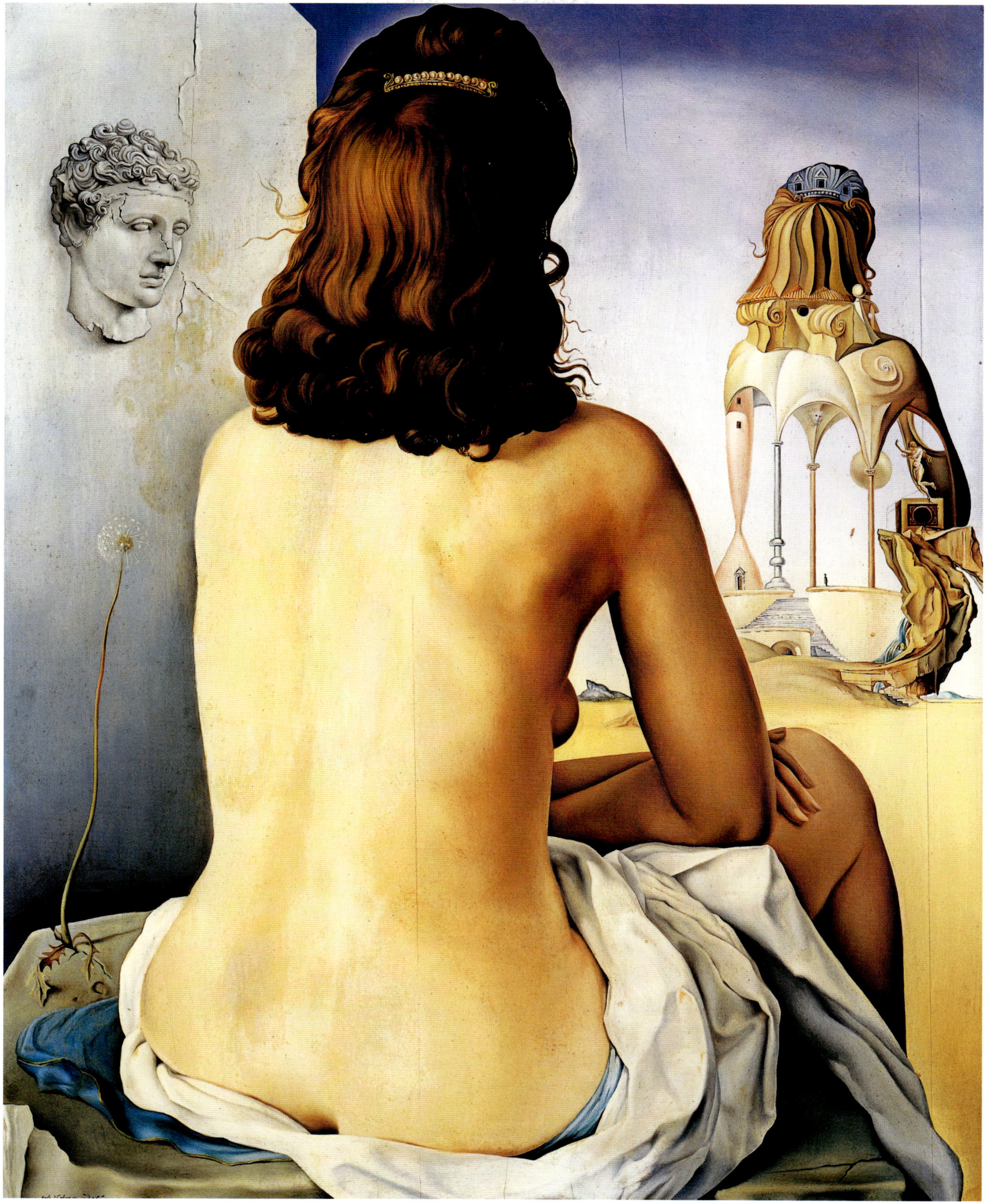

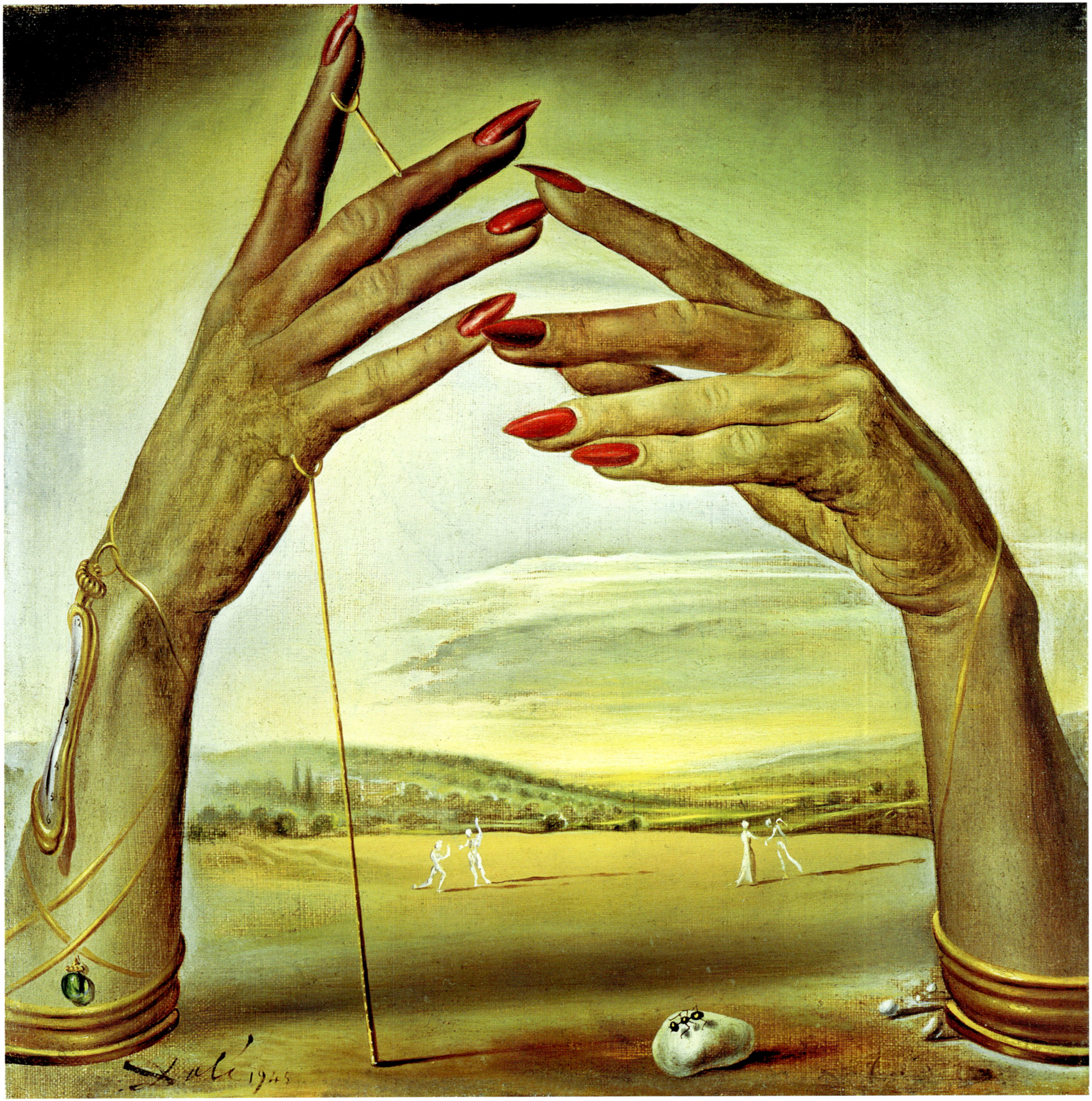
Dalí 1945

departed from the official line; even his father had turned towards the Church at the end of the Civil War, renouncing his own atheist beliefs. But Dalí's call to tradition – not only its historical meaning but its technical means – is not so different from the arguments he had used to dismiss his teachers at the San Fernando Academy in Madrid. What had changed in someone who had always kicked out at all the various father figures in his life was his willingness to swallow the dogmas of the Church and, ultimately, the Spanish State.

The Penitent Painter

In November 1949, Dalí was granted a brief audience with Pope Pius XII (1876–1958) in Rome, from whom he hoped to receive permission to marry Gala in the eyes of the Church. As Gala was a divorcée, the Pope insisted this was not within his gift, though in fact the obstacle would be removed just three years later when Paul Éluard, Gala's former husband, died at the very young age of 57. But Dalí's audience with the Holy Father seemed to be final confirmation to former friends and colleagues of his moral corruption. On hearing of it, André Breton wrote laconically of 'the first Dalí, who disappeared towards 1935 to give way to the personality better known as Avida Dollars, a painter of society portraits who has recently embraced the Catholic faith and "the artistic ideal of the Renaissance", and who now benefits from the felicitations and encouragement of the Pope'. Typically, Dalí greeted with perverse enthusiasm the ingenious anagram that Breton had made of his name, claiming in later years that it made him even richer. It is a position he sought to justify with seemingly infallible capitalist logic in *Diary of a Genius*: 'The simplest way not to have to make any concessions to gold is to have it oneself.'

'The face of my beloved Gala was born of the universal Brownian whirlpool, as the sacred image of the divine.'

It is a nice idea in the abstract, but by the same token those who have gold are often even more desperate to hang on to it. The couple had moved back to Spain in 1948, which by then had endured almost a decade of the repressive dictatorship of

(Left)

Portrait of a Passionate Woman (The Hands), 1945

Medium: Oil on canvas
Dimensions: 60 x 45 cm (23⅝ x 17¾ in)
Location: Private Collection

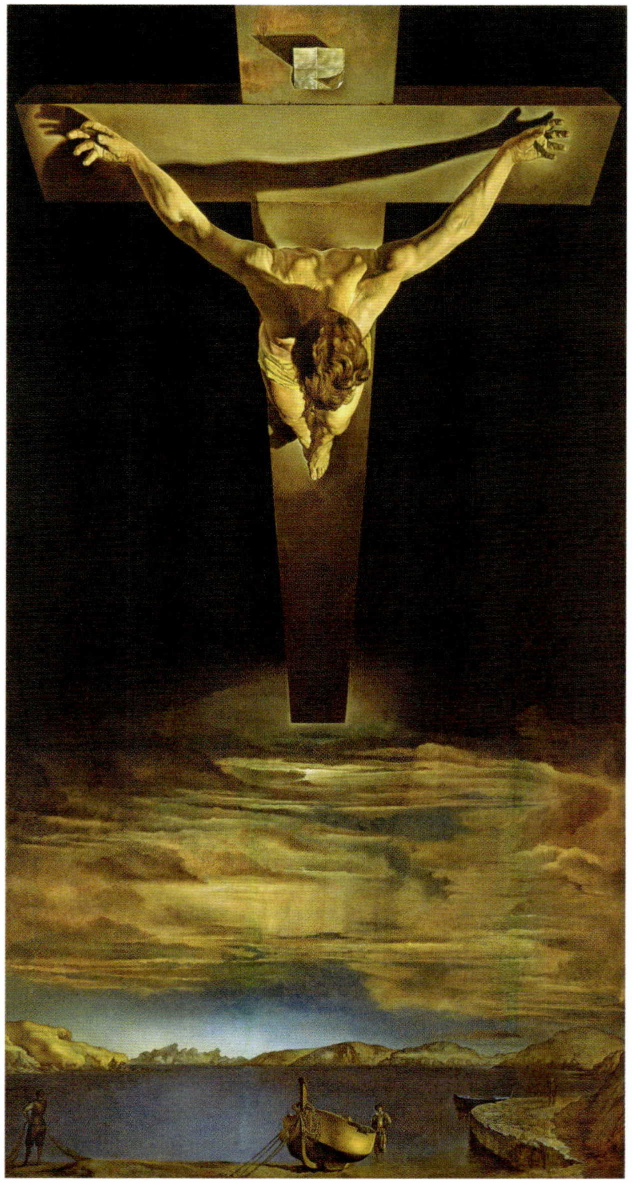

General Franco – a decade the painter had deftly managed to avoid. The government had already seen fit to ban the Argentinian version of *The Secret Life*, and it was not long after his return that Dalí found himself having to explain his past conduct and justify the content of his works. Indeed, despite his 'apolitical, ahistorical' position – what we might describe as an attitude of 'nothing touches' – it may have been the strong influence of the Catholic Church as an arm of the Franco regime that persuaded Dalí to issue decidedly political, historical statements that parroted the official propaganda about Spain's Catholic mission to the world, and led to the slew of religious works that followed over the next decade.

Madonna of Port Lligat

Dalí took the first of these, *Madonna of Port Lligat* (1949), to show the Pope – a Madonna with her midriff missing

> 'I am the Divine Dalí.'

which, according to the painter, Pius XII was inclined to admire. Certainly, the depiction as Madonna of the avaricious and increasingly promiscuous Gala, who wandered bare-breasted around the village and was rumoured to proposition the fishermen when she wanted to have sex, seems utterly preposterous even now; equally, the callous indifference she showed towards her own daughter, Cécile, makes a mockery of Dalí's choice of the Mother of God. The sincerity of the work, then, seems questionable, especially given the absence of faith that he honestly admitted. And it is also possible that beneath the cod reverence of the image, the cunning Catalan peasant he had once declared himself to be was asserting his claim to the

(Left)

Christ of St John of the Cross, 1951

Medium: Oil on canvas
Dimensions: 204.8 x 115.9 cm (80⅝ x 45⅝ in)
Location: Art Gallery and Museum, Kelvingrove, Glasgow

kingship he believed was his due through the supposed divinity of his wife. If she was the Blessed Virgin, what did that make him? Dalí's true motivations were always hidden behind his flamboyant and often contradictory pronouncements deployed deliberately to mystify the public and perhaps even himself. No matter how pithy and well-phrased, no matter how plausible, there is often the sense with Dalí that the dramatic impression his words created was more important than their meaning. As he put it himself to one journalist: 'I am here to confuse and cloud the issue, you to put matters straight.'

The Apotheosis of Gala

In any case, Dalí's need of religion was far less than his need of Gala, who had been so many things to him during their 20-year relationship: lover, mother, manager, muse. He once referred to her in Nietzschean

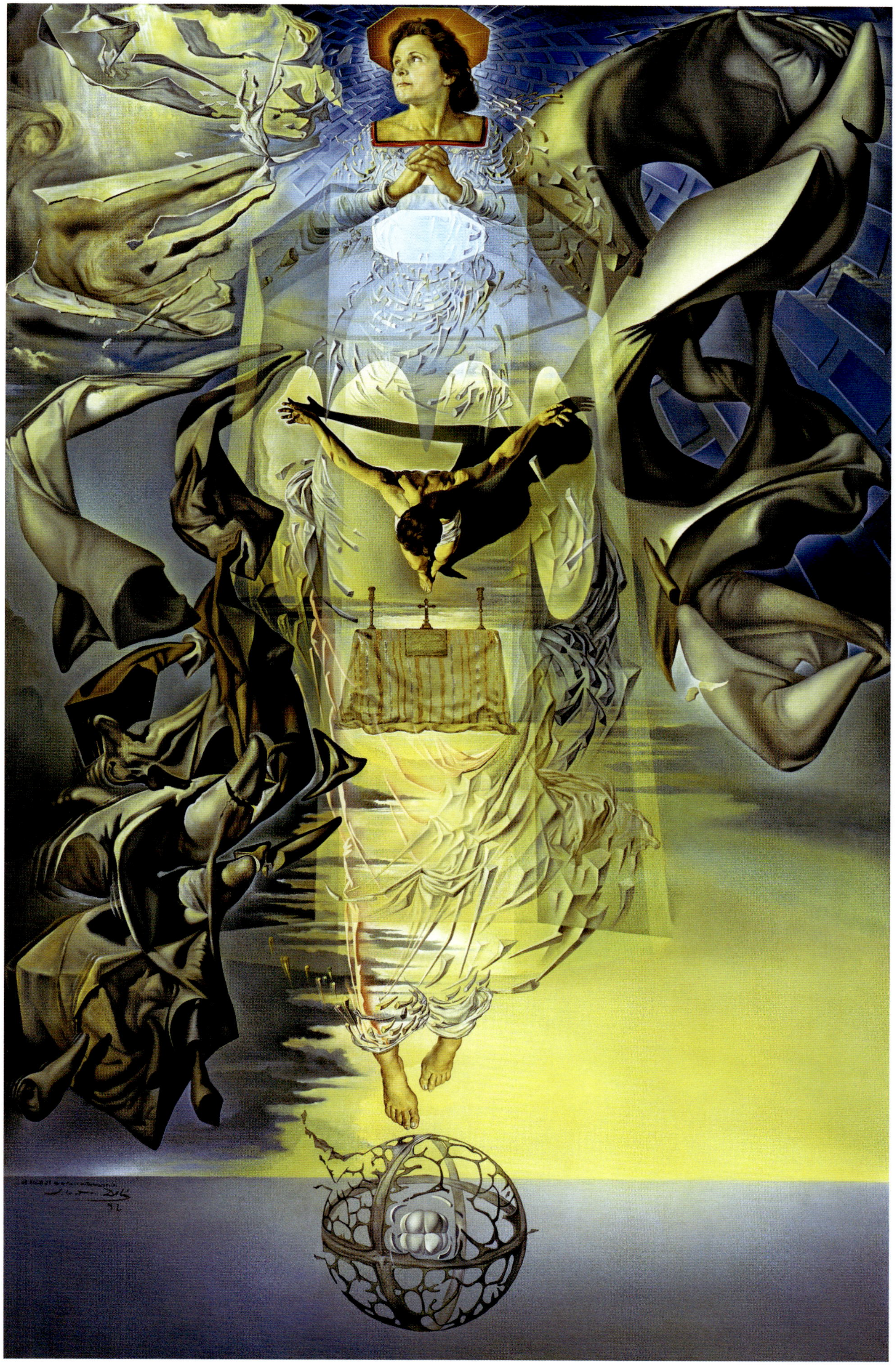

(Right)

Assumpta Corpuscularia Lapislazulina, 1952

Medium: Oil on canvas
Dimensions: 229.9 x 144.2 cm (90½ x 56¾ in)
Location: Private Collection

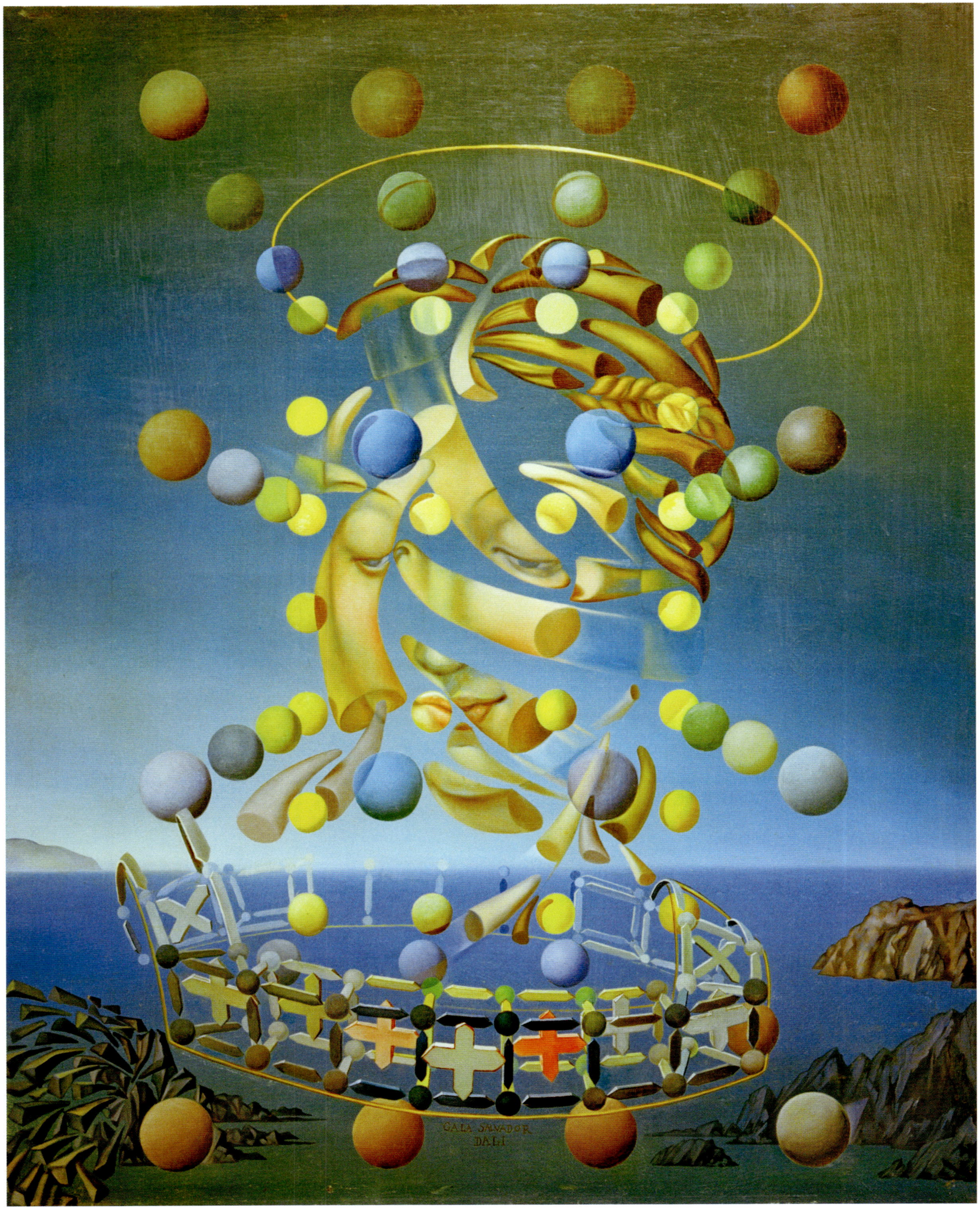
GALA SALVADOR
DALI

terms as 'the superwoman Gala'; so putting her on just such a pedestal as the one she is not quite touching in *Leda Atomica* (see page 131) and in the *Madonna of Port Lligat* was surely an effortless conceit. Dalí also seems to have been more than comfortable with her string of sexual conquests, which continued into her seventies, as his earlier pattern of onanism and voyeurism reasserted itself; he himself preferred not to touch. Dalí was still able to see Gala as a woman of flesh and physicality, as is clear from the confident eroticism of *Galarina* (1945), apparently modelled on Raphael's *La Fornarina* (1518–20), and even another work from the same year, the intriguing *My Wife, Nude, Contemplating her own Flesh Becoming Stairs, Three Vertebrae of a Column, Sky and Architecture* (1945, see page 135). But now apparently in the grip of trying to reconcile in the manner of the Old Masters the two opposite worlds of science and faith, it probably seemed a natural step to make the woman he worshipped a religious icon.

(Left)

Maximum Speed of Raphael's Madonna, c. 1954

Medium: Oil on canvas
Dimensions: 81 x 66 cm (32 x 26 in)
Location: Museo Nacional Centro de Arte Reina Sofia, Madrid

It was around the time of his audience with the Pope that Dalí's sister, Anna Maria, published her memoir, which in reducing him to the son and brother he had been in childhood and in offering a different version of the carefully controlled image of sociopathic genius he had cultivated in *The Secret Life*, earned the fury of Dalí.

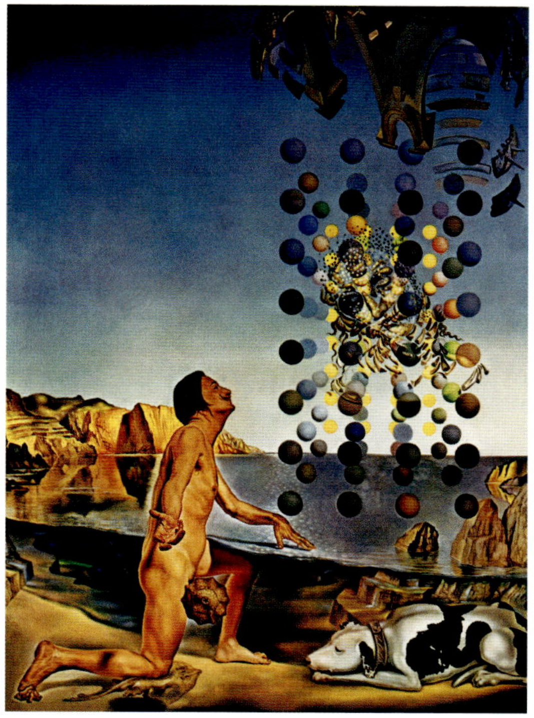

(Above)

Dali, Nude, Entranced in the Contemplation of Five Regular Bodies Metamorphosed in Corpuscles, in Which Suddenly Appears Leonardo's 'Leda', Chromosomatised by the Face of Gala, 1954

Medium: Oil on canvas
Dimensions: 61 x 46 cm (24 x 18 in)
Location: Private Collection

This was compounded when their father died in September the following year, leaving most of his estate to his daughter. Dalí, of course, did not need the money, but entered into protracted legal battles with his sister over the whereabouts of works of his left behind in the Port Lligat house when he had fled to America, which he believed she had sold behind his back. The two siblings were never reconciled.

The Saviour of Modern Painting

In the year 1951 Dalí published the 'Mystical Manifesto', in which he described himself as 'Salvador Dalí, inventor of the new Paranoiac-Critical mysticism and saviour, as his very name indicates, of modern painting'. In the same essay – which, in a gesture whose earnestness is inseparable from its irony – was published in both French and Latin, he also stated that

'I want my next Christ to be a painting containing more beauty and joy than anything that will have been painted up to the present. I want to paint a Christ that will be the absolute contrary in every respect to the materialist and savagely anti-mystical Christ of Grünewald!' Dalí here seems to refer to one of his most controversial but enduringly popular works, his *Christ of St John of the Cross* (1951, *see* page 138).

At first glance this dramatic painting seems like the ultimate act of egomania from a man who came to refer to himself as 'the Divine Dalí'. In fact, the view of Christ on the Cross from on high, as if seen through the 'eyes' of God, is based on a drawing done as a result of a vision experienced by the sixteenth-century Spanish mystic poet, St John of the Cross (1542–91), in which Christ is also seen from above. In Dalí's painting, the crucified Christ hovers over the bay of Port Lligat; again, it is not so much a statement of religious faith as it is a question to be asked. The painter himself said of this work that it resulted from a 'cosmic dream' in which the image represented 'the nucleus of the atom', which he considered 'the very unity of the universe'. As is typical with Dalí, the obscurantism of the explanation does little to clarify the meaning of the image and probably more to mystify it. An ambiguous work for both believers and non-believers alike, it continues to provoke extreme reactions, with one visitor to its home at Glasgow's Kelvingrove Art Gallery in 1961 physically attacking the canvas, inflicting significant damage that required extensive restoration. What is clear is that Dalí's mission to 'become classic' was succeeding thanks to his unerring ability to conjure images that imprint themselves on the mind, whether we like them or not.

> 'I cannot say it often enough: I am not mad.'

Support for General Franco

Whatever the possible subversions of his images, Dalí's public statements aligned themselves with increasing sycophancy towards the dictatorship of General Franco. It is possible that Dalí recognized in the despot a father figure who, for once, would not tolerate his contrarian ways. He had been indulged his whole life and had learned to treat all the soft forms of authority he had encountered with contempt; he could not do that now. At a lecture in Madrid in 1951, he made his support for the autocratic regime crystal clear, declaring that 'Before Franco, every politician and every new government only

(Right)

Portrait of Gala with Rhinocerotic Attributes, c. 1954

Medium: Oil on canvas
Dimensions: 39 x 31.5 cm
Location: Fundació Gala-Salvador Dalí, Figueres

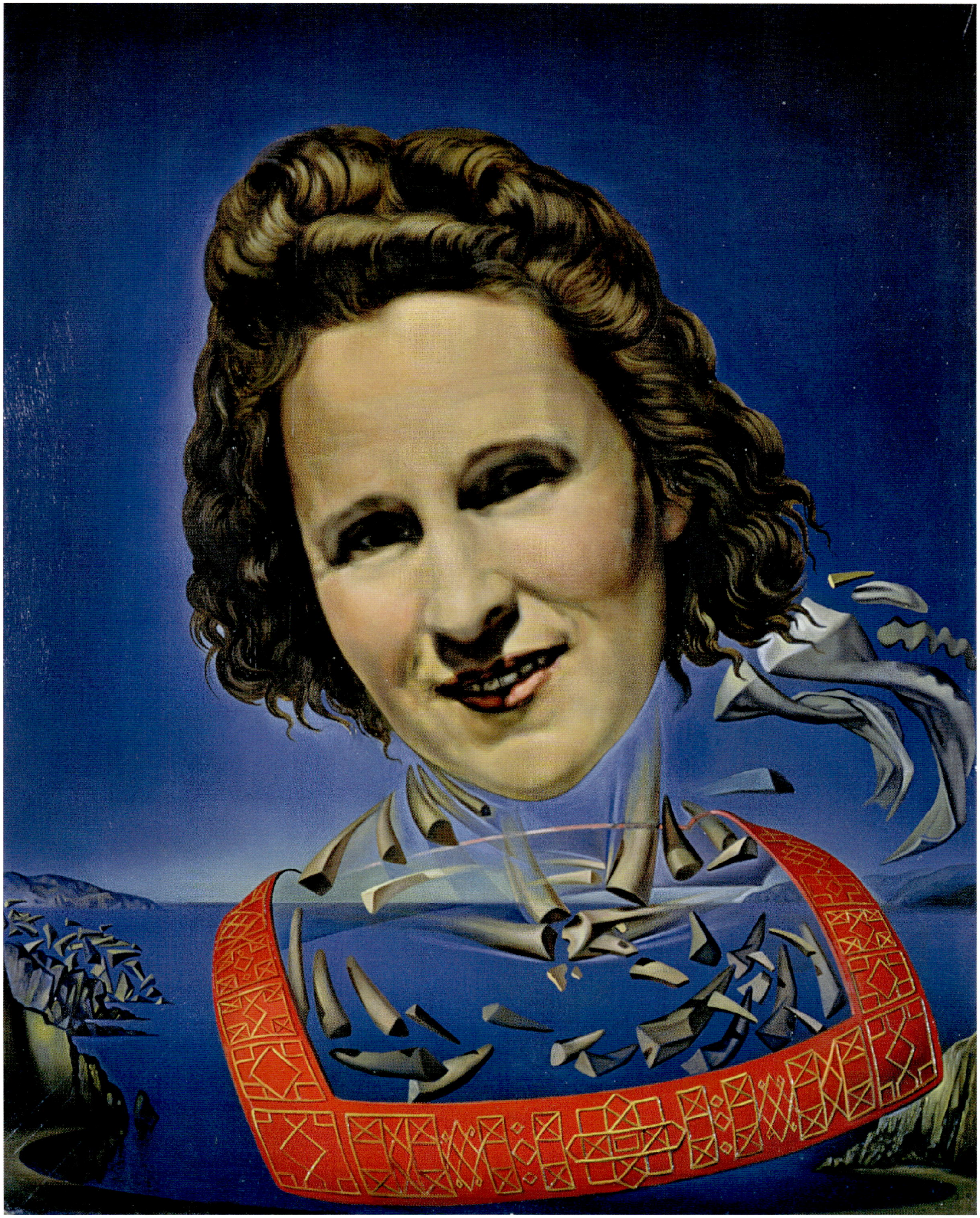

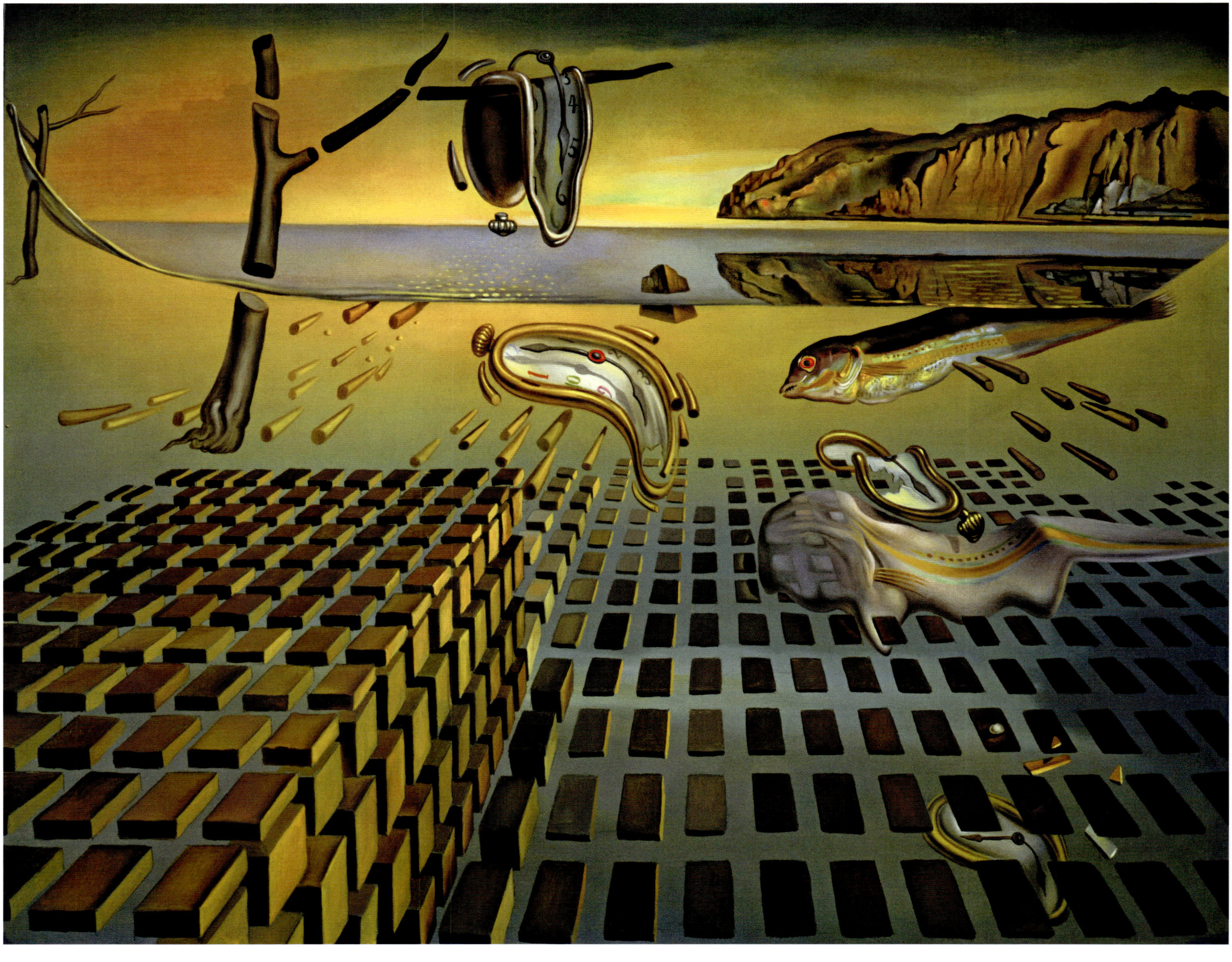

increased the confusion, the lies and the disorder of Spain. Franco broke violently with this false tradition, imposing clarity, truth and order in the country at a time when the world was experiencing its period of greatest anarchy.' For someone who was not political and not historic, this was quite a departure. As a statement of political allegiance and historical bias, it could hardly have been stronger.

More religious paintings followed, including *Assumpta Corpuscularia Lapislazulina* (1952, *see* page 139), where once again Gala appears as the Virgin, her body, in Dalí's explanation of the work, reintegrating in the heavens according to his own understanding of the doctrine of the Assumption, which had become official Catholic dogma as recently as 1950. For all his lapsing into political conservatism, Dalí had lost none of his curiosity for all areas of knowledge, albeit that such knowledge was seldom more than grist to his artistic mill – fed in at one end, improperly understood, before being fed out at the other in unlikely and often compelling images.

The Rhinoceros Horn

Dalí's tendency to fetishize objects that came into his orbit was also as strong as

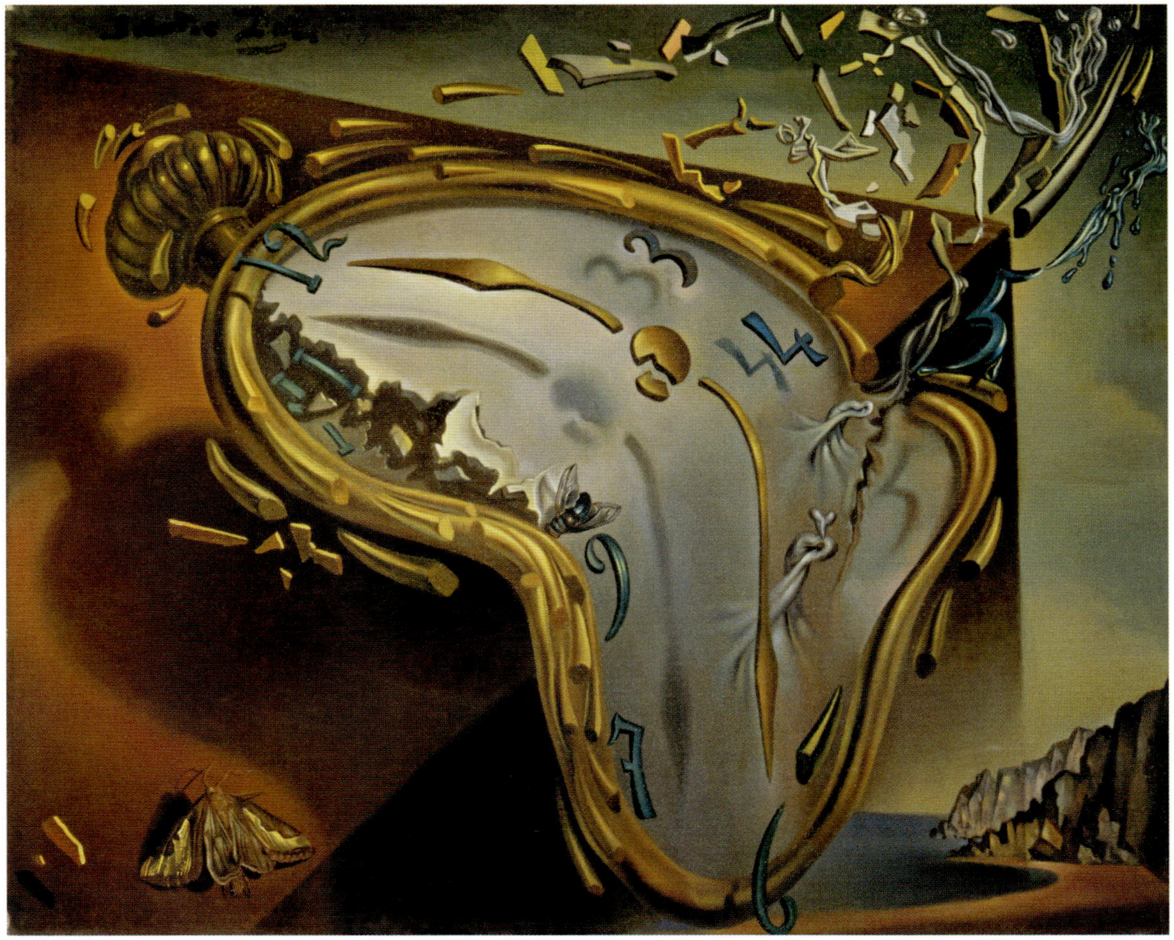

(Left)

The Disintegration of the Persistence of Memory, 1952–54

Medium: Oil on canvas
Dimensions: 25.4 x 33 cm (9⅘ x 13 in)
Location: Salvador Dalí Museum, St Petersburg, Florida

(Above)

Soft Watch at the Moment of Its First Explosion, c. 1954

Medium: Oil on panel
Dimensions: 20.5 x 25.7 cm (8 x 10 in)
Location: Private Collection

ever, although their importance to his imaginative universe was now structural, whereas in the 1930s it had been psychological. In 1950, Dalí was given a rhinoceros horn, whose logarithmic spirals with typical Dalínian solipsism he was soon proclaiming as a structural Rosetta Stone that only a genius such as the great Dalí could have recognized. As he puts it in *Diary of a Genius*: 'Artists, all through history have been tormenting themselves to grasp form and to reduce it to elementary geometric volumes. Leonardo always tended to produce eggs, which were the most perfect form, according to Euclid. Ingres preferred spheres, and Cézanne cubes and cylinders. But only Dalí, by the convolutions of his paroxysmal hypocrisy which had led him to an all-excluding obsession with the rhinoceros, has found the truth. All curved surfaces of the human body have the same geometric point in common: the one found in this cone with the rounded tip curved towards heaven or towards the earth, and with the angelic inspiration of destruction in perfection – the rhinoceros horn!'

It is a typical mixture of, if not quite the sublime, at least the brilliant with the absurd, an implausible theory which Dalí then demonstrates with his customary virtuosity in works such as *Assumpta Corpuscularia Lapislazulina* and *Raphaelesque Head, Exploded* (1951). This latter work is a reprise of the double images of the 1930s which in this case combines the face of a Raphaelesque Madonna composed of a constellation of rhinoceros horns with a scalp that is,

'Yes, I believe I am the saviour of modern art...'

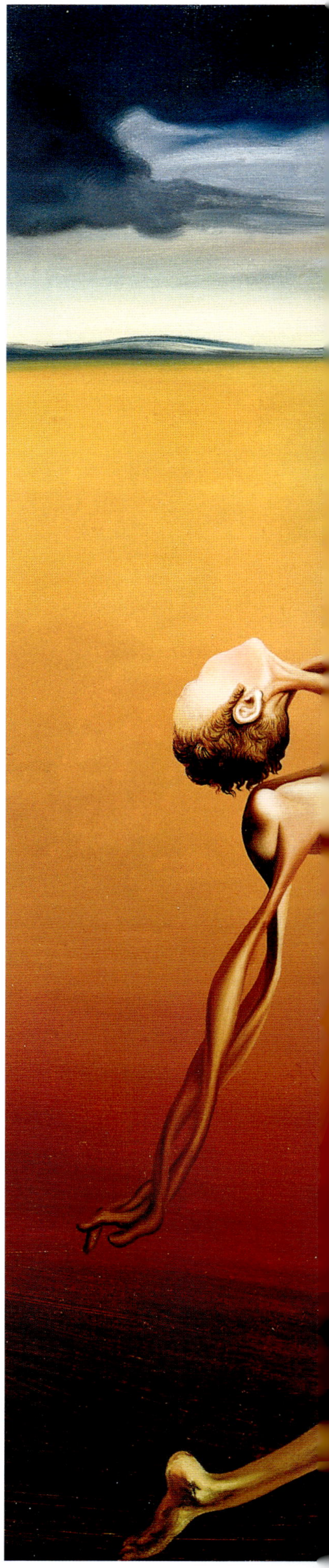

(Right)

The Dance (The Seven Lively Arts), 1957

Medium: Oil on canvas
Dimensions: 84 x 114cm (33 x 45⅛ in)
Location: Morohashi Museum of Modern Art, Fukushima

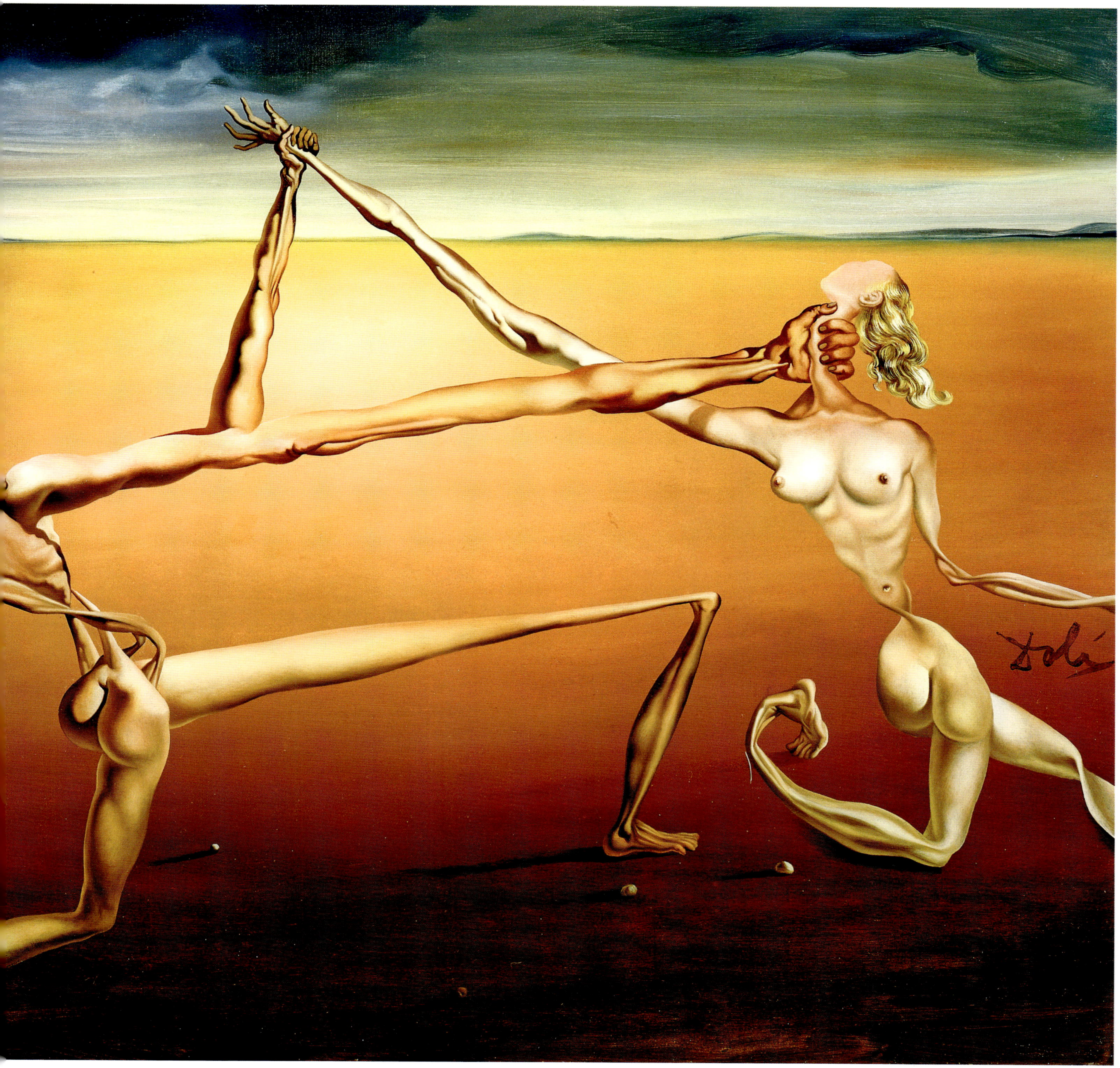
Dalí

in fact, the famous concrete ceiling and oculus of the Pantheon in Rome. An utterly brilliant piece of painting, it is nonetheless a confection whose meaning perhaps lies somewhere in the various convolutions of 'paroxysmal hypocrisy' that Dalí tells us led him to it. Quite what he meant by 'paroxysmal hypocrisy' might be deduced from a painting done a few years later, *Young Virgin Auto-sodomized by the Horns of Her Own Chastity* (1954). Based on a photograph he had seen in a pornographic magazine, in what is his most explicitly erotic major work rhinoceros horns become the fulcrums of an interest in the female backside which began with the Ingresque painting of his sister standing at an open window some 30 years earlier.

Galatea of the Spheres

Yet another bravura approach to depicting the human form occurs in *Galatea of the Spheres* (1952), in which Dalí depicts his wife composed entirely of 'atoms' disappearing in perspectival rows towards a 'vanishing point' located somewhere in the corner of her mouth. An example of portraiture behaving almost like landscape, of one mode of being in the form of another, it is perhaps the closest Dalí ever came to marrying the intellectual ecstasy of scientific understanding with what seems to be the religious rapture of mystic contemplation, of healing what he saw as a 'divorce' which had 'come about between physics and metaphysics', due to what he described as 'the almost monstrous progress of specialization without any synthesis' that was a consistent feature of the modern world. Dalí certainly saw himself as the only painter capable of bridging this divide, and *Galatea of the Spheres* was exemplary in that effort, a work he later described as 'synthesizing all of my new mystical science of painting and my technique of quantified realism, in which each element of the picture exists by itself but contributes to creating a cosmogonic whole that transcends it. The face of my beloved Gala was born of the universal Brownian whirlpool, as the sacred image of the divine.'

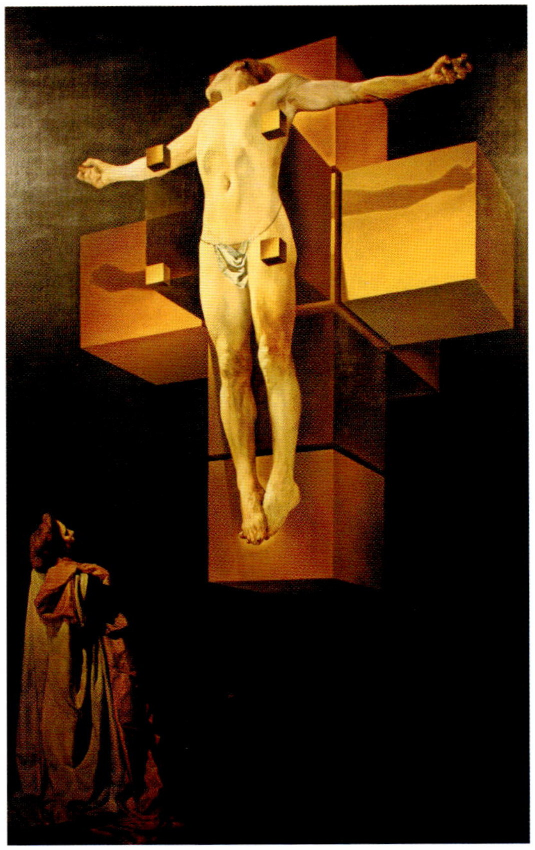

(Above)

Corpus Hypercubus, 1954

Medium: Oil on canvas
Dimensions: 194.4 x 123.9 cm (76⅝ x 48¾ in)
Location: Metropolitan Museum of Art, New York

Dalí and DNA

Dalí saw many of the analytical experiments of modernism, from Georges Seurat (1859–91) to Georges Matthieu (1921–2012), as in fact reinvigorating the tradition of painting they had sought to replace – a task he had taken it upon himself to achieve. In this pursuit, atoms and rhinoceros horns were followed in 1954 by molecules (which looked very much like the atoms), following the discovery of the structure of DNA by Francis Crick (1916–2004) and James Watson (1928–) the previous year. In the showpiece among these works, given the ridiculous title *Dalí, Nude, Entranced in the Contemplation of Five Regular Bodies Metamorphosed in Corpuscles, in Which Suddenly Appears Leonardo's 'Leda', Chromosomatised by the Face of Gala* (1954, see page 141), Dalí himself appears as naked as a desert hermit, though kneeling on the seabed with the surface of the water drawn up like a sheet across his knee. He also

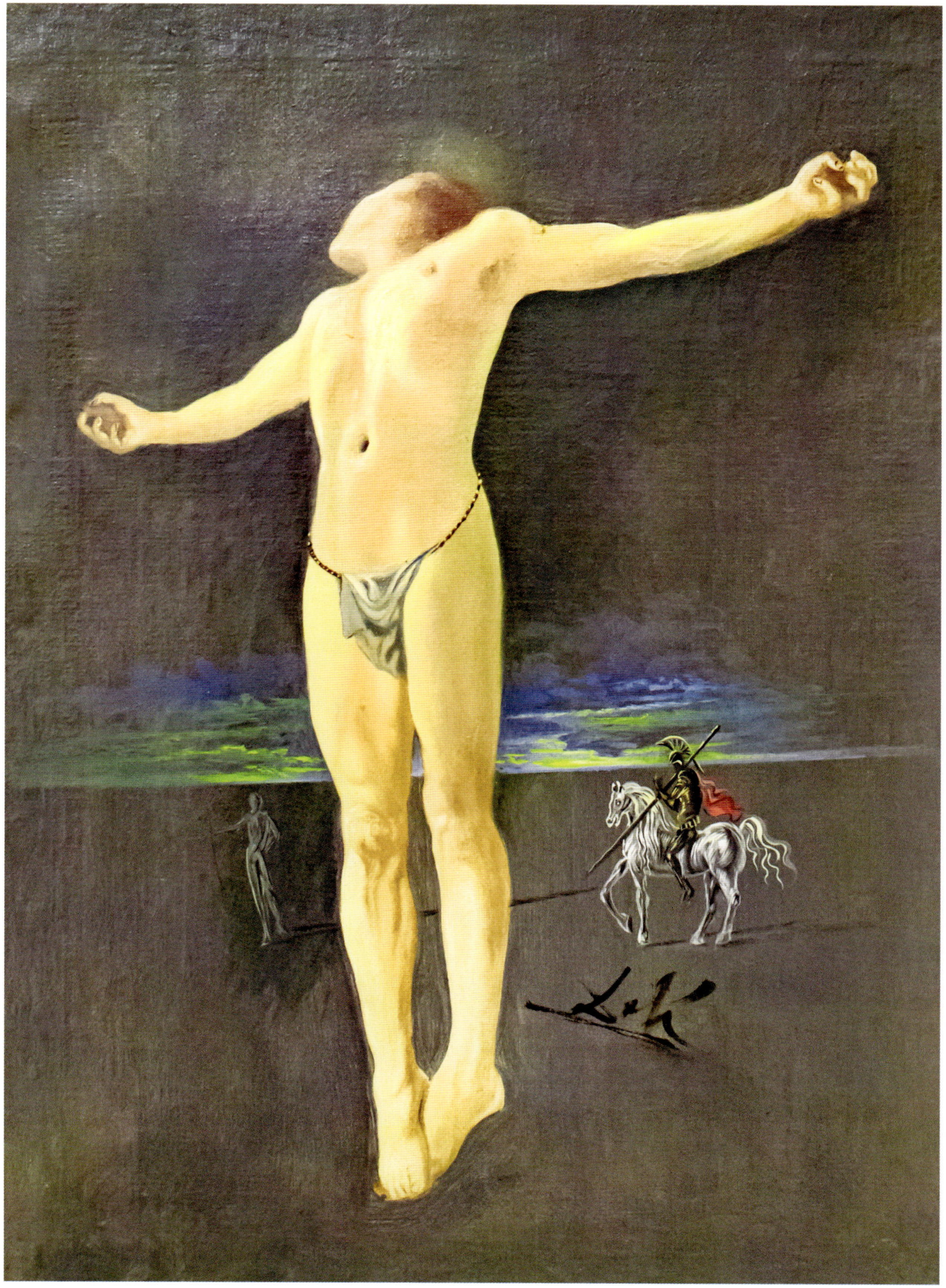

(Right)

Crucifixion, 1954

Medium: Oil on canvas
Dimensions: 40 x 30 cm (15¾ x 11⅘ in)
Location: Vatican Museums and Galleries, Vatican City

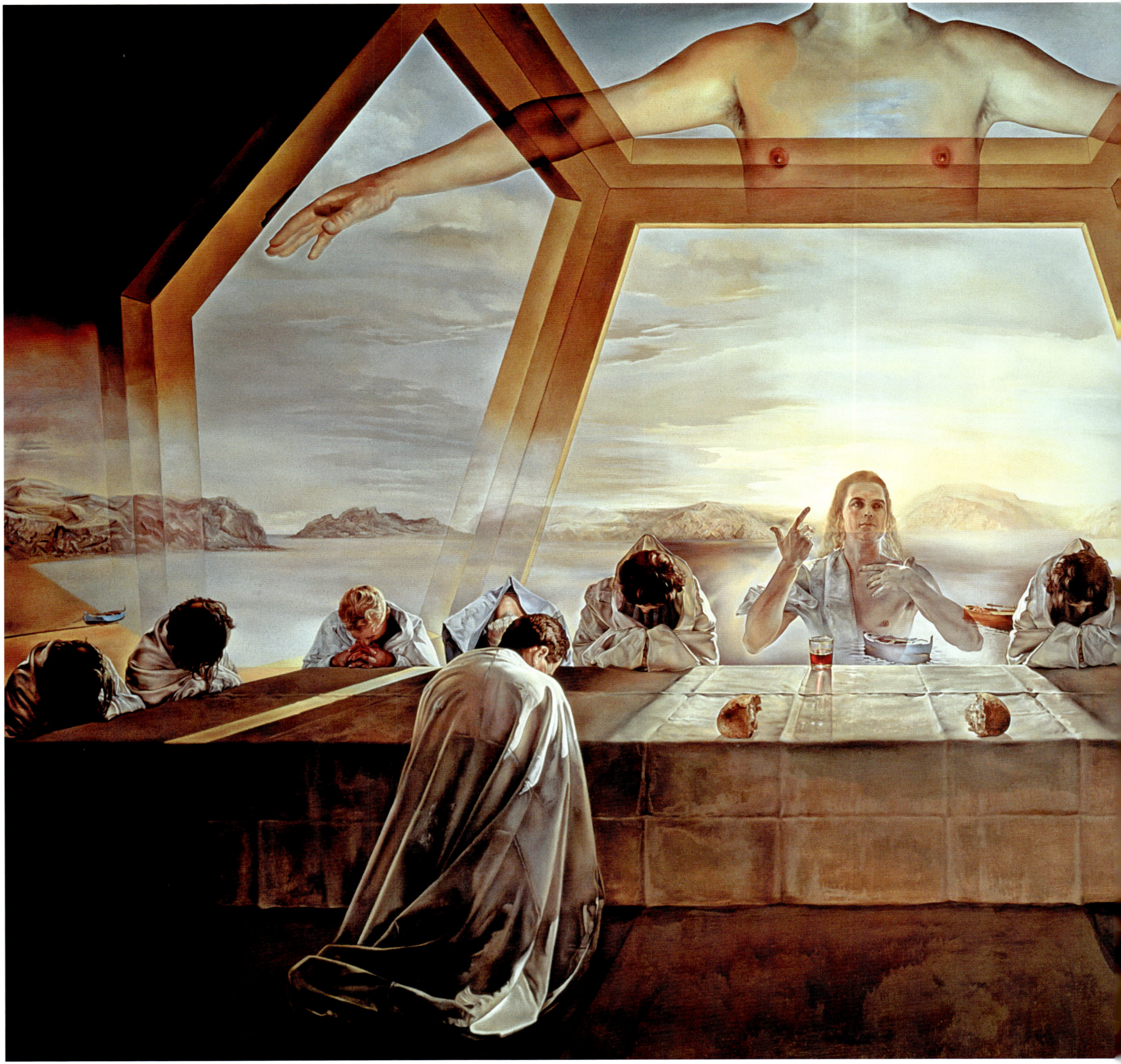

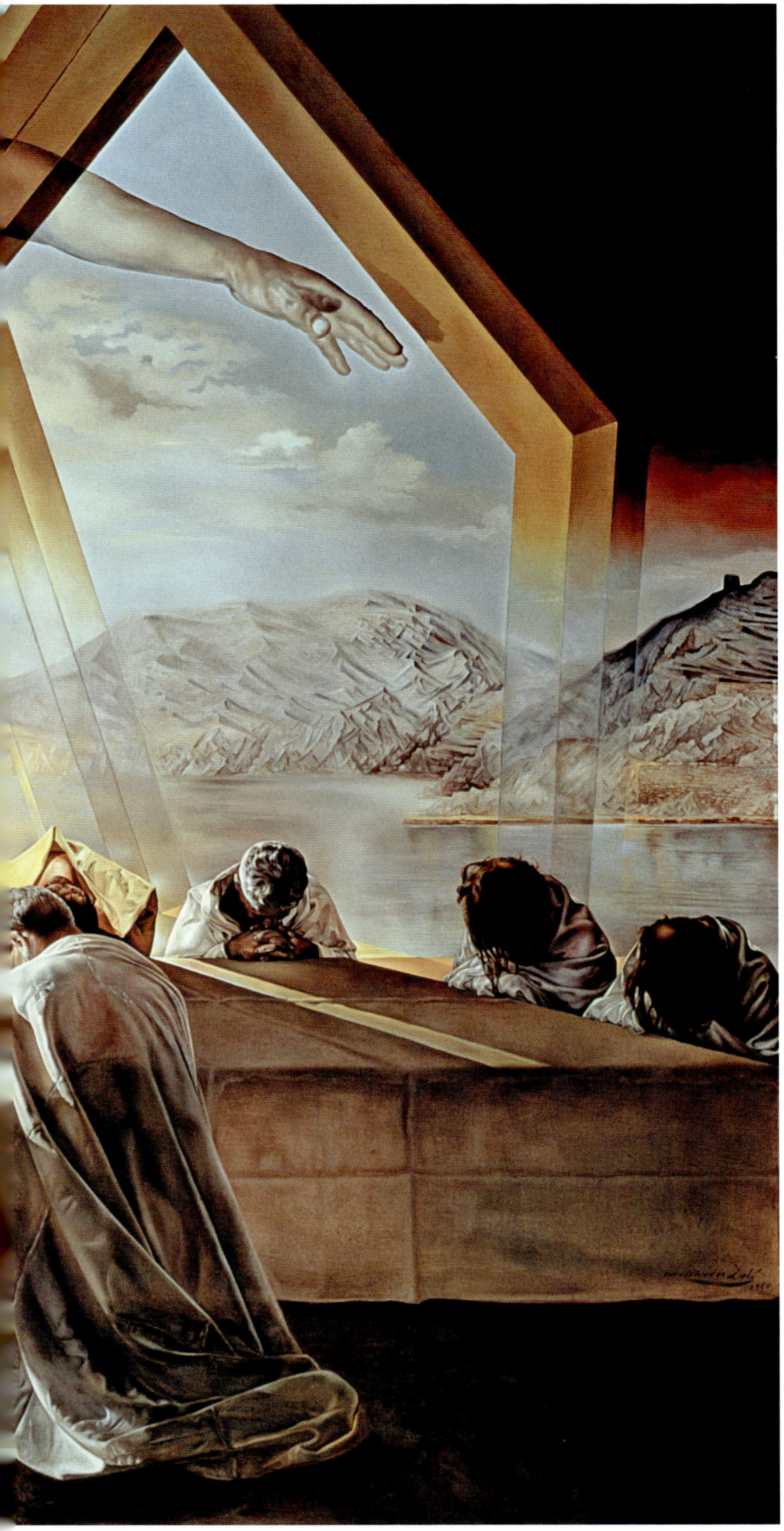

re-examines one of his greatest hits in the light of his thinking of the time in *The Disintegration of the Persistence of Memory* (1952–54, *see* page 144).

The Last Supper

But these scientific fantasias aside, this was above all a decade of religious painting, whose most significant achievement in Dalí's mind seems to have been *The Sacrament of the Last Supper* (1955, *see* left), a picture in which 'can be read all of my cosmogony: the union of time and space which is the secret of God'. Whether or not Dalí had indeed discovered the secret of the divine, he was nonetheless relying on others to help him realize it, by this point employing assistants to execute some of the complex perspectival structures he was using in his pictures. In 1955, he engaged Isidor Bea, an accomplished scenery designer who had forged a successful career working in the theatres of Barcelona but for some reason decided to throw in his lot with Dalí when approached. Bea would continue to work with 'the Master' until his very last paintings and was critical in executing *The Sacrament of the Last Supper*.

This very large canvas was bought in a froth of enthusiasm by the American millionaire Chester Dale (1883–1962), whose portrait Dalí would paint a few years later and who had already acquired another

(Left)

The Sacrament of the Last Supper, 1955

Medium: Oil on canvas
Dimensions: 166.7 x 267 cm (65⅝ x 105 in)
Location: National Gallery of Art, Washington D.C.

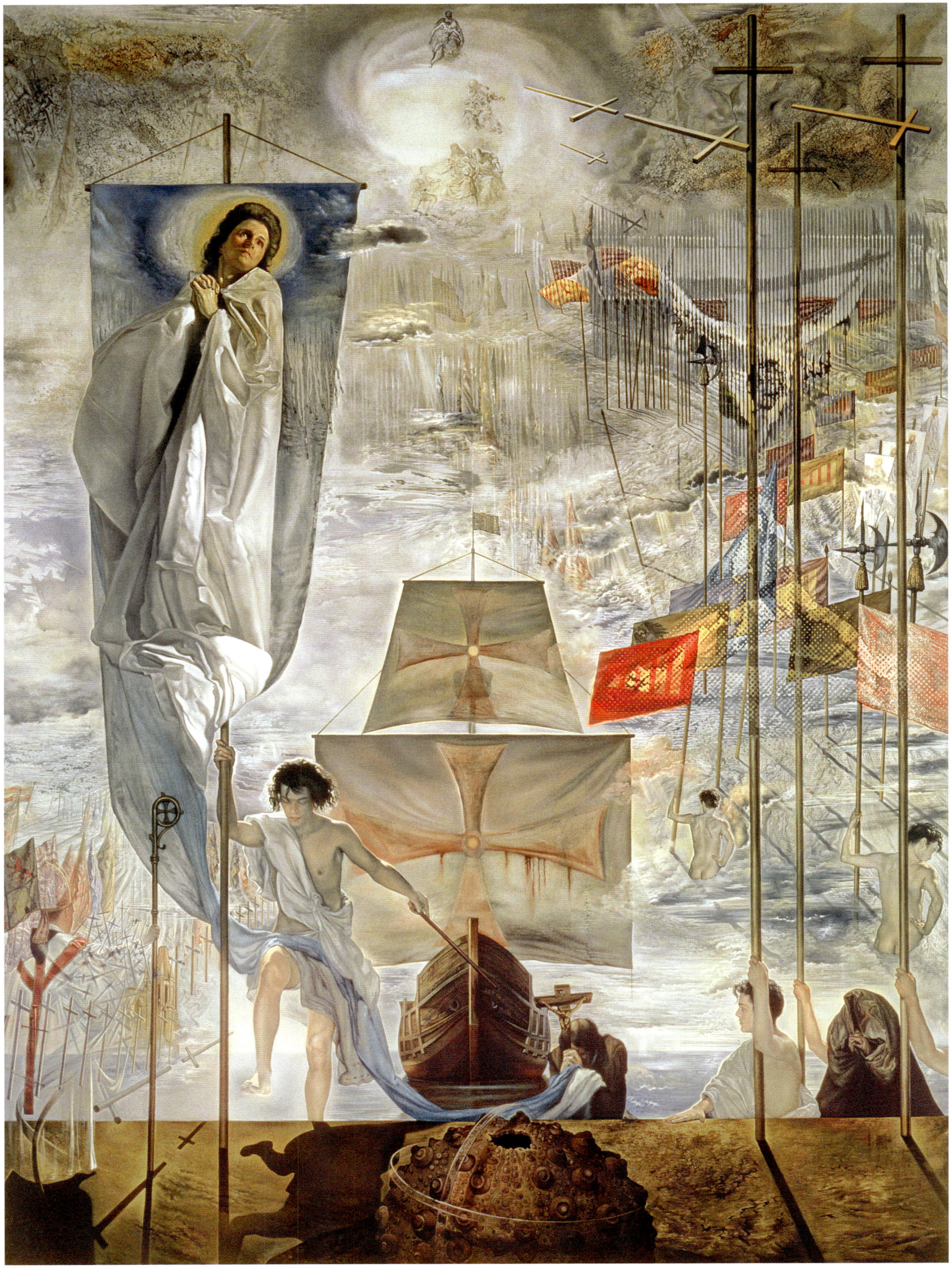

significant religious work, *Corpus Hypercubus* (1954, *see* page 148), secured for the collection of the Metropolitan Museum in New York City. *The Last Supper*, whose cloaked disciples look like privileged members of a masonic cult rather than humble fishermen, and whose Jesus has a physique that one distinguished theologian compared to a 'very good athlete on an American baseball team', was similarly donated to the National Gallery of Art in Washington, D.C. Over the years, successive curators, who like most critics have seen it as little more than a grandiose piece of religious kitsch, have gradually shunted it off to ever-more obscure locations within the building. Nevertheless, in an age with a yearning for the spiritual – albeit that the spirituality represented in *The Last Supper* is decidedly ersatz – the painting remains far more popular with the public, a point Dalí liked to confirm in sales of the image in the form of postcards bought at the museum.

The Discovery of America by Christopher Columbus

Towards the end of the decade, there were significant meetings – in 1956 with General Franco at his residence just outside Madrid, then in 1959 with the recently elected Pope John XXIII (1881–1963) – which in his own mind cemented Dalí's position as the leader of his one-man neo-Counter-Reformation, 'my crusade for the defence of Greco-Roman civilisation', as he put it as early as *The Secret Life*. Like so much art of that earlier campaign by the Church of Rome, many of Dalí's religious paintings can seem like a form of pictorial propaganda for the splendour of the Catholic faith rather than devotional images – a charm offensive of virtuosity over substance, though in Dalí's case we also need to ask who it was he was attempting to charm. A final large canvas of the 1950s will serve to illustrate the direction his painting and his political thought was taking at the end of the decade. *The Discovery of America by Christopher Columbus* (1958–59, *see* page 160), a history painting whose models were *The Surrender of Breda* (*c.* 1635) by his hero, Velázquez, and the works of Meissonnier, reinforces a sense of the retreat Dalí had made into political, spiritual and artistic conservatism. It had been commissioned by Huntington Hartford (1911–2008), an American business magnate, and as such it commemorates a moment of high significance to both Spaniards and Americans alike. Once again, Gala appears as the Virgin on the standard the young lad is bringing ashore; behind him, kneeling with a crucifix pressed to his forehead, is Dalí himself. What is he doing, we may wonder: giving thanks to God for safe passage to a new land, or to America, which had been so good to him? Or is the saviour of modern painting simply hiding behind the Cross?

(Left)

The Discovery of America by Christopher Columbus, 1958–59

Medium: Oil on canvas
Dimensions: 410.2 x 310 cm (161½ x 122 in)
Location: Salvador Dalí Museum, St Petersburg, Florida

The Jester as King

By 1960, Dalí's considerable global fame had been nurtured and then constantly lubricated by his insatiable need and his equally tireless ability to place himself constantly in the public eye, no matter what the reason: 'My motto is: "Dalí must always be talked about, even if nothing good is said about him."' Such exposure, coupled with what was still a prodigious work ethic during the spring and summer months he spent at Port Lligat, was generating a very large income indeed. The religious pictures of the previous few years had been sold for hundreds of thousands of dollars, huge sums for works by a living artist. For most of the previous three decades the task of negotiating sales and managing his affairs had fallen to Gala, but she was now tiring of an ever-more demanding role, and in any case her dalliances with various young men were an increasing distraction. The couple had, in fact, finally been married in the eyes of the Church in 1958, but by then their physical relationship seems to have been practically at an end.

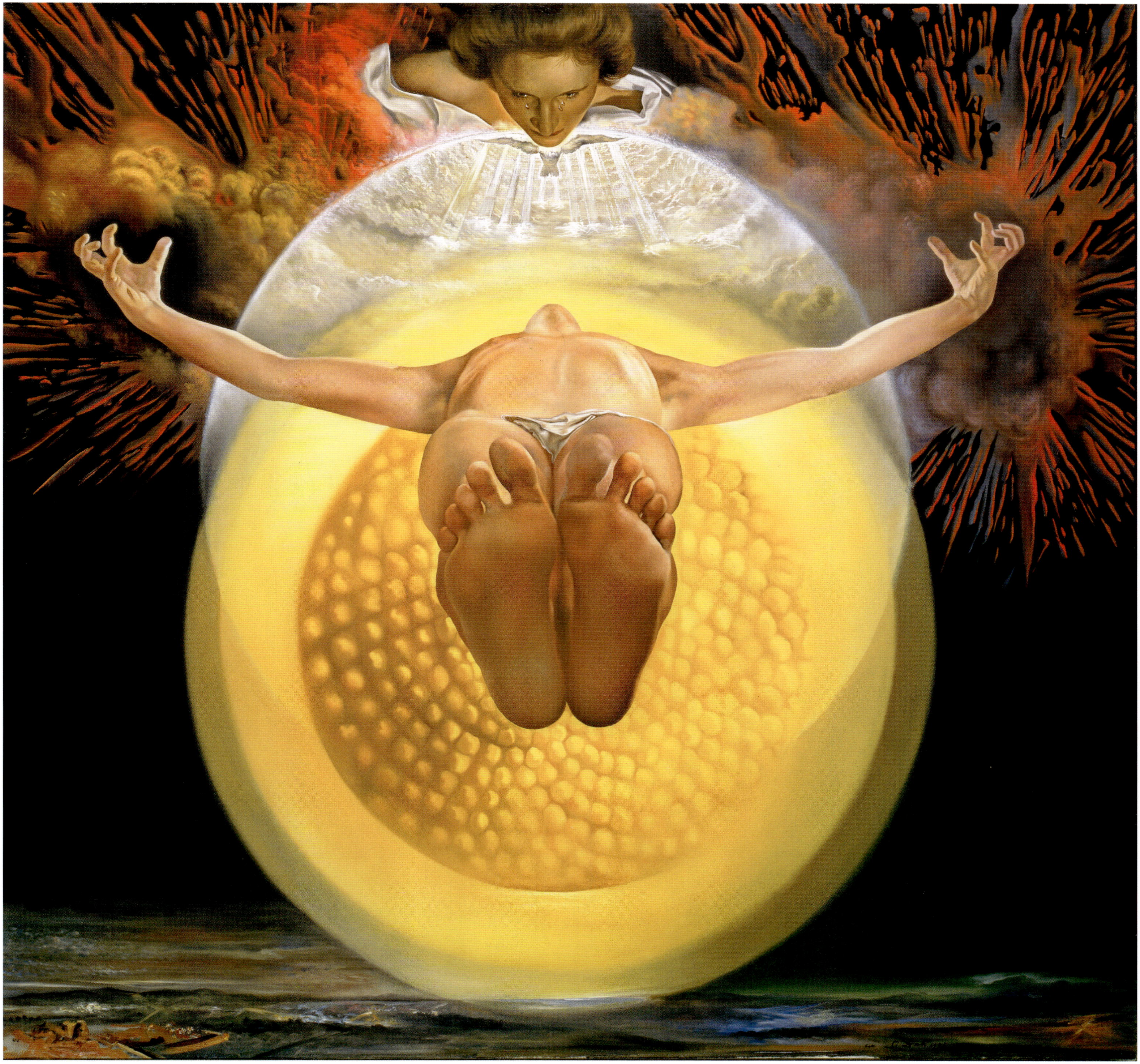

The Ascension of Christ (Pieta), **1958** | Medium: Oil on canvas | Dimensions: 115 x 123 cm (45⅓ x 48⅖ in) | Location: Private Collection

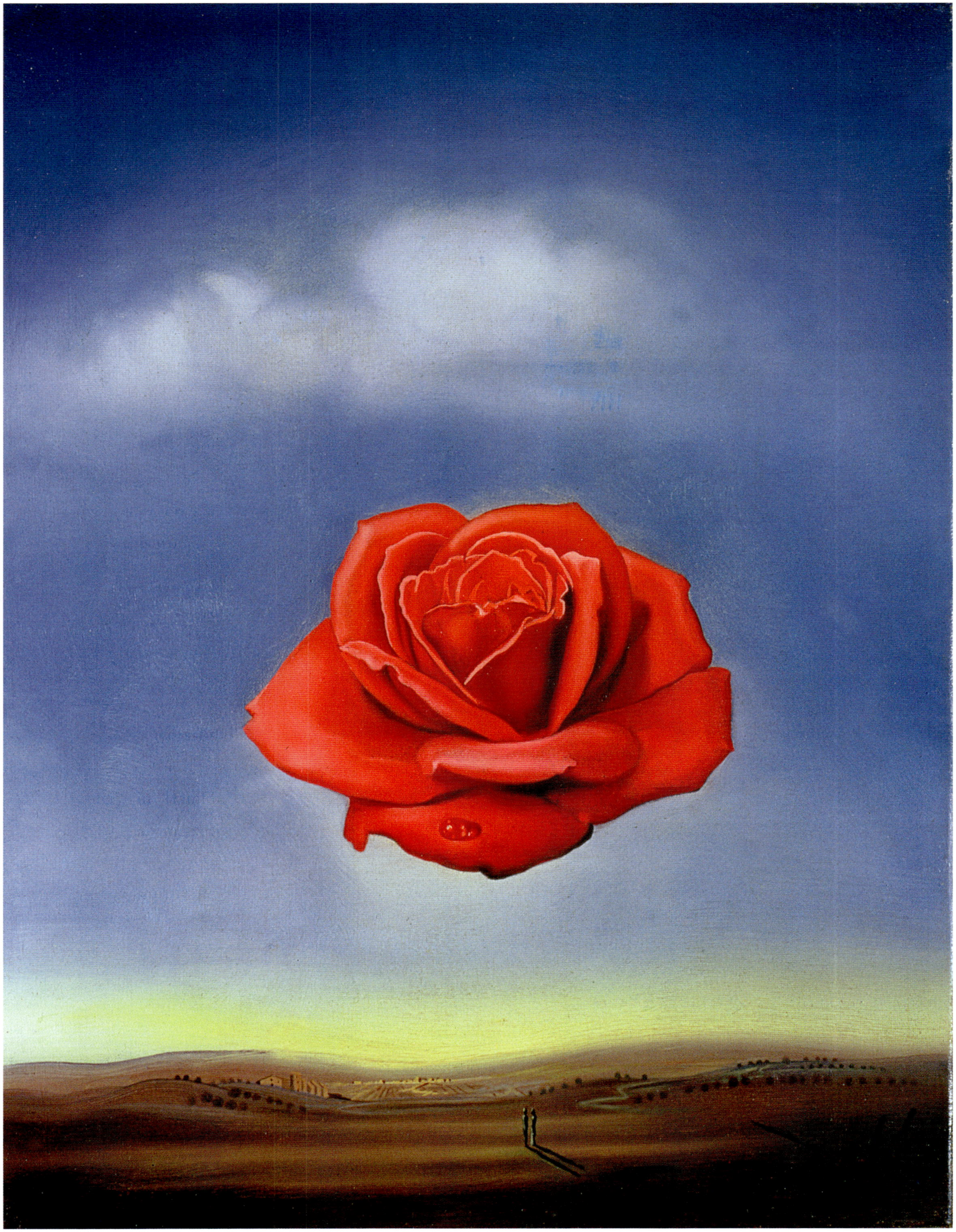

Pesetas Galore

Their enrichment, the ease with which increasingly it was achieved, was in many ways their downfall – as a couple and as individuals, too. Given a surfeit of available funds, Gala's runaway sex drive was granted almost unlimited licence, and the outlay she lavished on her youthful conquests, as well as a growing taste for gambling that she frequently indulged in the casinos of Monte Carlo, required a level of expenditure that took a sizeable chunk out of their burgeoning income. Although Dalí was less extravagant, the couple's regular annual itinerary saw them spending several months living in the hotels they had lodged in for years during the autumn and winter period – Le Meurice in Paris followed by the St Regis in New York – where routinely they entertained a doting entourage in fine and expensive style.

A succession of business managers would run their affairs over the next three decades on terms that were very lucrative indeed. Dalí and his wife had always demanded payment in cash – in pesetas, to boot. Given the growing sums his work commanded, this led to Gala stuffing ridiculous amounts of currency from their predominantly American buyers into their personal suitcases, which were then carried illegally through customs when the couple returned to Europe. Bizarrely, possibly in an attempt to avoid paying taxes, the money was often never deposited, with the result

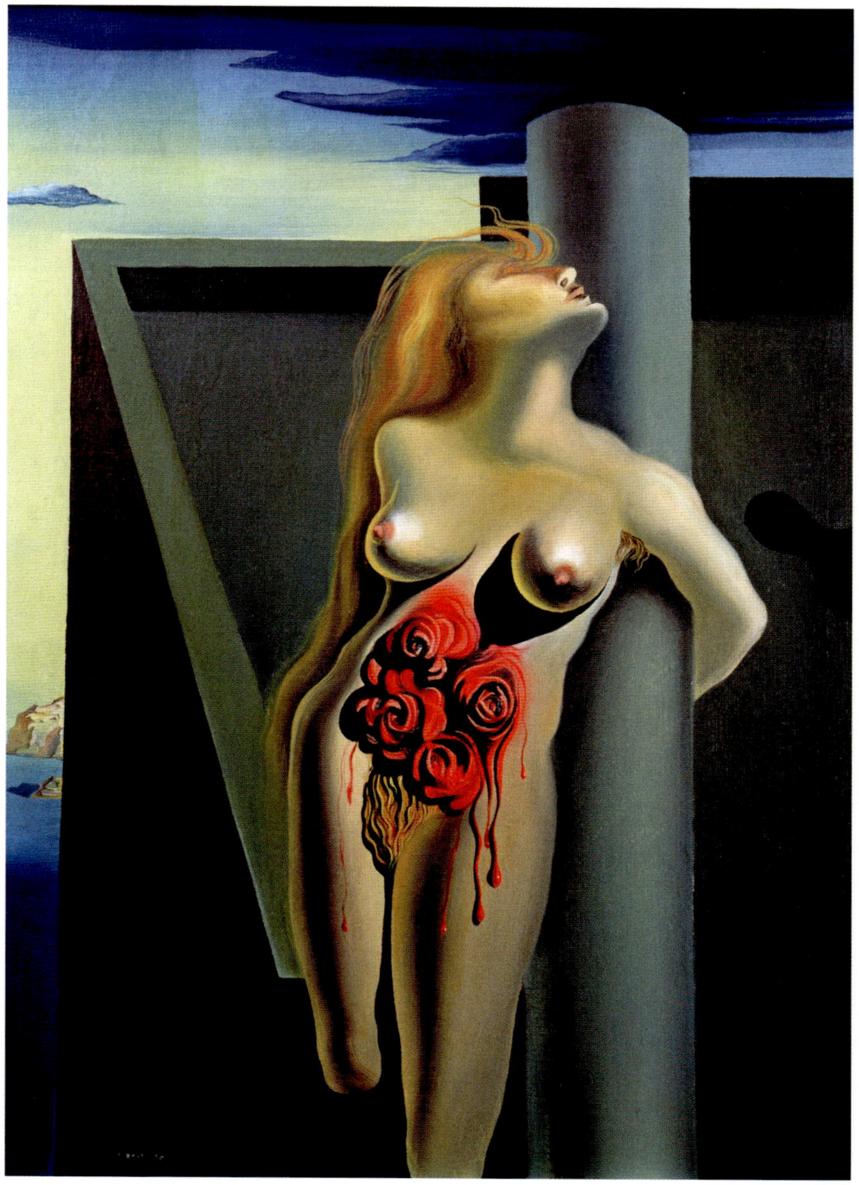

(Left)

The Rose, 1958

Medium: Oil on canvas
Dimensions: 37.5 x 30 cm (14¾ x 11 in)
Location: Private Collection

(Above)

The Bleeding Roses, 1930

Medium: Oil on canvas
Dimensions: 60 x 48 cm (24 x 19¾ in)
Location: Private Collection

that large amounts of unbanked and by then legally inadmissible tender was being discovered years later in items of luggage that had been brought home and apparently forgotten.

Avida Dollars

It did not seem to matter, as money flowed inexorably in their direction. As Dalí put it with unalloyed relish in the chapter 'How to Make Money' in *The Unspeakable Confessions of Salvador Dalí* (1973), 'I have always had a genius for making gold pop out'. This was Avida Dollars speaking, a name he said was 'a talisman that saw me through the doors of banks and safes', particularly in America, which 'recognized me as its prodigal son and threw dollars at my head like handfuls of confetti'. Neither did he feel any shame in milking the cash cow of his talent and notoriety in the form of ethically dubious practices in which he was willingly assisted by those who managed his affairs – first Captain Peter Moore (1919–2005) and then the even more avaricious Enric Sabater (1936–2013) – both of whom claimed their own commission on everything that was sold. Dalí did not complain, given the ease with which they enabled him to make ever larger sums. By the mid-1960s, Moore would bring Dalí two projects to dash off each morning after breakfast, prints for which he could now command a very high fee. He described the process with typically acquisitive glee. 'I like to start the day by earning twenty thousand dollars,' he said, referring to the prints he did for the Phyllis Lucas Gallery in New York, each of which took him half an hour and earned him $10,000.

Most notoriously, there was the question of multiples, reproductions of Dalí's prints by a large number of firms keen to make a killing from his fame. Not only did it not matter to Dalí that he had not printed these works himself, his cupidity drove him during the same period to what was a professional nadir, a course of action which has done great harm to his subsequent reputation. He agreed to sign blank sheets of paper, at $10 a signature, which earned him huge amounts of money for just a few hours' work – he set aside whole days at regular intervals to carry out this repetitive task – but which flooded a voracious market with thousands of fake Dalís.

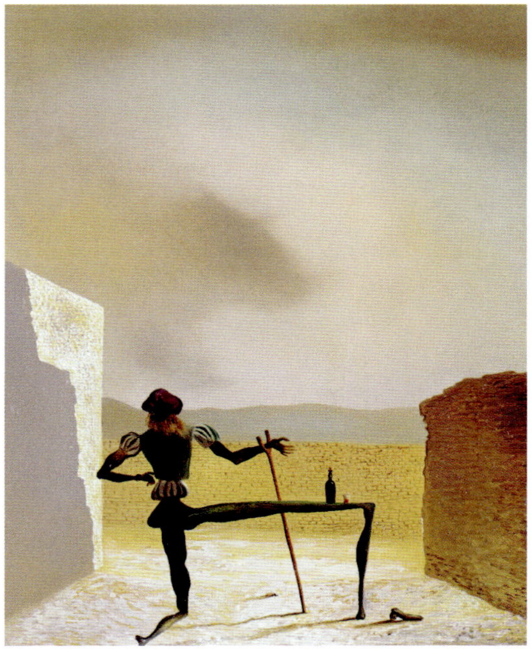

(Above)

The Ghost of Vermeer of Delft Which Can Be Used as a Table, 1934

Medium: Oil on wood panel
Dimensions: 18.1 x 13.97 cm (7 x 5½ in)
Location: Salvador Dalí Museum, St Petersburg, Florida

(Right)

Apotheosis of the Dollar, 1965

Medium: Oil on canvas
Dimensions: 400 x 498 cm (157½ x 196 in)
Location: Fundació Gala-Salvador Dalí, Figueres

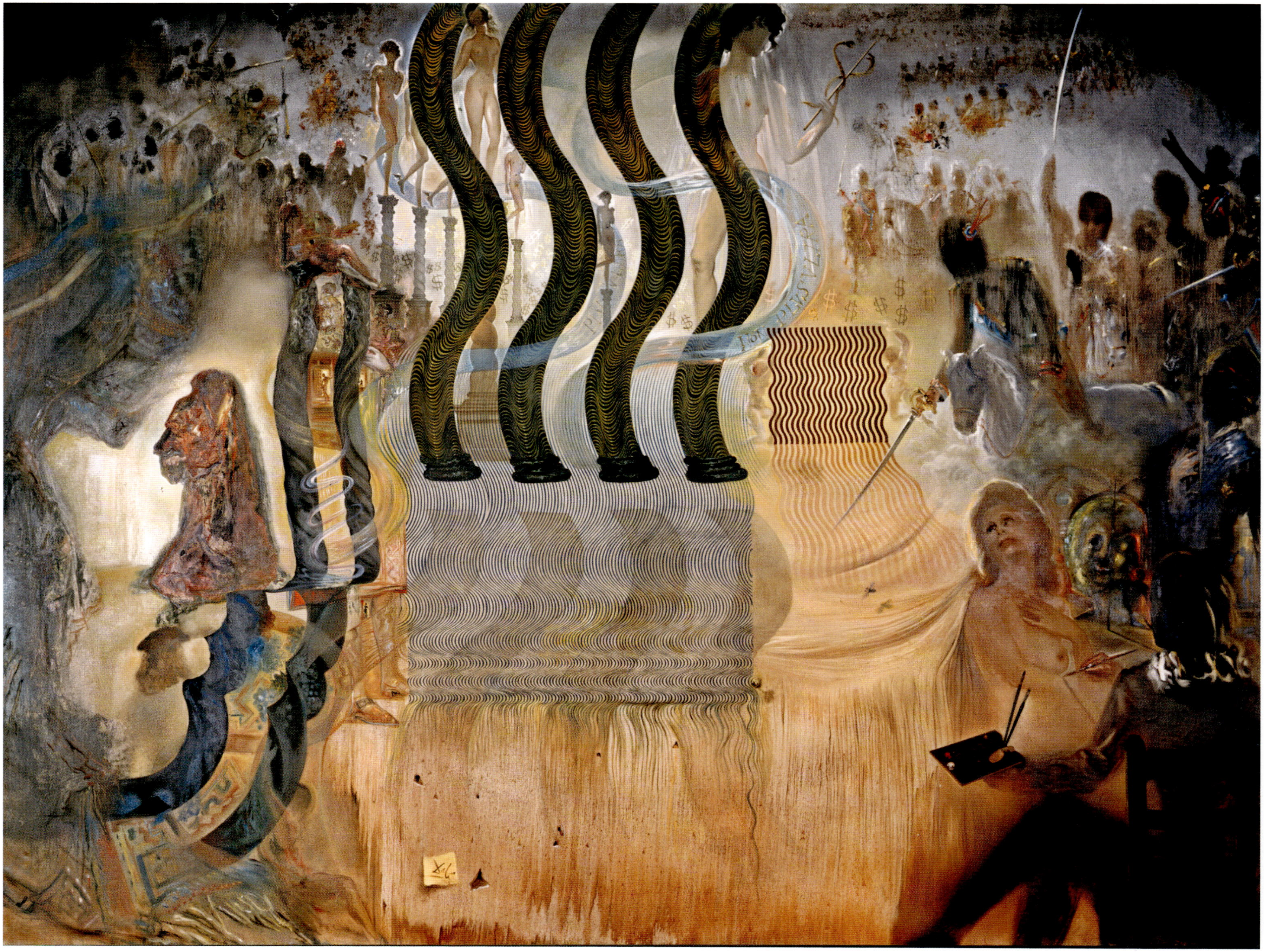

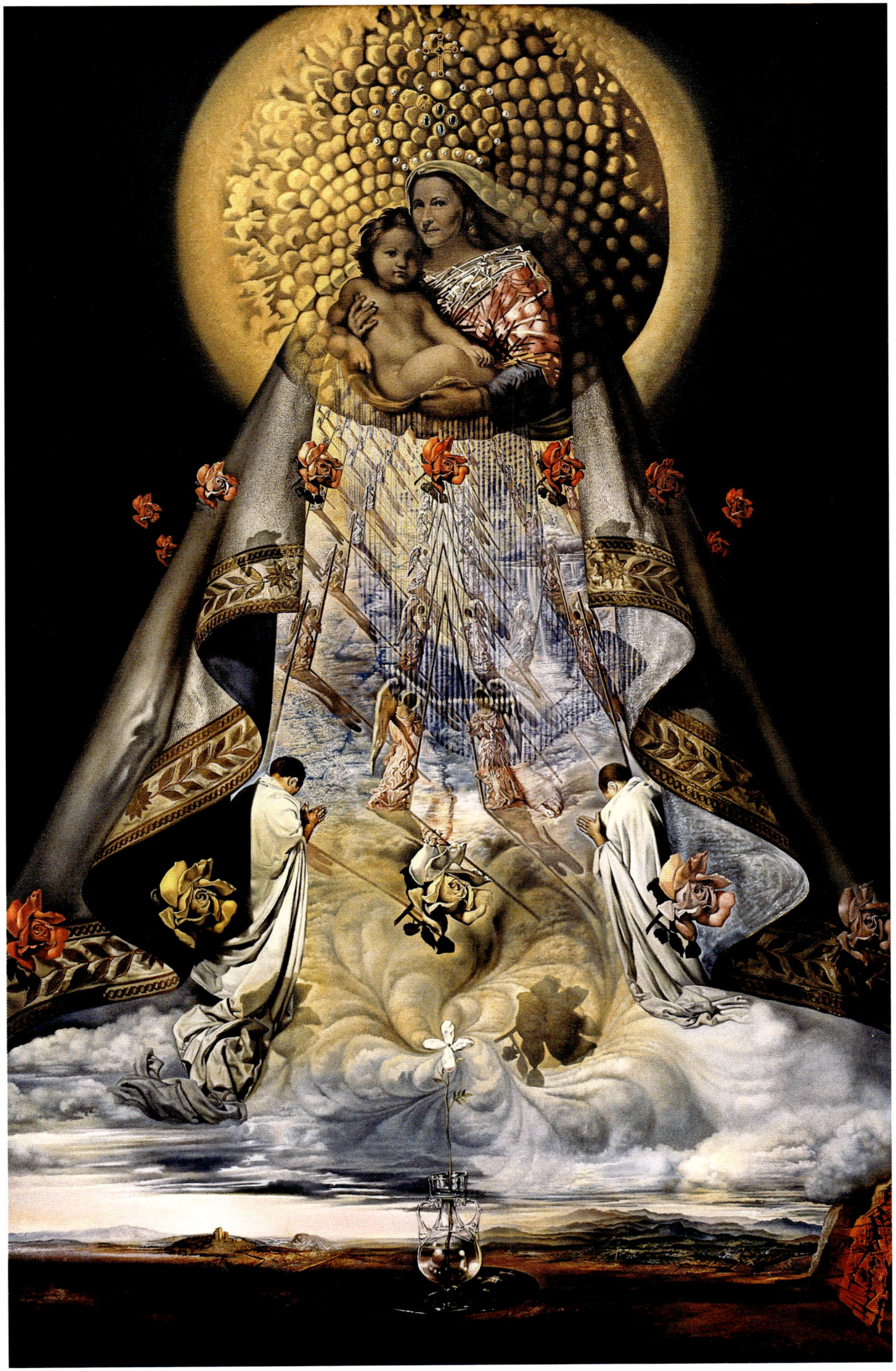

'My motto is: "Dalí must always be talked about, even if nothing good is said about him."'

(Left)

The Virgin of Guadalupe, 1958

Medium: Oil on canvas
Dimensions: 200 x 130 cm (78¾ x 51¼ in)
Location: Private Collection

New Approaches

Despite such naked greed, as witnessed by those around him who were not on the make, such as his builder Emilio Puignau, Dalí did in fact produce some fine work as a printmaker during his later years, above all a beautiful series called *Aliyah* (1968) whose subject was the Holocaust and the creation of the state of Israel. And he was also painting increasingly ambitious canvases that drew on a lifetime of technical know-how and a ceaseless quest for new expressive means. Indeed, just as in his 3D works he had anticipated postmodern irony decades before it became a commonplace, in his painting Dalí's natural curiosity led him to new techniques that also stole a march on others, as with the works that made use of the Ben Day dot system, beginning with *The Sistine Madonna* (1958, *see* page 167), three years before Roy Lichtenstein (1923–97) first used the technique, and including the haunting *Portrait of My Dead Brother* (1963, *see* page 168).

The Battle of Tetuan

In fact, Dalí's was a truly postmodern sensibility in that, given the ability to master any technique and any medium he chose to work in, he tackled so many works with the same mixture of frivolity and seriousness that characterizes so much contemporary art. Thus we have the monumental canvas *The Battle of Tetuan* (1962, *see* page 172), which Dalí painted to commemorate the centenary of an unfinished picture on the same subject by another of his more obscure nineteenth-century heroes, the Spanish painter Mariano Fortuny (1838–74). Dalí later described this painting as 'the product of indigestion' in which he had aimed at producing 'the most kitsch work imaginable'. Typically, the painting is a technical tour de force but also an aesthetic send-up, with battalions of horses sailing through the air above a charging brigade of Moroccan troops, in the centre of which ride Gala and Dalí, grinning inanely and wrapped in Moorish robes; it also appears to be Gala who, a huge standing figure, looms like a deity behind distant mountains, smiling benignly on the scene of carnage unfolding below. A pastiche nineteenth-century battle scene on which Dalí lavished so much work, partly in homage to Fortuny and partly because it must have tickled him to try it, it is also a painting that seems to revel in

'I like to start the day by earning twenty thousand dollars.'

its own absurdity. And the couple might well be grinning, as both knew that someone would buy it for a hefty price, in this case Huntington Hartford, the buyer of *The Discovery of America* (see page 152), for his Gallery of Modern Art in New York.

The Railway Station at Perpignan

Dalí's next significant work – in fact, a crucial reckoning with themes which had haunted him for decades – stemmed from a mystical breakthrough, a typically Dalínian revelation, which occurred the following year. At the end of every summer, the Dalís would decamp from Port Lligat to escape the grim winter and the pitiless *tramuntana* wind that whistles down from the Pyrenees with increasing frequency in the colder months. Their destination was always Paris, by way of a train from Perpignan, just across the border with France, on which the couple deposited their luggage before carrying on to the capital in their imported Cadillac. The station at Perpignan was a place where Dalí claimed to have had some of his best ideas, and on this occasion, on 19 September 1963, he writes in the entry for that day in *Diary of a Genius*: 'I had an exact vision of the constitution of the universe. The universe, which is one of the most limited things that exist, is, all proportions being equal, similar in its structure to Perpignan railway station, with the sole difference to be found near the ticket office, where in the universe there is that enigmatic sculpture whose engraved reproduction had been intriguing me for several days.'

'Eroticism is a royal road to the soul of God.'

From the ordinary insight that many before him have had that some of the best ideas come to us in the most unexpected circumstances, Dalí persuades himself that this is something altogether special, a heightened reality brought about in this instance not by eroticized metamorphosis but by mystical transformation. As if to confirm what was a numinous intuition, he later learned of a circumstance that did indeed seem to mark out this area as objectively special. As Dalí was to discover, in the late eighteenth century the standard length of a metre, a precise subdivision of the Earth's circumference, was determined at a site just north of Perpignan according to a geodetic calculation made by the French astronomer and surveyor, Pierre Méchain (1744–1804). The painter needed no further invitation

(Right)

Trinity (Study for Ecumenical Council), 1960

Medium: Oil on canvas
Dimensions: 58.4 x 66 cm (23 x 26 in)
Location: Vatican Museums and Galleries, Vatican City

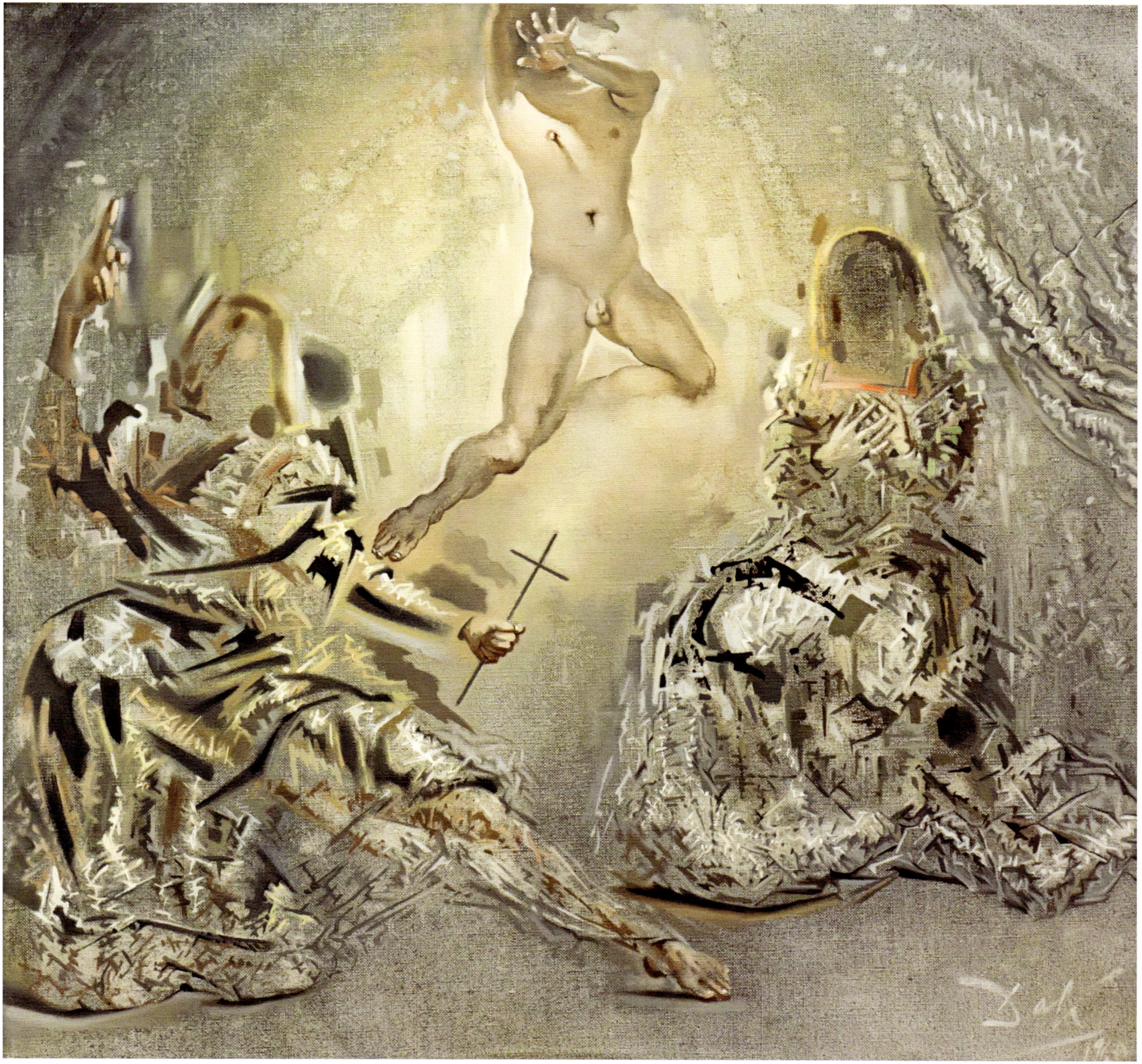

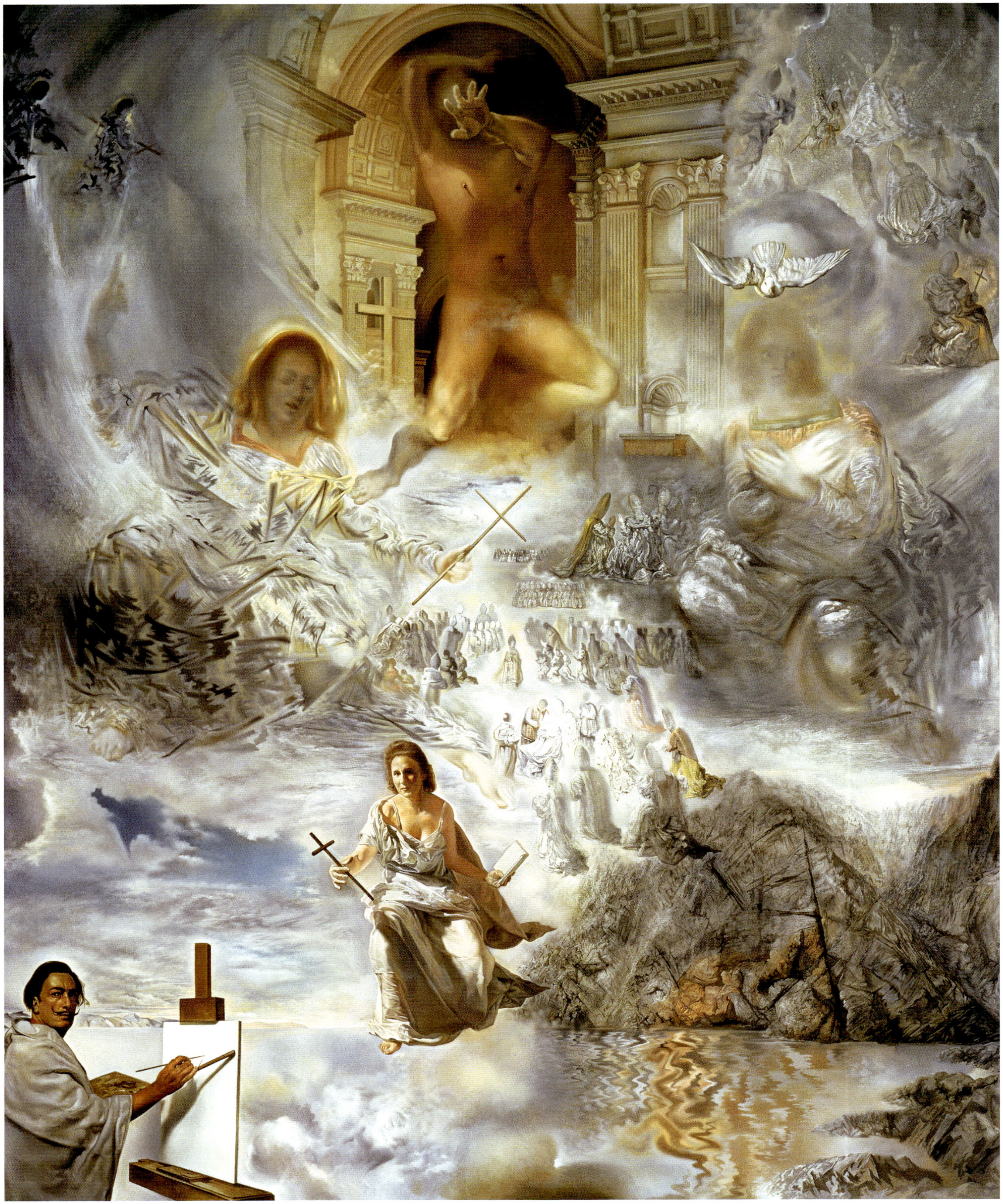

and proceeded to work on a picture, *The Railway Station at Perpignan* (1965, *see* page 171), which turns this moderately significant provincial location into a highly significant Dalinian one.

Towards a Mystical Vision

The familiar couple from Millet's *Angelus* are there in both their original and sexualized forms, framing a central square of light – apparently the skylight of the ticket hall at Perpignan station – from whose four corners radiate four celestial beams. A diminutive figure, who in fact is Dali himself, seems to be floating, legs and arms akimbo, towards the illuminated square, as if being drawn in by some irresistible force. And behind the square, his arms extended along the inclined plane of the two upper beams, his crown of thorns visible between the top of the square and the train that may be hurtling towards us or may indeed be leaving us behind, is Christ the Redeemer, the saviour from whose fundamental purpose in dying Dali, his dead father and his long-dead brother had taken their names.

'Some day, because of me, people will be forced to take an interest in my work.'

Beneath the clowning and the gradual corruption of his talent – the 'tragical sequence of exhibitionism' that he admitted had become the inescapable pattern of his life – did Dali really believe, after all, in a power that was greater than himself? This is not the vision of Saint John of the Cross with an all-powerful painter-god gazing down from some untouchable realm. For once, he seems utterly helpless, unable to control what will inevitably happen one day, in the same way that, as perhaps the figures from the *Angelus* reveal, he had been fundamentally helpless before the deepest forces of life. And who is that at the bottom of the picture – the boy who seems to stand in front of a sack like the one on the wheelbarrow from the *Angelus*? The younger boy in *The Spectre of Sex Appeal* (*see* page 175) did not have hair that long and wore a sailor suit, so perhaps the figure looking on in this case is not Dali himself but someone who has already crossed over – one of the many who had already left the station for the very last time.

(Left)

The Ecumenical Council, 1960

Medium: Oil on canvas
Dimensions: 302.2 x 254 cm (118 x 100 in)
Location: Salvador Dali Museum, St Petersburg, Florida

The Centre of the Universe

On realizing the significance of Perpignan, Dalí tells us: 'I then took a taxi and went slowly around the station, inspecting it as if it were some esoteric monument of which I had to find the meanings. The setting sun was ablaze and the flood of its light created flames on the façades and especially the central skylight of the station that seemed to become the centre of an atomic explosion. About the station I could see a radiating aura in a perfect circle: the metal trolley cables of the streetcars that ringed the edifice and gave it a crown of glinting light.'

And then, because as he himself once wrote, 'I go deeper into mysticism through erotic delirium,' he goes on with typical sexual frankness: 'My penis sprang to attention with joy and ecstasy: I had seized the truth, I was living it. Everything became overpoweringly evident. The centre of the universe was there before me.'

Of course, he knew that it was not, not literally, and he knew that we would know it, too. But he also knew that just as the hallucinatory phantoms of the unconscious mind can seem more real than the objective world, so the subjective intensity of mystical experience overrides whatever we may think we know of the world it momentarily transfigures; that the physical universe – 'one of the most limited things that exist' – is infinitely smaller than the one that exists in our minds. And the ability of the best of Dalí's art to remind us of the fundamental plasticity of the mind, its seemingly infinite capacity for creative transformation, is possibly its most lasting significance.

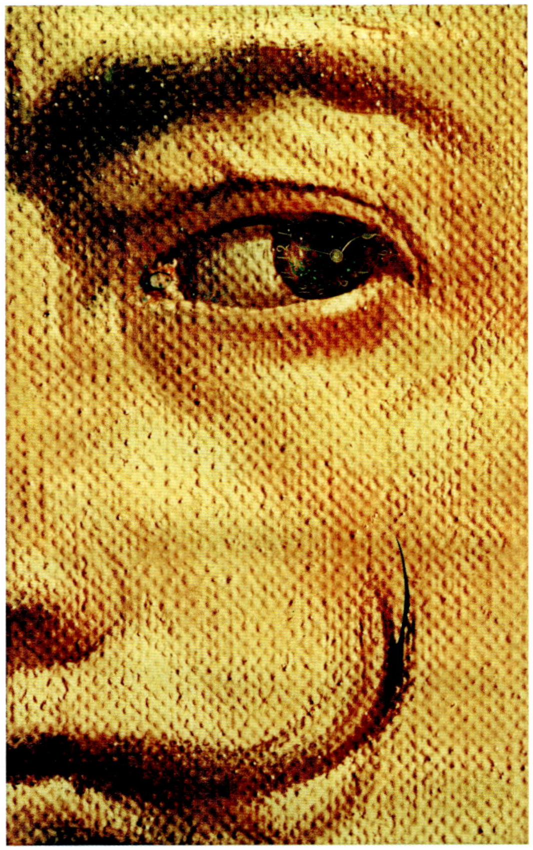

The Master of Ceremonies

But if Dalí was still able on occasions like this to draw from the sense of disturbance which had led to the great paintings of the 1930s, by the 1960s he was more often doing work of far less significance, distracted no doubt by the runaway gravy train of the blank sheets fiasco or the voyeuristic enjoyment of the orgies and erotic games involving beautiful young couples which he arranged for his onanistic pleasure; though

(Above)

Macrophotographic Self-Portrait with Gala Appearing as a Spanish Nun, 1962

Medium: Gouache on colour photograph
Dimensions: 76.5 x 48.1 cm (30 x 19 in)
Location: Private Collection

(Right)

The Sistine Madonna, 1958

Medium: Oil on canvas
Dimensions: 225.7 x 191.1 cm (89 x 75¼ in)
Location: Private Collection

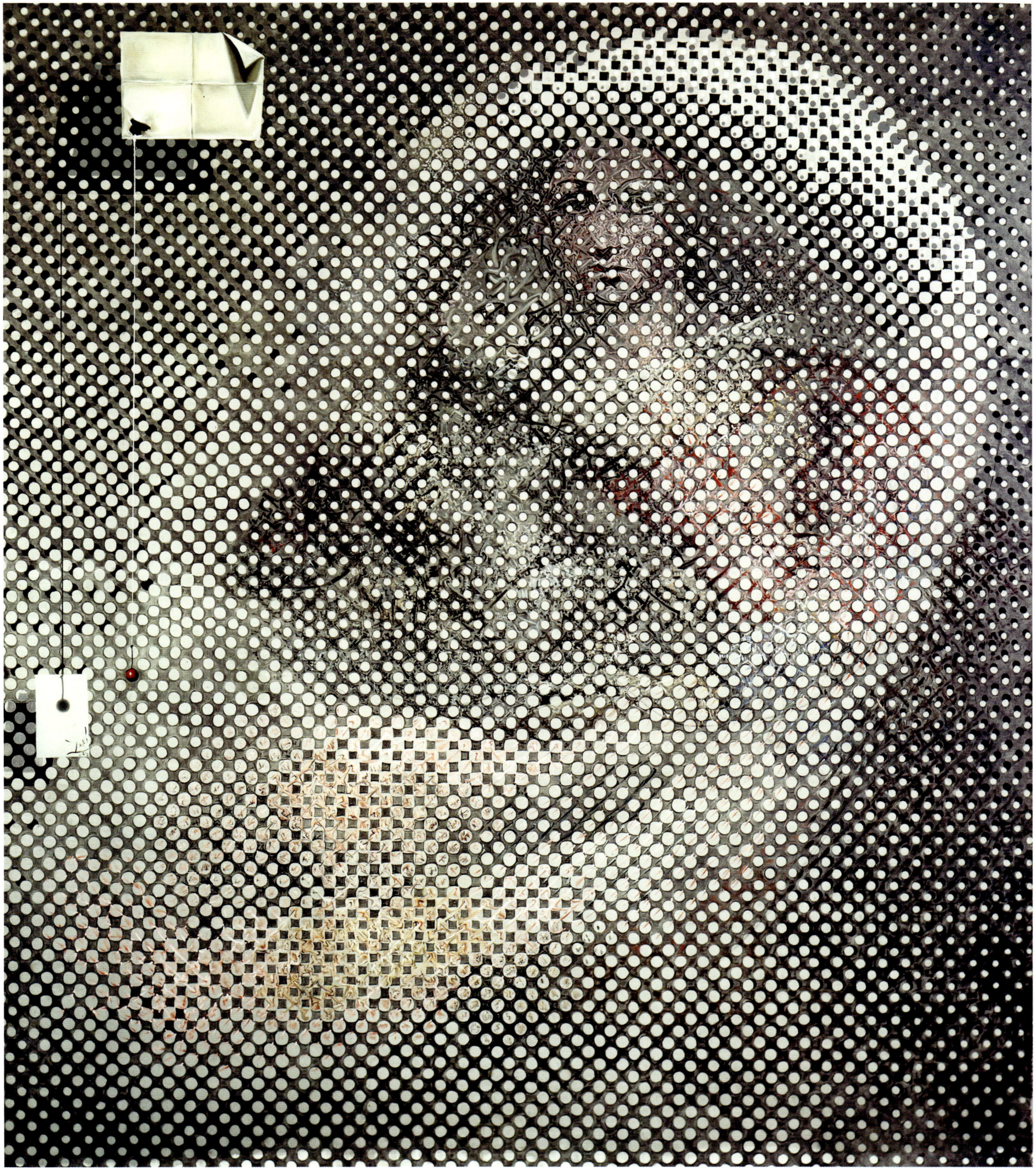

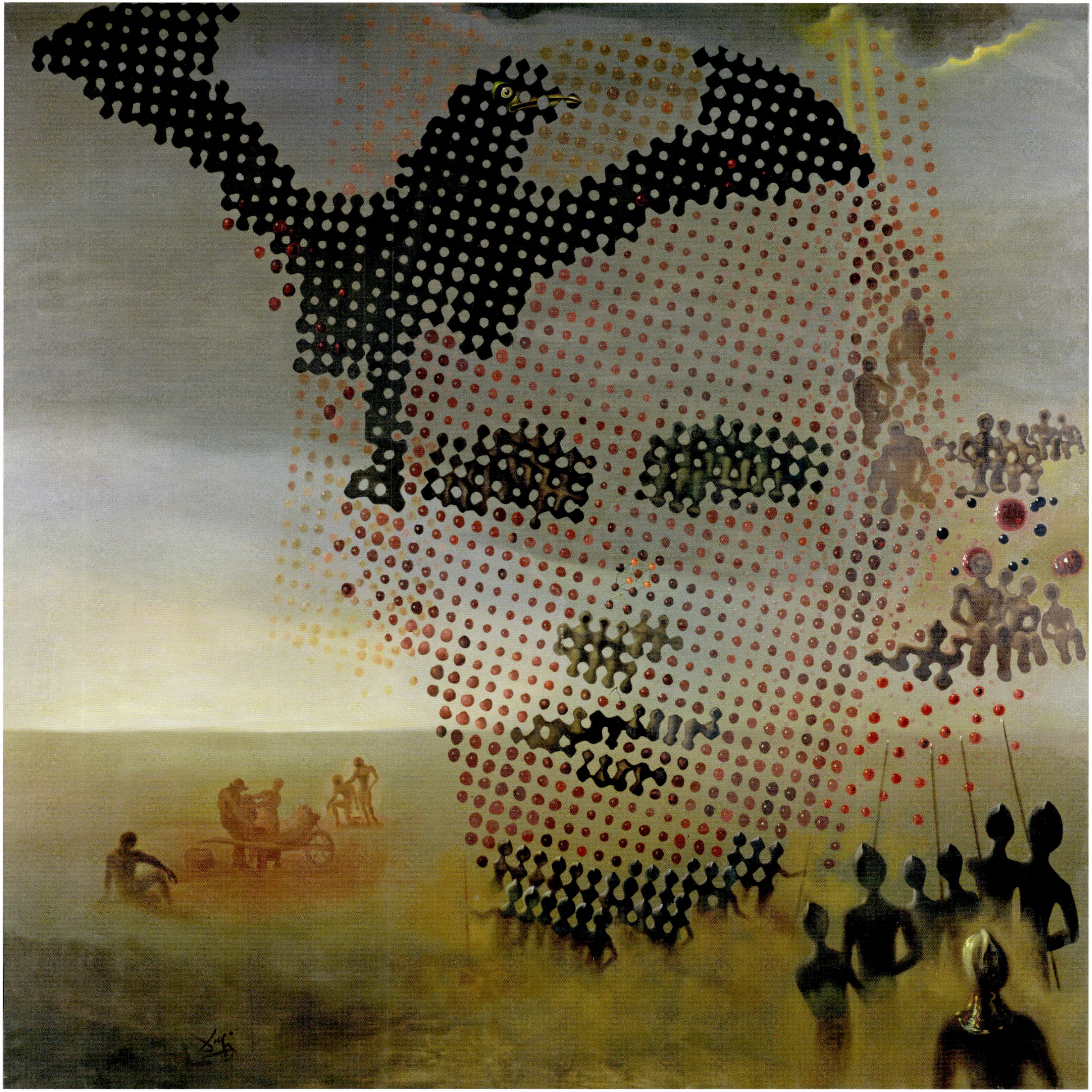

still the great masturbator never touched and was never touched in turn, having retreated to the only role in which he felt comfortable. These evenings of orchestrated debauchery he details with as much relish in his writings as he does in his paintings, just as he had always chronicled the details of his masturbation and his sex life with Gala. In these hedonistic experiments he found himself in step with the spirit of the 1960s, and Port Lligat seems to have become a stop along a branch line of the hippy trail, with Dalí in the role of louche, corrupting guru to the young.

With Gala now lost to an erotic world of her own, Dalí also had scope for valued female friendships, in particular with Amanda Lear, a transsexual who became an important model for Dalí in his later years; indeed, she was someone to whom at one point he drew so close that the two of them tramped up a mountain to consult a hermit at the sanctuary of Rocacorba near Girona, as to whether it would be possible for them to contract a 'spiritual marriage'. Dalí also adopted an ocelot, an exotic pet whose claws and teeth were filed down to stop it from harming anyone. And he missed no opportunity for a personal appearance, giving many interviews to journalists and filming opportunities to television crews throughout the 1960s and 70s. As he wrote: 'A picture's nothing compared with the magic which constantly irradiates from my person.'

'Every day I kill the image of my dead brother, with my hands, with kicks, and with dandyism.'

Tuna Fishing

Nevertheless, a painter he remained, and two large works from the late 1960s stand out as his most ambitious and perhaps his last major statements in the medium. The first, the huge, almost mural-sized *Tuna Fishing* (1966–67), subtitled *Hommage à Meissonnier*, is a Romantic spectacular, an orgy of slaughter based on his father's memories of the *almadraba* that had once taken place near Roses, the village with a long beach just south of Cadaqués, in which a school of tuna was forced into a narrow cove close to shore and then hacked to death by the fishermen; its other inspiration was a print of a painting by one of Meissonnier's *pompier* contemporaries depicting this very subject, which as a boy he had seen hanging in his father's office. He wrote of the work: 'It is the most ambitious picture I have ever

(Left)

Portrait of My Dead Brother, 1963
Medium: Oil on canvas
Dimensions: 175 x 175 cm (69 x 69 in)
Location: Private Collection

painted … a revival of representational art, which was underestimated by everyone except the Surrealists throughout the period of so-called "avant-garde" art…. What finally made me decide to take on the subject, which had been tempting me my whole life long, was my reading of Teilhard de Chardin (1881–1955), who believed that the universe and cosmos are finite – which the latest scientific discoveries have confirmed. It then became clear to me that it was that finite quality, the contractions and frontiers of the cosmos and universe, that made energy possible in the first place. The protons, antiprotons, photons, pi-mesons, neutrons, all the elementary particles have their miraculous, hyper-aesthetic energy solely because of the frontiers and contractions of the universe. In a way, this liberates us from the terrible Pascalian fear that living beings are of no importance compared with the cosmos; and it leads us to the idea that the entire cosmos and universe meet at a certain point – which in this case, is the tuna catch. Hence the alarming energy in the painting!'

A New Physicality

Tuna fishing as big bang, like Perpignan station before it; artistic apprehension as subjective mystical centre of the 'Dalí Universe', as those continuing temporary exhibitions are known which still move from city to city, showing his work across the world. But this is not mere Dalinian sophistry; it is also fundamental to the making or viewing of art – the ability to believe (or at least not to disbelieve) in that moment of creation or reception of the work that the experience in which we are involved and the place in which it is happening – namely, our minds – is the most significant there could possibly be.

'Have no fear of perfection – you'll never reach it.'

In Dalí's canvas, echoing his father's stories, the fishes' blood is the pervasive colouring of the picture, though the complex saturation of so much strong colour, applied with an expressionist freedom redolent of Abstract Expressionism or Tachism, its European variant, was a new departure for Dalí. In its violence, rendered through the chaotic upheavals of blood and water, and also in the savage intent of the naked fishermen with their Classical physiques, it also conveys a physicality and a potency of action that may have been what Dalí really admired in Meissonnier, a virility which in life he had always felt eluded him. In this regard, he was typically frank in describing his sexual impotence to Alain Bosquet around the time he was painting this picture.

(Right)

The Railway Station at Perpignan, 1965

Medium: Oil on canvas
Dimensions: 295 x 406 cm (116 x 159¾ in)
Location: Ludwig Foundation, Museum Ludwig, Cologne

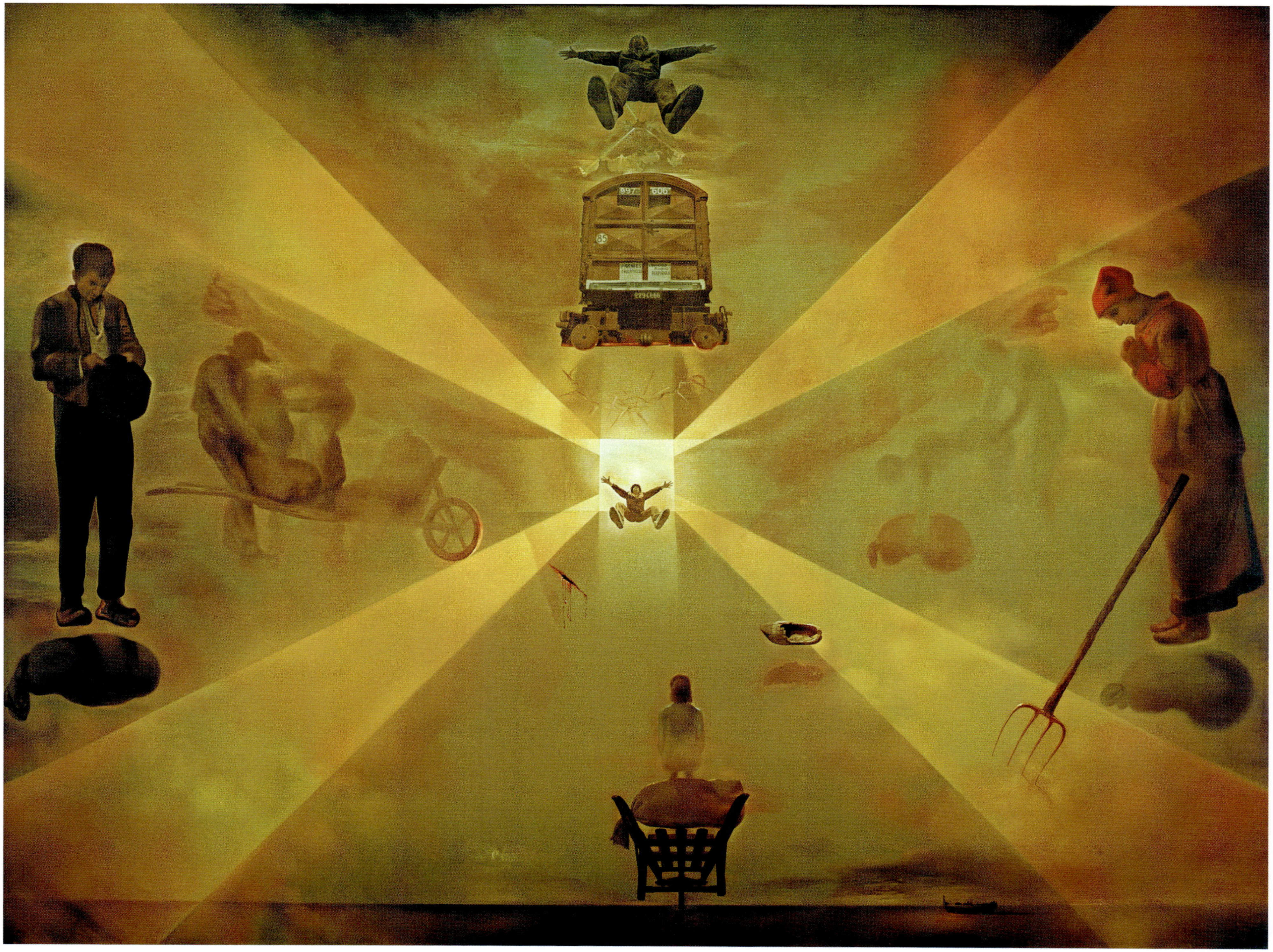

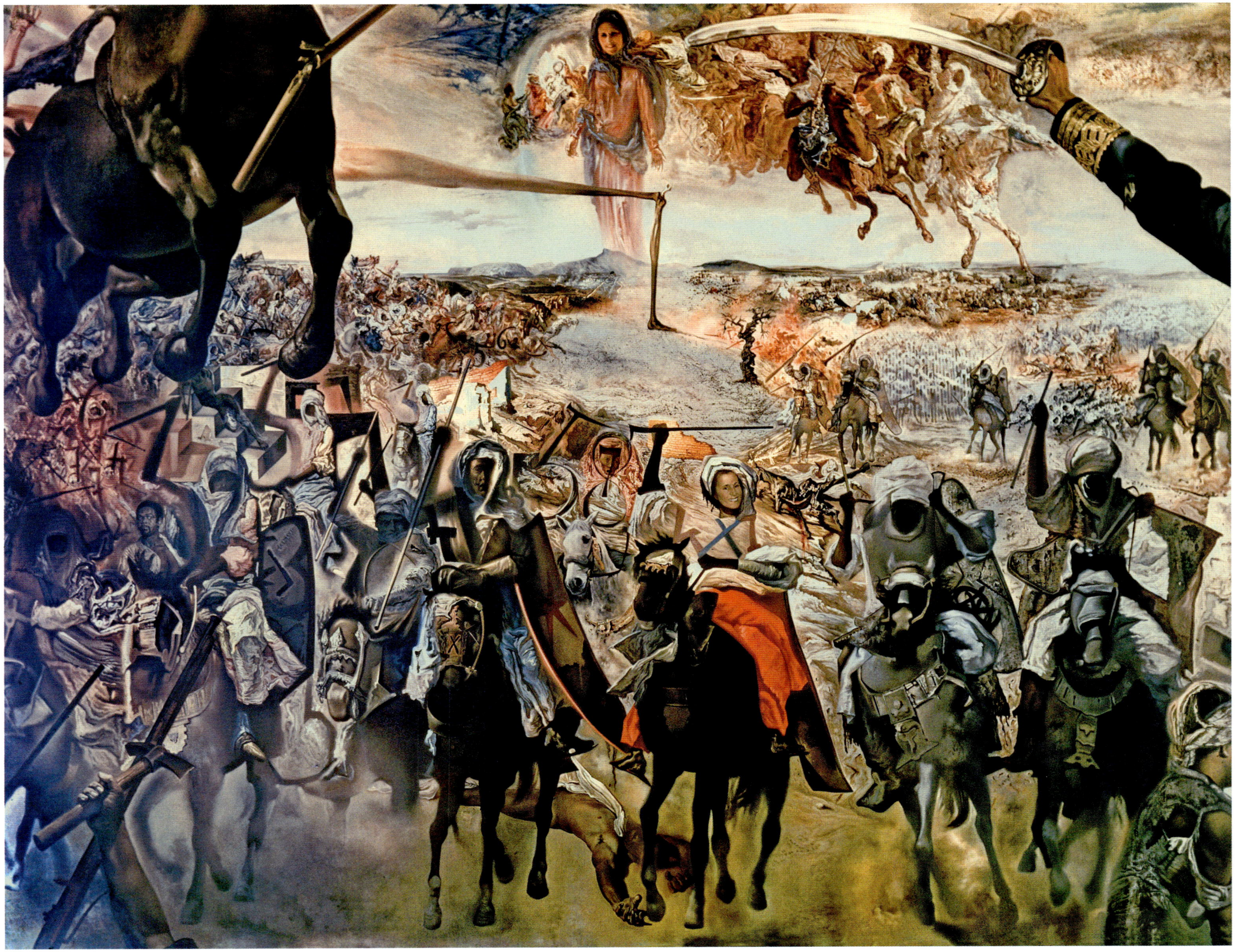

'I go deeper into mysticism through erotic delirium.'

Of course, because it was so alien, such physicality and potency also terrified him to the extent that Dalí had fled first the Spanish Civil War and then the European conflict that followed to avoid getting caught up in the blood-letting. So the picture is certainly an homage to the French painter but also quite possibly to the many fishermen of Port Lligat – some of whom had been his friends in their early years in the village – who had been murdered in the Civil War, and by implication perhaps those numberless others whose fate he had also escaped. It is not a *Guernica* by any means, but it was as close to a collective identification as Dalí would ever come. And, as we see from a work of the following summer, *Fisherman of Port Lligat Mending his Net* (1968), an astonishingly tender depiction, the subjects of *Tuna Fishing* were very much on his mind at this time.

The Hallucinogenic Toreador

If *Tuna Fishing* took two summers to complete, Dalí's next and probably last significant work took just as long. Another huge canvas, *The Hallucinogenic Toreador* (1969–70, *see* page 176) originated in the torso of the Venus de Milo printed on a box of pencils, in whose recessed shadows he saw the face of a bullfighter, creating yet another double image hallucination such as in the late 1930s he had been able to produce almost at will. Dalí himself declared that this new painting would be an anthology of all his work, but it is more than just a bravura exercise in stylistic virtuosity – or rather, the various styles in the painting are indivisible from the biographical anthology of Dalí's life that the work as a whole represents. Its content is indeed so rich and multifarious that it would need a whole chapter to fully describe it. The most salient elements are immediately apparent, in particular the face of the toreador as the shadow double in the second Venus. Dalí told one friend that this figure was a composite of various dead young men, including his dead brother, two suicides associated with Surrealism – Pierre Batcheff (1907–32) and René Crevel – and of course Lorca, the great modernist poet of the ancient soul of Spain and the person with whom Dalí had enjoyed the deepest male friendship of his life.

(Left)

The Battle of Tetuan, 1962

Medium: Oil on canvas
Dimensions: 304 x 396 cm (119¾ x 156 in)
Location: Morohashi Museum of Modern Art, Fukushima

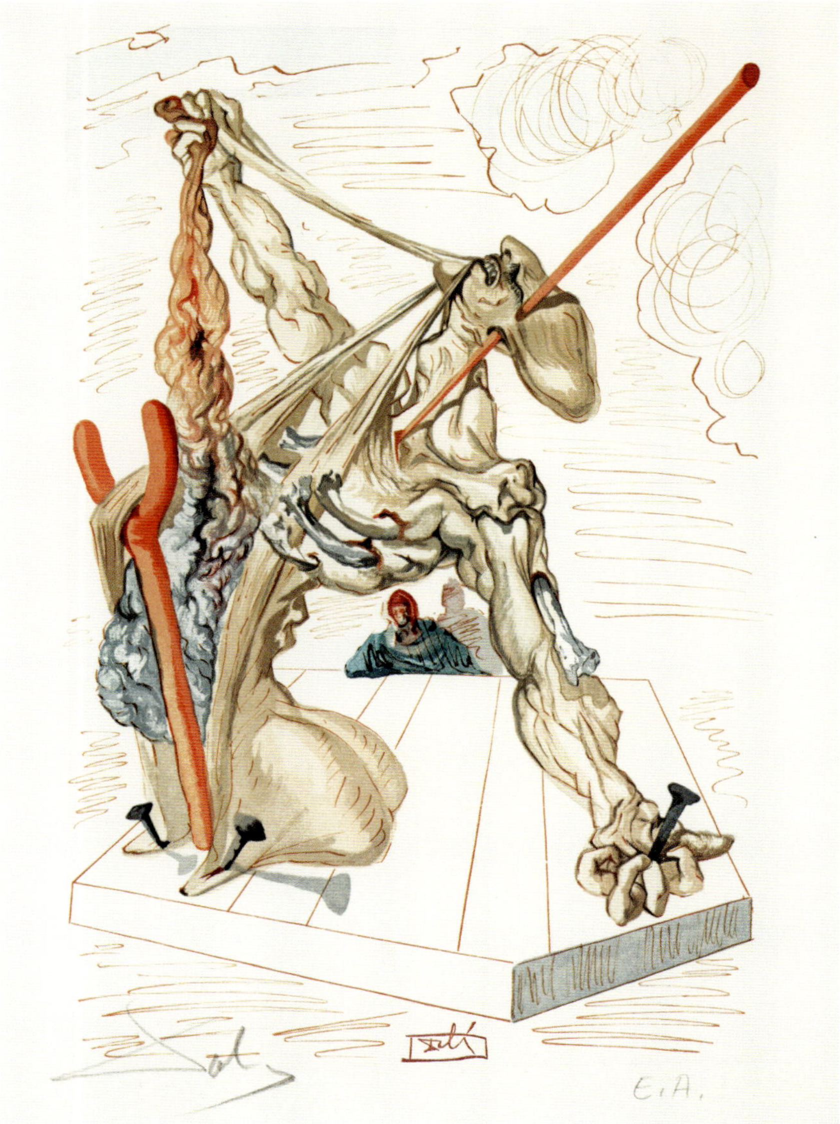

Lorca

When told of Lorca's death in 1936, Dalí's reaction had been to exclaim, 'Olé!', not in flippant dismissal of such a tragic event but almost certainly in a sense of shock which for once had rendered him speechless. His brother's ghost he had addressed over and over again, but the presence of the little boy from *The Spectre of Sex Appeal* (*see* right), looking up perhaps wistfully, perhaps longingly, from the right-hand bottom corner, as well as the bull and the bull ring – and the reference to a toreador – points to the presence of Lorca above all others in this shadow face.

We have already seen how much Dalí regretted not having persuaded the poet to come with him to Italy in the summer of 1936, but his grief at Lorca's death (*see* pages 103–05), despite their reconciliation in the preceding few months, was almost certainly sharpened by the rift which Dalí himself had caused with this undeniably noble human being. Lorca had also loved him deeply and had wanted to consummate that passion. Dalí had rejected him, so he tells us, but had loved him still. And given his lifelong difficulties as a heterosexual man, Gala's priceless intervention notwithstanding, we have to question whether out of his many acts of needless personal cruelty, for most of which he

(Above)

Canto 29 – The Personators, from Dante's Inferno, c. 1960

Medium: Woodcut
Dimensions: 33 x 27 cm (13 x 10½ in)
Location: Dallas Museum of Art, Texas

(Right)

The Spectre of Sex Appeal, 1934

Medium: Oil on wood
Dimensions: 17.9 x 13.9 cm (7 x 5½ in)
Location: Fundació Gala-Salvador Dalí, Figueres

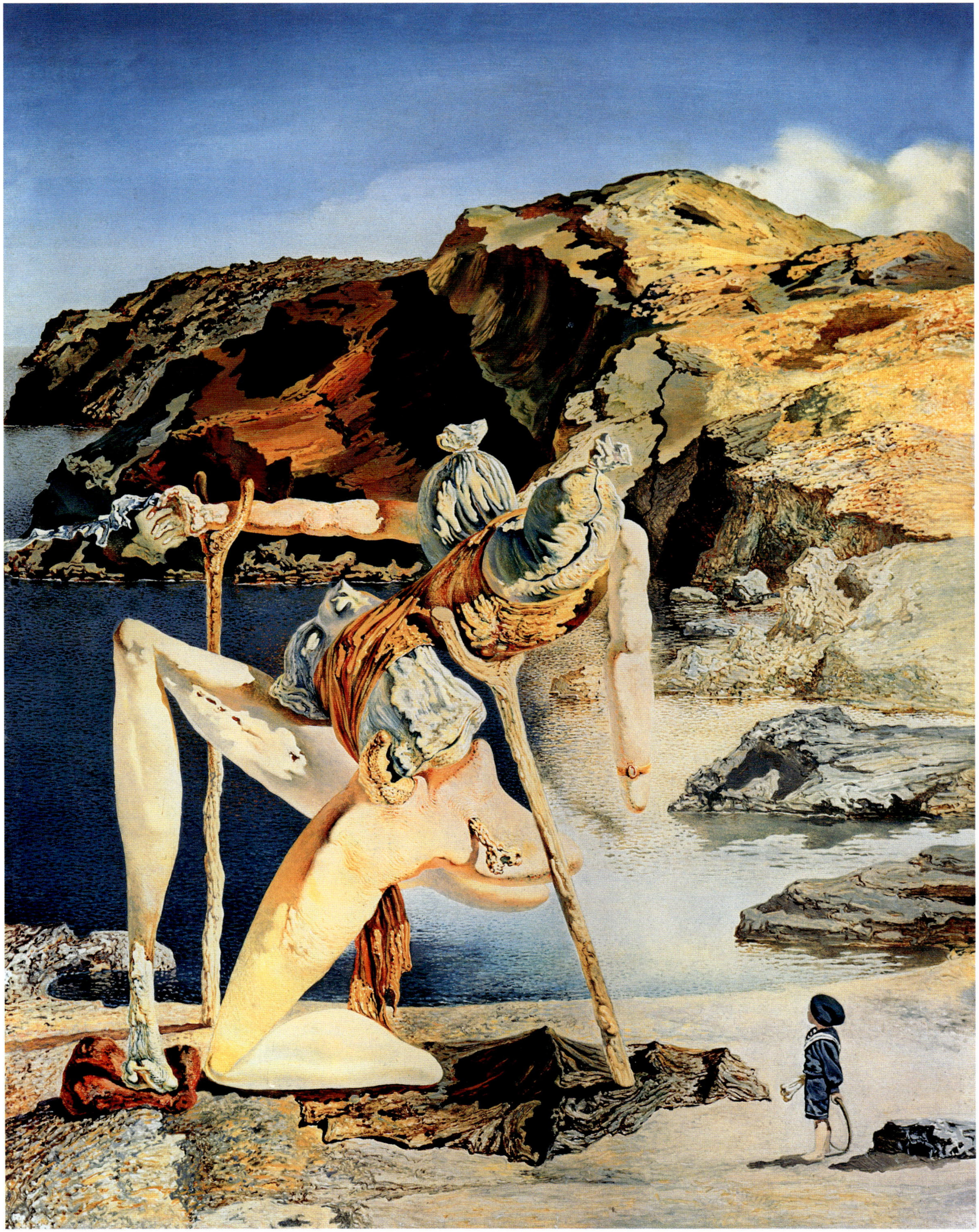

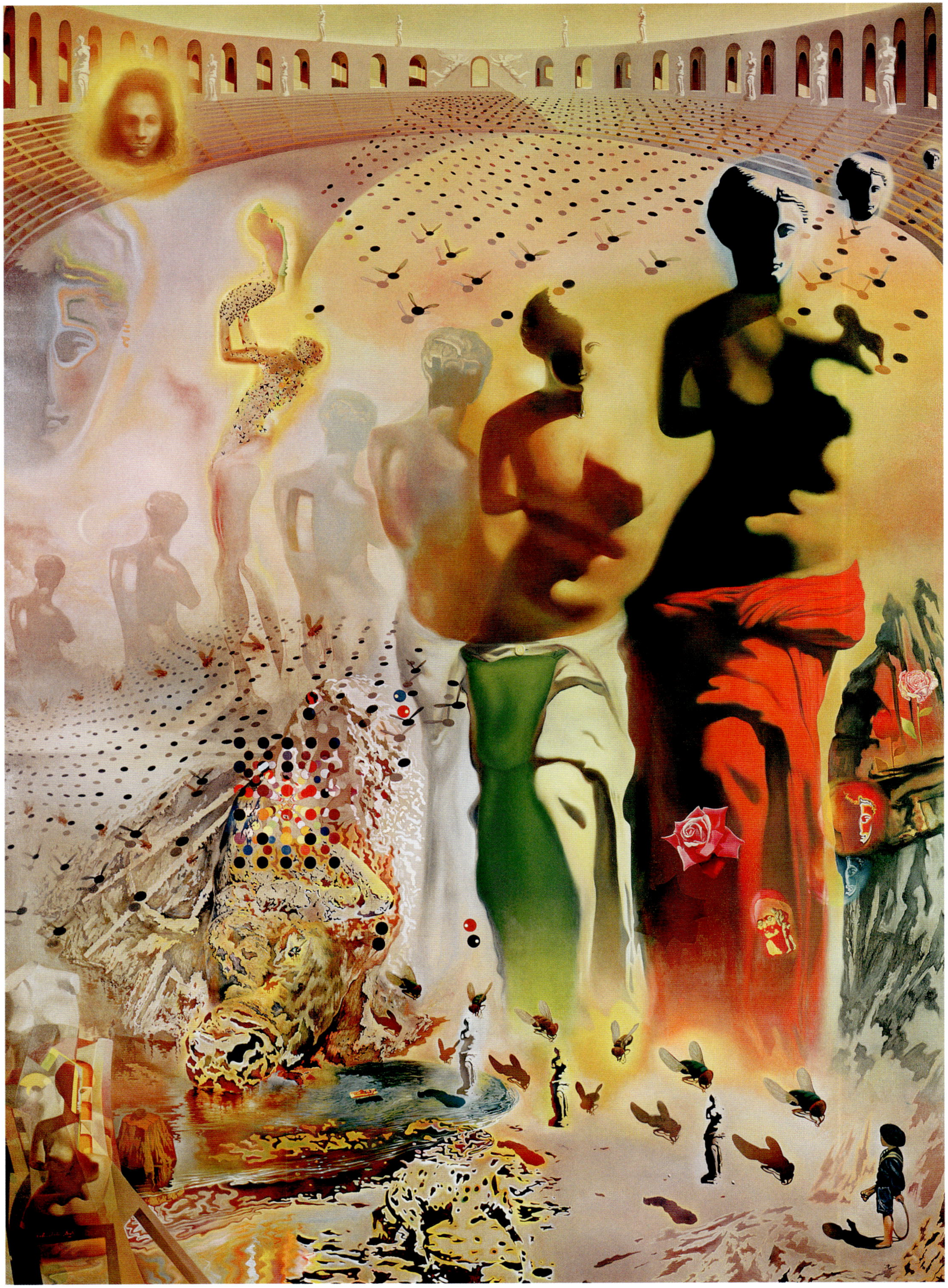

appeared to show no remorse, his rejection of Lorca was something to which he could never quite reconcile himself and may have regretted very deeply indeed.

A Pictorial Anthology

Certainly, the confusion over sex in the tiny 1934 canvas in which the boy gazes up at a monstrous grotesque of amputated limbs is here far more resolved: the child seems to look directly at the spectre of the toreador, perhaps able at last to acknowledge the source of the desire he had spent his whole life fetishizing in his art. And does the haloed face of Gala in the top left-hand corner of the canvas, the compassionate Madonna to his erotic Christ, seem to offer some kind of blessing or absolution? Of course, there are many other elements in the painting – the cubist chair, the rocks of Cap de Creus near his Port Lligat home,

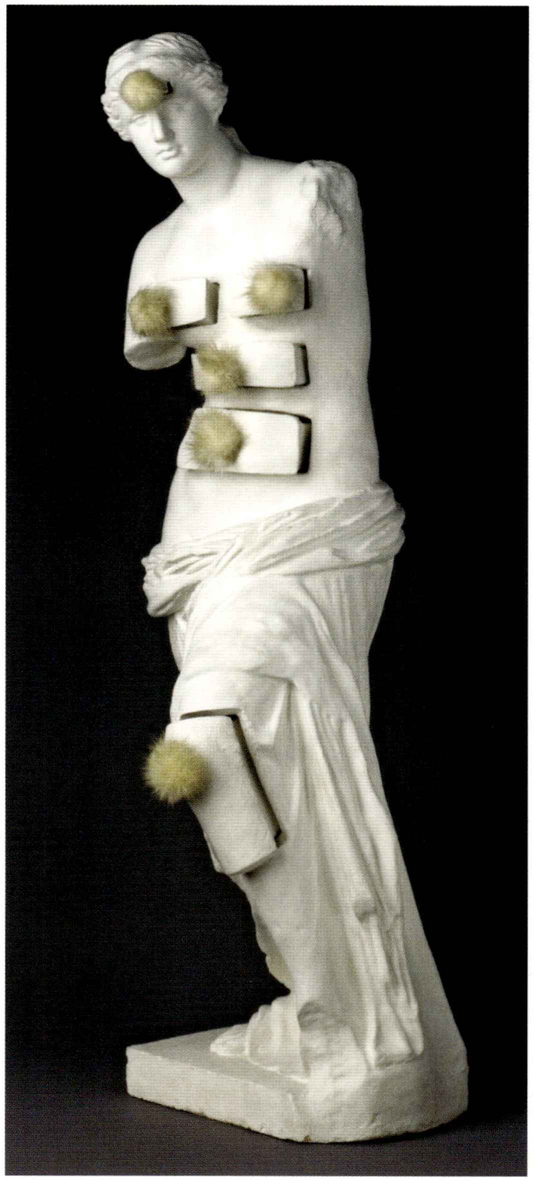

the spinning molecules of DNA, the head of Voltaire, and so on – that their interactions and relationships inevitably alter over repeated viewings of the image, making any definitive reading impossible. But it does seem perverse not to attempt one in a picture crammed with so many totems from the entirety of Dalí's artistic and emotional life.

Dalí never again attempted a painting of such ambition, though he continued his optical experiments, most notably in the field of holographic art, which for a short time seemed to him to be the future, until he realized that the technical sophistication he needed to make the holographic images in his mind would not emerge in his lifetime. But there were other diversions, in particular the stereoscopic images he made in the mid- to late 1970s, inspired by the work of seventeenth-century Dutch painter, Gerrit Dou (1613–75), whose results are perhaps not as interesting as Dalí thought they

(Left)

The Hallucinogenic Toreador, 1968–70

Medium: Oil on canvas
Dimensions: 398.8 x 299.7 cm (157 x 118 in)
Location: Salvador Dalí Museum, St Petersburg, Florida

(Above)

Venus de Milo with Drawers, 1936

Medium: Painted plaster with metal pulls and mink pompoms
Dimensions: 98 x 32.5 x 34 cm (38½ x 12⅘ x 13⅓ in)
Location: Art Institute of Chicago, Illinois

were. Above all, these optical games were products of his ceaseless curiosity, which often leaped far ahead of his artistic sensibility in these later years.

A Museum and a Castle

In any case, from the later 1960s onwards Dalí became increasingly preoccupied by a project that he soon came to view as the most important work of his life. The idea of a room devoted to his art in the Empordà Museum in Figueres had been suggested to Dalí as early as 1961 by the town's mayor, Ramon Guardiola Rovira (1920–91). The painter took up the suggestion with gusto, but wanted something much grander, something that was entirely suited to his exhibitionist personality and the protean nature of his work. He knew just the place: the ruins of the town's theatre, still mouldering after being burned out by Nationalist troops at the end of the Civil War – the very same theatre where as a teenager he had had his first exhibition. As he put it himself: 'Since everything about me is theatrical, I couldn't make a better choice.' Moreover, the empty shell was just across the square from the church of Sant Pere where the baby Salvador had been baptized (*see* page 36).

But the project was slow in getting off the ground and by 1968 Gala was demanding her own residence, the castle she had long dreamt of, where she might carry on her desperate assignations in complete privacy. By the summer of 1969, a suitable medieval ruin – one of the many such structures that punctuate the landscape of the Empordà, as they do the rest of Spain – had been located at Púbol, a village just a couple of dozen miles south of Figueres. In less than a year it was ready, and for the next decade Gala

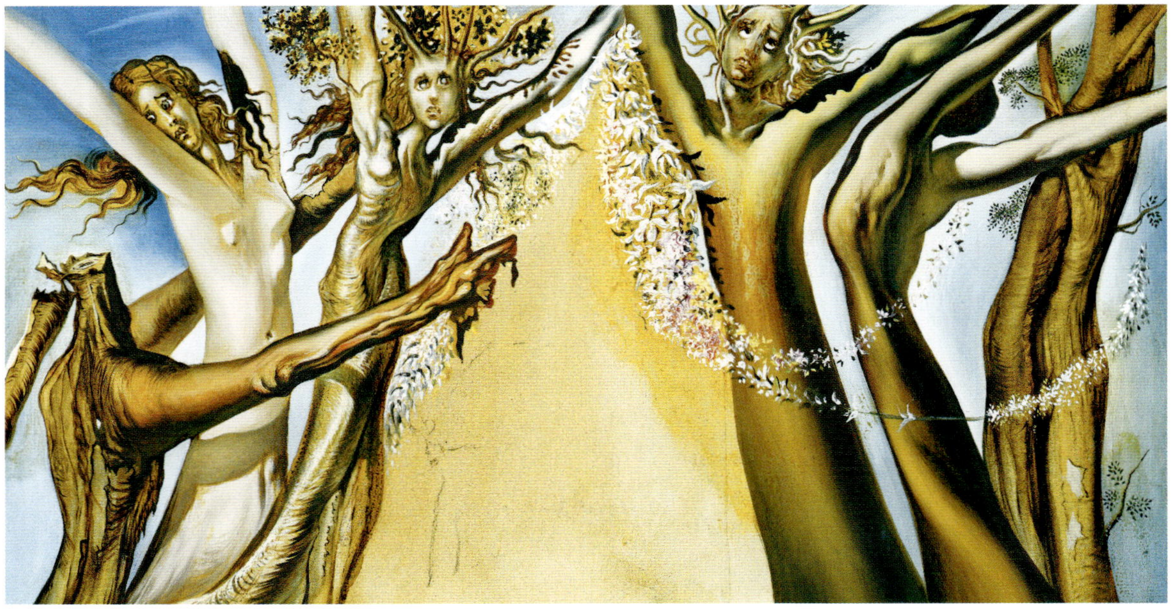

(Above)

Project for Mad Tristan, 1944

Medium: Oil on canvas
Dimensions: 26.5 x 48 cm (10¼ x 19 in)
Location: Private Collection

carried on her separate life at Castle Púbol, with Dalí supplying a huge ceiling mural and other decorations but otherwise only being able to visit his wife upon receipt of a written invitation. This very formal arrangement, holding Dalí at arm's length, was a restriction whose masochistic effect in fact delighted the painter, who was still very much her little boy.

The Theatre-Museum at Figueres

In October 1968, Dalí had been granted an audience with General Franco for the second time, but despite receiving the dictator's blessing for the Theatre-Museum, it was another two years before work began. What pleased Dalí most about the design was the geodesic dome, inspired by Buckminster Fuller (1895–1983) and designed by rising young architect Emilio Pérez Piñero (1935–72), which would sit

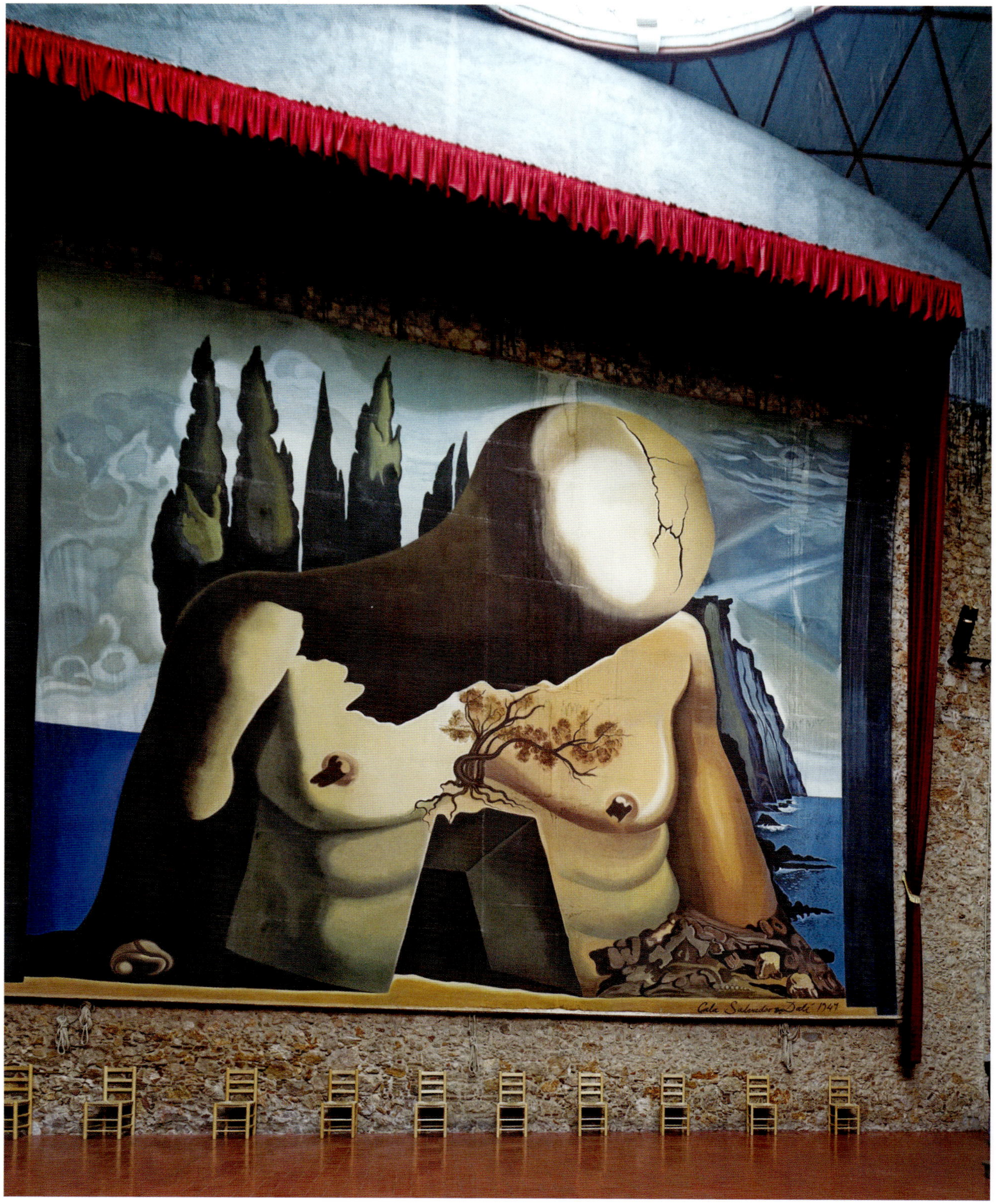

(Right)

Backdrop for Labyrinth, 1941

Medium: Tempera
Dimensions: 880 x 1300 cm ($346\frac{1}{2}$ x $511\frac{4}{5}$ in)
Location: Teatre-Museu Dalí, Figueres

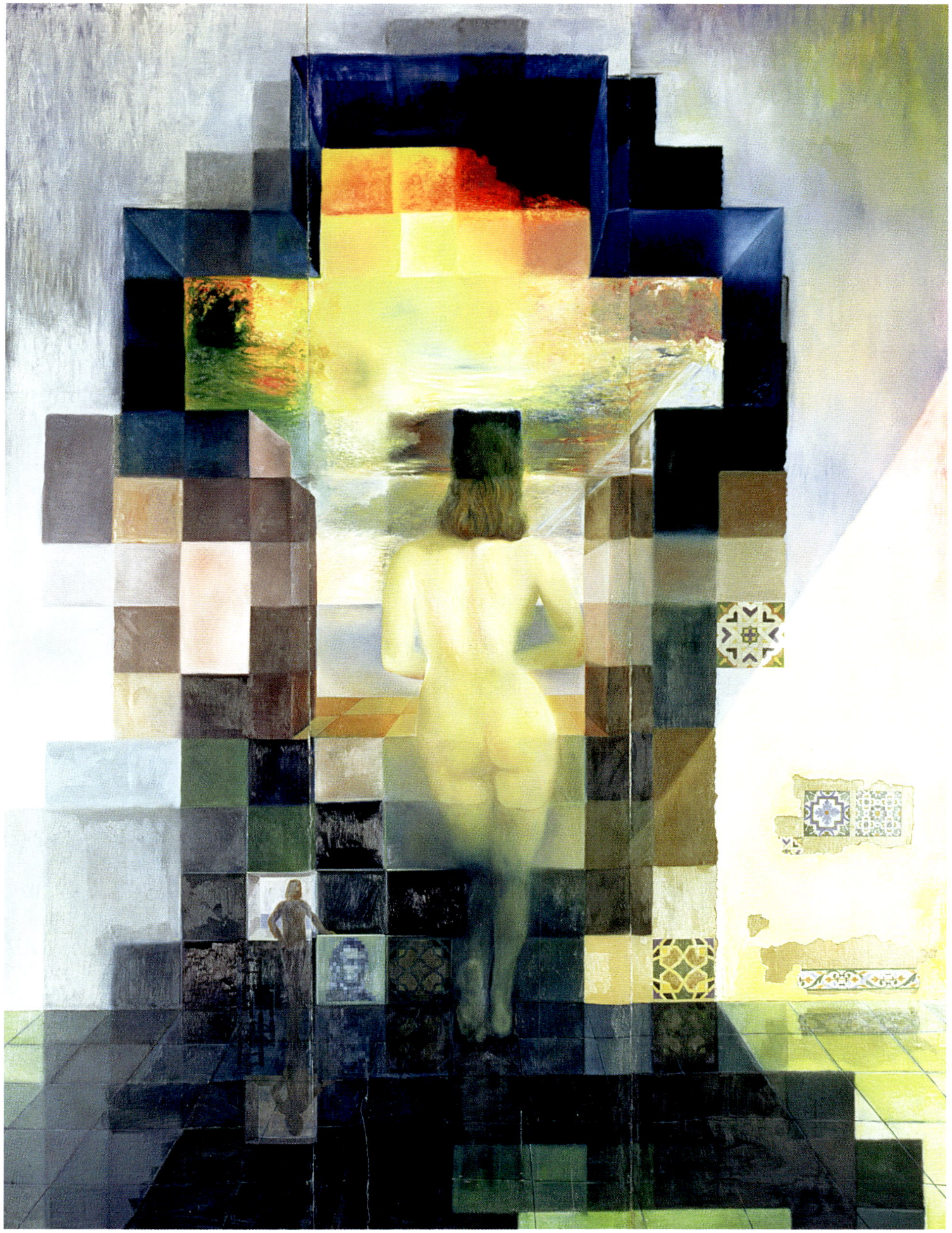

atop the former stage of the theatre, now serving as the new Theatre-Museum's capacious atrium. Dalí saw this exquisite structure as a cupola, which he insisted was a symbol of monarchy, and by this point in his life he was above all a believer in tradition and in monarchy.

The Theatre-Museum was officially opened on 28 September 1974, though without much interest beyond the local area, a reflection both of bad organization and Dalí's declining reputation in the art world at large. Then the following year, in one of his last acts as dictator, Franco ordered the execution of five alleged terrorists, among them three who belonged to the Basque separatist organisation, ETA. Dalí took the foolish decision to answer questions from a French news agency about this action. His supportive response, declaring Franco to be 'a wonderful person', 'the greatest hero of Spain', indicates not only his

(Left)

Gala Contemplating the Mediterranean Sea Which at Twenty Metres Becomes the Portrait of Abraham Lincoln – Homage to Rothko (First version), 1974–75

Medium: Oil on photographic paper
Dimensions: 445 x 350 cm (175¼ x 137¾ in)
Location: Fundació Gala-Salvador Dalí, Figueres

moral corruption by this point in his life but also an appalling lack of judgement. Digging himself an ever bigger hole, Dalí went on: 'Personally I'm against freedom. I'm for the Holy Inquisition. Freedom is shit, and that's why all countries fail when there's an excess of freedom.'

Dalí Goes Too Far

The international outcry against him this time was more than the ageing *enfant terrible* was used to getting. His remarks were widely disseminated through the world's media – he was Dalí, after all – and graffiti was scrawled on the walls of the house at Port Lligat and stones thrown at the windows. When the death threats began arriving in the post, Dalí decided to flee the country, travelling for the first time by air, first to Geneva then on to New York City, where he met with as much hostility from Spanish exiles living there as he had faced at home. Franco died in November that year, but Dalí was still in New York for his usual winter sojourn when a bomb was discovered beneath the chair he normally occupied at his favourite Barcelona restaurant.

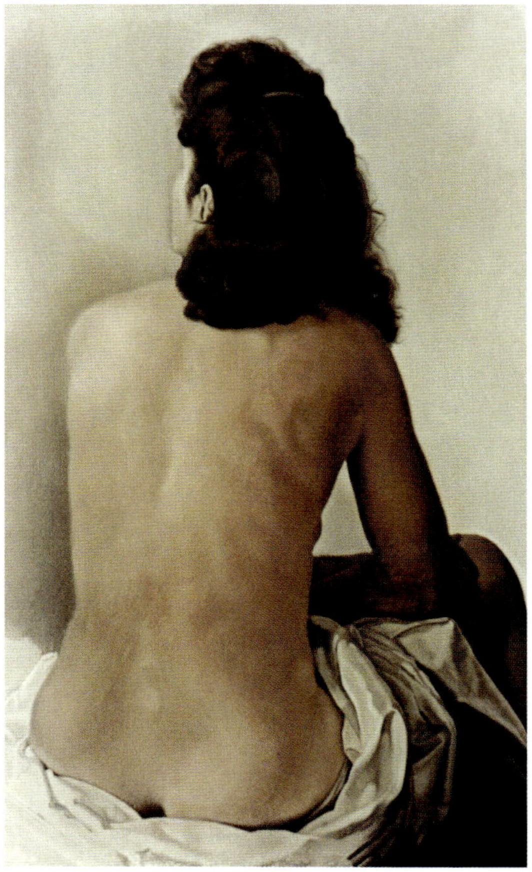

(Above)

Gala from Behind Looking in an Invisible Mirror, 1960

Medium: Oil on canvas
Dimensions: 41 x 31.5 cm (16 x 12⅖ in)
Location: Fundació Gala-Salvador Dalí, Figueres

Eventually, Dalí sneaked back home where, assured of the support of the restored monarchy – King Juan Carlos I (b. 1938) and Queen Sofia (b. 1938) – who would visit him several times in the coming years, he went back to making pieces to put in the still unfilled Theatre-Museum. One of these was the huge reproduced backdrop from his ballet, *Labyrinth* (see page 120), while a piece completed the previous year was yet another kind of double picture, given the self-explanatory title, *Gala Contemplating the Mediterranean Sea which at Twenty Metres Becomes the Portrait of Abraham Lincoln* (1976, see opposite page). This is an early example of pixelated art which is still displayed to its full advantage in the Theatre-Museum. By this time Dalí's secretary, Captain Peter Moore, had been supplanted by Enric Sabater. Moore had done well out of the prints debacle, but in exploiting the Dalí name Sabater would descend to a whole new level. In just five years at the helm of Dasa Enterprises, the company he set up, Sabater made himself a millionaire several times over in a paroxysm of merchandising that has become all too commonplace in the decades since.

Gala's Decline and Death

Despite the shenanigans, there were some at least who remembered that Dalí had once been a significant artist, and in December 1979 he was given a major retrospective at the Pompidou Centre in Paris – though Dalí and Gala were refused entry at the opening on account of a strike by museum staff. Gala was now in her mid-eighties and unable to live alone at Castle Púbol, her long-term gold-digging lover, Jeff Fenholt (b. 1951), having finally left her. Back at Port Lligat, Gala resumed her controlling ways with Dalí, dosing him with quantities of pills that may well have caused irreparable neural damage. In any case, Dalí's hand now trembled so much that he was unable to work without considerable assistance. Many, if not all, of the works from his final years have to be considered at least partly the creations of others, in particular the long-serving Isidor Bea.

In July 1981, Dalí and Gala returned to Port Lligat from Paris for the last time. The Theatre-Museum had become a roaring success, being now the second-most visited museum in Spain after the Prado in Madrid. In January 1982, King Juan Carlos awarded Dalí the country's highest decoration, the Grand Cross of the Order of Charles III, and on 20 March he received the Gold Medal of the Catalan Government, the highest honour his own region could bestow. Gala was having constant health scares and by early June was thought to be dying. Her estranged daughter, Cécile, drove from France to try to see her, but in a final act of cruelty, Gala refused to let her in. She died just a few days later at Port Lligat, but in a bizarre incident, having requested that her passing should take place at her castle, her corpse was driven in the early morning cross-country in the back of the Cadillac so that the doctor could pronounce her dead at Púbol. Dalí then made the strange decision to go on living at Gala's castle, having never been there before except by invitation. He never returned to Port Lligat.

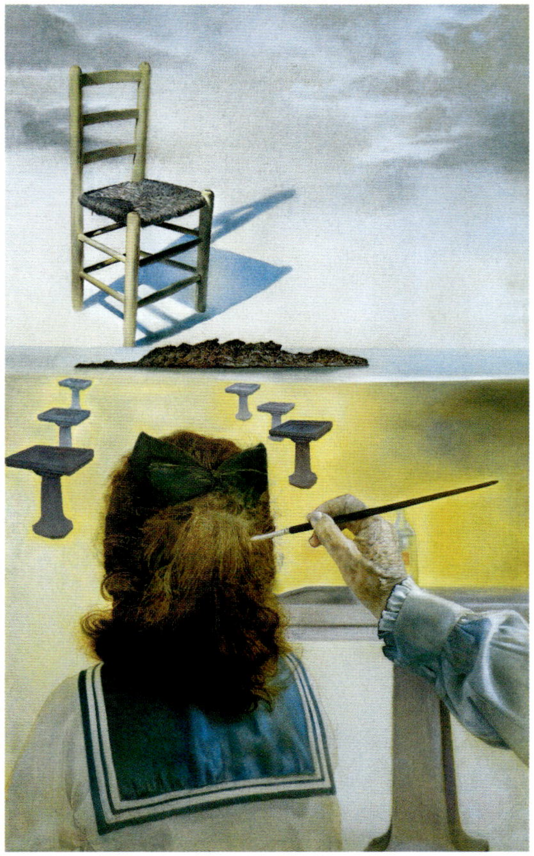

(Above)

The Chair (stereoscopic work, right component), 1975

Medium: Oil on canvas
Dimensions: 402 x 210.4 cm (158¼ x 82⅘ in)
Location: Fundació Gala-Salvador Dalí, Figueres

(Right)

Dalí Seen from the Back Painting Gala from the Back Eternalized by Six Virtual Corneas Provisionally Reflected by Six Real Mirrors, 1972–73

Medium: Oil on canvas
Dimensions: 60.5 x 60.5 cm (23⅘ x 23⅘ in)
Location: Fundació Gala-Salvador Dalí, Figueres

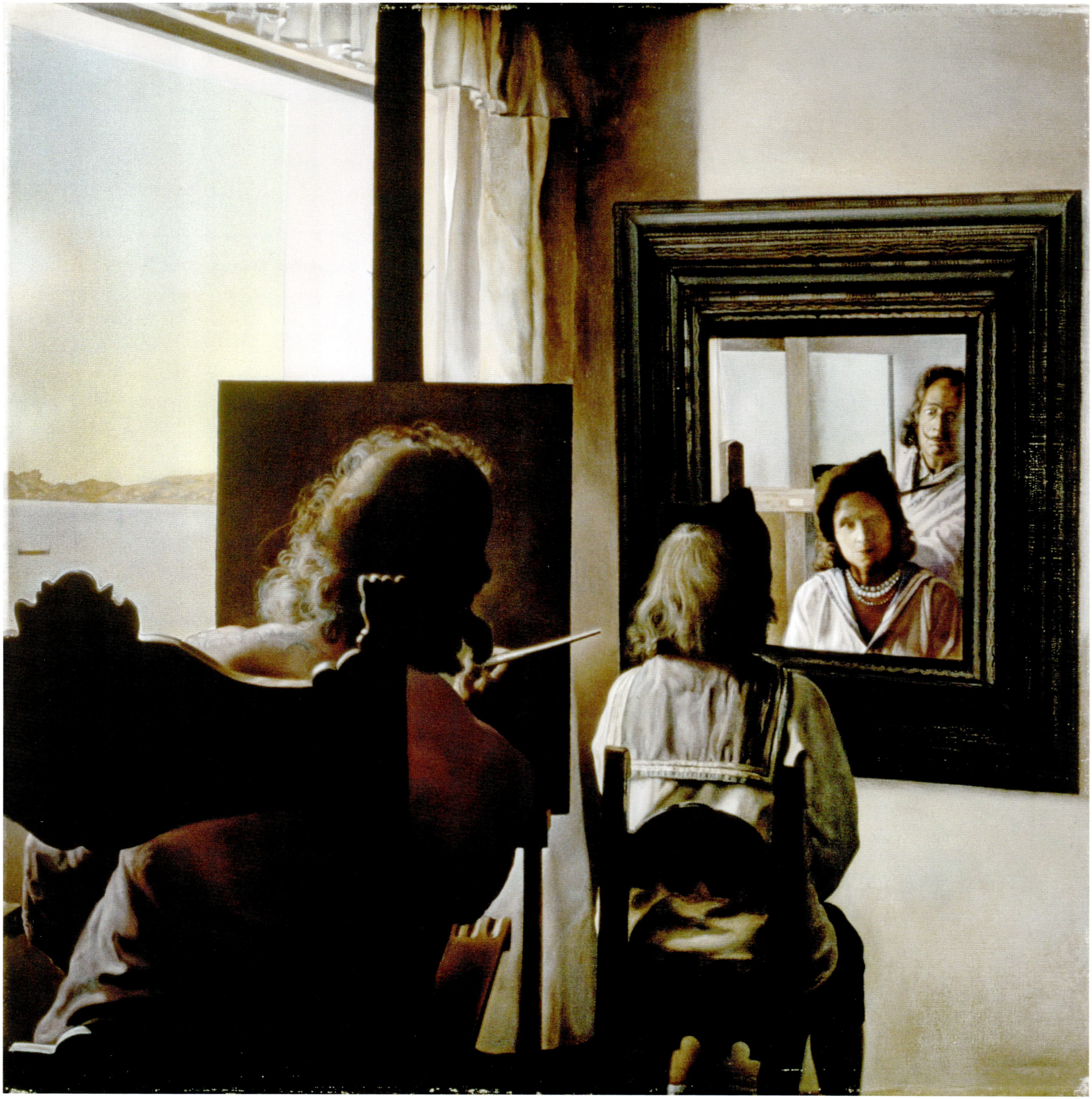

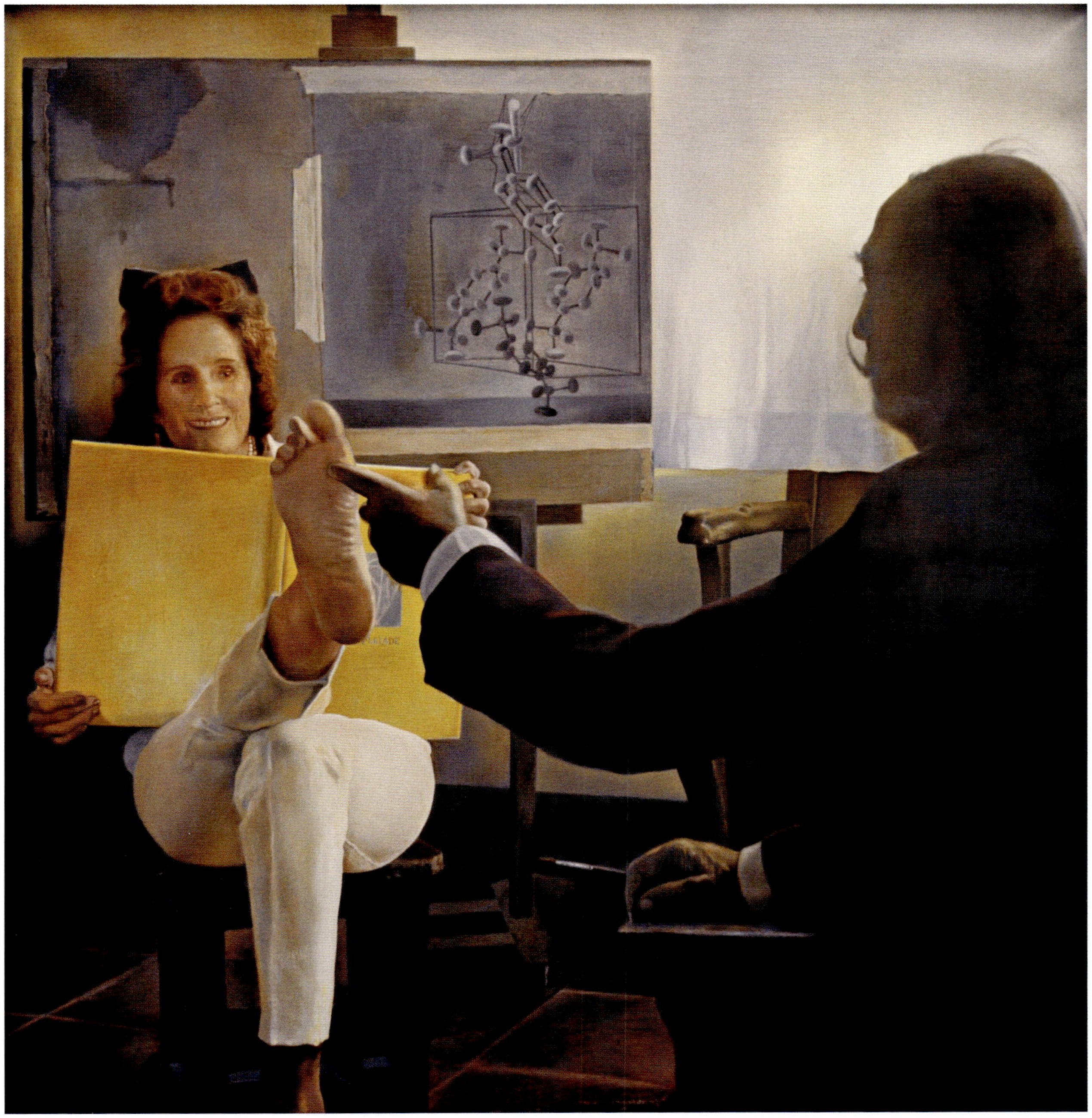

A Dismal Ending

In July Juan Carlos ennobled Dalí, granting him the title of Marquis of Dalí and Púbol, elevating this staunch supporter of absolute monarchy to the ranks of the aristocracy he had always admired. It made little difference to his state of mind, however, as over the coming months he declined alarmingly, hardly speaking, sobbing constantly and spending hours making pitiful animal noises. He also began experiencing hallucinations – involuntary ones this time – and believed that he was a snail. He became increasingly depressed and difficult to look after, declining to eat, spitting at his nurses and refusing to take his medicine. He also rang his bell incessantly, and it was probably a short circuit in this device that caused the fire in August 1984 which almost killed him. In the event, despite the smoke that was pouring from the room, Dalí was rescued by the policeman on duty and his then secretary, Robert Descharnes (1926–2014).

(Left)

Gala's Foot (Right Panel), c. 1975–76

Medium: Oil on canvas
Dimensions: 60 x 60 cm (23⅔ x 23⅔ in)
Location: Fundació Gala-Salvador Dalí, Figueres

He suffered 18 per cent burns to his body and needed skin grafts. His sister, Anna Maria, came to see him at the clinic in Barcelona, but he shrieked at her, sending her away with hideous insults; whatever she had done to him, he would never forgive her. In October, having recovered sufficiently, Dalí was taken back to his Theatre-Museum and installed in the adjoining tower, which he had named the Torre Galatea. He was now fed through a nasal-gastric tube and could hardly make himself understood.

Dalí continued to live in this secluded way, beside his beloved museum, for another four years, until his death on 23 January 1989. The funeral service took place in the neighbouring church of Sant Pere, where at the beginning of a century whose anxieties he had done so much to articulate, he had been baptized. It was the most inconspicuous of endings for someone who had lived so conspicuously throughout his remarkable life.

Dalí's Gift

But what are we to make of that life and of the work Dalí produced? Above all, perhaps, there is a sense that his very public attempts at explaining himself in both his paintings and in his writings were thwarted by the 'tragical sequence of exhibitionism' that was both his great gift and yet something of a curse in everything he did. Dalí created some of the most memorable images of his time and is still an artist who can reach a public that may otherwise have little interest in modern art. This gift to the world, the ability to communicate the darkest truths of the psyche to a mass audience, is not to be underestimated. A saviour of modern painting he may not have been, but in mining his own neuroses so unsparingly and then rendering their strange fruit with such an unflinching eye, at his best Dalí gave compelling, unforgettable form to the inexplicable phantoms that haunt the modern mind.

'I value death greatly. After eroticism, it's the subject that interests me most.'

‘A picture's nothing compared with the magic which constantly irradiates from my person.’

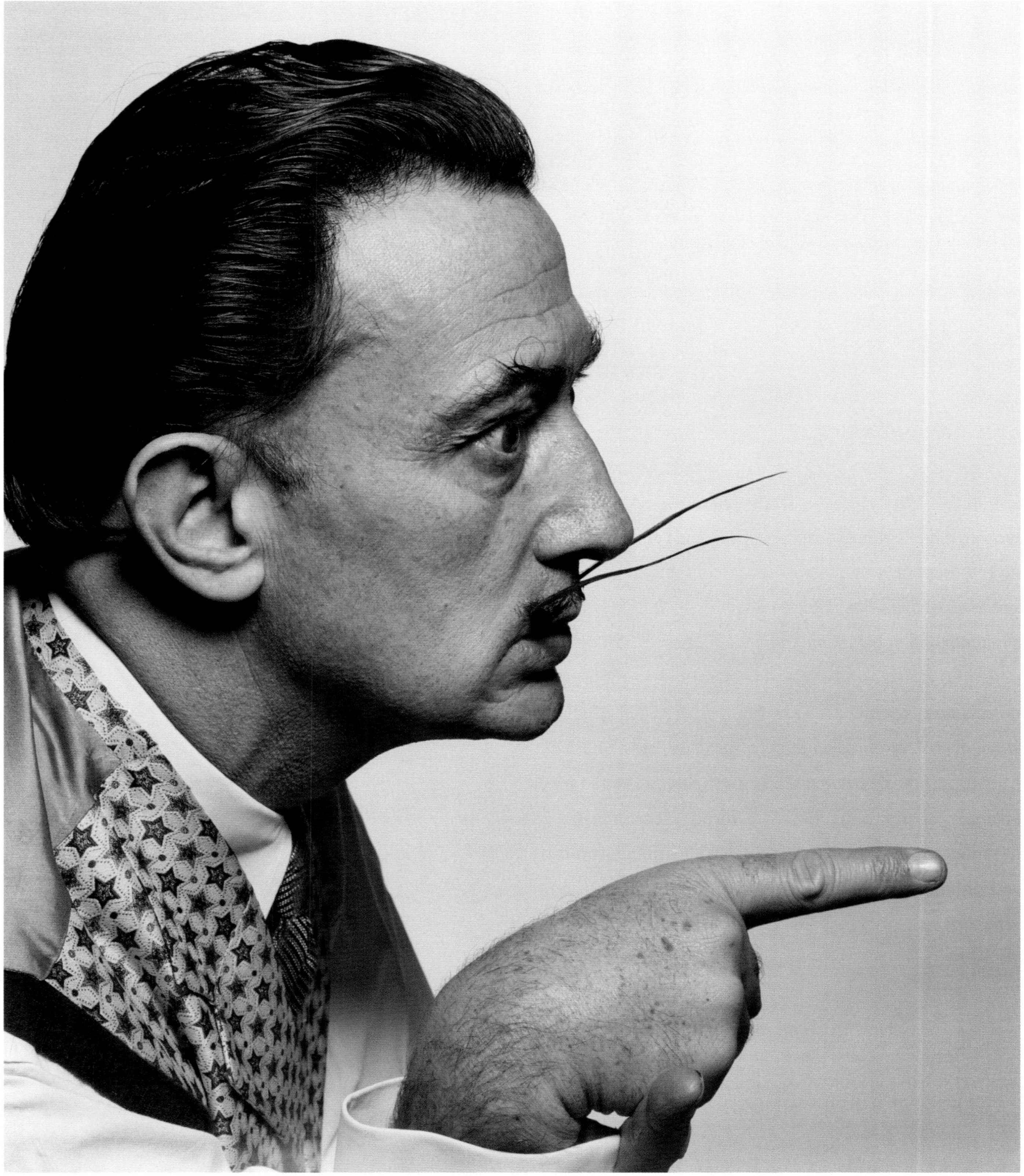

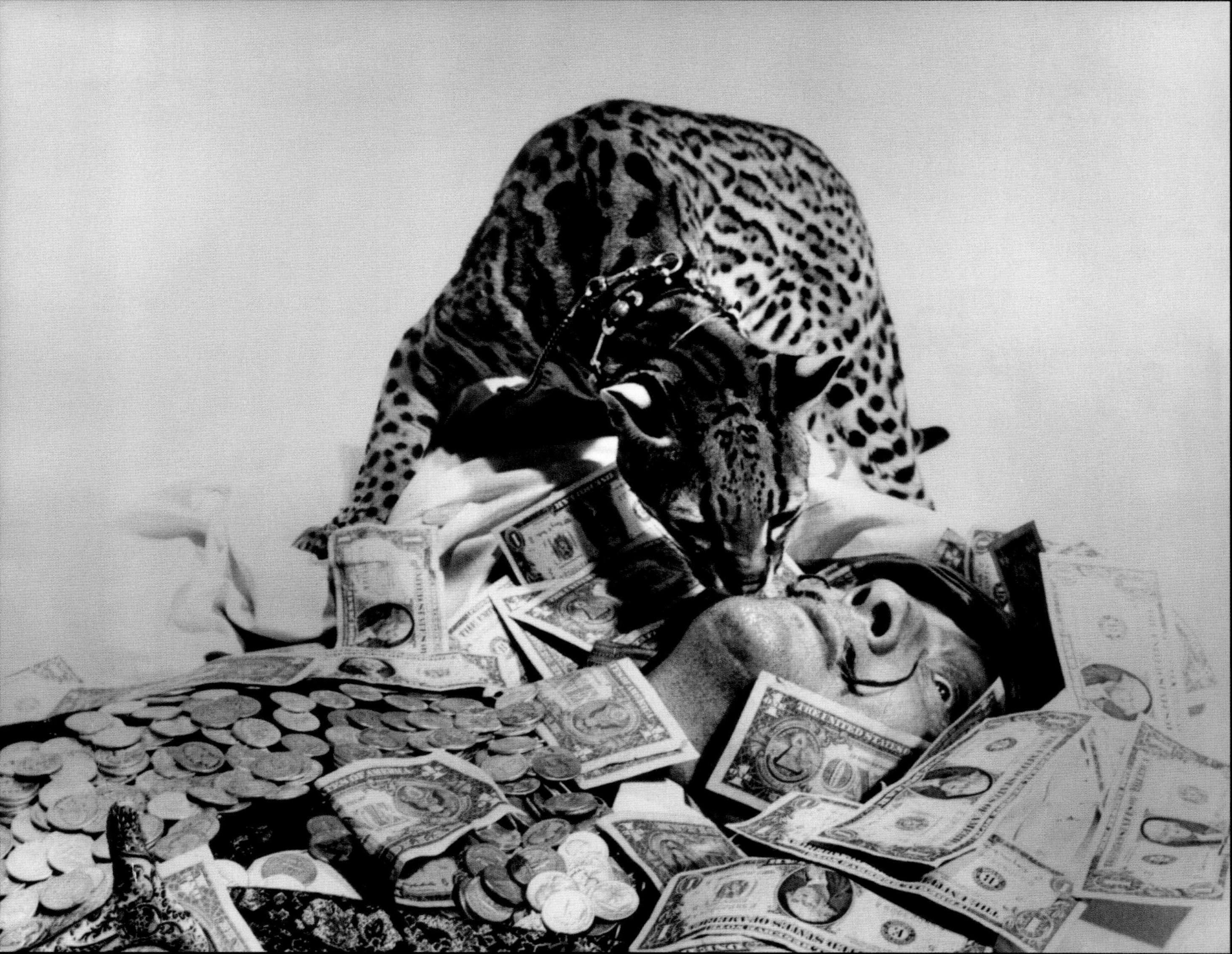

Liking money like I like it, is nothing less than mysticism – Money is a glory.'

Further Reading

Ades, Dawn, *Dalí*, Thames and Hudson Ltd, 1995

Ades, Dawn, and Bradley, Fiona, *Salvador Dalí: A Mythology*, Tate Gallery Publishing, 1998

Bosquet, Alain, *Conversations with Dalí*, translated by Joachim Neugroschel, E.P. Dutton & Co. Inc., 1969

Dalí, Salvador, *Diary of a Genius*, translated by Richard Howard, Pan Books Ltd, 1975

Dalí, Salvador, *The Secret Life of Salvador Dalí*, translated by Haakon Chevalier, Vision Press Ltd, 1973

Dalí, Salvador, and Parinaud, André, *The Unspeakable Confessions of Salvador Dalí*, translated by Harold J. Salemson, W.H. Allen, 1976

Descharnes, Robert, and Néret, Gilles, *Dalí, 1904–1989: The Paintings*, translated by Michael Hulse, Taschen, 1993

Descharnes, Robert, and Néret, Gilles, *Salvador Dalí, 1904–1989*, Taschen, 1998

Descharnes, Robert, *The World of Salvador Dalí*, translated by Haakon Chevalier and Albert Field, Macmillan, 1972

Finkelstein, Haim (tr. and ed.), *The Collected Writings of Salvador Dalí*, Cambridge University Press, 1998

Gibson, Ian, *The Shameful Life of Salvador Dalí*, Faber and Faber, 1997

Raford, Robert, *Dalí*, Phaidon Press Ltd, 1997

Schiebler, Ralf, *Dalí: The Reality of Dreams*, translated by Fiona Elliott, Prestel, 1995

Secrest, Meryle, *Salvador Dalí: The Surrealist Jester*, Weidenfeld and Nicolson, 1986

About the Author

JULIAN BEECROFT is a freelance writer specialising in the arts. He has previously written books on Monet and Renoir respectively, both for Flame Tree, and has also contributed to *The Guardian*, *The Telegraph* and *The London Magazine*, among other publications. In 2011, he travelled across Canada in search of Tom Thomson and the Group of Seven, writing about his journey for London's Dulwich Picture Gallery and for the Groninger Museum in the Netherlands.

Picture Credits

Index

Page numbers in *italics* refer to illustrations. Page ranges connected by hyphens take no account of intervening illustrations.

For further information about Dalí, Surrealism and associated art please visit our blog:

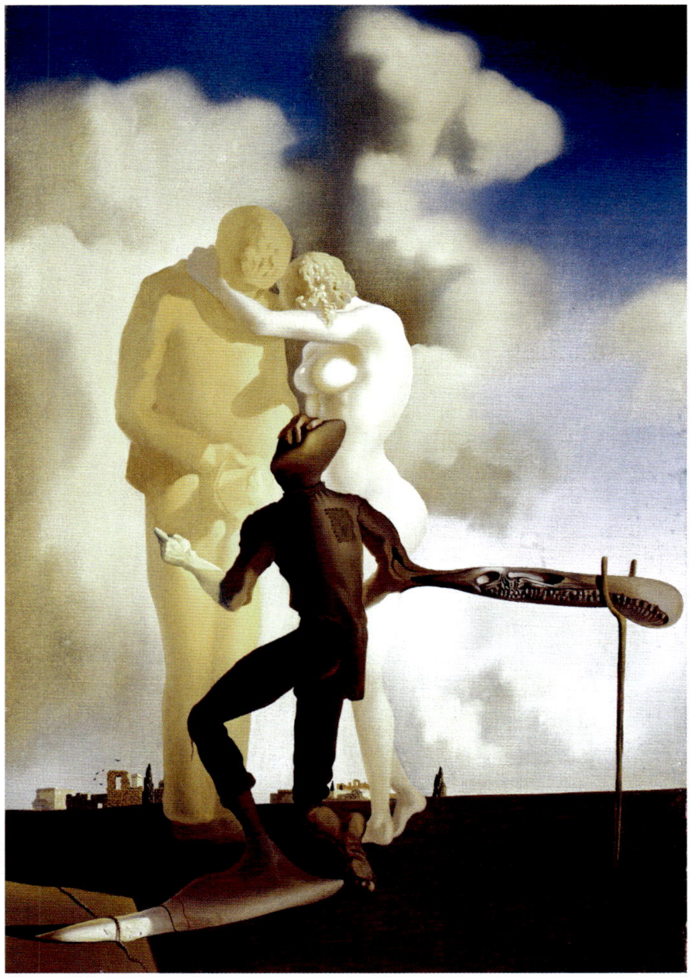

blog.flametreepublishing.com